John Taverner

Studies in Musicology, No. 5

Other Titles in This Series

John Taverner

Tudor Composer

by
David S. Josephson

umi
RESEARCH PRESS

Produced and distributed by
University Microfilms International
Ann Arbor, Michigan 48106

Library of Congress Cataloging in Publication Data

Josephson, David S   1942-
   John Taverner, Tudor composer.

   (Studies in musicology series ; no. 5)
   Bibliography: p.
   Includes index.
      1. Taverner, John, 1495 (ca.)-1545. 2. Composers—
England—Biography. I. Title. II. Series.

ML410.T186J7   783'.026'0924 [B]   79-12291
ISBN 0-8357-0990-6

To K. R. Eissler

CONTENTS

CONTENTS

LIST OF PLATES

LIST OF PLATES

ABBREVIATIONS

Printed Material

Benham, *LCM*	Hugh Benham, *Latin Church Music in England 1460-1575*
DNB	*Dictionary of National Biography*
EECM	Early English Church Music
ETSC	*Early Tudor Songs and Carols*, ed. John Stevens
Grove	*Grove's Dictionary of Music and Musicians*, 5th edition, ed. Eric Blom
Harrison, *MMB*	Frank Ll. Harrison, *Music in Medieval Britain*, 2nd edition
HMC	Historical Manuscripts Commission
LP	*Letters and Papers, Foreign and Domestic, of the Reign of Henry VIII*
LRS	Lincoln Record Society
MB	Musica Britannica
MCH	*Music at the Court of Henry VIII*, ed. John Stevens
MGG	*Die Musik in Geschichte und Gegenwart*, ed. Friedrich Blume
TCM	*Tudor Church Music*, eds. P. C. Buck, E. H. Fellowes, A. Ramsbotham, R. R. Terry and S. T. Warner
VCH	*Victoria County History*

Full references are found in the Bibliography.

Manuscripts

Cjc K.31	Cambridge, St. John's College Library K.31 (James 234)
Ckc 316	King's College, Rowe Music Library 316
Cm 1236	Magdalene College, Pepys Library 1236
Cm 1760	Magdalene College, Pepys Library 1760
Cp 471-74	Peterhouse Library 471-74 (*olim* 40, 41, 31, 32)
Cp 485-91	Peterhouse Library 485-91 (*olim* 44, 42, 43, 37, 45, 35, 36)
Cu Dd. 13.27	University Library Dd.13.27
Cu Hh.2.6	University Library Hh.2.6
CHe 1	Chelmsford, Essex Record Office D/p Petre 1
LIao	Lincoln, Lincoln Archives Office
Lbl 8 G.vii	London, British Library, Royal 8 G.vii
Lbl 11 E.xi	Royal 11 E.xi
Lbl 20 A.xvi	Royal 20 A.xvi
Lbl 24 d.2	Royal Music 24 d.2
Lbl 56	Royal Appendix 56
Lbl 58	Royal Appendix 58
Lbl 462	Lansdowne 462
Lbl 1210	Sloane 1210
Lbl 1709	Harley 1709
Lbl 3307	Egerton 3307
Lbl 4795	Harley 4795

Lbl 4900	London, British Library, Additional 4900
Lbl 5059	Additional 5059
Lbl 5242	Harley 5242
Lbl 5465	Additional 5465
Lbl 5665	Additional 5665
Lbl 11586	Additional 11586
Lbl 17802-805	Additional 17802-805
Lbl 18752	Additional 18752
Lbl 18936-39	Additional 18936-39
Lbl 19583	Additional 19583
Lbl 29246	Additional 29246
Lbl 31390	Additional 31390
Lbl 31922	Additional 31922
Lbl 34049	Additional 34049
Lbl 34191	Additional 34191
Lbl 35087	Additional 35087
Lbl 41156-58	Additional 44156-58
Lbl 47844	Additional 47844
Lcm 1070	Royal College of Music Library 1070
Lcm 2035	Royal College of Music Library 2035
Lcm 2089	Royal College of Music Library 2089
Lgl 4889	Guildhall Library 4889

Lpro	London, Public Record Office
MAk	Maidstone, Kent County Archives
NYpl 4180-85	New York, New York Public Library, Music Division, Drexel 4180-85
Ob 1-5	Oxford, Bodleian Library, Mus. e. 1-5
Ob 88	Bodleian Library, e. Mus. 88
Ob 376-81	Bodleian Library, Mus. Sch. e. 376-81
Ob 420-22	Bodleian Library, Mus. Sch. e. 420-22
Ob 423	Bodleian Library, Mus. Sch. e. 423
Ob 831	Bodleian Library, Ashmole 831
Och 45	Christ Church Library 45
Och 979-83	Christ Church Library 979-83
Och 984-88	Christ Church Library 984-88
Tsm 341-44	Tenbury, St. Michael's College Library 341-44
Tsm 354-58	St. Michael's College Library 354-58
Tsm 369-73	St. Michael's College Library 369-73
Tsm 389	St. Michael's College Library 389
Tsm 807-811	St. Michael's College Library 807-811
Tsm 1464	St. Michael's College Library 1464
Tsm 1469-71	St. Michael's College Library 1469-71
Tsm 1486	St. Michael's College Library 1486
WOw	Worcester, Worcester Record Office, Willmott MS

PREFACE

It was during a Columbia seminar given by Denis Stevens in 1964-65 that I encountered the enigmatic figure and glorious music of John Taverner. Professor Stevens generously and kindly guided the growth of that first interest into a doctoral dissertation prepared at Columbia seven years later.

This book is a revision of that dissertation. I have rewritten the text substantially, to account both for the remarkable recent growth in scholarship of Tudor music and for changes in my own thoughts on Taverner's life and music. Biographical chapters have been compressed somewhat, musical chapters considerably expanded. But I have not attempted in the latter chapters to treat at length general considerations of form, style, liturgy, ritual, or performance practice, where they have been the subject of published studies. Notable among these are Frank Ll. Harrison's *Music in Medieval Britain,* John Stevens's *Music and Poetry in the Early Tudor Court* and the editions associated with it, and Hugh Benham's *Latin Church Music in England 1460-1575.*

A new edition by Dr. Benham of Taverner's church music has been announced in the Early English Church Music series. Meanwhile, the older *Tudor Church Music* volumes remain both serviceable and available; discussions of Taverner's Latin compositions are accompanied by page references to them rather than by musical examples. The transcriptions of Taverner's English songs have been made at the original pitch, with note values halved.

In quotations from the documents of Taverner's period and from old secondary sources, spelling has been modernized and punctuation occasionally added. Song texts and figures found in accounts, however, are left in their original form, as are personal names, with the exception of Taverner's. His name is found in numerous forms and spellings, occasionally preceded by "Mr" or "Master," or by some form of "Johannes." There is no discernible pattern in this variety; often, several versions appear in the same manuscript. Therefore, it seems most sensible to refer to the composer simply as "Taverner" throughout.

The word "mass" is capitalized only when it refers to a musical setting. In references to the mass text, the "Qui tollis" of the Gloria is capitalized, "qui tollis" of the Agnus Dei is left in the lower case.

For reading parts or all of the original manuscript and providing critical insight, I am indebted to Professors J. M. W. Bean, Eugene Rice, Ernest Sanders and Piero Weiss of Columbia; Allan Melville Chapin,

Esq.; Professor Sears Jayne of Brown; Professor Neal Zaslaw of Cornell; and especially my good and patient friend Richard Goodman, whose sharp eye has spared the reader a great deal of obtuse argument and unnecessary bulk.

I record with pleasure the stimulating correspondence of Dr. Roger Bowers, Dr. Nigel Davison, Dr. Hugh Benham, Dr. G. R. Elton, Mr. John Harvey and Mr. Neil Ker. In addition, I express gratitude to Professor Margaret Bent of Brandeis for providing me with a photocopy of a Taverner fragment she unearthed; to Professor Philip Brett of Berkeley for helping untie John Baldwin's scribal knots; to Mrs. Dorothy Clarke for her assistance in the transcription and translation of public records; to Mr. Stephen Dydo, who copied most of the music examples; and to Ms. Joan Fink, who assisted selflessly and with great good humor and forbearance in the preparation of the present manuscript.

I wish to thank the librarians, archivists and staffs of the Town Hall, Boston, Lincolnshire; the Rockefeller Library of Brown University; the University Library and the Libraries of King's, Peterhouse and St. John's Colleges, Cambridge; the Essex Record Office, Chelmsford; the Lincoln Archives Office, Lincoln; the Guildhall Library, London; the Library of the Society of Genealogists, London; the British Library; the Public Record Office, London; the Kent Archives Office, Maidstone; the Bodleian Library and the Library of Christ Church College, Oxford; the Library of St. Michael's College, Tenbury; the Isham Library at Harvard University; and the New York Public Library. Especial thanks go to Mr. Thomas Watkins and his staff at the Music Library of Columbia, and to the staffs of Avery and Butler Libraries, Columbia.

For permitting photographs of manuscripts in their possession to be reproduced in this book, acknowledgement is made to the Bodleian Library, Oxford; the British Library; the Master and Fellows of Peterhouse, Cambridge; the Master and Fellows of St. John's College, Cambridge; and the Music Division of the New York Public Library, Astor, Lenox and Tilden Foundations. I am grateful for the permission of the Viscount de L'Isle, V.C., K.G., to examine and quote from the Tattershall College accounts.

In addition, I should like to express my appreciation to the George A. and Eliza Gardner Howard Foundation for a fellowship that contributed to my support during the work on this study.

To Professor Paul Henry Lang of Columbia for his inspiration, to my parents Pearl and Saul for their unwavering faith and support, and to my wife Sheila, who was engaged in greater labors as she encouraged me in mine, my debt is beyond words.

CHAPTER 1

INTRODUCTION

The visitor to the Cathedral Church of Christ in Oxford, the Parish Church of St. Botolph's in Boston, Lincolnshire, or the Collegiate Church of the Holy Trinity in nearby Tattershall, will find them in much the same condition as did the Henrician composer John Taverner more than four hundred years ago. But he will find no trace in these noble piles of the man who served them so well. Nor is the visitor likely to hear in their devotional services, or in any others in England, the music that Taverner wrote for their choirs. The reasons for this neglect are not difficult to find. Very little church music composed by Taverner and his contemporaries was copied, and none printed, in score during their lifetime. Most of the partbooks in which their music was inscribed were treated carelessly and later lost or destroyed. With the rapid religious and musical developments that followed the death of Henry VIII in 1547, the compositions of these men became liturgically irrelevant on the one hand and stylistically outdated on the other; compared with the melodic restraint and textural clarity of Elizabethan music, their work sounded old-fashioned, extravagant and impenetrably thick, and it was far more difficult to sing. From the beginning of the Elizabethan era to the end of the Victorian, the compositions of men such as Taverner, Robert Fayrfax and Nicholas Ludford remained unseen and unheard except by the occasional musical antiquarian.[1]

The name as well as the music of John Taverner has slipped in and out of the history of music with little acknowledgment until recent years. The first printed notice of the man appeared in John Foxe's *Acts and Monuments of Matters Special and Memorable Happening in the Church*, first published in 1563. Foxe noted that "Taverner of Boston," an organist who was "very singular in music," became involved in a heretical movement at Oxford in 1528, and was imprisoned for a brief time. In the 4th edition of his book, published in 1583, Foxe added in a marginal note: "This Taverner repented him very much that he had made songs to Popish ditties in the time of his blindness."[2] At the end of the sixteenth century, Frances Meres and Thomas Morley included Taverner in their lists of "excellent" musicians, and it is clear that Morley was familiar with several of Taverner's compositions.[3] In 1655, the church historian Thomas Fuller repeated Foxe's account of the Oxford heresy, but he mistook the composer for Richard Taverner, a colleague at Oxford who later gained fame as an early translator of the Bible.[4] Towards the end of the seventeenth century, Anthony à Wood went over the same ground, this time correctly, with his *Athenae Oxoniensis*,[5] and mentioned a set of partbooks compiled at Oxford while Taverner was there containing three of his Masses.[6]

When Sir John Hawkins published his *General History of the Science and Practice of Music* in 1776, he knew no more of Taverner's life than what he had read in Foxe and Fuller. His printing of an excerpt from Taverner's *O splendor gloriae*, however, was noteworthy: it marked the first occasion on which a sacred composition of Taverner's reached publication in its original form.[7] Six years later, in the second volume of his *General History of Music* (1776-89), Charles Burney printed two other Taverner works: a setting of *Dum transisset Sabbatum*, and a canon from the Mass *O Michael*.[8] After Burney, Taverner disappeared from view, and in 1895 the music historian Henry Davey had to admit that "nothing is known of his biography."[9] Such historiographical neglect was not unique to Taverner. It applied as well to his predecessors and to those of his contemporaries who had not lived to see publication of the first *Book of Common Prayer* in 1549, and with it the development and stabilization of the Anglican liturgy.

This neglect of three hundred years came to a sudden end in the second decade of our own century, with a generation of English musicians and historians determined to reclaim a long-lost heritage. Through the work of W.H. Grattan Flood, E.H. Fellowes, R.R. Terry, Dom Anselm Hughes, H.B. Collins and others, Taverner and his contemporaries finally emerged from the shadows of history.

Flood's first effort in 1913 resulted in a biography of the composer bearing little resemblance to the Taverner we recognize today.[10] Four years later, Davey published an essay that provided the first broad study of the sources of Taverner's music.[11] In 1920, Flood brought out a radically revised version of the biography, based on his study of recently published archival records of the reign of Henry VIII and on "the discovery of other first-hand sources" which he did not divulge.[12] Together with Davey's pivotal essay, it provided the foundation for the revival of interest in Taverner that followed. In 1923, Taverner's Masses were published in a modern edition in the first volume of *Tudor Church Music* with an editorial preface, a historical survey of Tudor music, an essay on sixteenth-century notation, and a biography;[13] in 1924, the rest of the church music followed.[14] These two volumes brought forth a spate of notable articles,[15] and in 1925 Flood issued his second revision of the biography.[16] In 1948, E. H. Fellowes, one of the original editors of *Tudor Church Music*, issued a supplementary volume updating the edition,[17] and six years later published an enormously influential essay on Taverner.[18] Despite their relatively recent date of publication, these two works belong in style, approach and method to the 1920s: they represent the last thoughts on Taverner of the Tudor revival of that period.

With the end of the Second World War, a second generation of scholarship in Tudor music gradually developed. It culminated in the late 1950s in the monumental work of F. Ll. Harrison, who produced comprehensive and detailed studies exposing the institutions, liturgy and music of medieval Britain to the light of modern scholarship. In 1961 Denis Stevens offered the first modern interpretive study to the subject;[19] his re-examination of Taverner in particular[20] was directly responsible for the genesis of this study. In 1962 there appeared the first volume of *Early English Church Music*, a series published by the British Academy under the General Editorship of Harrison, continuing where *Tudor Church Music* had left off. The scholarly energy released by Harrison's work has been extraordinary, resulting in an outpouring of articles, books, essays and editions of music that is transforming medieval English and Tudor musical scholarship.

We may ask, then, where does the study of Taverner now stand? Concerning the church music, we are reasonably well informed. We know, by and large, its sources, liturgical functions, and general stylistic properties. But of the songs, we know virtually nothing. As for the biography, we find ourselves in a quagmire that has led to a variety of conflicting hypotheses regarding Taverner's life, his development as a musician, and the chronology of his compositions.

At the root of the problem lies the fact that the documentary evidence heretofore uncovered yields a frustratingly sparse, indeed skeletal, biographical outline whose shape seems altogether peculiar. A reference to "Johannes Taverner" is found in a London guild of parish clerks in 1514; the identification of this reference with the composer remains uncertain. The first indisputable dated record of Taverner is as a clerk at Tattershall Collegiate Church in 1525. Taverner is found next at Oxford as choirmaster of Cardinal Wolsey's College by 1527, becomes involved with a Lutheran cell there in 1528, and leaves his post in 1530. Seven years later, he turns up in Boston as a member of a religious and social guild and as an agent of Thomas Cromwell. In the spring of 1545, he is appointed to the town council; a few months later, he dies, leaving a wife, two girls who have heretofore been considered his daughters, and a brother in Tattershall. Throughout the Boston years, there is no reference to him as a musician.

This skeleton has been fleshed out to form a generally accepted interpretation. Stated briefly, Taverner, born and probably educated in southern Lincolnshire, may have gone to London as a young man. After working as a musician in a provincial collegiate establishment, he was chosen to lead the choir of a magnificent college at Oxford newly founded by the most powerful man in England after the king. There, however, he was converted to Protestantism; two years later, he left Oxford and gave up composition. He spent the last years of his life as a married man back in Lincolnshire, occupied with politics and having nothing to do with music.

This interpretation will not do. If Taverner was indeed an obscure musician until the mid-1520s, why was he chosen for the prestigious position at Oxford? Was the reason for his departure from Oxford less than four years later a theological one? If so, why did he (or his superiors) allow two years to pass between his conversion in 1528 and his departure? If not, why did he leave? Finally, why did he renounce music at the height of his fame for religious reasons, and less than a decade later join a Catholic guild? Furthermore, how can we account for the creative development of a great composer, who left a substantial body of music displaying great variety and clear signs of growth, within a period of perhaps ten years, ca. 1520-30?

The interpretation that has raised such questions cannot answer them. It is quite literally incredible. How did we arrrive at it, and how have we tried to correct it? It began with John Foxe's reference to Taverner as a Lutheran heretic who later foreswore his "Popish ditties." Following so soon after the event, the reference was accepted as authoritative, and was repeated over and over until it became the central fact of Taverner's life. When Fellowes came to write the Taverner biography almost four hundred years later, he interpreted the composer's letters in the light of Foxe's statement, and discovered a "fierce fanatic" who was "compelled to abandon music under pressure of religious conviction," thereafter playing a malign role in the suppression of the monasteries in the late 1530s. Despite the contradictory evidence of Taverner's membership in a traditional religious guild during those years, Fellowe's interpretation gained wide currency, distorting judgments in so fine a work as Dom David Knowles' history of Tudor monasticism,[21] providing the foundation for Peter Maxwell Davies's opera *Taverner*,[22] and wreaking havoc on recent attempts to date some of Taverner's music.

With Denis Stevens's work, the task of correcting Fellowes and "rehabilitating" Taverner began. Stevens suggested, on the one hand, that Foxe's "Popish ditties" referred only to texts dealing with the veneration of the Blessed Virgin, and on the other, that Taverner's letters give evidence of a much kinder man than Fellowes allowed.

The next step was to admit the possibility that Taverner did not stop composing after leaving Oxford. At least one writer has taken that step in print, stating in a recent essay that

> it is unlikely that a man who had a wide reputation as one of the best composers in the country, and who must have been well known to Cromwell and many of the establishment figures of the 1530s, could not have been persuaded to return to composition in London circles, particularly when there was a real prospect that liturgical music might be steered in a Lutheran direction.[23]

This is a bold reading: Taverner, having quit composition because of his Lutheran beliefs, leaves Oxford for London. There he is "persuaded to return to composition" by the project of writing music for a Lutheran-influenced liturgy. It satisfies Foxe's history, his "Popish ditties" remark, Fellowes's interpretation that Taverner left Oxford for religious reasons, and Stevens's warning about the interpretation of those "Popish ditties." Reluctant to accept Taverner's permanent retirement from music, it has him return without compromising his assumed conversion to Lutheranism. This argument requires that Taverner be made to live "in London circles," disregarding the evidence of Taverner's last years in Boston in particular, and the course of Henrician England in general. Until the mid-1540s, the wandering *via media* of the Henrician institutional reformation and the music for the Sarum rite existed quite comfortably together, and within the music for that rite the "reform" was influenced not by Lutheran works, but by Franco-Flemish ones.

We are back, in other words, to Foxe and Fellowes for the last fifteen years of Taverner's life. Concerning the early years in London, we are scarcely better off. Only one composition, the prose *Sospitati dedit aegros*, has been tentatively ascribed to the London years, again by Stevens, but its technical sophistication argues strongly against its being an isolated work. Has nothing else survived from the early years?

In such questions lies the seed of this study. Its shape evolved quite naturally, often in directions and at lengths that I had not anticipated, from a desire to find psychological veracity and a sense of logical progression in an apparently contradictory collection of documents. There is a man behind this material, and both he and his music must be allowed to emerge free of the accretions of four hundred years.

Taverner's music has been recognized and treated generously in recent years. References are made at appropriate places to the studies and editions of Benham, Bray, Collins, Davison, Doe, Harrison, Denis Stevens and others; the reader is urged to consult them. Nevertheless, we remain far from a full understanding of his music, as well as that of his English contemporaries. A mastery of the manuscript sources is a prerequisite to that understanding, and we have barely begun to unravel their mysteries. Their provenance and filiation remain for the most part obscure. As a result, an accurate dating and reading of their contents is all too often a matter of guesswork. We are unable to attribute many anonymous compositions transmitted by them, but we cannot doubt that hidden among these are works by men whom we know well. On the other hand, we are not always certain of the accuracy of the attributions given in the manuscripts, but we lack the sure understanding of composers' individual idioms to positively verify or correct these attributions. We continue to be uncertain about the underlaying of texts to music, divided about the pitch at which this music is to be sung, and entirely in disagreement about the proper application to it of musica ficta. We have not yet analyzed the degree of its relationship and indebtedness to Continental music of the time. We remain largely ignorant about the compositional process fundamental to early Tudor music, and unsure about the way it is to sound. In sum, our conception of the style of Henrician polyphony, and our mastery of its sources is still an approximate affair at best.

As for Taverner's biography, many gaps remain, and one hopes that new material will be discovered for the years before 1524, and between 1530 and 1537. But I suspect that such discoveries will not change radically the outline of what is presented in this study.

I began the wandering course of reconstructing Taverner's life by probing the London episode. Why did Taverner go there, and what did he write there? He went to London to make his mark, and there he wrote his four songs, two superb antiphons of the Blessed Virgin, the *Western wind* Mass, and *Sospitati dedit aegros*. He was already a master musician. Where then did he receive his education? Taverner, we know, was born in southern Lincolnshire, and after his departure from London, the first place at which he is found is Tattershall, Lincolnshire--an unlikely place for a London musician to go to, unless he had had some previous association with it. Could he, then, have been educated there? It seems unlikely at first: Tattershall has long been an unimportant little village, and even in the sixteenth century it seems to have had only a modest reputation. However, an examination of the documents provides a startling answer. Tattershall was a first-rate establishment, protected by some of the great patrons of medieval England, provided with a college of well-educated and highly competent priests and singing men, and biased in its educational program towards a musical curriculum. We have every reason to believe that Taverner could have been educated there and come to London a fully formed musician. But the case for Tattershall has to be built at some length; without a thorough examination of its patrons, its masters, its architects, its musicians and its music, we cannot grasp the lively spirit, sophistication and excellence which marked Tattershall during the years of Taverner's youth. The case for London has to be developed with similar care, for it was in the capital that Taverner met many of his great contemporaries and was exposed to their music. Here, too, Taverner apparently came into contact with the court circle and discovered the fresh influences of secular music and courtly poetry. The songs and the *Western wind* Mass breathe the spirit of a courtly society. I have examined and analyzed the songs at particular length for they have been ignored by scholars of Tudor music. It has been our loss: they are the remains of wonderful songs.

The reasons behind my extended treatment of Oxford and Boston should be obvious, but it might help to add a few remarks at this point. Cardinal Wolsey's college at Oxford was not only a magnificent establishment, it was a center of liberal learning, and a seeding ground for many of the men who would later help Henry effect his Reformation. Foxe's remarks must be discredited on most counts. The Lutheran episode, if sharp, was short-lived. Taverner was only passingly involved, and was not imprisoned. Foxe's remark that Taverner repented his "Popish ditties" did not appear until the fourth edition of his *Book of Martyrs* in 1583; further, unlike most of his recounting of the Oxford story, he gave this remark no attribution, and pointedly placed it among the marginalia. If it was not his own invention, it came down to him third- or fourth-hand at best; in any case, it is a suspect piece of evidence and not to be trusted. What Taverner absorbed at Oxford was not Lutheranism but the new spirit of liberal learning and service to the king, which was to lead him ten years later to a political association with Thomas Cromwell. His leaving Oxford in 1530 had nothing to do with the heresy episode. Wolsey's college began to fail soon after the collapse of his personal power; faced with the loss of patronage and the decline of membership in his choir, Taverner quit, as any man in his position would have done. As for Boston, we need to note here only that the town gave Taverner ample opportunity to continue composing, and that like other Boston musicians who participated in the new politics of Cromwell's England, he took advantage of that opportunity. He contributed fully to the municipal and social affairs of his adopted town. During his life he was recognized by his fellow citizens, and, at his death, honored by them.

CHAPTER 2

YOUTH: TATTERSHALL

The precise date and place of John Taverner's birth are unknown. Although there are records of several Taverner families in the fourteenth and fifteenth centuries in Lincolnshire and Yorkshire, and isolated notices of other Taverners scattered throughout the rest of England, we have no genealogical evidence of the composer's ancestors or parents.[1]

The probable date of Taverner's birth has been given traditionally as ca. 1490 or ca. 1495. As the documentary evidence unfolds, we shall find ourselves inclining towards the earlier date or before (ca. 1485). An early document that may refer to the composer notes that one John Taverner and his wife Annes joined a guild of parish clerks in London in 1514. He is referred to as a "layman." If this man was our composer, he was probably a hired singer of junior rank, and was therefore probably in his mid-twenties when he joined the guild. A document referring to Taverner identifies him as a clerk at the collegiate church in Tattershall in 1525.[2] As far as we know, all the members of that establishment were local men; the college seems not to have attracted men from outside the district. All of the late references to the composer find him at Boston. His wife, at that time Rose, was a member of the Parrowe family of Boston.[3] A letter of his from 1540 identifies as one of his kinsmen a gentleman named Charles Yerburgh, who lived in northern Lincolnshire.[4] According to a document drawn up a year after the death of the composer in 1545,[5] his "next heir" was one William Taverner, "aged 40 years and more." This man is without doubt the William Taverner who died in 1556 at Tattershall,[6] a village situated between the cathedral town of Lincoln and the port of Boston in southern Lincolnshire.

We are impelled by these facts to conclude, as Grattan Flood did some sixty years ago, that Taverner was born in the vicinity of either Tattershall or Boston.[7] Of the two, Tattershall seems the more likely. A remote village noted only for its great manorial castle and collegiate church, it would not have attracted a musician unless he had had some prior association with it. The certainty that Taverner's brother William was a Tattershall man reinforces our hypothesis. Even if Taverner were not born in the area around Tattershall, he surely grew up there; for had his early association been with Boston he would have settled in early adulthood in the larger town, with its wider variety of musical, social and commercial opportunities, rather than in the close environment of Tattershall.

The precise location of Taverner's birth is not, however, of gripping significance; the nature of his training is what interests us, and any child born around Tattershall who displayed musical talents would have been sent to the collegiate establishment there. Since the names of boy choristers were not set down individually in the college accounts,[8] it is not surprising that there is no record of the young Taverner's presence at Tattershall. That he received his musical training there remains a substantial possibility, and that he was a musician there in the 1520s is a documented fact. It is therefore mandatory that we examine the history of the foundation and the nature of its musico-liturgical organization.[9]

A manor recorded in the Domesday Book (1086) around which a market village later grew, Tattershall came into the possession of Ralph, the first Lord Cromwell, in 1367. At his death in 1398, it passed successively into the hands of his son (1368-1417) and grandson (1403-1456) of the same name. It was the third Baron Ralph who remodeled Tattershall into a complex of castle, church, a college to serve it, a grammar school for sons of the manorial tenants and boys of the college.

Lord Cromwell had traveled to France with Henry V twice on military campaigns, and was chosen one of the Commissioners of the Peace of Troyes in 1420. Upon Henry's death in 1422, he sat on the Council of Regents which governed England during the minority of Henry VI. Dominating the Council were the Duke of Bedford, his brother the Duke of Gloucester, and their half-uncle Cardinal Beaufort. During the quarrels of the latter two while Bedford was in France, Cromwell emerged as mediator, and was appointed Treasurer of England in 1433. Bedford's death in 1435 left the unstable Gloucester in control, and the political fabric of England began to unravel. Finding his position on the Council even more precarious, Cromwell resigned as Treasurer in 1443 and died thirteen years later--barely eight months after the first battle of the War of the Roses at St. Alban's--just as his political fortunes seemed on the verge of collapse.

The year 1433 saw the inception of Cromwell's design to accommodate at Tattershall the 100 members of his household, and a collegiate foundation of more than thirty persons. It was executed "on an amplitude of scale and with an architectural splendour that has few parallels in the country."[10]

Cromwell began with the castle complex, adding a second moat and shaping a devious approach, with easily defended bridges, to the inner ward. He replaced and reconstructed the domestic buildings: the great hall with an annex, a kitchen, and a free-standing chapel to the east. The chapel, dedicated to the Virgin and to St. Nicholas, and rebuilt in the early years of the project, had been served for many years by a specially appointed and endowed chaplain.[11] Directly to the east of the great hall Cromwell built the monumental brick tower which to this day dominates the surrounding countryside. In function, style and plan the castle reflected the contemporary French chateaux which Cromwell saw while fighting alongside Henry V there. Much of its detail, however, is Germanic in provenance, and close study of the building accounts of the castle (of which examples survive from 1434 to 1446)[12] suggests that the German brickmason "Baldwin Docheman" was the architect responsible for Tattershall Castle.[13] Oblong and with turrets at each corner, the tower rises through five stories--each centered around a great hall or chamber--and a strong machicolated parapet to a height of 118 feet. The debt to earlier military architecture is immediately apparent. Yet this is no medieval keep, no self-contained defensive unit. The exposed western wall is a thin display-front of elegant proportions and symmetry; while large windows, ornate tracery, elaborate interior and lack of interior access between the ground and first floors all suggest a function unrelated to defense. Instead, Cromwell's tower was a residence for his family and personal retainers, one incorporated into a larger defensive complex of considerable age.

With the building of his castle under way, Cromwell turned to the formulation of detailed plans for the rest of his establishment. On 14 July 1439, royal letters patent licensed him to found and endow a collegiate church: he was to rebuild the existing parish church and

> to convert the said church, in honor of the Holy Trinity, the Blessed Virgin Mary, St. Peter the Apostle, John Baptist, and St. John Evangelist, into a collegiate, or college of seven chaplains, six lay clerks, and six choristers, one of which chaplains to be master, and to erect a perpetual alms house in their own ground, near the churchyard of the church aforesaid, containing ten acres of land, being parcel of the castle and manor of Tateshale, for thirteen poor of both sexes, with mansions, houses and buldings for the said master, chaplains, clerks, choristers, and their servants, with cloisters, enclosures, gardens, orchards, and all other conveniences; and to assign the same to the said master and chaplains; and they to be a body corporate, with all powers and capabilities as such, and that they might acquire lands, houses, tenements, or other revenues ecclesiastical and secular to the value of two hundred pounds per annum. . . .[14]

The master and six other chaplains would be responsible for the government and activities of the college, and maintain divine service and liturgical memorials for the souls of its founders. These seven men, priests all, would have been musically skilled only in the singing of plainchant. The six clerks and six boy-choristers would constitute the polyphonic choir at the collegiate church.

Soon after Cromwell created a trust with Cardinal Beaufort, the baron Sir John Scrope, Sir Walter Hungerford (the Admiral of the

Fleet), and two local gentry, William Paston (founder of the Paston family of Norfolk) and Walter Tailboys.[15] In November 1440 these five men signed a charter establishing the college.[16] During the following four years, a staff was recruited; having reached its statutory numbers, the college formally opened in March 1444, with William More its master or warden.[17] The men were temporarily housed in existing buildings adjacent to the tower and in the village.[18]

Around 1455, a series of draft articles concerning the foundation of the college was drawn up in the form of questions and answers. The master and chaplains could each receive "a benefice with cure" within the diocese of Lincoln, but were to reside at Tattershall at least forty-eight weeks each year. Annual wages were to be forty marks (£26.13.4) for the master, twelve marks (£8) for each chaplain, eight (£5.6.8) for each clerk, five (£3.6.8) for each chorister; the master of the choristers and the organist were to each receive an additional £2. Payments were specified as well to the verger, sacristan, steward, parish chaplain, and to the thirteen almsmen.[19]

Cromwell died in 1456, before he was able to issue his statutes in their final form. That task was left to his executors--William Wayneflete, Bishop of Winchester, Sir John Fortescue, Chief Justice of the Court of King's Bench, and Sir Thomas Tyrell--and carried out by them almost immediately. These final statutes kept close to Cromwell's license of 1439 and articles of ca. 1455, in general merely elaborating upon the earlier drafts by setting down the organization and various functions, responsibilities, and workings of the college in detail.[20]

But there was one critical novelty. By ca. 1455 the college endowments were yielding some £40 in annual income above what Cromwell had anticipated. At his suggestion, this added money was used for the recruitment not, as one might expect, of more chaplains, but rather of four more clerks "skilled in song and reading" and four boys "teachable in song and reading."[21] This disposition of funds, bespeaking a greater concern for the polyphonic music of the liturgy than for the liturgy itself, was very unusual, as was the resulting membership of the choir: seven chaplains (including the master of the college), ten clerks and ten boy choristers. Cromwell clearly intended Tattershall to be a musical establishment of distinction.

Elaborating upon the letters patent of 1439 and the articles of ca. 1455, they set out in considerable detail the posts and workings of the college and determined its organization and obligations. To preside over the daily schedule of the college a precentor and steward were chosen from among the chaplains and appointed for one-year terms on 30 September, (the day after Michaelmas). The precentor ordered weekly services, paid expenses, and took responsibility for "books, vessels, vestments, jewels, copes and other ornaments." The steward held analogous responsibilities in the college.[22]

The master received an annual salary of £20, in which commons and livery were included, somewhat less than the sum projected in the articles of ca. 1455. Chaplains received half that amount (£10), clerks one-third (£6.13.4).[23] In addition, the precentor received £2 extra for his work, as did the steward. The organist and master of the choristers each received an additional £2.6.8, while the annual stipend of each chorister was £2.16.8. The hierarchical structure of the community denoted by function and wage-scale further determined arrangements at table--master and chaplains sitting above clerks, and the boys eating separately--and the apportionment of living quarters.

The statutes set out the order of daily liturgical services. At 6:00 a.m. (and at 10:00 a.m.) chaplains said low mass. The choristers sang matins and lauds at 7:00 a.m. before going to school. Then high mass and Lady mass were celebrated, the former led by the master without music, the latter in the Lady chapel with polyphony and the playing of the organ ("cum canto organico et organis"). At 3:30 p.m. the choristers sang Marian vespers and compline, followed at 4:00 p.m. by regular vespers (and presumably compline). Only four chaplains and two clerks observed the minor office of prime, terce, sext, and none, also without music. The litany was sung on Tuesday, Thursday, and Saturday. The warden attended matins, mass and vespers on Sunday and important feasts. He or his deputy also celebrated mass at obits for the King and from Cromwell among the various exequies and anniversaries held during the year.[24]

The relative importance placed by Cromwell on these services seems clearly indicated by the musical observance (or lack of it) associated with them. Low and high mass and the four lesser offices were observed without music ("sine nota") at all; the four minor offices, with plainsong ("cum nota"). Lady mass alone received elaborate musical treatment. On holidays, of course, polyphony was sung more commonly; statutes indicated that the organist was to play "on Sundays, on greater and double feasts, and and at Lady mass."[25]

With the completion of the castle by 1455[26] and the promulgation of the statutes a year later, attention turned to construction of the college. By 1457 the hall and some living quarters were built;[27] in that year John Leynton of Lincoln's Inn, a resident of London and legal advisor to the foundation, had a room at the college. But this was a period of rapid change for Tattershall. Cromwell had died in 1456, leaving no children to continue his project; Warden More, in 1457; Baldwin Dutchman, in (or by) 1458.[28] Thus within three years the triumvirate responsible for building and directing the foundation were gone. Their plans remained far from completion: the college was unfinished, while work on the grammar school, almshouse and church had not yet begun. Thus the appointment of John Gigur as master in 1458 was a critical and, as it turned out, fortuitous one. A fellow of Eton and Merton College, Oxford, he alone guided the life and growth of Tattershall from 1458 until William Waynflete, Bishop of Winchester, came to his aid almost twenty years later. Gigur oversaw the completion of the college and construction of the grammar school, traveled to London to consult with executors and with Leynton on college business,[29] and maintained the statutory complement of college personnel. (During these years, from 1471 to 1482, he also served as warden of Merton College, Oxford, and in 1484 he directed the construction of Waynflete's grammar school, the Magdalen College School, at Wainfleet, Lincolnshire, the bishop's birthplace.[30]) In 1486, he arranged for and directed the construction of a new almshouse at Tattershall just north of the church.[31] After forty-four years as master, Gigur resigned in 1502; he died and was buried at Tattershall two years later. A man of broad scholastic culture, he left to the library of Merton College twenty volumes containing works by Aquinas, Augustine, Averroës, Bede, Jerome and others. To Tattershall he left treatises by Peter Lombard and William de Monte, as well as an early fifteenth-century grammar book of interest to us for the sixteen musical compositions found in its flyleaves-- fourteenth-century hymns, sequences and items from the ordinary of the mass.[32]

Had Gigur had to proceed alone as master of Tattershall beyond the 1460s, its future would have remained dim, for Cromwell's death had left the foundation with a diminshed source of patronage and an uncertain legal status. The manor had devolved upon his two nieces, Joan and Maud Stanhope. Joan married Humphrey Bourchier, son of the Earl of Essex, who inherited Cromwell's title. Bourchier seems to have been little interested in the college. But two events changed the course of the foundation once again. In 1471 he was killed at the Battle of Barnet, and the manor was forfeited to Edward IV. Now Crown property, its legal status was assured and its patronage secure. The second event was the intervention of William Waynflete around the year 1475. A Lincolnshire man educated at New College, Oxford, Waynflete had been master of Winchester College and provost of Eton. In 1447 he was appointed Bishop of Winchester, in 1456 Lord Chancellor of England. Two years later he founded Magdalen College, Oxford. The Lancastrian collapse in 1460 marked the end of his political career, although he remained in the good graces of Edward IV and Richard III.[33] As Magdalen neared completion, he turned as executor to the foundation of his late friend Cromwell, and in cooperation with Gigur tore down the parish church and oversaw the construction of its replacement.

It had been suggested that work on the collegiate church was begun as early as 1440,[34] but that is highly unlikely; no building accounts contemporary with those of the castle exist for it, and the castle accounts make no mention of materials for the church. Furthermore, it is utterly dissimilar to the castle in detail, materials and style, and betrays no sign of the work of Baldwin Dutchman. A more likely date is ca. 1475. The architect was John Cowper, who had been associated with earlier projects of Wayneflete's at Eton and in 1477-78, at Winchester and Magdalen College, Oxford. Shortly afterwards he moved to Tattershall, where he lived on and off until 1483,[35] supervising the completion of work on the collegiate church. Building accounts for the church exist for certain years from 1476 to 1482. The last account names Cowper; it also has entries for the staining of windows and for the bell-tower, so that by 1482 it must have been near completion.[36] Built expensively, yet simply, and on a large scale in Perpendicular style,[37] it has been called "the finest church of its period."[38]

With construction of the bedehouse in 1486,[39] the program of building came to an end, and the ensemble stood as Cromwell had first envisioned it some fifty years earlier. The scheme was unusual in its incorporation of an existing village and in the variety of elements from which it was composed. The central aim, however, was characteristic and its antecedents were numerous:

> The establishment of such bodies of priests in the neighbourhood of their principal residences was a common habit of the great noblemen of the fourteenth and fifteenth centuries, just as their predecessors had founded monasteries, and Edward III's colleges of St. George at Windsor and St. Stephen at Westminster gave a lasting vogue to the practice. It is noteworthy that in 1434 the rebuilding of the church of Fotheringhay had been begun for the service of the college and maintained close to their castle by the Dukes of York, and that in 1440 Henry VI was engaged in the foundation of his college at Eton, close to Windsor Castle, and its sister college at Cambridge. Just so, Cromwell, while converting Tattershall Castle into a Windsor of his own, prepared to establish at its doors a corporation of clergymen, whose first duty should be to celebrate mass daily for the benefit of his soul and those of his relations and ancestors, and for other purposes indicated by him. In addition to this the foundation had its educational side, principally on account of the six choristers who formed part of it, and thirdly, the priests had to look after the almsmen and almswomen, thirteen in number, whom Cromwell lodged in the bulding on the north side of the church. It should be realised that the warden and chaplains of Tattershall were not monks, but ordinary priests bound by no monastic rule; but it was intended that they should live together in one dwelling, similar to a college at Oxford or Cambridge, with a common hall, and with stipends derived from a common fund. . . .[40]

As construction of the last component of the college was nearing completion in 1486, Bishop Waynflete died and Tattershall lost its second great patron. This time, however, no crisis ensued. In 1487 the manor, to its good fortune, was given by Henry VII to his mother Margaret Beaufort, Countess of Richmond and Derby. Lady Margaret was an enlightened patroness of education and the one outstanding friend of learning and arts during the reign of her dour son. Under her aegis Tattershall flourished. When Gigur resigned as warden in 1502, she replaced him with her chancellor and the dean of her chapel, Henry Horneby, another Lincolnshire native, Doctor of Divinity from Cambridge and author of several books. Shortly before her death in 1509, at which time the manor reverted once again to the Crown, Horneby returned to Cambridge to assume the post of master of Peterhouse and to complete work on her foundation of St. John's College. He was succeeded at Tattershall by Edmund Hanson, a Cambridge graduate and canon of Lincoln Cathedral.[41] Within four years, however, Hanson was dead, and Horneby returned to the mastership of the college, where he remained until his death in 1518.[42]

If Taverner attended the school at Tattershall, as I believe probable, he would have gone there some time during the last decade of the fifteenth century or the first years of the sixteenth. Eight surviving accounts cover seven years of this period. Three are receiver's accounts (1492-93, 1495-96, 1507-1508), five are precentor's accounts (1495-96, 1496-97, 1498-99, 1500-1501, 1503-1504), found among the Tattershall manuscripts at MAk.[43] Extracts from them were published by the Historical Manuscripts Commission.[44] An examination of these accounts has yielded no positive sign of Taverner's presence there. But note that they include only seven years of a sixteen-year period. More significant is the fact that only once in all of this material is a boy chorister mentioned by name; and that case is exceptional, for he is a son of one of the clerks).[45] Every other notice refers to the choristers collectively and anonymously. Even when and if we discover the remaining accounts for this period, we should not expect to find Taverner's name mentioned in them. Its absence does not diminish the likelihood that he was at the college during these years.

These accounts prove to be a rich source of information about the musical and educational community of Tattershall. They indicate the financial health of the institution--income from endowments kept comfortably ahead of expenses during these sixteen years--and illuminate in their details the diversity of activities and functions at the college. Among the expenses relating to the keeping of anniversaries of the dead is £1.10.0 (listed in 1498-99, but occurring annually) for a mass for the soul of Lady Maud Willoughby, one of Cromwell's nieces; according to an indenture of 1487, in return for manors which she gave to the college:

> From Michaelmas next following they will keep a fit chaplain, either a fellow of the College or conduct [a hired chaplain], to celebrate mass daily for the good estate of the lady Maud, while alive, and for her soul after death. . . .After the death of the lady Maud, if she is buried in the Church or cemetery, the choristers of the College shall sing daily after vespers an antiphon at her tomb. Every future fellow of the College shall be sworn at admission to observe this deed, which at least once in every year shall be read before the fellows.[46]

The accounts give an interesting if incomplete picture of the observance of the statutes of ca. 1456. By the end of the century the position of warden required more time and work than had been foreseen in the original ordinances, and, as a result, by 1492-93 Gigur had two servants who were each paid £1. The statutory number of seven chaplains (including the warden) and six clerks was reached in 1495-96 and maintained thereafter. In 1501 the statutes were revised, mainly to compensate for the growing responsibilities of the warden. One revised statute allowed him a third servant and raised these men's salaries. Another freed him from the obligation of residence at the college.[47] As a result, the number of chaplains was raised to eight (including the warden) in order to maintain the original statutory number of resident chaplains at seven (including the warden). Furthermore, the additional salaries of the precentor and the steward (chosen from among the chaplains) were raised by 10s from the statutory £2.

In 1492-93 there were four chaplains besides Gigur: Master Thomas Gibon (d. 1506), Richard Lyon, Henry Porter (d. 1519) and Andrew Tott.[48] Three years later Lyon was gone, and three men-- Thomas Bundy, William Maltby and David Preston--had arrived to fill the statutory complement. In 1503-1504 Andrew Yonge is listed as the seventh chaplain, replacing Gigur, who had retired the year before. One finds various extra payments for duties such as repair of vestments and books, and keeping masses and altars, but no entries having to do with music. Given the context of medieval English foundations we may assume that these men were not musicians; their function was religious and their concerns were with ritual and liturgy. They were expected to be musically competent in plainsong, but usually nothing else. Their salaries were marginally lower than those stipulated in the original statutes: £5.6.8 in 1492-93 and £5.8.4 in 1495-96, compared with the proposed statutory stipend of £5.8.8. (The total of £10 mentioned above on page 13 included £3.18.0 for commons and 13s.4d for livery.)

The core of the musical establishment consisted of the clerks. In 1492-93 there were five of them: Robert Foster, Thomas Howard, Robert Lounde (Lunde), Robert Lynne (Lyn) and Edward Oky (d. 1519). By 1495-96 Foster was gone, while John Litster and John Pykering (Pikering, Pykryng) had arrived to fill the statutory complement. With the addition of John Charles in the following year, seven clerks were listed, an improbable number in view of the statutes: perhaps Howard resigned or died during that year and was replaced immediately, for his name did not appear on the lists of later years, and in 1507-1508 the anniversary of his death was one of those being celebrated.   The names of the other six men appear again in the lists of 1498-99 and 1503-1504, an indication of the stability of the complement of clerks (as of chaplains) at Tattershall.   The later fragmentary list of 1507-1508 mentions only three clerks: Charles, Lynne, and one Master Parker, the master of the choristers.

The salaries of the clerks, unlike those of the chaplains, had increased somewhat over the years.   The statutes of ca. 1456 had stipulated a basic stipend of £3.2.8 (commons as set at £3.0.8 and livery at 10s, for a total of £6.13.4): by the early 1490s it was £3.6.8.   The stipends for the organist and the master of the choristers were £2. Whether these two posts, as well as those of provost and sacristan, were rotated regularly among some of the clerks annually or were assigned on a long-term basis is difficult to ascertain because of the incomplete state of the records.   Only one (1495-96) mentions all four posts.   The information that we have is ambiguous.   The provost is named four times, the organist and master of the choristers three times each, and the sacristan twice.   The accounts show that the same men held a post in successive (but not contiguous) years, and that once replaced, he did not return to that post.

	Organist	Master	Provost	Sacristan
1492-93	Howard	Lynne	-	-
1495-96	Howard	Lynne	Lounde	Litster
1496-97	-	-	Litster	-
1500-1501	-	-	Litster	-
1503-1504	-	-	Litster	-
1507-1508	Lynne	Parker	-	Charles

Thus a pattern of tenure does seem possible.   Nevertheless, the words "this year" in the original payment entries seem to point in the opposite direction, namely, that the posts were given out on some sort of rotating basis. Thus the following entry in the Receiver's Account of 1495-96:

> And in the fee of Thomas Howard, clerk, keeper of the organ or occupying the office of organist this year 40s. And in fee of Robert Lynne, having care of the teaching of the choristers to be taught this year 40s. And in fee of John Litster, sacristan of the college there this year 26s.8d.

On the other hand, it can be argued that the term "this year" means nothing more than "during the year of this account," and does not preclude a man's having held the same post during the year of the past account, or of the following account. Certainly the term itself appears often enough to be considered merely a scribal mannerism with little further significance. All that we can draw from the accounts is that if rotation did occur, it seems to have been limited and irregular.

Concerning the other members of the musical establishment at Tattershall, our information is scanty and haphazard. The additional clerk-conducts (*clerici conducti*) stipulated by Cromwell--bringing the number of adult singers of polyphony to ten--are found in 1492-93. The men named (and the salaries paid them) in that year were Thomas Bedale (£1.6.8), Thomas Bennett (£3.0.10), John Litster (£1.13.4) and Thomas See (£1.6.8). By 1495-96 John Tonnard had been hired (13s.4d) to replace Litster, who was now a full member of the choir; Bedale, Bennett and See remained (Bennett at a reduced salary of £2.13.4). These salaries were not living wages, and therefore we must assume that the conducts were hired only for special occasions and important holidays. Their specific duties are rarely mentioned. Bennett is noted in 1496-97 as having assisted Litster in mending the organ bellows, and again in 1498-99 as having played the organ. In the accounts of those two years there is also mention of one Robert Decan (Deken), perhaps a conduct, who was apparently expert at binding and covering books.

The boy choristers are mentioned collectively throughout, usually in references to payments for their clothing and other provisions, and for the copying out of their grammar books. Frequent mention of those books leaves no doubt that their education was handled seriously. As stipulated by the statutes, a stipendiary chaplain was hired to be master of the grammar school. In 1492-93 and 1495-96 the master was Robert Edmundson; he was paid £2.13.4. But the statutes and accounts make it clear that the boys' primary task was to gain proficiency in music and to contribute to the celebration of the liturgy. Their number is never mentioned. In view of the fact, however, that the college had maintained its statutory complement of adults (chaplains, clerks and conducts), there is every reason to assume that it had also its statutory number of ten choristers--six boys who were endowed members of the foundation, along with four others brought in to aid them at services of particular importance. Support for this assumption is found in entries in the two earliest accounts of payments "for fitting, sewing and making 10 cloaks . . . for the aforesaid choristers." The entries immediately following these indicated payments for the purchase of "xij Bonnettes . . . [1492-93:] for the same choristers."

The clerks and conducts named in the known extant accounts seem to have come from Lincolnshire or the surrounding counties. None of those named is known to have been at any establishment other than Tattershall.[49] If any of them were composers, their music has not survived in any known manuscript. None brought a reputation with him to the college and none later achieved recognition beyond its walls. One might have expected a provincial little society of men who fulfilled the terms of Cromwell's statutes with devotion, but little distinction, in return for a quiet and secure living; certainly, one would have expected to find little courtly music at Tattershall. Yet these accounts provide massive evidence of a thriving professional community with catholic and discriminating tastes. Its repertory was drawn from a wide variety of sources both sacred and secular, encompassing complex polyphonic liturgical works and simple song. Some of the music shares a common patrimony with the Eton choirbook, and at least one work seems to be of continental origin. A substantial number of entries refer to secular polyphony: apparently, the chapel singers acted as "court musicians" in the household of the manor. One wonders how this little society developed its musical sophistication. Perhaps it was through Gigur, who, as we know, spent much of his time away from the college and frequently traveled to London. Perhaps it was through the interest of Robert Lounde, the clerk who was entrusted with almost all of the copying and compiling of music for the college manuscripts--music of a complexity that would demand practical and theoretical knowledge as well as a sure hand, whether in the writing out of a discant exercise for the boys or setting out a seven-part antiphon.

    The extracts of the accounts published by the Historical Manuscripts Commission give only a partial picture of the musical activity at Tattershall. The originals are altogether more revealing. They identify, among others, settings for the mass and various liturgical hours or offices, votive antiphons, two songs and a few works that have eluded identification.[50] There are several entries for the copying of manuscripts, and a few that deal with organs and organ-playing. Lounde was responsible for virtually all the scribal work except in the case of two procesional antiphons, which were copied down by John Charles. The amount of money paid to the copyist for each composition (or manuscript) must reflect the amount of work done, and therefore the length or complexity of the music; I have noted that sum, and then the year of the account in which the reference is found, in the parentheses that follow the name of each work (or the manuscript).

The Mass setting is "Missa de Gaudent in celis," apparently the mass ordinary for the Feast of Relics and Martyrs[51] (3d; 1496-97). The relatively small payment argues against an extended polyphonic setting. One item for the proper of the mass is found, an "Alleluia with verse *Confitemini iiij parts* of the compilation [i.e., composition] of R. Lyn" for high mass on Easter Eve (1½d; 1496-97).

The settings for the offices are connected mostly with Eastertide: a "versus prophete" (1498-99) for the Palm Sunday procession;[52] four lessons at Tenebrae (one at 1d in 1496-97, and three at 2d in 1498-99) at matins on the three nights preceding Easter Sunday; and three processional antiphons for Easter Sunday. These are *Sedit angelus* and *Christus resurgens* (2d; 1498-99),[53] sung following the hymn *Salve festa dies*, and "Laudate pueri in iv parts" (2d; 1498-99). The one reference to a respond, "iiij Scrowes [scrolls] de Audivi vocem" (the eighth respond at matins on the Feast of All Saints, with its verse *Media nocte*; 2d; 1498-99), indicates that the music was read from parts rather than from a choirbook such as the one at Eton.[54]

The votive "Ant[iphona] Domine celi et terre in v parts" (5d; 1498-99) is almost certainly Richard Davy's *O Domine caeli terraeque* in five parts, written at Magdalen College, Oxford, in ca. 1490 and found in the Eton choirbook.[55] The other three are Marian antiphons on a large scale (as the payments indicate): a *Salve regina* in six parts (6d; 1496-97), a "Gaude in vij parts compiled by M. Bawlewyn" (6½d; 1498-99). These texts were frequently set in pre-Reformation England. Out of a total of ninety-two compositions in the Eton choirbook, fifteen settings are of *Salve regina*, and eighteen are Marian antiphons beginning with the word "Gaude."[56] "Bawlewyn" also suggests a link with the Eton manuscript, for that is the only musical source of the period in which his name is encountered.[57]

The three remaining references to religious works are to two settings of unidentified texts--"one song [or chant; the Latin original is *cantus*] called Alma parens"[58] (5½d; 1498-99), and "Rex benedicte" (2d; 1496-97)--and to "another song commonly called 'Flos florum'" (10d; 1495-96). The only known setting of the motet *Flos florum* is by Guillaume Dufay; it was composed ca. 1415-23 and is not found in any extant English manuscript.[59] Its presence in the Tattershall repertory would be remarkable.

The two secular songs named in the accounts are a "threefold song called Maydens of London" (copied for 2d in 1496-97) and "a current song of iiij parts called the Cry of Caleys" (11d; 1495-6). The larger sum paid for the copying of the latter song indicates that it was an extended one. Its title points to a long tradition of urban "market" songs, not previously suspected, which culminated in the extended London "Cries" of the early seventeenth century. Neither of the songs has a known concordance.

Entirely beyond identification at present are a "bass and tenor song called Seculorum of Richard Davy" (1d) and "countertenor of the same song with others" (1½d; 1498-99) and "iij *Seculorum* of the compilation of Richard Higons, Turgins and Burtons" (22d; 1496-97). These odd entries tell us almost nothing about the music, but they testify unequivocally to the breadth of the musical repertory at Tattershall. Richard Davy (d. ca. 1516) had entered Magdalen College, Oxford, in 1483. By 1490 he was organist and choirmaster there. From 1497 to 1506 he was at Exeter. Richard Hygons was organist and choirmaster at Wells Cathedral. Both he and Davy are represented in the Eton choirbook. On the other hand, Edmund Turges, whose music is also found in the Eton book, and Avery Burton were associated with the royal court chapel in London.[60]

The series of miscellaneous entries in the accounts confirms our ideas about the nature and activity of the chapel community; payments for the notation of "vj booklets with various chants" (4s; 1498-99) and of "various chants ordered for the choristers learning descant" (9d; 1492-93); for the covering and binding of "one pricksongbook [i.e., a choirbook of polyphonic music] (6d)," of "viij burdons" (6d), and of various breviaries and graduals (1498-99); for repairing the organ bellows (10d; 1496-97); and a payment "to Thomas Benett playing on the organ for iij principal feasts at the time of the offertory" (3d; 1498-99).

These accounts, then, though few in number and scattered over a relatively brief period of time, establish Tattershall as a thriving center of musical activity. It may have owed its excellence during these years in good measure not only to Gigur's activities and evident interest in music, but also to the concern of Margaret Beaufort, the Queen Mother and patroness of the college from 1486 until 1509. But whatever the reason, it would have been the magnet for a young musician from the vicinity, and Taverner would have received a fine education here. Robert Edmundson would have taught him grammar and would have been in charge of his general education. As master of the choristers, Lynn would have instructed him in the fundamentals of musical theory and composition, and trained him to sing polyphony, both improvised (descant) and written, and plainsong. As provosts of the choir,[61] Lounde and Litster would have introduced him to the music of past and contemporary composers.   Finally, the organists, Howard and Lynne, would have instructed him in the art of playing the organ, and perhaps the clavichord as well.

Indentures of musicians at two similar, if larger, provincial establishments indicate that musical education in pre-Reformation England was both standardized and broad.   At nearby Lincoln Cathedral in 1477, vicar William Horwood was appointed to teach the choristers "plainsong, pricksong, faburdon, discant and counter, as well as in playing the organ and especially those whom he shall find apt to learn the clavichords."[62]   In 1508, Thomas Ashewell was appointed to the same post.   Five years later, he entered into an agreement with the prior and convent of Durham to

> teach assiduously and diligently and as well as he can, those monks of Durham and eight lay boys whom the Prior of Durham or his deputy assign to him; and he shall freely and to the best of his ability teach them both to play organ, and to learn plain and harmonized chant by practising plainsong, pricknote, faburdon, discant, squarenote, and counter.

The account continues:

> The said Thomas Ashewell shall also be found to personally attend all masses, vespers, and *Salve Regina* in the choir of the cathedral of Durham with pricknote, discant, faburdon, and harmonized chant together and separately, from the first of these chants until the last, unless some legitimate cause impedes him from so doing.   If it be necessary, he shall play the organ, sing the tenor part of the chant or any other part suitable to his voice or assigned to him by the precentor.   And he must attend daily the mass of the blessed Virgin Mary in Galilee celebrated with music, singing plain or harmonized chant at that mass as well as he can. . . . In each year of his tenure, the said Thomas shall be bound to compose a new mass of four or five parts, or something else equivalent to it . . . in honor of God, the blessed Virgin Mary, and Saint Cuthbert. . . .[63]

If evidence of the statutes and accounts of the college points undeniably to a vital musical tradition at Tattershall--one which would have encompassed many if not all of the facets of the above indentures-- a visitation of Tattershall several years later, in 1519, documents its continuation well into the sixteenth century.   William Atwater, Bishop of Lincoln,[64] visited the college on 6 July of that year.   Shortly afterwards, he issued a brief report stating that he found the college in good order except in two matters.   One of these (the first one) concerned the boys' instruction:

An instructor in grammar is to be provided for, as the present
instructor teaches the boys only music, and little or no grammar.
The Lord enjoins that henceforth, after the boys are versed
adequately in song, they ought to be taught grammar diligently as
well.[65]

It is instructive to note that in his proposed correction of the situation,
Atwater asked only that the boys be given grammar lessons *after* they
had achieved proficiency in music. He seems to have recognized the
direction and purpose of education at Tattershall.

The record of Atwater's visitation included no names of the
persons at the college in that year. Had it done so, however, it almost
certainly would not have have included Taverner's. His formal education
had long since ended, and in embarking on his career as a professional
musician he headed, I believe, for London.

CHAPTER 3

FIRST FRUITS: LONDON

The association of Taverner's presence in London during the second decade of the sixteenth century was made first, I believe, by Hugh Baillie only some twenty years ago.[1] It was based on an entry in a register of the guild of parish clerks in the city, the Fraternity of St. Nicholas, where the names of John Taverner and his wife Annes are found in a list of persons who joined that society in 1514. Baillie saw no reason to question the identification of that Taverner with the composer, and his view has been widely accepted.[2]

Treated on its own merits, Baillie's assertion remains open to some doubt. The register entry stands apart from the rest of our biographical evidence in splendid isolation: the earliest dated document we have concerning Taverner,[3] it is separated from the second dated document by eleven years. It mentions a wife about whom we know nothing, while we do know that he was considering marriage in 1526, and that he was married to a woman named Rose in 1537. It identifies him as a lay member of the guild, while the overwhelming majority of musicians in the guild were clerk members. Finally it is corroborated by no other piece of dated archival evidence that the composer lived or worked in London. On the other hand, it seems to be supported by a setting by Taverner of the prose prayer in honor of St. Nicholas, *Sospitati dedit aegros*. An analysis of the fraternity register relationship to the musicians of London, the Taverner entry, and the prose will demonstrate that while that entry may well refer to our composer, it alone does not contribute secure proof of Taverner's presence in the capital.

But it is not alone. There is a great deal of evidence, musical and archival, that when examined and connected makes the case for Taverner's presence in London. This evidence falls into three areas. One involves a series of isolated partbooks containing works by Taverner and their dating. A second concerns Taverner's surviving songs, their texts, their style, and the significance of their manuscript and printed sources--an area of Taverner research hitherto entirely ignored. A third relates to the *Western wind Mass*, whose musical relationship to the court of the young Henry VIII has been discussed inconclusively, and whose fragmentary presence in a London manuscript has been all but overlooked.

This evidence is not dependent upon the identification of the fraternity register entry, nor does it necessarily verify it; but it may be taken reasonably to support it. While we must submit the pieces of our evidence successively, they do not refer to one another in successive fashion. While no one piece proves Baillie's assertion, conversely no one piece, if found to be invalid, would collapse the case. Rather, the components begin to interlock as they accumulate, and collectively make, I believe, an irrefutable argument that Taverner spent much or all of the period ca. 1510-20 in London.

Within this framework one can submit reasons for his coming to London and his leaving it, which, if not susceptible to substantiation, are certainly plausible. The implications of Taverner's presence in the city as a young man are most suggestive, for it was the center of musical life in England, yet small enough for him to have met many of his colleagues and absorbed their music, and that of many foreign musicians. But we must begin our argument by reviewing the musical institutions in London and examining the guild of parish clerks.

"All the beauty of this island is confined to London," wrote a Venetian visitor at the turn of the sixteenth century.[4] Like most visitors to England, he saw little else of the country: Dover, Canterbury, the Kent countryside on the road to London, and perhaps Oxford or Cambridge. With its population of some 70,000,[5] it was the commerical, financial, cultural and social center of England, as well as the seat of her government. Archepiscopal York had long since waned: Thomas Wolsey, Archbishop of York for some fifteen years, never once set foot in that city. Bristol, the second city of the kingdom, and Norwich, the third, had declined recently with the curtailment of Continental trade because of foreign wars.[6] Only trade with the Low Countries flourished through the fifteenth century, and with it flourished London.

Within the city walls were over 100 parish churches and monasteries. Rising above them were St. Paul's, with its grammar and song schools, and the Tower of London, which housed the Chapel Royal of St. Peter. On the south bank of the Thames lay Southwark and its Priory of St. Mary Overy. The royal palaces of Greenwich and Westminster marked the eastern and western limits, respectively, of suburban settlement around London, while just upstream from Whitehall were the government complex at Westminster, the Benedictine monastery there, and the adjacent royal collegiate chapel of St. Stephen.[7] The king's country seat at Richmond lay five miles southwest of Westminster, Wolsey's palace at Hampton Court another two miles southwest. These imposing structures were centers of musical life in a city that offered virtually unlimited opportunities to musicians of every class.[8]

Published records indicate that the parish churches, monasteries, guilds, hospitals and colleges of London also fostered active musical establishments, through either their own financial resources or the generosity of their wealthier members. Patrons provided the means for musical display, founding schools in which boys were taught music, and endowing chantries at which priests sang for the souls of them and their families.[9] Pre-Reformation inventories from the sixteenth century suggest that in over a dozen London parish churches polyphony was performed regularly, with the aid of conducts (professional singers) to augment their choirs at important festivals and during the Christmas and Easter seasons. A few churches engaged conducts on a long-term basis: St. Mary-at-Hill, for instance, hired three singers in 1514-15, five in 1532-33, and nine (among them, Thomas Tallis and Richard Wynslatt) in 1537-38.[10] Organists here included John Thorne, Robert Okeland in 1533-35, Philip ap Rhys and his successor in 1547, William ap Rhys.[11]

A polyphonic choir was established at Westminster Abbey by the latter part of the fifteenth century, and in 1479-80 there were enough boys to necessitate the appointment of William Cornysh senior as master of the choristers. At the dissolution of the monastery in 1540 and under the new foundation there were ten choristers, one of whom in 1542-43 was William Mundy.[12]

A "great chapter"--the Bishop of London, a dean and thirty canons--presided over St. Paul's, while a college of minor canons led by a subdean was responsible for its music. Early in the sixteenth century the choral establishment consisted of twelve minor canons, six vicars-choral supplemented by sixteen chantry priests, and ten boys; among its members were William Whytbroke, subdean from 1531 to 1535, Philip ap Rhys and John Redford.[13] State occasions of especial pomp and importance took place at the cathedral, and for them its fine choir was supplemented by other singers (usually from the Chapel Royal) and by instrumentalists.[14]

Six waits were retained by the city of London to sing and play the shawms and sackbuts. They automatically gained the freedom of the city in the Company of Musicians, and received a basic wage of £11.6.8 along with two sets of livery annually. They augmented their income through private performances for city officials and companies, by playing at church dedication days and major religious feasts, and by assisting at a variety of affairs from banquets to weddings and guild dinners.[15]

Independent musicians, "the wardens and commonalty of the fellowship of minstrels freemen of the city of London," received a charter in 1500. Supported by membership dues (3d quarterly) and governed by a master and two wardens, this Company of London Musicians dedicated to St. Anthony, exercised the functions common to all city guilds: fraternal, religious, governmental, educational and economic. Because of the disappearance of many of its records and accounts, we know nothing of its religious and fraternal life. Concerning its musical activities, however, we are better informed. Each master could teach one apprentice (as well as interested gentlemen and merchants), instructing him to play on various instruments and to sing. Apprentices had to be free-born and unmarried; after completing a seven-year term, and upon reaching the age of twenty-four, they joined the guild and received the freedom of the city. Aside from providing a tradition of secular musical education, the company fostered professional standards of performance, settled disputes among its members and sought to provide security and prosperity for musicians by achieving a monopoly on secular performances in the city. Amendments in 1518 to the charter list their activities at "triumphs, feasts, dinners, suppers, marriages, guilds . . ., taverns, hostelries or alehouses"; to these we can add playing at religious festivals, in the streets during the evening, and probably too in the fledgling theater.[16]

Certain of the wealthy London nobility maintained their own chapels. Lady Margaret Beaufort, for example, had a household chapel until her death in 1509; among its members were the composers Thomas Farthyng (d. ca. 1520?) and Hugh Aston (d. 1522). But the two outstanding household chapels in the area were Thomas Cardinal Wolsey's and the king's. Wolsey's gentleman usher and first biographer, George Cavendish, has given us what little we know of the legate's chapel:

> Now will I declare you to the officers of his chapel and singing men of the same. First, he had there a dean, who was always a great clerk and a divine; a subdean; a reporter of the choir; a gospeller; a pistoler; and twelve singing priests. Of seculars he had first a master of his children, twelve singing children, sixteen singing men, a servant to attend upon the said children. In the revestry a yeoman and two grooms. Then were there divers retainers of cunning singing men that came at divers sundry principal feasts.[17]

Unfortunately, we have no record of the membership of Wolsey's chapel. The Cardinal constituted and began to staff it some time between his elevation to the see of York in 1514 and his appointment as chancellor of England late in the following year. He chose Richard Pygot as master of his choristers, and by 1518 had fashioned it into a musical organization excelling the king's. He spared no cost on behalf of his chapel, and attempted, rashly and in vain, to resist the king's conscription of his prized treble chorister, a boy named Robin, for the Chapel Royal.[18] (In 1524 he would lose Pygot, too, to the king's chapel.) Fine music, ceremony and luxurious appointments were symbols of power to Wolsey. He built a court "far more magnificent than that of the king," wrote Ludovico Falier, the Venetian ambassador, in 1531.[19] Similar pretensions were to be evident as we shall see later, when Wolsey established his college at Oxford.

Still, the royal presence dominated London and patronized its finest musicians. Through the fifteenth century, kings hired minstrels to serve them on significant personal and state occasions, rewarded them with regular wages and livery, and allowed them a limited jurisdiction over other minstrels. Some fifteen musicians served the royal household under Henry VIII. At the beginning of his reign, Henry VIII established them as the King's Musick, to attend him on a permanent basis as members of the Royal Household. By 1540 the King's Musick numbered thirty-seven men; by 1547, forty-two. These men were often exempt from taxes, subsidies, impression on juries, and other civic duties. They received gifts and monetary rewards, as well as special licenses and favors. In return, they gave concerts, played at dinner, taught the royal children, trained boys for royal service, played at masques and royal ceremonies, and assisted in some services of the Chapel Royal.[20]

As the King's Musick formed the secular musical arm of the court, the Chapel Royal formed the religious arm. It had been formally incorporated by Edward IV in 1483, after more than a century of informal existence, with a dean and three canons, twenty-four chaplains and gentlemen-clerks, a gospeller and episteller, and eight boys under the tutelage of a master. (By 1525-26 there were nine chaplains, nineteen clerks, and twelve boys). The master of the choristers, armed with a warrant to seize promising boys from any establishment except St. Paul's, Windsor and Westminster Abbey, recruited choristers, housed, fed and clothed them, and taught them to sing. The offices of gospeller and episteller often were given to choristers after their voices had changed, as duties preliminary to their appointment as gentlemen; graduate boys who found no place in the chapel were sent to a royal foundation at Oxford or Cambridge for study until a chapel post was found.

Henry VIII's enthusiasm for music during the early years of his reign is well known. Under his generous patronage, the Chapel Royal flourished as an instrument of both the king's divine worship and state diplomacy, and its members were treated handsomely, receiving £11.8.1½ in annual wages, along with board and livery. Some gentlemen of the chapel retained posts in the cathedrals from which they had come. Extra payments for weddings, progresses and other occassions were common, as were grants of crown lands, prebends, and leases in reversion. Henry particularly favored William Cornysh junior and William Crane, whom he rewarded with huge sums of money and commercial monopolies, and Robert Fayrfax, to whom he made three known New Year's Day payments for books of polyphony: £13.6.8 in 1516, and £20 in 1517 and 1518.[21]

There were foreigners in the King's Musick when Henry ascended the throne in 1509,[22] and he added to their number, bringing among others the Venetian organist and political agent Dionisio Memmo from 1516 to 1525,[23] the lutenist Peter van Wilder, and his relative Philip van Wilder, under whose co-stewardship with one William Lawes the king built a collection of more than 300 instruments.[24]   Henry also employed Pierre Alamire, a Dutch composer at the court of Marguerite of Austria, as a secret agent between 1515 and 1528.[25]

Such royal concern bore fruit. On 24 August 1514, for instance, a visitor to London attached to the Venetian Embassy wrote of a high mass "performed with great pomp and with vocal and instrumental music, which lasted until 1:00 p.m."[26]   A high mass offered on 6 June 1515 at Richmond in honor of the Venetian ambassadors elicited this praise from Sagudino, secretary to Giustiniani:

> So they went to church, and after a grand procession had been made, high mass was sung by the king's choristers, whose voices are more divine than human; *non cantavano ma giubilavano*; and as to the counterbass voices, they probably have not their equal in the world.[27]

Contacts between English and Continental musicians were facilitated by state visits. The royal choirs of Marguerite of Austria (led by Pierre de la Rue)[28] and Henry met at Lille in October 1513. When Charles V came to England in 1520, he brought some court musicians, including the organist Henry Bredemers, who gave a banquet for the English royal choir at Canterbury.[29]   During a second visit by Charles two years later, his musicians performed at court.[30]   In 1527, Wolsey took his chapel to France for two months; among the musicians was Avery Burton, a gentlemen of the Chapel Royal apparently on loan to the Cardinal.[31]

The most noteworthy and best known such occasion was the meeting between Henry and Francis I of France in June 1520 at the Field of Cloth of Gold. For two weeks there was a succession of feasts, jousts, tilts and dancing. Then on Saturday 23 June, in "a goodly and large chapel which was richly behanged and garnished with divers saints and relics," Wolsey celebrated a mass of the Trinity, assisted by all the bishops of France and England, choirs of the chapels of both kings,[32] their organists, and a complement of fife, cornett and sackbut players. The choirs sat in an open space between the altar and the royal pews, each singer at his desk, and performed sections of the mass proper and ordinary in alternation--"chaplains of both the kings did sing mass sometime and one and sometime the other, which was a heavenly hearing"--with each group singing with its own organist. Pierre Mouton was the French organist. It was reported that he "played the Kyrie with the French singers," and that sackbuts and fifes accompanied the Credo. The latter report is of particular interest, as it indicates the presence of wind accompaniment in a choral mass. The practice seems to have been extremely rare, and we must assume that the extraordinary occasion was responsible for it. One account identifies "Perino" as the composer; he was probably Mouton.[33]

Such travelling cost Henry dearly, and in 1526 he ordered that only the master of the choristers, six other singing men and six boy choristers, along with certain vestry officers, should accompany him on his journeys. This rump chapel celebrated Lady mass daily before noon, and on Sundays and festivals it also sang the mass of those days and a votive antiphon in the afternoon; "for which purpose no great carriage, either of vestments or books shall be required."[34]

A smaller royal chapel existed in London, St. Stephen's at Westminster. Incorporated by royal charter in 1348, this collegiate church had a dean and twelve canons, thirteen vicars, four clerks and six boy choristers. The composer Nicholas Ludford was a clerk there. Richard Sampson, a diplomat and composer, was dean there from 1520 to 1523, when he became dean of the Chapel Royal.[35]

One other community whose membership included many practising musicians existed in medieval London: the fraternity of parish clerks.[36] Although a parish clerk had duties such as keeping the church in order, assisting the priest at services, and preparing records of births, baptisms, marriages and deaths, his primary function was musical. Often he would hire one or two other clerks, as well as a small number of conducts, to assist him at services.

No records exist for the early years of the fraternity of the London parish clerks. These men came together, probably some time during the thirteenth century, for social and religious reasons--to support their aged and poor colleagues, to provide charity, and to ensure masses and prayers for the souls of their late colleagues--as well as to gain the political rights, notably the freedom of the city, that came with membership in a guild. Slowly the brotherhood, whose patron saint was Nicholas of Myra, assumed more formal shape. By 1422 the parish clerks were renting the brewers' hall for the meetings. An act of Parliament passed in 1437 required all fraternities to bring returns and register their charters and ordinances.[37] In response to this act, and sensing the need to declare the form of the organization and invest in property, the company sought formal incorporation. In January 1442, Henry VI confirmed by royal charter the foundation of "The Fraternity or Guild of the Principal and Chief Parish Clerks of the Collegiate and

Parish Churches of London."[38] This charter established a corporate community having two masters and two chaplains, the latter

> to celebrate divine service each day for our good estate whilst we live and for our soul after we have departed from this life and for the souls of all faithful deceased, and seven poor persons to pray and beseech for the estate and souls aforesaid before the Most High. . . .[39]

In return, it conferred upon the fraternity the legal right to hold lands and tenements, to sue and be sued, and to receive gifts up to the value of £140 annually. In 1444 the corporation of the city of London recognized that membership in the Fraternity of Parish Clerks gave one the freedom of the city.

The company was re-incorporated several times. In February 1449 a fresh charter was received. It provided for the annual election of the masters by the members of the fraternity and gave them the right to appoint two chaplains, who conducted services in the chapel of St. Mary Magdalene by the Guildhall.[40] A further charter, granted in July 1475 by Edward IV, extended the jurisdiction of the fraternity to the suburbs of London, and relieved it of the expense of maintaining one of the chaplains. Four years later the company was granted arms.[41] A set of ordinances adopted in 1530 reflects the earlier practices of the company-- whose purpose was to maintain a continuing governing body that would protect the professional monopoly of its membership--and sets out the obligations which its members were called upon to fulfill.[42] Two masters, elected annually, were responsible for the financial transactions of the fraternity. Two wardens, chosen annually by the masters to assist them, were to maintain the hall, almshouse and tenements of the guild, and to call quarterly business meetings to be attended by the brothers of the fraternity.

Membership was compulsory for all parish clerks and conducts in the city and its environs at the cost of 1s in annual dues:

> No clerk nor conduct in parish nor college shall take upon him to keep any masses, evensong, anthems, and processions, within the city of London or the suburbs of the same, but only in the parish or place where he hath his principal service, but if so be a brother of the said fraternity.

No clerk or conduct who was a member could assist a non-member at another church, and no member could have an outsider assist him at his own church if a member was available. Threats of heavy fines accompanied these rules.[43]

Members had several professional duties. Each year at Michaelmas, after the election of the lord mayor, all of the parish clerks, collegiate clerks and conducts gathered at the Chapel of St. Mary Magdalene at the Guildhall to sing the mass of the Holy Ghost "with solemn music" in the presence of the mayor and aldermen. On the Sunday before Whitsun, the clerks and conducts came to their chapel to sing evensong. On the following day they sang mass and then walked formally attired in procession to their hall for dinner. They assisted at funerals of their deceased brothers and sisters and those of wealthy Londoners, at civic processions and at the dedication days of the city's parish churches. They held feasts for the induction of new members, "which they celebrated with singing and music; and then received into their society such persons as delighted in singing or were studious of it."[44] Four times a year, too, they gathered at the Guildhall chapel and there did

> solemnize by note, a dirge and mass of Requiem for the sake of our said sovereign lord King Henry VIII, our sovereign lady Queen Catherine his wife, and for the souls of the said our late sovereign lord King Henry VII, and for the brethren and sisters of the said fraternity, and for all Christian souls. . . .[45]

Finally, the parish clerks played a vital role in the early history of the English theater. They performed miracle plays in parish churches on the feasts of St. Nicholas (6 December), St. Catherine (25 November) and the Holy Innocents (28 December). Along with the London waits and independent musicians, they contributed to the writing and performance of secular pageants sponsored by the city. They also trained choristers as actors and participated in the services on St. Nicholas Day and Holy Innocents.[46]

The company was not only a professional guild, but also a social fraternity for freemen and nobility who wished to study and patronize music. A list of the membership for the years 1449 to 1521, contained in a large, handsome parchment volume (Lgl 4889), records in annual entries the names of over five thousand members who joined the fraternity and those whose deaths were reported in each year: kings and queens, lay nobility, bishops, abbots and priors, mayors and aldermen, monks, priests, masters of the fraternity, clerks and their wives, laymen and their wives, and laywomen.[47]

The great Lancastrian patrons of music are here: Henry V, his son Henry VI, his brothers John Duke of Bedford and Humphrey Duke of Gloucester, and Cardinal Beaufort. The list of Yorkists is virtually exhaustive, from Richard Duke of York through Edward IV and his wife Elizabeth Woodville, to the Duke of Clarence and Richard III. Of the Tudor house, however, Lady Margaret Beaufort alone is represented.

The list of other eminent persons in English history is long and distinguished,[48] but it is the list of musicians that is really striking. The yearly calendar is usually, though not always, divided into members who have joined and those who have died, as well as into sub-classifications of priests, clerks and laymen. Virtually every practising musician who lived in London for any extended period of time between 1449 and 1521 and worked in a church or chapel of parochial, collegiate or royal foundation joined the fraternity. Composers who were members of the company when the roll was begun in 1449 include John Bedyngham, John Benet, John Burell and John Plummer. During the next forty years, the following composers joined the fraternity: Gilbert Banester (1456), Walter Frye (1457, clerk), Edmund Turges (1469, clerk), William Newark (1476, layman), William Cornysh senior (1480, layman) and Sir William Hawte (1488). Nicholas Sturgeon was an early member, as his death was recorded in 1455. So, too, was William Horwood of Lincolnshire, who joined in 1464 and was one of the masters of the company in 1474.[49]

The number of known composers and singers seems to increase substantially in the last thirty years during which the register was kept. Many, though not all, are included in an index of Tudor London musicians recently published by Baillie.[50] The following selective list, based on an examination of the original register, excludes several men noted by Baillie and includes some not found in his index. It is limited to members of the fraternity whose names are found in Harrison's "Register and Index of Musicians"[51] and who can be identified positively as London musicians from other sources. It excludes names that are not susceptible to positive identification, either because they are common ones[52] or because the dates given in the register do not fit comfortably with the known facts about a musician of the same name.[53]

SELECTIVE INDEX OF MUSICIANS IN THE FRATERNITY OF PARISH CLERKS, LONDON, 1491-1521

The first column following each name classifies the man as priest (p), clerk (c), layman (l), or of unknown status (u). The second column indicates whether he was a member of the Chapel Royal. The third, fourth and fifth columns indicate entries for the musician in *Grove, MGG,* and in the *Royal Musical Association Research Chronicle* (2: 18-47), respectively. The reader might note that Baillie's index contains the name of many minor musicians not recorded in this index or in Harrison's.

Joined-Died	Musician	1	2	3	4	5
1491	John Cooke	c	x			x
1496	Thomas Appulby (Appleby)	p		x	x	x
1498-1502	William Edmunds	c	x			x
1502	William Corbronde	c	x	x		x
1502	William Cornyshe, senior	c		x		
1502-1521	Robert Fayrfax	c	x	x	x	x
1502	John Gyles	1	x			
1502-1514	Henry Prentys (Prentyce)	c	x			x
1506	William Crane	c	x	x		x
1509	Robert Johnson	p		x	x	x
1510	Robert Cowper	p		x	x	
1513	William Pasche	c		x		x
1514	John Taverner	1		x	x	
1518	Thomas Byrde	-	x			
1519	John Darlington	c				
1519	Robard Johnys (Robert Jones)	c	x			x
1520	Benedictus de Opitiis	1	x	x		
1521	Nicholas Ludford	c		x	x	
1521	John Norman	-				

The name of John Taverner is recorded with that of his wife Annes.[54] Both joined in 1514 as lay members of the fraternity. If this man is the composer, we have in the fraternity register our first dated documentary evidence of him. But the identification of this entry as a reference to the composer is problematic.

There are several references to the name John Taverner in London during the reign of Henry VIII. Among them are a warden of the Company of Tallow Chandlers recorded in November 1516;[55] a stationer paid by the king in April 1521 for binding books of the Chapel

Royal;[56] a "high collector" for the parish of St. Mary Overy in
Southwark mentioned in February 1524;[57] a witness in the proceedings of
the legatine court concerned with the possible annulment of the king's
marriage, in July 1529;[58] and finally, a man granted lands in London and
Hertfordshire by the king in September 1544.[59]

While two of these five entries may refer to one man, none of
them refers to the composer. A professional musician would be neither a
chandlers' guild warden nor a royal stationer. By 1524 he was at Oxford,
and at his death in 1545 he left no lands outside Boston; therefore none
of the last three entries can refer to him. It is certainly possible that the
Taverner recorded in the fraternity register may be one of these men
rather than the composer, as membership in the fraternity was open to
any citizen of London interested in music. And the Taverner in the
register was listed as a layman, the classification appropriate to any of
these men.

The lay classification raises a second problem. Of the
approximately 120 London musicians identified in Baillie's index as
members of the fraternity between 1485 and 1521, all were noted as
clerks, excepting only one priest and seven laymen. These seven were
Robert Scarlette,[60] Owen Bromsden,[61] Thomas Foster,[62] Dunstan
Chechelly,[63] Stephen Holt,[64] Thomas Man,[65] and Richard Fawconer.[66] In
none of these cases is the identification of fraternity member with
musician beyond question. With Foster and Holt it is probable; with
Scarlette, Bromsden, Chechelly and Man, possible; with Fawconer,
unlikely. Of the nineteen men named in the list on page 35, eleven were
noted as clerks, three as priests, and only two, aside from Taverner, as
laymen: John Gyles and Benedictus de Opitiis.

The overwhelming number of professional church musicians in
the Fraternity of St. Nicholas, then, joined it as clerks. Conversely, the
great majority of lay members of the fraternity were not professional
musicians. We do not know why a musician like Taverner would have
entered the fraternity as a lay member. We can cite, however, the
positive evidence of Benedictus, Gyles and some of the men in Baillie's
list, as well as the lay membership of two eminent musicians whose
names are found earlier in the fraternity register--William Newark
(joined 1476) and William Cornysh senior (joined 1480)--in asserting that
musicians occasionally, though not commonly, joined the parish clerks'
guild as laymen.

There is yet another problem: virtually every identification of a
fraternity member with a known musician is based upon the
corroborating evidence of an institutional affiliation in London, usually
with a royal or household chapel or with a parish church. In Taverner's
case, no such evidence exists. We should note that the majority of
membership records of London institutions have disappeared. For parish

churches, for example, perhaps one-third of the records remain;[67] the rest are gone, and with them the names of many unknown musicians in early Tudor London. One of these lost names may be Taverner's,

On balance, we may conclude that it is possible, but far from certain, that the John Taverner who joined the Fraternity of St. Nicholas in 1514 was the composer. But were this the only evidence for our argument that the composer spent some part of the second decade of the sixteenth century in London, that argument would hang by a thread. It is not our only evidence. The musical evidence we shall gather is sufficiently compelling so that should we rule out altogether the 1514 entry in the guild register, we would still have little doubt that Taverner was in London during this time.

We must note first a musical manuscript known as the Fayrfax Book, Lbl 5465.[68] Copied in ca. 1505, this songbook contains forty-nine songs and carols (missing folios account for two others now lost). Composers represented in it are the Prince of Wales, later Henry VIII, and five gentlemen of the Chapel Royal: Fayrfax (1464-1521) and William Newark (d. 1509), with seven works each; (William?) Browne (d. ca. 1511?) and William Cornysh junior, with three each; and Gilbert Banester (d. 1487), with one. Other composers included Hampshire (Hamshere), a clerk at the royal foundation at St. George's, Windsor; Richard Davy, whose music, judging from its frequent presence in the London manuscripts of the time, was well known in London circles; and Edmund Turges (d. after 1502), a member of the London parish clerks' guild whose contribution to Lbl 5465 (a prayer celebrating the marriage of Prince Arthur to Catherine of Aragon in 1501) suggests an association with the court. (About two other contributors, Thomas Phelypps [Philipps] and John Tuder [Tutor], we know nothing.) Two songs, Prince Henry's *Pastime with good company* and Fayrfax's *Somewhat musing*, are found in a slightly later court songbook, Lbl 31922 (King Henry's Manuscript, ca. 1515).[69] In sum, all the known composers in Lbl 5465 were associated with or familiar to the London musical community, and in terms of both composers and repertory, there is a clear connection between this songbook and the royal court.

While Taverner is not represented in Lbl 5465, his song *The bella, the bella* is found on fragments of a related songbook containing fifteen works and surviving as a pair of flyleaves attached to the early seventeeth-century partbooks, NYpl 4180-85.[70] Five songs found here-- two by Davy, one each by Fayrfax and Newark, and one anonymous[71]-- are also in Lbl 5465. One of these, Fayrfax's *Somewhat musing*, is also found in the court manuscript Lbl 31922. Two songs, perhaps three, seem to be carols related to the devotions of Jesus,[72] a genre heavily represented in Lbl 5465. Two others are associated indirectly with John Heywood, a composer and playwright at the royal court by 1514.[73] One song fragment has words suggesting the marriage of James IV of Scotland to Henry's sister Margaret in 1503.[74] While too little of the original manuscript remains to enable us to determine its provenance precisely, enough survives to compel the conclusion that it was copied in London, inscribed by a musician familiar with the composers and repertory of the court at about the time of the compilation of Lbl 5465, or a few years later. In other words, we find a song of Taverner's copied into a manuscript in London for some time roughly during the period ca. 1505-1510, or perhaps ca. 1515 at the latest.

    Other manuscript evidence pointing to Taverner's presence in London later in the second decade is found in two partbooks that have survived from an original set of five, now at Cambridge: the countertenor book Cu Dd.13.27 and the bass book Cjc K.31 (James 234).[75] They are divided into two sections. The first contains a *Te Deum* by Hugh Aston and a *Stabat Mater* by Davy (found also in the Eton choirbook), along with nine votive antiphons: *Ave Dei patris filia* (which opens the manuscript), *Lauda vivi Alpha et O*, and *Aeterne laudis lilium* (usually dated ca. 1502) by Fayrfax; *O bone Jesu* and *Plaude potentissima* by Stephen Proweth; *O Domine caeli terraeque* by Davy (found in the Eton choirbook, and recorded in the Tattershall accounts; composed in 1490); *Maria dum salutaris* by (Thomas?) Lovell; and Taverner's *Ave Dei patris filia* and *Gaude plurimum*. The second section, containing five Masses, opens with *Regali* and *O bone Jesu* of Fayrfax, followed by Aston's *Te Deum* Mass, William Pasche's *Christus resurgens* (found in the Caius choirbook) and Thomas Ashewell's *God save King Harry*. At the end of the manuscript the *Magnificat Regali* by Fayrfax has been added in a later hand.

    These Cambridge partbooks do not have any illuminations with royal badges or coats of arms, and perhaps for that reason have not been identified with the Chapel Royal. Yet such a connection seems certainly possible. Large and elegantly inscribed, they seem to have been a "presentation" set for a chapel of some wealth and prestige. Fayrfax's *Lauda vivi Alpha et O* contains a prayer for Henry VIII ("pro rege nostro ora henrico octavo inclito"), and the "King Harry" of Ashewell's Mass must refer to Henry VIII, or possibly his father Henry VII.

    We may infer some connection between these partbooks and Fayrfax, who headed the list of gentlemen at Henry's coronation in 1509 and again at the Field of Cloth of Gold in 1520, the year before his death. Five of the sixteen original works, and the added *Magnificat*, are his. Two of them inaugurate the manuscript, two others introduce its second section. Perhaps the original set was one of those for which

Fayrfax was paid by the king on New Year's Day in 1516, 1517 and 1518. Since Fayrfax died in 1521, we may suggest the date of its compilation as ca. 1515-21. A later date is possible but unlikely, given the generally conservative repertory of its music.[76]

Davy and Fayrfax were active from the last decade of the fifteenth century, possibly earlier, until their deaths in ca. 1516 and 1521, respectively. Lovell is possibly the Thomas Lovell who led the trumpeters and minstrels at the wedding festivities of Prince Arthur and Catherine of Aragon in 1501, and died in Wells in 1524.[77] These men represent the old generation of composers in the manuscript, and account for nine of the seventeen works. Of Proweth, nothing is known. The younger generation, who contributed six works, includes Ashewell, born ca. 1480, whose last recorded appointment was at Durham in 1513; Aston, who became a canon at St. Stephen's, Westminster, in 1509, was B. Mus. at Oxford in 1510, and was master of the choristers at Newark College, Leicester, in 1525;[78] Pasche, evidently a Welshman, who joined the Fraternity of St. Nicholas in 1513 and remained active as a musician until at least 1537;[79] and Taverner.

Of the six known contributors to the Cambridge partbooks aside from Taverner and Proweth, four of them--Aston, Fayrfax, Lovell and Pasche--lived in London; Davy's music was widely known there; and Ashewell was at Windsor for probably a decade before his removal to Tattershall in 1502. All, as far as we know, were established composers by the second decade of the century.

Possibly related to the Cambridge partbooks is the mean partbook Lbl 1709, the sole survivor of an original set of five partbooks containing twenty-one Marian antiphons, two Jesus antiphons, two settings of *Stabat mater*, and a *Te Deum*. While this partbook is altogether too humble to suggest a connection with a royal or aristocratic chapel, it is in all probability, like the Cambridge books, the work of a London scribe. Davy is represented by four works; Fayrfax by three; Ashewell, Ludford and Taverner by two each; and Thomas Tallis, Aston and Thomas Hyllary by one each. With the possible exception of Hyllary, about whom nothing is known, every one of these men aside from Taverner is known to have had a London connection, and all of them but Davy worked at one of the royal establishments. Taverner's exception in this regard would be remarkable.

The relationship between the Cambridge and Harley partbooks is one of repertory. Six of the seventeen Cambridge works are found in Lbl 1709: Davy's *O Domine caeli terraeque* and *Stabat mater*, Fayrfax's *Ave Dei patris filia* and *Lauda vivi Alpha et O*, and Taverner's *Gaude plurimum* and *Ave Dei patris filia*. The order and placement of these six works is so different in the two sets that their relationship is probably not direct, but rather through a now lost common source. The presence of

Fayrfax's *Lauda vivi*, with its prayer for Henry, in both sets is noteworthy: it survives in no other source before ca. 1540.[80] The Harley set is clearly the later one; the weight of its repertory has shifted to music current in ca. 1515-25. Especially interesting is the inclusion of Tallis's *Salve intemerata*. If he was born in ca. 1505 as is usually assumed, or perhaps a few years earlier, the Harley partbook could not have been inscribed before ca. 1525. But the strong representation of earlier music argues against a date much after that year: by ca. 1535 music such as Davy's would have been old-fashioned. (Fayrfax, exceptional among composers of his generation, remained strongly re-presented in manuscripts throughout the sixteenth century.)[81]

Lbl 1709 is of interest to us not only because two of his antiphons are found there, but also because of their position in the manuscript. *Gaude plurimum* and *Ave Dei patris filia* were buried in the middle of the Cambridge set, coming eleventh and ninth, respectively. But in the later source they are given pride of place, coming first and second, respectively, in the manuscript. We may interpret this placement as evidence that by ca. 1525 his music was recognized and admired in London.

Gaude plurimum is found again in Lbl 34191, a lone surviving partbook of an original set of five. This handsomely inscribed book includes three Masses and ten other Latin works, mostly Marian antiphons. We encounter familiar names--Ashewell, Aston, Cornysh, Davy, Fayrfax, Pygot and Taverner--as well as the new one of Robert Jones, boy chorister of the Chapel Royal during the reign of Henry VII and one of its Gentlemen from 1512 until his death in ca. 1536. Two compositions are found in the Eton choirbook: Cornysh's *Salve regina* and Davy's *Virgo templum*. Two others (besides Taverner's) are in the Cambridge partbooks: Fayrfax's *Magnificat Regali* and *O Maria Deo grata*, here subtitled *Albanus*. Aston's *Gaude virgo* is found, with *Gaude plurimum*, in Lbl 1709. One anonymous setting, *Potentia patris*, has a prayer for Henry VIII.

The date of Lbl 34191 is commonly given as ca. 1540-47, apparently to account for its several items for the reformed English service of early Edwardian years. But these were clearly later additions fitted (rather roughly, with accounts of food purchases) into folios left empty by the original scribe. The composers and repertory of the first layer suggest a date similar to that of Lbl 1709, possibly earlier: there is no Tallis here. Circa 1525 is certainly a reasonable assumption, and if we are correct, it would indicate that *Gaude Plurimum*, for one, was achieving wide circulation in London before Taverner was offered his prestigious post at Cardinal College, Oxford.

Another London document containing music by Taverner is the book of *XX songes*, of which only a bass partbook has survived, printed there in 1530. It is a decidedly old-fashioned production. The texts, metric schemes and musical style of its songs bespeak the influence of the early Tudor court, closer to the songs of the Fayrfax Book (ca. 1505) than to those of Henry VIII's Manuscript (ca. 1515). The men represented are London composers: Ashewell, Cornysh, Robert Cowper, Fayrfax, John Gwynneth,[82] Jones, and Pygot. Three of Taverner's songs are found here; *The bella, the bella, Love wyll I and leve,* and *Mi hart my mynde.* (A fourth extant song, *In women is rest / No season,* is found only in a commonplace book compiled at Windsor at the end of the sixteenth century.)

Two other works can be ascribed tentatively to London. One is the prose *Sospitati dedit aegros.* Its text is an insertion into the ninth respond at matins (*Ex eius tumba*) on the Feast of St. Nicholas. Six late medieval settings of this text are extant: five are found in the late fifteenth-century manuscript Cm 1236 at Magdalene College, Cambridge, while Taverner's setting is found in no contemporary manuscript. Two outstanding musical institutions in England--King's College, Cambridge, and the Fraternity of St. Nicholas in London--were dedicated to Nicholas, and it is likely that all six settings came from these two establishments. The only attributed setting in the Pepys manuscript is Walter Frye's, and he was a member of the London guild. An inventory of music books taken at King's College in 1529[83] mentions several composers and their music. Two passages from this inventory note settings for the Feast of St. Nicholas: "vi books of parchment containing Turges masses and anthems *Pontificem. O per omnia. Summe dei . . . Qui tres pueros*"; and "Haycomplaynes *Gaude. Congaudentes. . . .*" All of these "anthems" except the *Gaude* are items for the Nicholas feast.[84] Turges, like Frye, was a member of the London guild, while Hacomplayne was at Cambridge.[85] Judging from the layout of the inventory, it is not at all certain that any but the first piece or pieces following a composer's name belong to that composer, but in the case of Turges it is possible. Thus, every Nicholas item for which we have a possible attribution comes from the pen of a composer at King's or the London guild. Since we know of no association between Taverner and King's, it is hardly improbable to assume that he set *Sospitati dedit aegros* for performance by musicians of the Fraternity of St. Nicholas on the feast of their patron saint.

For the *Western wind* Mass, the evidence pointing to London is substantial. For all its extrovert athletic quality, it shares with the other Latin works mentioned a grounding in traditional roots; and, like them, it is ambitious in scope and cunning in technique. The evidence concerning is origins lies in Lbl 58, compiled in London over a

considerable period of time and completed by ca. 1540.[86] It was begun
as a tenor partbook with some twenty courtly songs by Cowper, Cornysh,
Daggere, Henry VIII and others (six of which appear complete in
Lbl 31922), then evolved into a commonplace book, with tenor parts to
Latin works, a couple of English devotional songs, and instrumental
pieces.   One tune found in its earliest layer is a setting of a charming
single quatrain:[87]

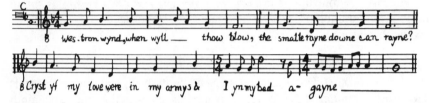

It has been called a "courtly-popular song," that is, courtly in origin and
popular in destination.[88]   Far removed from the melodic ingenuities of
Lbl 5465, it is similar to the simpler tunes in Lbl 31922, sharing with
them a smooth contour, limited melodic range, and four-square phrases.
The tune is, in fact, remarkably akin to some of Henry's own songs, its
opening measure identical to those of *Though some saith* and *Pastime
with good company*.[89]   One suspects that the young king heard this tune,
and then wrote his own, probably by 1515.

It was on a version of the *Western wind* tune that Taverner, and
later John Sheppard and Christopher Tye, wrote Masses. This version is
considerably more sophisticated than the original, however, and one
wonders whether it could have been simply an outgrowth--a popular
elaboration through oral transmission--or whether it was deliberately
fashioned from the original by Taverner (without doubt the first of the
three composers to set *Western wind* as a Mass).

The altered version of the tune is more susceptible of
contrapuntal expansion and elaboration than is the original. The melodic
contour of both phrases is now sharply defined; the tension created by
upward thrusts of an octave or a fifth released gradually by descending
steps.   A slight melodic elaboration at the end of each phrase allows
harmonic variety at these points in a polyphonic setting. Most striking,
the second phrase is repeated, with subtle modifications that now give it
a feeling of greater repose.   This repetition is integral to the entire

design; for the altered version of the tune, with the greater melodic range and spring of its opening phrase and the leap to its second phrase, demands an extended return to equilibrium. The repetition gives it that extension, that postponed release of tension.

Seen in this light, the elaborated tune is surely not an outgrowth of popular oral transmission, but rather a conscious and shrewd reworking of the original by Taverner: by repeating the second phrase, he has upset the balance imposed on the tune by the poem, and has instead created a formal musical structure (*a-b-b¹*) quite independent of the poem. We might note that the altered version is found nowhere in the manuscripts as a tune, but only as a kind of cantus firmus (stripped of its words) for the three Masses that bear its name.

In summary, the manuscript and musical evidence indicates that Taverner heard the *Western wind* tune during his sojourn in London, either through its circulation among London musicians or through his own contact with composers in the court circle. He then took the tune, expanded it into a suitable cantus firmus, and wrote a four-part Mass upon it.

But why did Taverner do so? Was he so taken with the tune that he set it for his own pleasure? That would seem hardly likely; composers were professional craftsmen who wrote music for specific occasions. Did he write it for performance in a parish church? One doubts it: its jaunty secular tune repeated thirty-six times and always prominently displayed seems hardly appropriate for a parochial service on a solemn feast-day. I find a third hypothesis more attractive. The *Western wind* Mass is the only extant Mass of Taverner's based on a song and one of very few extant English Masses so based. The setting would have had immediate impact on only those persons to whom the original tune was familiar, that is, persons who had at least some association with the royal court. Furthermore, this Mass is the most tightly organized of all Taverner's major works. It is a technical *tour de force*, and one moreover that flaunts its ingenuity. Might it have been a "presentation" or "demonstration" piece for the king, composed by a man hoping to gain a position in the royal musical establishment? True, it would have been an unusual kind of display piece, lacking the profound tone and canonic complexities of John Lloyd's Mass *O quam suavis* or Fayrfax's *O quam glorifica* and *Albanus* Masses: on the other hand, its charm and vigor might well have appealed to the young Henry, and the source of its ideas would have amused, not to say flattered, the composer of *Pastime with good company.*

This speculation is not the only possible one.[90] If we accept it, moreover, we must ask why the *Western wind* Mass failed to achieve its aim, why Taverner did not get a post at court when many lesser men had done so, at a time when Henry's support of music at his court was lavish.

We cannot answer the question. We might speculate, however, that failure to gain a position at court would lead Taverner to quit London and return to his native shire.

Whatever the circumstances leading to the composition of the *Western wind* Mass, we cannot doubt that it was written in London. The very idea of a secular cantus firmus setting may betray a continental influence and presupposes a lively and sophisticated musical environment such as London's.

Manuscript evidence, too, points to a London provenance. A version of the original tune is found, as we have seen, in the London manuscript Lbl 58. A keyboard version of the treble and tenor voices of the opening section of the Agnus Dei of the Mass (arranged, we must suppose, from a manuscript now lost) is found in another London compilation, Lbl 56,[91] a commonplace book sharing with Lbl 58 complementary parts to five chansons and a hymn (four of them occurring in the same order in both sources) as well as several instrumental works. Lbl 56 was copied over some period of time, probably during the 1530s. While the anonymous arrangement of an extract from Taverner's *Western wind* Mass certainly had nothing directly to do with Taverner, it does indicate that the Mass was known in London during this period.

Aside from this keyboard excerpt, there is no surviving source of the *Western wind* Mass, or for *Sospitati dedit aegros*, dating from Taverner's lifetime. But we must assume that both were probably written in London during his stay there. The dates of that stay are not precisely ascertainable. The evidence of the songs indicates that he arrived there by ca. 1510. The evidence of the 1514 entry in the register of the Fraternity of St. Nicholas, uncertain in itself but supported by the rest of our argument, may indicate that Taverner was married and fully involved in London musical life by that year. The manuscript evidence for *Ave Dei patris filia* and *Gaude plurimum* suggests that he was still in London in ca. 1520. We know that he moved to Tattershall by 1525 at the latest, and perhaps several years earlier than that date. We have no evidence that he ever returned to live in London after ca. 1525. We may assign to the *Western wind* Mass--without doubt a London composition--therefore the approximate date of ca. 1510-1520; the connection between the original tune and several melodies in Lbl 31922 reinforces this hypothesis. Probably other known works of Taverner's were written in London as well; the loss of contemporary manuscripts renders their identification impossible.

CHAPTER 4

A CLERK AT TATTERSHALL

Taverner left London probably some time early in the 1520s. We have speculated that he may have left because of his failure to gain a position at a royal establishment or perhaps--if our Taverner was indeed the married man who joined the Fraternity of St. Nicholas in 1514--his departure was linked to the death of his wife Annes, for by 1526 he was contemplating (another) marriage. Whatever his reason, the decision to leave London for a position at a musical establishment in the provinces was not unique to Taverner, as we have seen, and Bishop Atwater's visitation report of 1519 gave evidence that the collegiate church at Tattershall was an excellent post for a musician.

Taverner is found at Tattershall as a clerk-fellow (*clericus socius*) in an account recorded by John Rayne, chancellor to John Longland, Bishop of Lincoln, during a visitation of the college on 17 May 1525.[1] According to Rayne's report,[2] John Cunstable[3] was warden; the six chaplains were William Butler, Thomas Lawney,[4] John Mershall,[5] John Ramesey,[6] Richard Sotheby[7] and William West;[8] the six clerks were Thomas Banaster, Robert Hayloke, John Litster (who had been at the college for more than thirty years), John Porter, John Sewell and John Taverner. Also noted were a few stipendiary chaplains and the chaplains of two chantry chapels, those of the Holy Cross and of St. Nicholas.

Cunstable was absent at the time of the visitation (he may have been at the cathedral at Lincoln, where he was dean from 1514 to 1528) and submitted no statement to the visitors; neither did Butler. Of the eleven other men, three reported that all was well (*omnia bene*), three disclosed nothing (*nihil detegit*), two accused two others of gaming (*solet frequentare ludos alearum*). One clerk, Sewell, complained that certain clerks who should have rooms had none. Taverner noted only that the room of Master John Clerk, stipendiary chaplain, was run down (*est quidem camera magistri Clercke ruinosa*).

At the end of his short report, Chancellor Rayne found it necessary to issue six injunctions. The warden, for his part, was to observe the statutes and see that the other fellows observed them. No one was to leave the college without the express permission of the warden or the precentor. Any fellow who did not attend divine service had to pay the statutory fine for his absence. All fellows were to take part in processions, unless they could give legitimate reasons for their absence. The receiver was to be responsible for the finances of the college once the account was completed and publicly declared at the end of the year. Finally, the clerks had to abstain from further gambling.

There is no reference to the complaint in Bishop Atwater's report that grammar was inadequately taught to the choristers; apparently the fellows of the college had taken care of that problem.   For the rest, the foundation seems to have operated without difficulty, and the fellows seemed satisfied with their work and living conditions.   "In short, the college was open to the ordinary temptations which beset such institutions, and it does not seem as if they had attacked it very seriously."[9]

Two later sources, the Subsidy returns of 1526 and the *Valor Ecclesiasticus* of 1534, supplement the visitation document.   According to the Subsidy returns, all but one of the six chaplains had remained at Tattershall; Thomas Lawney, who had gone to Cardinal Wolsey's College in Oxford in ca. 1528, had been replaced by Robert Bere.[10]   William West was precentor, John Ramesey, steward; John Clerk, John Monke and William Tonnard[11] were the stipendiary chaplains.   Each chaplain was paid £10.   The returns also note stipends of £6 each to six clerks, £4 each to three conducts, and £3.6.8 to ten choristers.[12]   Additional payments were made to the master of the grammar school (£9), the master of the choristers (£2), and the organist (£2). These numbers are virtually identical to those of the college at the turn of the century.

The *Valor*, a compilation of assessments of clerical incomes and benefices in England, yields valuable information only about the chaplains.[13]   George Hennage[14] had replaced Cunstable in 1528 as warden of the college (and dean of Lincoln as well), and William Tonnard had replaced Mershall.   The five other chaplains remained. Ramesey was now precentor, John Clerk, master of the grammar school. John Robynson[15] was chaplain of the chantry of the Blessed Virgin and St. Nicholas in the castle, William Wayd was chaplain of the Holy Cross chantry in the collegiate church, and Thomas Jordan[16] was chaplain of a second chantry in the church.   Three other members of the college held positions in parishes in central Lincolnshire: John Monke and John Smyth as chantry chaplains at Driby, and John Snarry as vicar of Burwell.[17]   The thirteen almsmen stipulated in Cromwell's statutes were still being provided for; the number of clerks, mentioned only collectively, remained at six.

This evidence points to the continuing prosperity and stability of the collegiate and musical establishment at Tattershall.   When in October 1526 Taverner was given the magnificent opportunity to take charge of the musical establishment at Cardinal Wolsey's new college in Oxford, he showed no inclination, at first, to do so, citing "the assurance and profit of his living at Tattershall."   He was ensconced securely in a pleasant community, contemplating marriage, and working with competent musical colleagues.   One understands his reluctance to leave.   Behind the general air of security and satisfaction at Tattershall was the patronage and protection of Henry Brandon, the Duke of Suffolk and brother-in-law of the king, who had been granted the manor in 1520 and spent a part of each year there. The castle, now his, stood as the lone symbol of royal authority in southern Lincolnshire, and was used as such in a critical moment during the Lincolnshire rebellion of 1536.[18]   But while the castle was the physical bulwark of Tattershall manor, the collegiate establishment was the source of its spiritual luster.   And so, after the dissolution of the college in February 1545, the manor gradually receded into the provincial backwater that it has remained ever since.

CHAPTER 5

RECOGNITION: OXFORD

While Taverner was living quietly at Tattershall, an event occurred 100 miles southwest of his home which was to draw him into the mainstream of intellectual life in England, hurl him into the midst of a religious controversy eating away at the fabric of English society, and bring him, finally, the promise of generous patronage to which every musician aspired.

On 15 July 1525 Thomas Cardinal Wolsey issued a charter for a college bearing his name at Oxford, to be built on the site of the Augustinian Priory of St. Frideswide, ground revered since the eighth century. Wolsey had the full support of the university in his suppression of the priory and his plan to use its endowments for a new academic college, for although St. Frideswide's was a major landlord in the town, it neither submitted to the jurisdiction of the university nor offered facilities for academic training.[1] Moreover, he found solid precedents for his action. Large-scale suppressions of monasteries first occurred at the beginning of the fifteenth century, when, as an outgrowth of the Hundred Years' War, Henry IV dissolved priories owned and controlled by French mother abbeys. The ease with which he executed this action encouraged later kings and prelates to suppress weak monastic foundations and bestow their property and revenues on new colleges and collegiate churches--that is, to transfer the assets of communities of regular canons to colleges of secular canons--which would not only memorialize their patrons and founders but also use the land and funds for the purpose of education.[2]

Wolsey had maintained ties with Oxford ever since his early days at Magdalen College, where he had earned several degrees and been master of Magdalen School. As his political star rose he became a generous benefactor of the university. In 1517, he had planned to establish a permanent series of daily lectures there, and by 1518, to endow chairs in civil law, Greek, humanity, mathematics, medicine, philosophy, rhetoric and theology. In 1519, he obtained from Pope Leo X the enormous power of *legatus a latere* in England, giving him, among other privileges, jurisdiction over all dioceses and most religious orders in the land, as well as the right to grant degrees in the arts, medicine and theology.[3] During the next five years, while engaged in sporadic attempts at religious reform, he evolved a grand scheme of attaching the planned professorships to a new college, which would stand as a visible memorial to himself, and then establishing grammar schools that would prepare scholars for the college.

Having determined upon his plan by the end of 1523, Wolsey gathered a group of brilliant clerics and lawyers, exploited his legatine power to suppress the regular clergy and transfer their assets, and proceeded to execute his design in a series of swift, bold strokes. Early in 1524, he sent agents to survey St. Frideswide's and applied for papal permission to suppress it. On 3 April, Pope Clement VII signed a bull authorizing the cardinal to dissolve the priory and transfer its canons to other Augustinian houses. A royal writ approving the action came one month later, and Wolsey took over St. Frideswide's with the intention of using its property and annual revenues of £220 as the nucleus of his college. Early in September he obtained a second bull, authorizing him to dissolve monasteries with fewer than seven members, on the grounds that these foundations could not maintain divine worship adequately. On 11 September Wolsey received a draft license to incorporate for the use of his college the revenues and property of twenty-one religious houses, and obtained permission to annex the dependencies of St. Frideswide's.[4] By the turn of the new year, he was sending agents to take possession of these "exile and small monasteries," half of which in fact supported fewer than four active members.

The legal proceedings did not end there. From 1524 until 1529, there was a long succession of documents attesting to his unceasing energy on behalf of the college: royal writs serving notice to local authorities to turn over property to the college; papal bulls and royal ratifications appropriating parish churches controlled by the religious houses and incorporating their benefices; papal bulls for further suppressions; foundation and endowment grants; and gifts for the building and general funds--gifts given freely, gifts tendered in return for favors from Wolsey and most commonly, forced gifts.[5] The suppressions, if they had legitimate precedents, certainly exceeded them in scope and abused them in execution. They involved the dislocation of about one hundred persons and the transfer of annual income of some £1700 to the college. Many individual suppressions appear to have been uncanonical, and the behavior of some of the cardinal's agents elicited open protests in its harshness.[6] No scruple deterred him until finally the king was forced to intervene and bring a halt to the rampant bribery and blackmail. Later these abuses would be brought as evidence against the cardinal; now, however, they were mere expedients in a program as grand in its way as were the diplomatic ventures of this international statesman and prince of the church.[7]

By the beginning of 1525, Wolsey had chosen John Higden, president of Magdalen College, Oxford, as dean of his new college, and received loyal confirmation of its foundation charter.[8] Now he felt ready to send Bishop Longland, his chief deputy for affairs concerning the university, to present his plan for the college to the king and queen.

Longland described the meeting in a fascinating letter to Wolsey on 5 January. He assured an enthusiastic Henry VIII that the cardinal's college would serve both state and church: "Many should there be brought up, which should be able to do His Grace honorable service." Then he reported Wolsey's plan to cut off the importation and distribution of Lutheran books and to suppress the new religion. After dinner, the letter continues, Longland

> went with the lords into the Queen's chamber, where the King came with the Queen towards where I stood, and said to the Queen these words: "Madame, my Lord of Lincoln can show of my Lord Cardinal's College at Oxford, and what learning there is and shall be, and what learned men in the same." And so the King departed; and I showed to the Queen's Grace the effect of all, and what great good should come of the same, as well to conservation of Christ's Church and faith, as to the realm, where all good learning and letters should be; whereby resort should be out of all parts of Christendom to the same for learning and virtue. And [I] showed her of the notable lectors that should be there, and of the exercitations of learning, and how the students should be limit by the readers to the same; likewise in the exposition of the Bible; and expressed to Her Grace the number of your Hours, and divine service of your college, and of the great suffrages of prayer you have made. . . . And Her Grace was marvelous glad and joyous to hear of this your notable foundation and college, speaking great honor of the same.[9]

During the early months of 1525, Wolsey and his aides, notably Thomas Cromwell and Stephen Gardiner, began to work out the design of the college. They labored on drafting a license for its foundation, a set of statutes, and inventories of the property and revenues of St. Frideswide's. They drew up plans for the reconstruction of the site, began to staff the college and its chapel,[10] and drafted estimates of the annual cost of the establishment.[11] (This last matter proved difficult to work out. A petition was drawn up by "the whole company of the college" requesting more generous stipends than those laid down in a "book of annual charges," and it required over a dozen drafts before "the yearly charge of my lord Cardinal's College in Oxford, when the number therein shall be fully accomplished," was settled.) On 13 July 1525, Wolsey received a license to found his college and endow it to the annual value of £2000. Two days later he issued his foundation charter, and Bishop Longland laid the foundation stone of the new institution.[12]

Preliminary work on the site had begun late in January 1525 under the supervision of Higden and Nicholas Townley, the Master of the Works and controller of the college. They arranged for adequate amounts of stone and timber to be prepared and carried to the site. Lime-kilns were built, tools purchased and lathes made. Masons and laborers, carvers, carpenters, slaters and rough-layers were hired. Within ten days the foundations were dug, and construction of walls of the proposed buildings began immediately. By the end of June expenses had exceeded £400 and the payroll listed 112 persons.[13]

Three master masons--William Jonson, John Lubyns (Lovyns), and Henry Redman--designed the buildings and drew up scale plans. These men were the outstanding English architects of their age; Lubyns and Redman were royal masons, and Redman was responsible for Wolsey's two other monumental projects, Hampton Court and York Place in London. They planned to raze the entire priory as well as some surrounding tenements, part of the city wall and the adjacent church of St. Michael Southgate. In their stead, an integrated cluster of buildings would rise around a great closed quadrangle larger in scale than its model at Magdalen College. Included in the plan were a library, lodgings, a gateway surmounted by an imposing tower, a chapel and cloister on the north, and a hall (its entrance topped by a second tower) and kitchen on the south.[14] At once traditional in design and path-breaking in scale, Wolsey's college was to be "the apotheosis of the Gothic college in England."[15]

The work went quickly. By the end of 1526 some lodgings on the west and south sides of the quadrangle were completed, as were the lower part of the gate-house, the kitchen and its accessory buildings (the servants' quarters, stables, the larder and pantry, and the fish and slaughter houses). Work had begun on the hall, while the foundation of the chapel and cloister was level with the ground. The college functioned even in the midst of this construction. John London, warden of New College, wrote in sycophantic admiration:

> I think Almighty God is not more duly, more devoutly nor better served in any church in Christendom, both working day and holy day, and in their learning they be the flower of my Lord's University. . . .

> In the ordering of their lands all other places may and do take example of them. If you were a continual dweller in Oxford, and did take a watchful regard unto that young college, but yesterday in manner begun, you should not think but it were a very old foundation, established in everything as though it had been founded two hundred years past; only the buildings not yet finished showeth it to be a new foundation.[16]

Wolsey intended that this chapel should rival in size and appointments the chapel of King's College, Cambridge. As early as 1526 he ordered bells to be sent for it.[17] Two years later he had an immense timber roof designed and built by Humphrey Coke, the royal master carpenter who had designed the superb extant roof of the college hall. In 1529, with the other buildings virtually completed, a scaffolding arose around the monastic chapel in preparation for its destruction and replacement. Although Wolsey's fall later that year spared the ancient church and chapter-house (as well as the refectory and two sides of the cloister), and prevented completion of the master plan, what had been achieved so far deeply impressed his contemporaries. The scope and pace of the program of construction were astounding. In one month, April 1527, 500 workers labored at the site. Almost £9000 were spent by the end of that year, another £5000 in the ensuing ten months, and over £8500 in the final account from November 1528 to October 1529--over £20,000 altogether.[18] The monumental scale of Cardinal College elicited eloquent testimony from a man so ill-disposed to Wolsey as the historian John Foxe, who spent some years in Oxford during the early 1530s:

> How large and ample those buildings should have been, and what sumptuous cost should have been bestowed upon the same, may easily be perceived by that which is already builded, as the kitchen, the hall, and certain chambers, whereas there is such curious graving and workmanship of stone-cutters, that all thing on every side did glitter for the excellency of the workmanship, for the fineness of the matter, with the gilt antiques and embossings, insomuch that if all the rest had been finished to that determinate end as it was begun, it might well have excelled not only all colleges of students, but also palaces of princes.[19]

The architectural splendor of Cardinal College reflected the excellence of an academic community which, in its brief life, served as a vital link in the history of English humanism. The quality and tone of its intellectual activity were influenced largely by Wolsey's interests and by the nature of his career, and that activity in turn influenced the course of the Henrician revolution. This bare statement is the thesis of Gordon Zeeveld's brilliant account of the development of the theoretical foundations of the royal supremacy, a development that marked the demise of medieval England. Wolsey's significance as a patron of education lay largely in the example that his life set for ambitious young men of the next generation: a man of humble stock, he rose in the world through tenacity and intelligence, using his legal training and ecclesiastical preferments to achieve the political and diplomatic ends of the crown. Scholarship and knowledge were for him neither goals in themselves nor signposts on the road to churchly eminence, but means instead to achieve positions of power in the affairs of state. Cardinal College, as the embodiment of Wolsey's spirit, attracted some of the finest minds among the sons of the landed gentry and the urban middle class. In Zeeveld's words, it

> represented the culmination of an habitual partronage of scholarship within his own household, marked by an unprecedented liberality both in a material and an intellectual sense . . . Wolsey's occupation with political business was precisely the element that lent impetus to those who, in benefiting by his generosity, were shrewd enough to see that his patronage of scholarship was a way to fortune.[20]

When Henry later unleashed the English reformation, it was to these men of letters and the law that he turned for the philosophical and legal underpinnings of his actions. In this light, Cardinal College is seen to have played a major role--along with Reginald Pole's household in Padua during the 1520s and early 1530s--in transmitting a humanist tradition that was handed down by John Colet and Erasmus, threatened by the snuffing out of Thomas More and John Fisher, and revived during Elizabeth's reign by Roger Ascham, John Cheke and Matthew Parker.

    The future role of Cardinal College could not have been foreseen by Wolsey, of course, when he drafted its statutes in 1525. His intentions, as embodied in those statutes, were traditional and conservative; their novelty lay in their unparalleled scale. Dedicated to the Holy Trinity, St. Frideswide and All Saints, Cardinal College was to consist of a dean, sixty senior canons (fellows), forty petty canons (junior scholars), and public professors in canon law, civil law, humanity, medicine, philosophy and theology. From among the fellows there were chosen a subdean, four censors (the equivalent of deans in other colleges), three bursars and four "private" professors who were to lecture daily in humanity, logic, philosophy and theology. The junior scholars were to be at least fifteen years old upon admission and were superannuated either after completion of five years in college or at the age of twenty-five, unless they had already been promoted to fellows. Twenty of them were to be commoners supported out of endowment funds. Suitable observation of religious obligation was to go hand in hand with education. So that divine office might be celebrated frequently and with highest respect (*honorificentissime frequentissimeque*), the academic community would be augmented by a large company of hired servants of the chapel: thirteen chaplains (*presbyteri conductitii*) and twelve clerks skilled in polyphony (*clerici conductitii*) along with sixteen boy choristers (*pueri chorustae*)[21] to serve in the hall as well as the chapel, and a music teacher and choirmaster (*informator*) for the boys (*unus aliquis musices peritissimus qui eosdem instruat et musicam artem commode doceat*). One man, skilled in playing the organ (*scitus et peritus organorum pulsatorem*), would be chosen as organist from among the clerks.[22] Finally, among the supporting members and servants of the college were a librarian, an auditor, stewards, bailiffs, receivers, household servants, keepers of the horses, cooks, a barber, butler, porter, launderer, pantryman and butcher. Such numbers betokened a community of exceptional prestige. Medieval England had seen nothing approaching its projected scale, aside from the royal court.

According to a late sixteenth-century source[23], eighteen men were canons of Cardinal College at its foundation in July 1525. The following list gives their names in alphabetical order, along with some data on their education up to that date, where available.[24]

> Thomas Baggard (New Inn, Oxf.; B.C.L. 1521)
> Thomas Baggarre[25]
> Richard Barker (Brasenose, Oxf.; B.A. 1516; M.A. 1520)
> William Battenson (Oxf.; B.A. 1509; M.A. 1513)
> Edward Bete
> John Brysett (Magdalen, Oxf.; B.A. 1511; M.A. 1516)
> Walter Buckler (Oxf.; B.A. 1521; M.A. 1524)
> Thomas Cannar (Magdalen, Oxf.; B.A. 1513)
> Richard Champian (Lincoln, Oxf.; B.A. 1520; M.A. 1524)
> John Crayford (Queen's, Camb.; B.A. 1512; M.A. 1515; B.D. 1523)
> Richard Langrege (Merton, Oxf.; B.A. 1520; M.A. 1523)
> Edward Leighton (Oxf.; M.A. 1521)
> Thomas Newton (Oxf.; B.A. 1523)
> John Pierson (Magdalen, Oxf.; B.A. 1520; University Coll., Oxf.;
>   M.A. 1524)
> Thomas Reynolds (Merton, Oxf.; B.A. 1519; M.A. 1521)
> Andrew Stockton (Oxf.; M.A. 1522)
> John Tucker (Exeter, Oxf.; B.A. 1521; M.A. 1523)
> William Weston (New Coll., Oxf.; B.A. 1525)

Most of these men went on to earn higher degrees in divinity and took posts as rectors and curates. Champian became a chaplain to Archbishop Cranmer; Crayford, master of Clare and then University College; Baggard, chancellor of the diocese of Worcester. Few went into secular life. Pierson left the college in 1529 to practise medicine in York, while Buckler later served the king in state affairs. The fact that at least four canons came from Magdalen calls attention once again to its links with Cardinal College. Wolsey, Longland and Higden were Magdalen fellows: Higden, president of Magdalen before coming to Cardinal College, chose Cannar, formerly of Magdalen, as his subdean. Three chaplains and agents of Wolsey's--Laurence Stubbes, Robert Carter and Richard Stokes--were Magdalen men, and Wolsey rewarded Stubbes for his services with the presidency of Magdalen in 1527.

The original eighteen canons, while loyal, solid and orthodox, were not a particularly brilliant group. Wolsey would find better as he augmented their number. He turned to Cambridge, the center of the "new learning" or Erasmian humanism. Dr. Robert Shorton,[26] brought from the sister university as dean of the college chapel in October 1525, was charged with bringing promising young Cantabrigians to the college.[27] Zeeveld speculates that Shorton's massive importation of Cambridge scholars was directed by Edward Fox, a servant of Wolsey's, graduate of Eton and provost of King's, who was to act as a royal agent in 1530 in the matter of the king's divorce and to write on behalf of the royal supremacy four years later. Citing these later activities, Zeeveld reasons that the scholars, several of them Eton and King's men, came to Oxford under his patronage "would reflect his opinions as of 1527, and . . . those opinions would be liberal."[28] But whoever was responsible, the list below attests to the success of Shorton's commission--every one of these "second generation" canons at Cardinal College was a Cantabrigian--as well as Wolsey's ambition of creating in the college a center of secular, state-oriented thought. (In this list, the last date in each entry is the date of the scholar's incorporation as a petty canon in the college.)[29]

> John Clark (Pembroke Hall; B.A. 1519; M.A. 1521; 4 November 1525)
> John Fryer (Eton; King's; B.A. 1521; M.A. 1525; 4 November 1525)
> Geoffrey (Godfrey) Harman (Eton; King's and Gonville Hall; B.A. 1522;
>   M.A. 1525; 4 November 1525)
> John Frith (Eton; probably King's; B.A. 1525; 7 December 1525)[30]
> Richard Cox (Eton; King's; B.A. 1524; 7 December 1525)
> Henry Sumner (Eton; King's; B.A. ca. 1523; 7 December 1525)
> William Betts (Gonville Hall; B.A. 1524; 7 December 1525)
> Winmer Allen (B.A.; 7 December 1525)
> John Aker (B.A.; February 1526)
> John Bayley (B. Can. L. 1526; February 1526)
> Edward Staple (Peterhouse; B.A. 1511; M.A. 1514; March 1526)
> Edmund Wotton (Corpus Christi; B.A. 1525; 17 July 1526)
> Michael Drumme (B.A. 1525; 21 June 1527)
> Richard Shirrey (Magdalen, Oxford; 21 June 1527)
> Richard Taverner (Corpus Christi; 21 June 1527)
> John (?) Goodman (B. Can. L.; date of incorporation unknown)
> Richard Morison (probable date of incorporation 5 November 1528)[31]
> Gervase Tyndale (date of incorporation unknown)[32]
> Thomas Lawney (?; education at Cambridge; chaplain at Tattershall
>   Collegiate Church in 1525; date of incorporation unknown)

Many of these men achieved distinction and positions of authority in later years. Fryer rose to eminence as a physician and eventually presided over London's College of Physicians; a skilled lutenist, he never lost his interest in music, for in his service was a noted organ-maker Thomas Howe.[33]   John Frith was a scholar of outstanding intellect; his friendship with William Tyndale would set him on a path of Lutheran writing that would arouse the ire of Sir Thomas More and cost him his life at the age of thirty.   Cox became, successively, headmaster of Eton, tutor to Prince Edward, chancellor of Oxford, and Bishop of Ely. Betts served as chaplain to Anne Boleyn.   Staple became a royal chaplain, and was one of the men sent by Henry VIII to introduce the reformation to Ireland.   Drumme became an active reformer, corresponding with the Swiss Protestant Heinrich Bullinger, and later returned to the Roman Church (as did Fryer).   Richard Taverner, a protégé of Archbishop Cranmer, was to write several books on behalf of the reformation and would publish a translation of the Bible. Morison became one of Thomas Cromwell's closest advisers and a leading propagandist for the reformation.

Wolsey's efforts were not, however, completely successful. According to one source,[34] he failed to bring to Oxford four of the most promising Cantabrigians: Cranmer, Walter Haddon, Matthew Parker and John Skip.   Yet the reasons given for Cranmer's refusal to leave Cambridge throw light on the larger success of Wolsey's plan:

> Though the salary was much more considerable [at Cardinal College], and the way to preferment more ready, by the favour of the Cardinal, to such as were his own scholars; yet [Cranmer] refused to go, choosing rather to abide among his old fellow-collegians, and more closely to follow his studies and contemplations here: though he were not without danger for his incompliance with this invitation, giving them that were concerned great offence hereat.[35]

All told, then, here was the community that Wolsey had had in mind when he founded Cardinal College.   Supplemented by seven eminent public professors, among whom was the great Spanish humanist Juan Luis Vives (professor of civil law),[36] Wolsey's foundation had achieved academic distinction within a year of its inception.

Construction of buildings and incorporation of scholars were two of the three components in Wolsey's plan for Cardinal College.   The third was the staffing of the chapel with singing men and boys, for which Bishop Longland was responsible: it was carried out with the vigor characterizing the entire project.   Wolsey, as he noted in his letter of 4 September to Longland, originally scheduled the formal entry of the dean and canons into the chapel of St. Frideswide's for "our Lady Day next coming," presumably the Feast of the Nativity of the Virgin on 8 September 1526.   In preparation for that event, Longland had arranged for the arrival of "certain priests, singing men and choristers" by that date. Wolsey now postponed the ceremony until the Feast of St. Frideswide on 19 October:

> My lord I commend me unto you in my most hearty manner. And like so thank you for the pains and labors which by your letters I perceive you have taken in providing such ministers for the choir as should be meet to be in my college at Oxford. And whereas upon certain considerations I have deferred the entry of the dean and canons till about the Feast of Saint Frideswide, by the which time I trust to have all things conveniently provided for the said entry, the delay whereof being to you unknown, you, according to my first determination made in that behalf, have appointed certain priests, singing men and choristers to repair th[i]ther by our Lady Day next coming. Your provisions notwithstanding the alteration of my purpose doth very well content me, and I reckon your opinion to be right good that the dean of my said college shall give them for their commons and allow them for their wages according to the rate unto such time as the said entry and taking possession shall be made. And as touching the informator for the choristers whom you intended to have provided out of the college of Leicester if his commodity might have stood therewith, whom considering his great wages which he allegeth in perpetuity there you would not remove from thence but upon further knowlege of my mind in that behalf, adding moreover how you doubt not but that of singing men, I shall be sufficiently furnished by such as be near at hand. As hereunto my Lord with most hearty thanks for your pains I remit the whole ordering of those affairs to your wisdom and discretion as to that person in whom I have and do put my confidence and trust, not only in that provision of the said informator but also of all other persons meet and convenient choosing and election of such persons as shall be in the same, you will have special regard according to the trust that I have in you.[37]

As Wolsey noted, Longland had offered the post of master of the choristers to Hugh Aston of Newark College, Leicester.[38] His offer rejected, he turned to John Taverner, who declined it because of his involvement with a woman and the security of his post at Tattershall. At a loss to find someone else of sufficient stature, Longland wrote to Wolsey on 17 October, urging the appointment of an interim choirmaster from among the singing men in the chapel, and listing the qualifications for the post. He expressed the hope that with the singers obtained from William Crane, Master of the children of the Chapel Royal, that a full choral complement would participate in the opening ceremonies:

> It may please you to understand [that] Taverner, a singing man whom I sent for by Dene of the king's commission to have been informator of the children of your chapel in your honorable college at Oxford (who no doubt of is very meet for the same), I can in no wise have his good will thereunto. He allegeth the assurance &

profit of his living at Tattershall; and that he is in way of a good marriage which he should lose if he did remove from thence. In consideration of these premises it may please your grace to appoint some one man of your honorable chapel meet for the same number there, for I cannot now tell where shortly to have one meet therefore out of your chapel. And it shall be meet for him that your grace will appoint thereunto to have both his breast at will, the handling of an instrument, pleasure, cunning and exercise in teaching; and to be there iiij or v days before your appointed day for the ordering of his children, to feel them, to know them and to be acquainted with such songs as shall be the day of the solemnity there sung. I trust and doubt not but you shall have an honorable good choir there of singing men & children, as well in breast as in cunning, and hope to have the whole number complete with those that your grace hath sent for to Crane. And I beseech your grace I may be so bold to put you in remembrance of your rector's staves & cross staves and of a good pair of organs. You must need have two pair, less cannot be there well. Thus I am over bold to encumber your grace with this matter saving that I would have all well & for your honor which I beseech God increase.[39]

Longland set out the qualifications in the most general terms. The interim choirmaster would have to be a competent singer ("have his breast at will"), and organist ("handling of an instrument"), and a skilled ("cunning") and experienced teacher. Furthermore, he would need four or five days to work with the children and learn the music for the opening ceremony.[40] A deed of appointment for a permanent *informator* suitable to the college chapel would have been far more detailed, and the duties listed there more onerous.[41]

We do not know who filled the position on a temporary basis. But apparently negotiations with Taverner continued and he was persuaded to accept the position[42] as *informator chorustarum*, organist, and director of the chapel's music. If the responsibilities were substantial, however, so too was the authority of the post and the prestige accruing to the man who exercised that authority at Cardinal College. The position carried a salary of £15 including commons and livery,[43] a sum greater than that paid to any member of the college except the dean and subdean; the cantor and the public professors, and far exceeding the salary at a college such as Tattershall.

Taverner arrived to find a flourishing community, with buildings continuing to rise on every side, and scholars arriving from Cambridge and visitors from London and other towns. The college had already achieved a reputation for learning.[44] Wolsey was negotiating in Italy for the acquisition of books from Rome and Venice, and for copies of Greek manuscripts that had formed part of the collection of Cardinal Bessarion, the eminent fifteenth-century neo-Platonist and scholar.[45] For the chapel and its officers he spared no cost. As early as October 1525 he had

Stubbes bring a magnificent collection of vestments and service books from Hampton Court.[46] Two later shipments from London,[47] and further acquisitions by means fair and foul--the most spectacular being Wolsey's crude procurement in 1528 of the splendid collection of service books that had belonged to the household chapel of Henry Percy, the fifth Earl of Northumberland[48]--attest to the grandeur of the chapel at Cardinal College. It was here that Taverner, responsible for providing music for the liturgy, teaching the boy choristers and leading the musical portions of devotions and services, spent what must have been the richest and most active years of his creative life.

One can gain some idea of how active those years were from the ambitious daily schedule of services in the chapel.[49] The boys began the liturgical day at 5:00 a.m. with the chanting of Marian matins and hours, and an hour later the chaplains and clerks sang first matins and prime (*cum cantu et nota*). These finished, the choirmaster with his choristers and certain clerks sang Lady mass in polyphony, in the finest possible manner (*cum nota et intorto cantu, modo optimo qui sciverint*). Six chaplains and six clerks then celebrated requiem mass at the high altar *cum nota et cantu*. At 9:00 a.m., the minor offices having been said, the entire company of chaplains, clerks and choristers sang the daily mass. At 3:00 p.m., the boys said Marian vespers; one hour later, the twenty-five chaplains and clerks celebrated vespers and compline with solemn song (*solemniter cum cantu*). Immediately afterwards, three antiphons were sung in polyphony: one to the Trinity, another to the Virgin, and a third to St. William, an ancient predecessor of Wolsey's as Archbishop of York (died 1154, canonized 1226). At 7:00 p.m. the choirmaster returned to the chapel with his choristers and several chaplains and clerks to sing polyphonic settings first of *Salve Regina* with the versicle *Ave Maria*; then of *Ave Maria*, in three sections separated by the ringing of bells (*trina vice, campanae sonitu intervalla distinguente*);[50] and then of the Jesus antiphon *Sancte Deus, sancte fortis*. Finally, he was to lead the choristers in commemorations of the Trinity, St. Mary, All Saints, and St. Frideswide. On days when these prayers were omitted, he was to give music lessons to the choristers.

On Sundays and principal and double feasts, the dean and canons were to join the clerks and boy choristers in chapel for all the offices as well as processions, masses and the sprinkling of the holy water. On greater double feasts (which included the Feasts of St. Frideswide and St. William) the dean would lead services; on lesser double feasts the subdean would replace him. Furthermore, the entire community met in chapel for weekly exequies for Wolsey's parents, and for his and their benefactors, and for his soul and the souls of the king and queen after their deaths, as well as for quarterly requiem masses for Wolsey's parents.[51]

Taverner held the responsibility of providing and ordering the music for this rigorous schedule of services, as well as the duty of teaching and training the boy choristers. Undoubtedly, he filled some of his requirements with the music of his contemporaries, and with his own earlier works. Just as certainly, he composed a great deal of new music specifically for the chapel at Cardinal College. It is unwarranted to entertain the notion, as Fellowes did, that Taverner "wrote all his fine church music" during his three and a half years at Oxford;[52] but certainly much of Taverner's music must have been the product of those years. How much of that music survives, however, and which of the extant works come from Oxford, are questions we cannot answer at present. The motet *Jesu Christe pastor bone* and the Mass for the Feast of St. William of York derived from it can be attributed with virtual certainty to the Oxford years. So too can *Ave Maria* and *Sancte Deus, sancte fortis*, both settings of texts prescribed in the college statutes, and the antiphon *O splendor gloriae*, whose text could have served devotions to both Jesus and the Trinity. The antiphon *Mater Christi*, whose text conforms to the general requirements for antiphons stipulated in the statutes, is probably also an Oxford setting.

By chance, a set of six partbooks (Ob 376-81) produced for the use of the chapel choir at Cardinal College has survived. It is the only source of Taverner's music copied during his lifetime that remains complete today. Known as the Forrest-Heyther collection, it opens with Taverner's *Gloria tibi Trinitas* Mass and continues with ten other Masses: Fayrfax's *Regale*, *Albanus, O bone Jesu* and *Tecum principium;* Avery Burton's *Ut re mi fa sol la;* John Marbeck's *Per arma justitiae*; William Rasar's *Christe Jesu*; Hugh Aston's *Te Deum*; Ashewell's *Jesu Christe;* and John Norman's *Resurrexit Dominus*. With Norman's Mass, the scribal hand ends abruptly. It is clear from the layout of the partbooks that the cessation of that hand represents not an intended completion of the manuscript but its interruption.

An inscription in the manuscript tells us that at this point it changed hands, coming in 1530 into the possession of William Forrest, who was then a petty canon at Cardinal College. Some time afterwards-- it is assumed during the 1550s, when he was chaplain to Mary Tudor and had reason to expect performances of the music--Forrest took up where the first scribe had left off, adding seven more Masses, including Taverner's *Corona spinea* and *O Michael*. He died in ca. 1581, leaving his work unfinished. The set came into the possession of John Baldwin, a musician at St. George's Chapel Windsor, who completed it.[53]

The fine hand that inscribed the first eleven Masses may have been Taverner's. If he did not copy them, however, someone did so under his supervision. The opening of *Gloria tibi Trinitas*, which is given pride of place in the manuscript, is illuminated in three books by a portrait of a man's face, to which a ribbon is attached bearing Taverner's name. We must assume that these three portraits are (admittedly clumsy) likenesses of him. (Smaller, unidentified portraits open the Mass in two of the other three partbooks.) No other composer or composition is accorded similar treatment.

The first layer of the manuscript was copied, quite obviously, for performance by the chapel choir. Taverner, as director of the choir, chose its repertory. Therefore, we can identify the ten Masses (aside from *Gloria tibi Trinitas*) of the first layer as music that he knew and respected. The man he seems to have admired most was Fayrfax, who was also a native of southern Lincolnshire and whom he surely had known in London. We might note that three of these Masses--Fayrfax's *Regali* and *O bone Jesu*, and Aston's *Te Deum*--were inscribed with his own antiphons *Gaude plurimum* and *Ave Dei patris filia* in Cjc K.31 and Cu Dd.13.27.

The interruption of the copying after Norman's Mass may have been related closely to Taverner's apparently sudden decision in the spring of 1530 to leave Cardinal College. As we shall see, there was considerable confusion at that time. If Taverner was the scribe, he might nevertheless have regarded the books as college property and left them there, incomplete. If someone else was the scribe, that man would have halted his work temporarily, to await the instructions and decisions of the new choir director, who might well choose a different repertory. By whatever means, and in the sequence of events unknown to us, Forrest acquired the partbooks that same year. He did not forget Taverner. He began his own copying with the Mass *Corona spinea*, and later added *O Michael*. Taverner is the only composer accorded two Masses in the second layer of the Forrest-Heyther set.

At some point late in 1527 or early the following year, Taverner became involed in a bizarre episode at Cardinal College centering upon the activities of Thomas Garrett,[54] a restless cleric engaged in the selling of heretical books, and the subsequent discovery and destruction by the authorities of a Lutheran cell at Oxford. The traditional reading has had Taverner convert to Lutheranism, play an active role underground, leave Cardinal College in 1530 for ideological reasons, and then cease composition altogether. Misunderstanding of the nature of his involvement and exaggeration of its degree have bedeviled the composer's biography for 400 years. A detailed study of the entire episode, and of Taverner's last two years at the college, will refute its every point, and allow us not only to see the Oxford years in a fresh light, but also to provide a foundation through which we may understand the difficult documents of Taverner's later years in Boston.

Cells of heretical Lollards had been active in England since the propagation of John Wycliffe's beliefs late in the fourteenth century, and their numbers--along with attempts to destroy them--had increased markedly towards the end of the fifteenth. Since Lollard thought anticipated virtually every Lutheran tenet except justification by faith, and fostered a vigorous spirit of critical dissent and anti-clericalism, these cells provided a suitable market for Lutheran book-agents after the publication of the German reformer's three revolutionary tracts in 1520. Given the common outlook held by supporters of both movements, it is difficult to separate one sect from the other. Together they formed the source of English Protestantism, and when William Tyndale's published translation of the New Testament arrived in England in 1526, the organization of a heretical cell at Oxford could be considered by the authorities unfortunate but hardly surprising.[55] Yet Wolsey's men were caught unaware and disorganized. The Oxford episode reveals a widespread disaffection among promising young scholars as well as the spiritual rot that was undermining the Roman church in England. It is all the more symbolic for having centered upon the magnificent foundation of the cardinal and papal Legate.

The catalyst of the Oxford incident and founder of the group espousing heresy was John Clark, one of the Cambridge scholars brought to Cardinal College by Dr. Shorton. While at Cambridge, Clark had undoubtedly been a member of the group of dons and students who patronized the White Horse Inn, commonly called "Little Germany," and absorbed Luther's ideas there. By the time he came to Oxford in November 1525, his ideas were formed and his convictions sturdy. Once there, Clark preached daily and delivered lectures in theology which attracted scholars from the colleges and halls of the university. He gathered around himself a community of young men known for their intelligence and industry--ironically, just the men with whom Wolsey, unaware of the depth of their alienation from the church, wished to staff his college. They included Bayley, Betts, Drumme, Frith, Fryer, Goodman and Sumner. A number of singing men from the chapel joined this group, among them a clerk named Radley, possibly John Mayow and Taverner. Others, too, were involved, men who avoided notice when the inevitable crisis exploded and whose names are therefore not recorded. Nevertheless, despite Clark's daily lectures and the widening coterie, Dean Higden seems to have made no connection between the Cambridge group and the dissemination of Lutheran ideas, for he continued to recruit scholars from the sister university until late in 1527.

The underground spread to scholars at other colleges at Oxford. Among those whose names have come down to us were Sir John Dyott

(Diet; B.A. 1526) and Nicholas Udal (M.A. 1524; afterwards master of Eton and servant to Catherine Parr), both fellows of Corpus Christi College; William Edon (B.A. 1524), a fellow of Magdalen; Sir James Fitzjames (B.A. 1509, M.A. 1511, B. Theol. 1516), son of the chief justice of England and a chaplain at St. Alban's Hall, a residence in the lease of Merton College; and Anthony Dalaber, a young scholar living at St. Alban's Hall.

The Oxford group maintained connections with Lutherans at Cambridge (among the Cantabrigians eventually arrested at Oxford were Jeffrey Lome, a former porter at St. Anthony's School, and Sygar Nicholson, a student at Gonville Hall and later a university stationer), in London, and in the west country. Along with Cambridge, Oxford was a prime market for the English book-agents who obtained Lutheran tracts from German merchants in London. This book trade thrived despite official efforts to suppress it. Copies of Tyndale's translation of the New Testament began to arrive in London almost immediately after it was printed in Germany. It found a wide readership and became so popular that Tyndale published a second edition within a year; pirated editions were published for export in the Netherlands. The man responsible for bringing it to Oxford was the Lincolnshire cleric Thomas Garrett.

An account of the short-lived turmoil that Garrett precipitated was narrated some thirty years after the event by Anthony Dalaber to John Foxe, who set it out in his passionately anti-Roman *Acts and Monuments*. Dalaber's account is neither objective nor entirely trustworthy, for by 1562, when he related it to Foxe, his memory of dates and persons was no longer accurate. Furthermore, he died before finishing the narrative, and Foxe's reconstruction of the rest of it (from sources he does not cite) is unconvincing. A dozen entries in the *Letters and Papers of Henry VIII*--abstracts of letters written from late February until mid-April 1528--not only allow us to correct the Dalaber-Foxe account; they transform the melodrama Foxe gave us into a poignant story of ideals, courage and ineptitude.[56]

During the Easter season of 1527, Garrett went up to Oxford from London, apparently at Clark's invitation, to sell copies of Tyndale's translation of the New Testament and Lutheran books on Scripture to scholars at the university. Having received a sympathetic response, he returned with a second shipment on Christmas Eve.[57] Wolsey and Bishop Tunstal of London, who were dealing now with heresy of baffling proportions in the capital, apparently had Garrett followed and were aware of the purpose of his journeys to Oxford. Biding his time, Wolsey brought Dean Higden to London, probably to discuss events in Oxford, then sent him back with orders to remove Garrett from Radley's rooms at Cardinal College and send him to London. Once in Oxford, Higden enlisted the aide of Dr. London, the warden of New College, and Dr.

Cottisford, master of Lincoln College and commissary (i.e., vice-chancellor) of the university. With them, he began "a privy search" for Garrett. The reformers were tipped off, however, by Arthur Cole, a proctor of Magdalen who warned Garrett to run. Dalaber, who had bought books from Garrett and had spent the previous summer attending Clark's lectures (given without proper license in the town of Poughley, as an epidemic had struck Oxford), now gave Garrett documents enabling him to find employment as curate to his brother, a rector in Dorset, until an opportunity to flee the country should arise.

On the morning of Wednesday, 19 February 1528, Garrett left Oxford and headed west. He lost his courage, however (perhaps having second thoughts about serving Dalaber's brother falsely), and by Friday night had smuggled himself back to Radley's rooms, where he was immediately discovered, arrested and removed to the rooms of Dr. Cottisford, who intended to keep him prisoner and then send him to Wolsey on Sunday. On Saturday afternoon, however, Cottisford carelessly left Garrett unguarded while he went to vespers. Garrett fled forthwith to Gloucester College, and was taken to Dalaber's room. But Dalaber had only recently transferred to that Benedictine house and, still engaged in moving his belongings, had not heard of Garrett's sudden return and arrest. He was taken aback by the rapid turn of events and, as he listened to Garrett's story in the presence of a strange and perhaps hostile monk, realized that he himself was now implicated in the conspiracy. Dalaber could not harbor the hunted man. Garrett would have to leave Oxford again.

> But now, with deep sighs and plenty of tears, he prayed me to help him to convey him away; and so he cast off his hood and his gown, wherein he came unto me, and desired me to give him a coat with sleeves, if I had any; and told me that he would go into Wales, and thence convey himself into Germany, if he might. Then I put on him a sleeved coat of mine, of fine cloth in grain, which my mother had given me. He would have another manner of cap of me, but I had none but priestlike, such as his own was. Then kneeled we both down together upon our knees, and lifting up our hearts and hands to God, our heavenly Father, desired him, with plenty of tears, so to conduct and prosper him in his journey, that he might well escape the danger of all his enemies. . . . And then we embraced, and kissed the one the other, the tears so abundantly flowing out from both our eyes, that we all be-wet both our faces, and scarcely for sorrow could we speak one to another.

Alone now and in danger, Dalaber turned to the tenth chapter of the Matthew Gospel, in the hope of renewing his strength:

> Behold, I send you forth as sheep in the midst of wolves; be ye
> therefore wise as serpents, and harmless as doves. But beware of
> men: for they will deliver you up to the councils. . . . But when
> they persecute you in this city, flee ye into another. [King James
> translation]

He hid Garrett's clerical robes among his own and left his room,
intending to go first to Corpus Christi to speak to Dyott and Udal, and
then to Cardinal College to tell Clark of Garrett's escape. On the way he
met William Edon of Magdalen, another "brother," and, after telling him
his astonishing story, went directly to find Clark in the college chapel.

> Evensong was begun, and the dean and the other canons were there
> in their gray amices; they were almost at Magnificat before I came
> thither. I stood at the choir door and heard Mr. Taverner play, and
> others of the chapel there sing, with and among whom I myself was
> wont to sing also, but now my singing and music was turned into
> sighing and musing. As I thus and there stood, in cometh Dr.
> Cottisford, the commissary, as fast as ever he could go, bareheaded,
> as pale as ashes (I knew his grief well enough), and to the dean he
> goeth into the choir, where he was sitting in his stall, and talked
> with him very sorrowfully; what I know not; but whereof I might
> and did well and truly guess. I went aside from the choir door to
> see and hear more. The commissary and dean came out of the choir,
> wonderfully troubled as it seemed. About the middle of the church
> met them Dr. London, puffing, blustering, and blowing, like a
> hungry and greedy lion seeking his prey. They talked together a
> while; but the commissary was much blamed by them for keeping of
> his prisoner so negligently, insomuch that he wept for sorrow . . . .
> The doctors departed, and sent abroad their servants and spies
> everywhere.

Clark had watched all of this from his choir stall; something was
amiss. Towards the middle of compline, after the uproar had died down,
he left his stall, brought Dalaber to his rooms, and sent for Sumner and
Betts. Dalaber again related his story.

> Then desiring them to tell unto our other brethren what had
> happened, for there were divers other in that college [Cardinal
> College], I went to Corpus Christi College, to comfort our brethren
> there, being in like heaviness. When I came to Corpus Christi
> College, I found together in Diet's chamber, tarrying and looking for
> me, Fitzjames, Diet, and Udal. They knew all the matter before by
> Master Eden, whom I had sent unto Fitzjames, but yet I declared
> the matter unto them again. And so I tarried there, and supped
> with them in that chamber, where they had provided meat and drink
> for us before my coming; at which supper we were not very merry,
> considering our state and peril at hand. When we had ended our
> supper, and committed our whole cause with fervent sighs and hearty
> prayers, unto God our Heavenly Father, Fitzjames would needs have

me to lie that night with him in my old lodging at Alban's Hall.
And so I did, but small rest and little sleep took we there both that
night.

Returning early on Sunday morning to his rooms at Gloucester
College, Dalaber found that they had been thoroughly searched; the
monk who had accompanied Garrett had gone to the prior of the college,
Anthony Dunstan, and told him about the conspiracy. Dalaber's fears
had been justified. He was brought to Dunstan and questioned about
Garrett's flight.

> I told him that I knew not where he was, except he were at
> Woodstock. For so, said I, he had showed me that he would go
> thither, because one of the keepers there, his friend, had promised
> him a piece of venison to make merry withal the Shrovetide, and
> that he would have borrowed a hat and a pair of high shoes of me,
> but I had none indeed to lend him. This tale I thought meetest,
> though it were nothing so. Then had he spied on my finger a big
> ring of silver very well double gilt, with two letters, A.D., engraved
> in it for my name. I suppose he thought it to be gold. He required
> to see it. I took it unto him. When he had it in his hand, he said
> it was his ring, for therein was his name, an A. for Anthony, and a
> D. for Dunstan. When I heard him so say, I wished in my heart to
> be as well delivered from and out of his company, as I was assured
> to be delivered from my ring for ever.

Dalaber now was removed to the chapel of Lincoln College for
interrogation by Cottisford, Higden, and London, "the rankest papistical
Pharisee of them all." There he admitted having known Garrett for
almost a year and having seen him the previous afternoon. He repeated
what he had told Dunstan; but---he claimed falsely to Foxe--he would
admit nothing else, though threatened with torture and confinement in
the Tower of London. After two hours, he was taken to a room in the
college and put in stocks. It is at this point that Dalaber's narrative ends,
having omitted the fact "that on examination he betrayed twenty-two of
his associates."[58]

Dalaber's confession broke the secret cell wide open. In
Radley's room, some of Garrett's books were found; and in John
Mayow's, a list of books that Garrett had advised him to buy. So widely
had the heresy spread that among the men implicated were two monks of
Bury and one of Glastonbury. Still, Garrett eluded the good doctors.
Gentle Cottisford, "being in extreme pensiveness," consulted an
astronomer, who declared, after a faulty reading of the stars, that Garrett
had fled in a tawny coat towards the southeast and was in London. Dr.
London's reaction was characteristically harsh: "It were a gracious deed
if they were tried and purged and restored unto their mother from

whence they came." But he correctly identified the root of the immediate problem in the activities of the London booksellers, sought to help Wolsey identify them, and in two letters to Longland, pleaded the cause of the young scholars: these "most towardly young men in Oxford" had long tired of Garrett's books and had brought them back to Dalaber, in whose keeping they were found on Tuesday 25 February after a three-day search.[59]

Cottisford, meanwhile, recovered his wits and sent word of Garrett's flight to the western ports of Bristol and Chester as well as to various ports in southeastern England. On the night of Saturday 29 February (1528 was a leap year), just one week after his escape and disguised in courtier's coat and buttoned cap, Garrett was captured and arrested near Bristol by Cole's father-in-law. Taken immediately to the county jail at Ilchester (some thirty miles south of Bristol)[60], he broke down and confessed, implicating his fellow heretics: Clark, Dyott, Frith, Fryer, and Dalaber in Oxford; the prior of Reading, to whom he had sold some sixty books; and the London book-agents John Gough[61] and Robert Farman (rector of All Hallows, Honey Lane in London) with Goodale his servant, who were Garrett's sources. Bishop Longland assumed control of the operation of arresting and interrogating these men. He delegated responsibility for the London group to Bishop Tunstal, and for the Oxford scholars to the heads of their respective colleges.

In London, Gough protested his innocence and denied any knowledge of Garrett, while Farman admitted importing Lutheran books, but only, he declared, in order to be able to refute the cause that they advanced. Tunstal found this argument unpersuasive, and in a heresy proceeding he forbade Forman to celebrate mass or to preach. Goodman admitted only to having studied under Garrett.[62] The purpose of these interrogations was not only to dissuade suspected and known heretics but also to uncover the broad underground of still-hidden heretics; the discovery and arrest of John Fryer in London on 4 March may have been one result of these sessions.[63] Farman, however, escaped to Antwerp, and was not caught until July.[64]

Now Dean Higden arrested and interrogated the involved persons at Cardinal College. It is in connection with this specific event that Foxe wrote two paragraphs which have ever since separated the Taverner biography from fact. In Foxe's words,

> To these [dissidents] join also Taverner of Boston, the good musician, besides many others called also out of other places, most picked young men, of grave judgment and sharp wits; who conferring together upon the abuses of religion, being at that time crept into the church, were therefore accused of heresy unto the cardinal, and cast into a prison, within a deep cave under the ground of the same

[Cardinal] College where their salt fish was laid; so that through the filthy stench thereof they were all infected, and certain of them taking their death in the same prison, shortly upon the same being taken out of the prison into their chambers, there deceased.

. . . Taverner, although he was accused and suspected for hiding of Clark's books under the boards in his school; yet the cardinal for his music excused him, saying that he was but a musician: and so he escaped.[65]

Foxe's account is ambiguous. It can and should be read: Taverner and others joined these young men, who were accused of heresy and imprisoned. But because of his music, Wolsey excused him from punishment; and so he escaped *imprisonment*. Instead, it has been taken to mean that Taverner was imprisoned for his part in the heresy and was then released on Wolsey's orders. Foxe added in a marginal note, inserted into the seventh edition in 1583:

This Taverner repented him very much that he had made songs to Popish ditties in the time of his blindness.

This marginal note, ascribed to no contemporary source, was added by Foxe probably on the basis of secondary oral sources. Furthermore, although quoted often to support the claim that Taverner ceased composing after 1530, it is not corroborated by the actual text in any way. Denis Stevens has pointed out that the phrase "Popish ditties" must refer to the large-scale Marian antiphons rather than to the Latin mass, which remained inviolate until the last years of Henry's reign.[66]

The truth of the matter is clearly stated in a letter from Higden to Thomas Byrton, a chaplain of Wolsey's, on 15 March 1528:

Master Byrton, I pray you to ascertain my Lord's Grace that according to His Grace's commandment by his letters I have kept in ward Master Clerke, Master Sumnar, Master Bettes and Sir Frithe, being canons *primi ordinis* [senior canons], and Sir Baylye being a canon *secundi ordinis* [a petty canon], also Sir Thomas Lawney, a priest of the chapel, as they being suspect to have books suspect of errors; and I with the assistance of Master subdean, ij censors, and a notary, have examined them in certain articles and here send to my said Lord's Grace their very answers to every article by their oath of the holy evangelist. As for Master Taverner I have not commit him to prison, neither Radley, because the register of the university at his being with my Lord's Grace, their names among other suspect sent up by the university, His Grace said to him, as for Taverner and Radley, they be unlearned, and not to be regarded. As for Master Taverner, the hiding of Master Clerke's books and being privy to the letter sent to Master Clerke from Master Garrett after he was fled be the greatest things after my mind that can be

> laid to his charge. And for Radley, he did sell diverse of Master
> Garret's books and hid diverse books suspect, and to his house to
> Master Garret was the resort of all.[67]

Wolsey had excommunicated the dissidents some time earlier, but had made no attempt to bring them to justice. Therefore, Higden, in the same letter, asked that they be released and absolved, as Easter was approaching.

Garrett was brought to Oxford, interrogated at the Church of St. Mary's by Cottisford, Higden and London, and was convicted of heresy. A transcript of the proceedings was sent to Longland, who in turn sent it to Wolsey on 1 April with an accompanying letter that noted the discrepancies between Garrett's answers and those of the other scholars, and described him as "a very subtle, crafty and an untrue man,"[68] despite the fact that he had recanted.[69] Soon afterwards--probably between 8 April (when Longland wrote to Wolsey asking that most of the imprisoned men be released) and Easter Sunday (12 April)--all those who were accused or suspected of heresy were compelled to walk in procession, carrying faggots from St. Mary's to St. Frideswide's. As they passed the top of Carfax, each man, in a symbolic act of repentance, cast a book into a bonfire which had been set there.[70] Garrett and Dalaber then were sent to the prison at Osney, and a few unrepentant scholars were returned to the fish cellar at Cardinal College. The others were freed and allowed to resume their normal lives.

Seven weeks had elapsed since Garrett's first flight, and Cardinal College was now back to the quiet, if not the untarnished promise, of its early days. Indeed, a semblance of normality had existed for some time, as a letter of Thomas Cromwell's to Wolsey on 2 April attests:

> The building of your noble college most prosperously and
> magnificently doth rise in such wise, that to every man's judgment
> the like thereof never seen nor imagined, having consideration to the
> largeness, beauty, sumptuous, curious, and most substantial building
> of the same.

> Your chapel within the said college most devoutly and virtuously
> ordered, and the ministers within the same not only diligent in the
> service of God, but also the service daily done within the same so
> devout, solemn, and full of harmony, that in mine opinion it hath
> few peers.[71]

The next few months passed quietly. The environment was so peaceful--and Wolsey and Higden so lenient--that Clark was able to obtain a petty canonry for his brother.[72] Then, at the beginning of August, Cardinal College suffered a second setback. The sweating sickness, a virulent disease whose symptoms differed from those of the plague but had an equally devastating effect, attacked Oxford. It descended with particular severity on Wolsey's foundation,[73] killing two scholars (one of them, Clark's brother) in the first week and infecting several others. Baylye and Sumner were fatally stricken in the fish cellar; although they refused to recant in the face of a threat of eternal damnation, they did repent for their offenses and, after their deaths during the week of August, were given Christian burial.[74] A shaken Higden persuaded Wolsey to release the three surviving prisoners--Betts, Frith, and Lawney--on the condition that they remain within ten miles of Oxford. Frith broke his word and escaped to the Continent where he worked with Tyndale. Fryer, who was pardoned by Wolsey and whose letter to the cardinal, written from a cell in the Fleet in London, sheds a kinder light on Wolsey than Foxe would have allowed, remained quiet after his release, and later traveled to Italy to study medicine in Reginald Pole's household in Padua.[75] Garrett returned to London and remained close to the Lutheran community there. Farman was held in Antwerp for six months, while English agents there attempted to persuade Wolsey to bring charges of high treason against him. Wolsey, however, would have nothing to do with such harassment, and eventually Farman was released.

Aside from Goodman, who "was had out [of the prison] and died in the town,"[76] the erstwhile dissidents who remained in Oxford returned to the fold of the church and university. For almost all of them, and their colleagues in the heresy, radical religious beliefs were to remain a thing of the past. Only two of these men--Frith and Garrett-- would go to the stake as heretics. The rest would follow the wandering course of Henrician theology and remain content to serve their king and church.

Compared with these men's activities in the Oxford incident, Taverner's were trivial. As Higden had noted, the most serious charges that could be laid against him were that he had hidden some of Clark's books and knew of a letter sent by Clark to Garrett. No doubt, then, he was sympathetic to the leaders of the cell, and to their cause: his favor to Clark and Clark's trust in him leave no doubt of Taverner's interest in the new religious ideas circulating among the Oxford scholars. But his involvement with them was mild, and the notion that he ceased composing because of his involvement with the Lutheran cell is without foundation. We will remember that this notion had its origin in Foxe's marginal statement, added twenty years after his first published account and more than fifty years after the fact, that Taverner regretted having set "Popish ditties in the time of his blindness." Fellowes interpreted this to mean that he stopped composing after leaving Oxford in 1530. Had Fellowes been consistent, he would have had Taverner give up his association with music in early 1528, rather than remain as director of the chapel's music for two more years. But there is no evidence whatever

that Taverner gave up music. On the contrary, positive evidence that
Taverner remained active as a musician in Wolsey's service comes from a
hitherto unnoticed source, one that deals once more with a school of
Wolsey's.

      In the spring of 1528, Wolsey engaged in a second educational
project, one directly related to the needs of Cardinal College: a college
of secular canons attached to a grammar school, to be built on the site of
the Priory of St. Peter and St. Paul in the town of Ipswich, Suffolk,
where the cardinal was born. The religious function of the foundation
was to maintain divine service and to pray for the king and cardinal as
well as for Wolsey's parents. Its secular function was to prepare scholars
for entry into Cardinal College, in a tradition established by the
associations of Eton with King's and Winchester with New College,
Oxford. Once again, then, Wolsey set his ambitions on a traditional
path.
      Wolsey established this new institution much as he had done
with his college at Oxford. First, in May 1528, he sought and received a
papal bull and royal confirmation for the suppression of the Augustinian
priory, with its seven active members and income of about £80, and the
foundation of his new college, to be called the Cardinal's College of St.
Mary in Ipswich. There quickly followed bulls appropriating five
churches in the town and several monasteries whose incomes would be
put towards the raising of funds for the undertaking.[77] On 15 June,
Bishop Longland laid the foundation stone, and on 28 July Wolsey
received a royal license to found the college and endow it to the annual
value of £100 for the maintenance of anniversaries and the erection of
chantries. Its membership was to include a dean, twelve priests, eight
clerks, eight boy choristers and poor scholars, thirteen poor men, and a
grammar master for the boys.[78] William Capon was brought from
Cambridge and appointed dean of the college, and Richard Ducke, a
graduate of Exeter College, Oxford, and chaplain of Wolsey, was made
dean of the chapel. During the summer, virtually the entire clerical and
musical complement ordered in the statutes was recruited and brought to
Ipswich. Wolsey chose the Feast of the Nativity of the Blessed Virgin
(8 September) for the ceremonious inauguration of the college chapel.
He had food and other gifts for a formal dinner sent to the college by
such eminences as the Dukes of Norfolk and Suffolk, and sent as his
deputies to the ceremonies Thomas Cromwell, Stephen Gardiner (later
Bishop of Winchester) and Edward Lee (who would succeed Wolsey as
Archbishop of York). Cromwell arrived on 6 September with the others,
bringing the altar cloths, copes, plate and vestment to appropriate the old
monastic church to its new function, and remained for four days to

supervise the arrangement of the furniture and tapestries of the hall. On the eve of the feast-day, according to Capon,

> I, with all the company of Your Grace's college, as the subdean, Mr. Ellis, vj priests, viij clerks, and ix choristers with all our servants, when we had finished our evensong in our college church, then immediately after we repaired together to our Lady's Chapel there sang evensong as solemnly and devoutly as we could. And there accompanied with Mr. Stephyns, Doctor Lee, and Mr. Crumwell, with Mr. Humfrew Wyngfylde, (to whom all we of Your Grace's college be much bounden unto for his loving and kind manner showed unto us,) the bailiffs of the town, with the port-men and the prior of Christ's church, all the which accompanied us that same night home again to Your Grace's college with as loving and kind manner as I have seen; and at their coming thither they drank with me both wine and beer, and so that night departed. On the next day, which was our Lady's Day, the viijth day of September, a day of very foul weather, and rained sore continually, so that we could not go in procession through the town to our Lady's Chapel according to our statute by Your Grace made; but we made as solemn a procession in Your Grace's college church as could be devised. Insomuch there were xl of your copes worn there, and as much people as could stand in the church and in the churchyard. Also all the honorable gentlemen of the shire were there . . . to the number of xxiiij gentlemen of the country, besides the bailiffs, port-men of the town, the prior of the Christ's Church, the prior of Butley, Doctor Grene, vicar of Alborough, as commmissaries both to your Grace and to the Bishop of Norwich, and the Duke of Norfolk's almoner Mr. Hege, all the which were there, with as good will and diligence as they could to do Your Grace honor that day; and they all took repast at dinner in Your Grace's college, and as I trust well entertained with good fare, and such fashion as we could devise, wherewith they were right well contented as I supposed.

The singers of the choir were first-rate:

> Furthermore as for your singing men been well chosen, very well chosen, very well breasted with sufficient cunning . . . and some of them very excellent.

Nevertheless, the musicians lured from wealthier establishments by extravagant promises of wages and commons, were unhappy with conditions at the college, and protested openly and with some persistence.

> [They] will not serve here with their good wills for that wages, alleging for their self how they had much better wages there from whence they came from. Moreover they will have breakfasts every day in as ample and large manner as they have had in other places. I fear that their commons allowed by Your Grace will not suffice

> them as yet: for we can make no provisions neither for beefs nor
> for muttons for want of pasture near unto us. . . . I have entertained
> them according to Your Grace's commandment with good words and
> plenty of meat and drink, promising to some of them that be
> excellent more wages, for they grudge sore at their wages as Mr.
> Doctor Stephyns and Mr. Crumwell can show to Your Grace more
> at length.

Other problems beset the chapel. The yeoman of the revestry
could not handle his many duties, and so Capon hired a sexton to assist
him until Wolsey further advised on the matter. Nor could six priests
(one of whom, the subdean, was occupied in overseeing the construction
of the new buildings) keep the three daily masses prescribed by the
statutes. Capon requested either that more priests be brought in or that
one of the masses, either the requiem mass or the Lady mass, be
temporarily dispensed with. In fact, order seems to have been kept in
the chapel only by the presence of one man, a musician of outstanding
abilities about whom we know almost nothing, curiously, aside from
Capon's letter:

> And but for Mr. Lentall we could in a manner do nothing in our
> choir. He taketh very great pains and is always present at matins
> and all masses with evensong, and setteth the choir in good order
> from time to time, and faileth not at any time. He is very sober
> and discrete, and bringeth up your choristers very well: assuring
> Your Grace there shall be no better children in no place of England
> than we shall have here, and that in short time.[79]

Unfortunately for Capon, Wolsey fully recognized Lentall's value, and
sent for him in December in order to transfer him to the more
prestigious college at Oxford.[80]   In a letter of 28 December Capon
expressed his sense of great loss at the removal of Lentall, who was the
key of his choir, "and set everything in so good order, and made us very
good children."[81]

The loss and ensuing difficulty, however, only presaged the
melancholy fate of the young institution altogether. Although the
grammar school grew so quickly that by January 1529 the school house
no longer had adequate room for its students,[82] and new construction--
"much of it above the ground, which is very curious work"--proceeded at
such a clip during the summer that laborers had to work day and night,[83]
Wolsey's fall in October of that year brought a sudden and disastrous
end to the college. King Henry took over its property as he did with the
cardinal's other works at Hampton Court, Oxford and York Place; but
whereas he appropriated these magnificent structures for his own use and
prestige, the more modest foundation at Ipswich held no attraction for
him. By the end of November 1529, less than two months after Wolsey's

fall, royal agents had stripped the foundation of its plate and vestments, and proceeded to dissolve it. The canons, hired men, boys and servants of the college were scattered. In the following year, the king granted the site to Thomas Alvard, a former servant of Wolsey's and now gentleman usher of the king's chamber.[84] Some of the property was granted to Eton College and Waltham Abbey, the stone of the destroyed buildings was brought to London for the building at the king's palace at Whitehall (formerly Wolsey's residence, York Place). In a final degradation, the site of Cardinal College, Ipswich, became a garbage dump of the town.

A letter from the halcyon days of the college, which has remained obscure despite its publication in abstract form some forty years ago, shed light on Wolsey's foundations at Ipswich and Oxford, on the architect John Molton, and on Taverner. It was written at Oxford on 28 July 1528 (the day on which Wolsey received a royal license to found his college at Ipswich) by Nicholas Townley, and sent to Thomas Alvard.

> Mr. Alford in my full hearty manner. I commend me unto you desiring you to ascertain my Lord's Grace that there is no vestments for priest, deacon nor sub-deacon of the best blue cloth of gold here at His Grace's college. Whereas His Grace's pleasure is to have ij children for His Grace's college at Ipswich, Master Taverner will be at Hampton Court himself on Saturday next with His Grace and bring with him iiij children that be very good to that intent my Lord's Grace may hear them sing and then to choose such ij as shall stand with His Grace's pleasure. Master Taverner will bring with him at the same time all those books of songs that Lentall did leave with Master Gouff. I do send unto you here enclosed a bill indented containing the just measure for the hangings of the hall here and do keep the counterpane with me to that intent whosoever shall be the provider of the same hangings shall be sure of the just measure, and not to lay the fault in me if the hangings be not justly provided according the said measure. I pray you remember my Lord's Grace to send to the dean of Saint Stephens for his mason whose name is Molton, and that he may be sent to Oxford with speed. My Lord's Grace did promise me that His Grace would write to the dean for him. If we may have him here he shall do my Lord's Grace great pleasure. Thanked be Jesus there is little or no sickness here. This week we have come to the work at most twenty more masons than we have before. I do not doubt but we shall have many more this same week. The works go well forward here, and plenty of stuff cometh in abundantly every day, as stone, timber, lime, etc. Thanked be God we shall want no manner of stuff, with a great remain at the end of the year. Thus fare ye well from Oxford, the xxviij[th] day of July.[85]

There is much of interest here. Construction at Cardinal College was proceeding so rapidly that the number of masons on the site had to be augmented weekly. The great hall, now completed, lacked only hangings, while the chapel required only vestments "of the best blue cloth of gold" for its senior members. The reference to the master mason John Molton establishes that at this time he was in the service of the dean of the chapel of St. Stephen in Westminster Palace, where he may have been continuing work on the cloisters of that church begun by William Vertue, the royal master mason who had died in March 1527. It was to Molton that Wolsey turned immediately after the death, on 10 July, of Henry Redman, his principal architect and the man responsible for the superb design of Cardinal College. But eighteen days later Molton still had not arrived at Oxford, and the urgent tone of Townley's request for him undoubtedly stemmed from his fear that any further delay in replacing Redman would slow the rapid pace of work and upset what must have been a complex and carefully gauged schedule of construction.[86] We may note, too, that there were no signs of the spiritual disease which had recently afflicted the college. When read alongside Cromwell's letter of 2 April, with its astonishing report that all was running smoothly at the college even then, Townley's letter seems to confirm the fact that Cardinal College returned to peace as quickly as it had exploded.

Townley's remarks about Taverner overshadow in importance everything else in the letter, for they are the only contemporary evidence concerning his service as a musician, aside from a few account entries, that has come down to us firsthand. (Remember that even Dalaber's reference to Taverner's playing the organ in St. Frideswide's chapel reached us via Foxe. And there is no evidence that Foxe ever met or knew Taverner, even though as a boy in Boston before 1532 he may have heard of the local musician.) They make doubly clear the fact that Taverner remained active both in the musical life of Cardinal College, and in Wolsey's service. Only four months after his involvement in the heresy episode, he rode with four boys and, presumably, some servants of the college to Hampton Court in order to audition his gifted singers personally for Wolsey and to give the cardinal "all those books of songs"--sets of partbooks containing liturgical music--"that Lentall did leave with Master Gouff." We can only guess at the meaning of this last phrase. Lentall must have passed through Oxford on his way to his post as *informator chorustarum* at Ipswich; while in Oxford he visited Cardinal College and left several sets of partbooks, which he had probably brought from his former place of employment, in the custody of Gouff (a chaplain at the college), who in turn gave them to Taverner to bring to Wolsey. These music books could not have been for use at Ipswich-- even though one might assume that a choirmaster would bring the materials necessary to establish a repertory for a choir that he would have to build and train, and though the time sequence strengthens that assumption (Lentall had passed through Oxford some time before 28 July, the date of the foundation of the college)--for otherwise Lentall would have undoubtedly taken the books to Ipswich himself. More probably they were destined for Wolsey's household chapel choir. But Lentall would have entrusted Gouff with these music books only because Taverner was not there at the time.

Townley's letter indicates, too, that Wolsey took an active interest in the choirs of his foundations, as he did in their statutes, endowments, staffing, architectural design and furnishings. He had built the choir of his household chapel to preeminence and resisted the king's efforts to raid it, and had borrowed singers from the Chapel Royal to augment the musical establishment at his Oxford college during its early days. Now, beginning to staff the choir at Ipswich, Wolsey sent for Taverner and four boys trained by him in order to choose two--the minimum number needed for "gimel" passages--those duets for two voices, usually boys', found frequently in early Tudor music. It is striking that a man so preoccupied by affairs of church and state, and now mired in the complexities of a royal annulment proceedings that would lead to his collapse, would not leave this relatively minor task to the dean or choirmaster of the new foundation. Such personal concern attests to the cardinal's recognition of the symbolic role that music played in the projection of the status of his foundations and, by extension, of his own status. Taverner served a function by no means insignificant in Wolsey's strategy. As a trusted servant, he could expect that the patronage that so often flowed from powerful persons to their valued musicians would come one day from the cardinal.

Such a possibility, however, was cut short in 1529. At the beginning of that year Taverner was at the peak of his career: active and secure in his post, responsible for the music of the most promising college in Oxford, and at the head of a first-rate choir. Nine months later, his future, and that of Cardinal College, seemed suddenly to disintegrate. Wolsey's collapse was to change the course of his life.

Wolsey's fall may be studied as a personal disaster that broke his spirit and hastened his death, or in broad terms as a symbol of the demise of medieval England. Its significance, however, is neither personal nor symbolic: it is political. His collapse was a matter of state.[87] A century and more of dynastic strife and political instability had impressed on Henry the necessity of a male heir who would insure a secure line of succession in the Tudor house; and Catherine of Aragon's failure to produce that heir drew the king by the early 1520s to the possibility of dissolving his marriage. For some years he studied Biblical texts, theological arguments and canonic precedents, and gained support from numerous canon lawyers who questioned the dispensation of Pope Julius II that had permitted his marriage to the widow of his older brother. In the spring of 1527, goaded by his infatuation with Anne Boleyn and the decline in diplomatic relations with Emperor Charles V, the nephew of his wife, Henry initiated formal legal proceedings for annulment under Wolsey's guidance. Although he might have derived encouragement from the easy divorces granted to his sister Margaret, Queen of Scotland, and his brother-in-law, the Duke of Suffolk, Henry encountered only frustration and delay. On the one hand, Catherine displayed stubborn integrity and canny manipulation of her diplomatic leverage in refusing any compromise; and, on the other, Charles exerted over Pope Clement VII a growing control that was hostile to Henry's cause. After a hastily convened tribunal to test the validity of the marriage had ended in disaster, Wolsey studied the canon law of annulment as well as documents of the royal marriage, and discovered the one loop-hole through which Henry might escape his bond: an insufficiency in the original papal bull, which granted a dispensation of the impediment of affinity that would have been incurred had Catherine's first marriage been consummated, but neglected to dispense with the lesser impediment of public honesty incurred by the non-consummation which Catherine had always claimed. Yet Henry ignored Wolsey's argument in favor of his own weaker one, taken from two Levitical injunctions forbidding a man to sleep with the wife of his brother, which complicated the case and delayed its resolution.

But if Wolsey found his hands tied by Henry's stubbornness, he added to his own difficulties in an uncharacteristic misjudgment of his king's determination. During a long trip to the Continent in the summer of 1527, Wolsey gave the distinct impression of handling the royal divorce case with far less energy than that with which he pursued his dream for a European peace conference and treaty. Worse still, the cardinal so thoroughly underestimated the role of Anne Boleyn, whom he held in contempt, that he began to look for prospective brides for the king. Only upon his return from Europe in September did Wolsey discover that Henry had deceived him and engaged in secret divorce actions of his own. He now realized that his own position was in jeopardy. In desperation, he drafted one commission after another for papal approval, sent several embassies to Rome, and succeeded in getting three bulls by the spring of 1528: a commission to Wolsey and another papal legate to examine the validity of the marriage, a general commission to Wolsey and a second English bishop, and a dispensation for Henry to marry Anne once his first marriage was annulled. None of these was sufficient; he needed a specific, decretal commission to state the canon law of the matter and apply that law to Henry's marriage. Having little choice, however, Wolsey settled on the first bull and awaited the papal legate, Cardinal Campeggio. After a summer of postponements, the legate arrived at the end of September and proceeded to engage in a series of delaying actions. In December Catherine produced a copy of a second dispensation which seemed to correct the errors of Pope Julius's first bull and threatened to destroy Wolsey's argument. When in the early months of 1529 Campeggio secretly asked the Pope to revoke the case to Rome, and one last embassy to Rome failed to move Clement, Henry was lost. The legatine court headed by Wolsey and Campeggio was opened in mid-June, only to be adjourned, after it had bogged down a month later, until October.

Certain revocation of the entire question to Rome signalled Henry's total failure and public humiliation. He did not have to look far for a scapegoat. As Wolsey's argument for annulment collapsed, so too did his grand scheme for European peace. The foundations of his power began to disintegrate. In August 1529 an aristocratic clique took over the affairs of state. On 21 September he surrendered the chancellor's great seal, and soon after he was accused and found guilty of *praemunire*. Though pardoned by Henry, he was stripped of the bishopric of Winchester, the abbacy of St. Alban's, his college at Ipswich, and his palace at York Place. Sent to York in April 1530, he set out for his see with a great retinue, summoning a Northern Convocation of the Church to meet there for his enthronement in November. But his ambition led him to establish secret contacts with foreign agents. These were discovered and he was arrested for treason on 4 November. With his power now finally broken, Wolsey's health collapsed, and he died twenty-five days later before reaching London and the king's justice.

The impact of Wolsey's fall on Cardinal College, Oxford, was disastrous, for he had never given that college the corporate autonomy that would have separated its legal status from his. If the events beginning in 1527 and leading to Wolsey's demise suggest to us a "decline and fall," they did not assume that shape at the time. In 1528 he spent over £5000 at Oxford, a sum greater than that of any of the previous years, and founded Cardinal College, Ipswich. The sum for the first nine months of 1529 was half again as high. If at the beginning of July 1529 certain lords felt strong enough to accuse Wolsey of transgressions, among them illegal seizure of land for Cardinal College, Oxford,[88] the erosion of his position was not yet reflected in the situation at the college. Almost £500 was spent there during the fortnight of 5-18 July, shortly before the adjournment of the hopeless legatine tribunal, and for the final fortnightly account of 11-24 October the sum of £1400. Wolsey had resigned as chancellor on 19 September, and *praemunire* charges were brought against him on 9 October; this last great expenditure, therefore, may reflect a frantic attempt to complete as much work as possible before the final collapse of his position. On 27 October he was convicted of the *praemunire* charges, and his goods and property were declared forfeit. Henry quickly appropriated the cardinal's palace at York Place, and rumors circulated concerning the fate of his other foundations.

The king's original plan evidently was to bring an end to both of Wolsey's colleges. It was rumored, according to the Imperial Ambassador Eustace Chapuys in early November,

> that the King has very lately issued orders for all priests and ecclesiastics appointed by the Cardinal to quit the place forthwith, as part of it is to be demolished, were it for no other purpose than that of removing the Cardinal's escutcheon, which will be no easy work as there is hardly a stone from the top of the building to the very foundations where his blazoned armorial is not sculptured.[89]

Such rumors eventually reached the cardinal, and when in April 1530 the king announced his intention to suppress Ipswich, Wolsey moved to save the larger foundation at Oxford. He begged Cromwell some time in late June or early July of 1530 to see that his colleges were not destroyed, for they were, he noted, *opera manuum tuarum*, the work of your hands; to which Cromwell replied that Henry was determined to dissolve them, and might refound them as his own colleges.[90] On 20 August Wolsey wrote an anguished letter to Henry directly, "to recommend unto your excellent charity and goodness the poor college of Oxford," and followed it with similar pleas to several of the king's agents.[91] His fears were well based. When Dean Higden went to court in mid-August to plead for his college, he was told by the Duke of Norfolk, one of the triumvirate that had replaced Wolsey, that Henry intended to take from the college all its property except that which had belonged to St. Frideswide's, to dissolve the college and to tear down its buildings. Only a few moments after that interview, however, the king met Higden personally and told him:

> Surely we purpose to have an honorable college there, but not so great and of such magnificence as my lord Cardinal intended to have, for it is not thought meet for the common weal of our realm, yet will we have a college honorably to maintain the service of God and literature.[92]

Although Henry's statement did signal his final purpose, he would not act upon it for over a year, and the period since Wolsey's fall in September 1529 must have been dispiriting and full of uncertainty for the men at Cardinal College. A manuscript list of weekly payments to its canons and chapel members for the fifth year[93] documents the attrition in their numbers, and offers convincing proof of the decline of the college during this time of indecision. The list is divided into four terms (*primus terminus / quinti anni, secundus terminus,* etc.) of thirteen weeks each, starting around the beginning of October, January, April and July, respectively. The year covered is 1529-30.

The decline in the number of canons was relatively slight. Eighteen senior canons and eighteen canons were paid in the first week, while sixteen and fifteen, respectively, were paid in the last. Although fluctuations occurred below more often than above these numbers, we would still see no trend in them were it not for the decline in the membership of the chapel. From the beginning of the first term in October 1529 to the end of the last, the number of chaplains decreased from thirteen to three, of clerks from nine to eight, and of boy choristers from sixteen to eleven. The membership of the chapel thus dropped by more than a third, from thirty-eight to twenty-two. If we remove the figures for the boy choristers, who were probably not as sensitive to political winds as adults, the proportionately greater attrition--a drop of half, from twenty-two to eleven--gives clear evidence of the eroding impact Wolsey's ill fortune was having on the college. Moreover, the decline was not sudden; the figures show that it was steady and inexorable. From the beginning of the period, despite some evidence of musical activity and payments for books of polyphony,[94] attrition ground away at the size and morale of the musical establishment at Cardinal College (see table).[95]

By the early months of 1530, then, evidence of decline was seen at every turn. Wolsey's protectorship of the college and its men had collapsed along with his power. His conviction of *praemunire,* furthermore, nullified the legality of all his acts since he had become papal legate, and therefore undercut the status of Cardinal College from its very foundation. The vestments and other valuables of the chapel had been confiscated and taken to London, ostensibly to have Wolsey's arms removed; they were never returned. This stripping of the chapel must have depressed Taverner and his colleagues profoundly. It was also a clear symbol of what was to come. Ipswich had already been suppressed, and for six months now rumor spread that Cardinal College would follow.

Taverner therefore made the decision to quit the college. It had nothing to do with political or religious motives. The membership of his choir was shrinking. There was no longer a source of patronage here, or even a secure personal future. His decision was practical and realistic. At the end of Hilary term, he was paid £5 for two terms' work,[96] and, collecting the sum of 29s paid to him for a bill,[97] he left the college.

Weekly List of the Number of Chapel Members at Cardinal College, Oxford, Receiving Payment in "The Fifth Year"

First Term

Senior canons	18	19	16	16	14	12	17	18	15	17	17	17	17
Junior canons	18	18	18	18	18	17	17	19	24	17	17	16	16
Chaplains	13	12	12	11	11	12	12	13	11	11	11	11	12
Clerks	9	7	6	5	5	4	6	7	6	6	7	7	6
Boy choristers	16	16	16	16	16	16	16	16	16	15	14	14	14

Second Term

Senior canons	18	18	17	16	14	16	16	16	15	12	14
Junior canons	18	18	18	18	18	18	18	18	18	17	15
Chaplains	12	12	11	11	12	12	12	9	9	10	9
Clerks	6	6	5	5	6	6	6	9	*	8	9
Boy choristers	15	15	14	14	13	13	13	13	13	13	13

Third Term

Senior canons	14	16	16	15	17	17	17	15	15	15	15	15
Junior canons	17	18	18	18	18	18	18	17	17	17	17	15
Chaplains	10	10	9	9	8	8	8	8	6	6	6	6
Clerks	9	9	8	8	8	9	9	9	9	9	8	9
Boy choristers	12	12	12	14	10	10	10	10	10	11	11	11

Fourth Term

Senior canons	17	16	16	16	17	17	17	17	17	17	17	16
Junior canons	16	17	16	14	16	16	16	17	17	17	15	15
Chaplains	6	6	7	7	6	6	7	4	3	4	4	3
Clerks	7	8	9	8	9	9	9	8	8	8	8	8
Boy choristers	11	11	11	11	11	10	10	11	11	11	11	11

*scratched out in the manuscript

After a hasty search, John Benbow of Manchester, perhaps a fellow of the collegiate church of St. Mary the Virgin there, was engaged to succeed him. The college sent 10s to Benbow on 29 May in anticipation of his arrival;[98] three weeks later, William Whytbroke, one of the remaining chaplains, was sent by Higden to bring him to the college.[99] Benbow began his tenure as choirmaster at the beginning of the fourth term.

Nothing is known about either Benbow or the other members of the chapel aside from Whytbroke--who later went to London and became a canon and later subdean at St. Paul's[100]--but their next years were spent in a depressing climate. Although the college was referred to as King's College as early as January 1531,[101] Henry's plans concerning it were still uncertain and his patronage fitful. By December of that year, any hopes which the canons had entertained of completing Wolsey's design for the college had vanished.[102] In addition, receipts no longer covered expenses, and the men complained of poverty and hunger.[103] When Henry finally refounded the college seven months later, he organized it as a purely ecclesiastical foundation similar to Cardinal College in its liturgical provisions. The statutes given to King Henry VIII's College, Oxford, on 18 July 1532,[104] called for a corporate body of a dean and twelve canons, as well as eight chaplains, eight clerks, eight choristers and twelve poor men. Like Cardinal College, it was dedicated to the Blessed Virgin, the Holy Trinity, and St. Frideswide. Its statutes called for the singing of daily mass, Lady mass, requiem mass and the major offices, and a daily polyphonic rendering of the antiphons *Sancte Deus, sancte fortis* and *Ave Maria.*

The resemblance was superficial. Prayers for Wolsey and his parents were replaced by numerous prayers for Henry and Anne Boleyn, as well as for Henry's parents. Membership in the college was substantially reduced by the statutes, and even these were projected figures: there were ten canons at the foundation of the new college, only two of whom, Thomas Cannar and Edward Leighton, remained from the original group at Wolsey's college.[105] Deprived of most of its former sources of income and dependent upon the wayward generosity of the king, the college had to operate on a diminished financial basis lacking many of its old valuables and the servants necessary for the upkeep of its buildings and grounds. What most dimmed its luster, however, was the lack of any provision in the statutes for education.[106] Having no professors, visiting scholars, or students, it resembled a cathedral chapter without a cathedral. It became a backwater in the life of the university town it had so recently dominated, until in 1545 Henry refounded it again, this time in the dual capacity of college and cathedral of the newly-formed see of Oxford. It maintains those functions today as Christ Church, Oxford.

CHAPTER 6

THE LAST YEARS: BOSTON

Not a shred of evidence has been discovered about Taverner for the six years following his departure from Oxford. Several documents have survived, however, from the last eight years of his life, 1537-45. They are the membership list of a guild in Boston that Taverner joined in 1537; various letters, including three from Taverner to Thomas Cromwell, concerning the suppression of the friaries, in 1538-39; another letter in Taverner's hand concerning a kinsman of his; an *Inquisition post mortem* for the composer in 1546; the wills of his widow in 1553 and brother in 1556; and a mutilated document from ca. 1579 which involved his widow's descendants. These documents, and others relating to the major guilds of Boston, yield a great deal of information. They do not answer directly, however, the questions of when and why Taverner settled in Boston, and how he earned a living there. The obvious destination for a musician of his caliber was London; but there is no record of his having gone there. It is possible of course, that he did go to London from Oxford, and that his presence there went unrecorded, as it did in the second decade of the century. But there is a difference: in ca. 1510-20 Taverner was starting out, a young man who might not have been recognized widely, but in 1530 he was a musician and composer to be reckoned with. This time we should accept the lack of documentary evidence at face value. Taverner, I believe, went elsewhere, back to the district of his original home, his family and his personal connections, which he had left four years earlier. A return to Tattershall was out of the question: he had outgrown the little musical community at the collegiate church; the rest was a village. But nearby Boston was an obvious choice, an important commerical center with institutions offering Taverner ample opportunity to remain musically active.

When Taverner settled in Boston in the 1530s, it was a town of some 2000 citizens and a small community of foreigners, situated on the banks of the river Witham thirty miles downstream from Lincoln and six miles from an extension of the North Sea known as The Wash. Built on the site of a monastery founded in the seventh century by St. Botolph, medieval Boston (Botolfston, from "St. Botulf's stone")[1] was dominated by the solid homes of its old merchant families, the buildings and gardens of its four friaries, a thriving market place next to the immense parish church of St. Botolph's, the halls of its wealthy guilds, and its riverside warehouses and wharves. These--rather than any castle, college, monastery or cathedral--gave evidence of a society reflecting its mercantile history as a port for the hinterlands of central England.[2]

Boston had grown quickly from its early Norman beginnings into a marketing and trading center, as prosperous North Sea routes developed in the twelfth century; by the end of that century it was, after London, the wealthiest of English ports. The Hanseatic League established a "Steelyard"--a trading post and community of German merchants and their families--and built a lucrative trade in corn, while some twenty monastic foundations set up agencies there for the export of wool. An annual fair was founded, and local merchants made fortunes in the trading of leather, Scandinavian wood, iron, pitch and seal oil, Italian cloth and Flemish manufactured goods. Increasing affluence attracted the orders of preaching friars, and brought the establishment of craft, mercantile and religious guilds, which regulated industry and commerce, promoted the interests of their various memberships, and contributed to the municipal, educational and religious services of the town. Their grandest achievement was the construction, begun in 1309, of an enormous parish church, still standing, between the marketplace and the river. In 1369, Boston, which now handled more than a third of all English trade with the Continent, received the privilege of the staple of several goods, notably wool. Its continued prosperity during the fifteenth century was reflected in a series of elaborate additions to the tower of St. Botolph's until by the end of that century, it reached almost 300 feet high. Completion of the tower (an intended spire was never added, and so it became known as the "Stump") coincided ironically with the onset of Boston's decline, caused by the silting of the Witham, the growth of the English cloth industry and consequent decline of the wool trade, and the shifting trade patterns that followed the discovery of America and the passage around the Cape of Good Hope to the East Indies.

An account of the town during the period of Taverner's residence there has come down to us from John Leland, a royal chaplain and antiquarian. Leland passed through Boston in 1538 during his travels through England to collect books for the royal library from the recently suppressed monasteries. His perceptive entries invariably drew attention to the outstanding qualities and points of interest in the towns he visited. So for Taverner's Boston

> Botolphstone standeth hard on the river of Lindis.[3] The great and
> chiefest part of the town is on the east side of the river, where is a
> fair market place and a cross with a square tower. The chief parish
> church was at St. John's, where yet is a church for the town. St.
> Botolph's was but a chapel to it. But now it is so risen and adorned
> that it is the chiefest of the town, and for a parish church the best
> and fairest of all Lincolnshire, and served so with singing, and that

of cunning men, as no parish is in all England. The society and brotherhood [belonging] to this church[4] hath caused this, [and now] much land belongeth to this society.

The steeple being *quadrated turris,* and a lantern on it, is both very high and fair, and a mark both by sea and land for all the quarters thereabouts. There is a goodly font, whereof part is of white marble, or of stone very like to it.

[There] be 3 colleges of Friars, Gray, [Black] and Augustines. There is al[so a hos]pital for poor men, and in the [town, or] near to it the late Lord Hus[sey had a] place with a stone tower. All the bu[ilding] of this side of the town is fa[ir,] and merchants dwell in it; and [a staple] of wool is used there. There is a pile of stone [set in] the middle of the river. The stream whereof is sometimes as swift as it we[re an arrow].

On the west side of Lindis is one lon[g street], and on the same side is the White [Friars].

The main sea is 6 miles of Bost[on. Diverse good ships and other vessels ride there.][5]

But by this time the decline of the post had progressed considerably. Leland was told by Thomas Paynell, a leading citizen, that

since that Boston of old time at the great famous fair there kept was burnt that scant since it ever came to the old glory and riches that it had: yet since hath it been many fold richer than it is now.

Leland noted further that "the steelyard is little of nothing at all occupied,"[6] because of the decline of international trade through the post. But Boston remained a center of local and regional trade, and retained some of its earlier affluence.

To discern the nature of the Boston community, and Taverner's place in it, we must examine the crucial role of the guilds of freemen who came together to promote their common interests and establish institutions for the government of their town. At the beginning, each of the five incorporated guilds of Boston, was well as ten small unincorporated companies, derived its distinctive functions and characteristics from the particular body of artisans and merchants that formed it. But with the gradual establishment of commercial monopolies and standards of industrial production, their mercantile character and functions declined. The necessity of exclusive membership based on professional interest gave way to a heterogeneous caste, and the energies of the guilds focused more and more in common on the government and welfare of the town, the repair of its public buildings and its dikes and sewers, its wharves and warehouses. They bought, managed and leased tenements and farms, produced pageants and plays, dispensed charity among the poor, paid the town waits and supported hospitals and grammar schools. When the town was incorporated and raised to the rank of a free borough in 1545, the aldermen of the guilds became its burgesses, and from among their number were appointed the mayor and aldermen of the municipal corporation. These guilds, then, were influential and powerful institutions, their members chosen from among the prominent citizens of the community. Election to one or more of them signified the attainment of some commercial, social or political success.

It is of particular note to us that these guilds were religious fraternities as well, responsible for the maintenance of divine worship in the parish church on behalf of their members and benefactors. It was they, not the parish churchwarden, who supported the liturgy, music and choirs of St. Botolph's, hiring chaplains and clerks to conduct services there and see to the burial and commemoration of the dead. It is in their registers and records that we would find the evidence of music and musicians in Boston. Unfortunately, only one register of members has survived, that for the Guild of Corpus Christi. John Taverner was elected to the Guild of Corpus Christi in 1537, was appointed one of its two treasurers in 1541 and remained in that post for three successive terms.[7] Evidence that we shall examine in the course of our argument suggests strongly that Taverner was connected with another fraternity as well, the Guild of the Blessed Virgin. In that capacity he had the opportunity to compose for and sing in St. Botolph's, which, as Leland noted in 1538, "was served so with singing, and that of cunning men, as no parish is in all England."

The Guilds of the Blessed Virgin (founded 1260) and Corpus Christi (1335) were the largest and wealthiest in Boston. Together their memberships embraced every Bostonian of note, and the most affluent citizens joined both of them. The older guild was spectacularly affluent: its income in 1526 was £1347, of which almost £300 came from endowment revenues and the rest from entrance and membership fees.[8] The value of its property and goods, according to the Chantries Commission report in 1548, was three times that of Corpus Christi and greater than that of all its sister guilds combined.[9] An inventory, taken in 1534, of goods belonging to the Guild of the Blessed Virgin attests to its wealth. The kitchens, buttery and larderhouse of the guildhall were stocked with brass cooking utensils weighing over 1000 pounds, pewter dishware and iron spits, while its chambers and common rooms were lavishly furnished, carpeted and supplied with linens and hangings. One of the hall tables had a parchment cover "noted with Anthems of Our Lady, with 3 collects." In the revestry were valuable relics, testimony to those idolatrous beliefs and practices which so offended the Protestants, among them stones from Calvary, bones of Saint Christina and of the Holy Innocents, two reliquaries containing "part of the milk of Our Lady," and "a relic of part of the finger of Saint Ann, closed in a hand of silver and gilt." For services in the parish church of St. Botolph's and its lady and chantry chapels, the fraternity possessed organs, silver and gold candlesticks, censors, chalices and crosses, a large inventory of plate, altar cloths, and vestments of damask, silk and velvet. It also owned some three dozen books, mostly liturgical, among them "the principal mass-book, with 2 clasps of silver and gilt, with 2 roses with pins of silver gilt."[10]

The value of the religious possessions of the Guild of the Blessed Virgin reflected the prestige of its ecclesiastical establishment. An amusing story told by Foxe recounts that in 1510 it sent an emissary to obtain a renewal of its indulgences from Pope Julius II. Traveling through Antwerp, he met Thomas Cromwell, who was then on his way to Rome, and enlisted his aid. To gain an audience with the Pope, Cromwell prepared "certain fine dishes of jelly after the best fashion made after our country manner here in England." One day as Julius was returning from the hunt, Cromwell approached him with these jellies and had them "brought in with a three man's song (as we call it), in the English tongue, and all after the English fashion." The Pope succumbed. Henceforth pardons granted on major holidays in the Lady chapel at St. Botolph's to brothers of the guild would rank in efficacy with those given at Scala Celi and S. Giovanni. (Among English churches, only Westminster Abbey and the church of the Austin Friars at Norwich could claim this distinction.) Absolution came, of course, at a price: the donation of 5s.8d (with the promise of an additional 1s each year thereafter) for the support of the seven chaplains, twelve clerks, thirteen bedesmen, the supply of candles, and the grammar school run by the guild.[11]

An account of guild expenses for the fiscal year 1514-15[12] includes some payments to the religious and educational establishment mentioned by Foxe. The sum of £1.10.5 was paid to the "rood singers" in St. Botolph's; the master of the Boston grammar school, a chaplain named George Watson, received a stipend of £9 with 8s.4d for his livery; Thomas Watson and five other clerks were given £44 in stipends and payments for extra services; and £18.13.2 was paid out for "provisions and vestments" (commons and livery) for the choristers. Bailiffs' accounts from 1518-19[13] add some information. George Watson remained master of the grammar school, and Nicholas Blewet and Richard Hykkes were two of the clerks. Among the disbursements were 8s.8d paid weekly for the support of thirteen poor persons in the almshouse, and 7s.ld paid to eight men who carried Noah's ark (*Naviculm Noie*) at the celebrations on the Feasts of Corpus Christi and Whitsun.

Two later accounts give more specific information, placing the Guild of the Blessed Virgin in an astonishing light as a patron of education, religion and music. According to the account of 1525-26, it supported ten chaplains, ten singing clerks (*clerici cantatores*) and a number of choristers,[14] all of whom presumably served at St. Botolph's. One chaplain served as master of its grammar school, being paid £10 as his stipend--the same as the salary of the master at Eton--and £1 for livery. He was Thomas Garrett, the recent university graduate and cleric who would play so prominent a role in the Oxford heresy in 1528. Three chaplains were paid stipends of £8, £6, and £5.13.4, while the remaining six were paid £5.6.8 each;[15] these men also received 13s.4d for livery. Two of them held services at the Hospital of St. John in the South End. The clerks were better paid than the chaplains, an unusual practice testifying to the esteem in which polyphonic music was held by members of the guild. One of them, Robert Westwood, received £13.6.8 as master of the choristers, as well as £3.6.8 for giving them singing lessons, £13s.4d for livery, and 6s.8d for the maintenance of his garden--a sum considerably higher than that paid to Taverner at Cardinal College. The organist John Wendon also received £13.6.8; three clerks received £10, three others £5.6.8, and one £8. John Broke, keeper of the Lady chapel at St. Botolph's, received £3.6.8 for that service, 1s.4d "for seeing the choristers say their matins every day," and other payments bringing his salary to £4.4.8. The choristers' livery cost £7.4.9, their commons, £17.6.8. Ten shillings were paid to the Corpus Christi Guild for the rental of a building that served as their song school (*domus cantationis*). Although the number of boy choristers is not specific in the account, it was probably eight or sixteen: if eight, the commons paid to each boy (£2.3.4) would have been equal, and the livery about twice that paid to the boys at the Cardinal College; if sixteen, the commons (£1.1.8) would have been half, and the livery about equal to respective sums paid at Cardinal College. In the latter case, the small sum for commons might have been augmented by the support of another of Boston's religious guilds.

The second account, given by the commissioners of the Chantries Act of 1548,[16] names eleven chaplains and seven clerks. William Harrisoon, master of the grammar school and *ludimagister*,[17] received a salary of £10.12.0. Of the other chaplains, Andrew Headley was paid £6.2.0, Robert Richardson £6, Ralph Cokeler and Robert Ellingtoune

£5.13.4, Richard Robinsoon, Richard Spensley and John Welles £5.6.8, and one Christopher (his surname is not given) who served at the Hospital of St. John, £1.13.4.[18] There are separate entries for payments to two chaplains: John Gillmyn, £1.13.4 for singing in the Lady chapel, and William Warde, £2.3.4 for playing the organ there. Of the clerks, Richard Gillmyn and Richard Goche received £8.13.4, William Neudik £7.10.0, Nicholas Blewet and Stephen Mighell £6, John Broke £1.16.0, and John Newman 13s.4d. The guild paid £6.17.10 for the maintenance of the choristers and £10.16.0 for their commons. Once again their number is not recorded, though the sum indicates that it had declined since 1526, and individual payments had been lowered as well. There were probably six or twelve: if six, their commons was £1.14.4 each; if twelve, 17s.2d. The latter sum is so low that we must assume that the number of choristers was six; and probably, therefore, that their number in 1525-26 was eight.

The erosion of financial support by the guild for music at St. Botolph's is made clear by the payments to the men. No longer is there an *informator*, or a separate post for organist. There are fewer clerks, and they are paid less well.

These remarkable documents indicate that it was the Guild of the Blessed Virgin that was primarily responsible for the maintenance of the choir of St. Botolph's, and that it supported divine service there with polyphony as splendid--for a time--as was its inventory of ecclesiastical books, vestments and plate. The guild was responsible as well for Boston's song and grammar schools. In 1525-26 the song and grammar masters, organist and clerks were paid generously, and the choir was a large one. Even in its reduced state in 1548, two years after the guild had surrendered title of its goods and property to the municipal corporation, and when its very future was in doubt, the size of the choir compared favorably with those at Eton, Winchester and the ambitious new college at nearby Thornton established by Henry VIII (see table).

Two men supported by the Guild of the Blessed Virgin, John Wendon and Richard Gillmyn, are of particular interest to us. Both were accomplished musicians. Wendon was a political associate of Taverner, Gillmyn a trusted friend; their lives shed substantial light on his. Wendon was born probably in or around Boston about the year 1490. Some time after receiving his Bachelor of Music degree from Oxford in 1509, he returned to Boston to serve as clerk and (by 1525-26) organist at the chapel of the guild.[23] He did not come from a landed or titled family--no hired clerk did--but his success in that post, or his association with the guild, apparently brought him social position and commercial advantages. By 1534 Wendon was receiving, or expecting to receive, favors from Thomas Cromwell, in return for which he sent Cromwell "a fat swan and a fat crane" in January 1535.[24] Through

COMPARATIVE LIST OF CHAPELS AND CHAPEL PAYMENTS AT SELECTED COLLEGES AND AT THE GUILD OF THE BLESSED VIRGIN MARY, BOSTON

	Chaplains				Clerks				Choristers		
	No.	Stipend	Livery	Commons	No.	Stipend	Livery	Commons	No.	Livery	Commons
Guild of the B.V.M. (1510)	7	–	–	–	12	–	–	–	–	–	–
Guild of the B.V.M. (1525-26)	10	£61.13.4	£7	–	10	£88.4.8	£6.13.4?	–	8 or 16?	£7.4.9	£17.6.8
Guild of the B.V.M. (1548)	11	£55.0.8	–	–	7	£39.6.0	–	–	6 or 12?	£6.17.10[22]	£10.6.0
Cardinal College, Oxford (1526)	12	£80	£12	£52	13	£82	£8.13.4	£56.6.8	16	£7.4.0	£34.13.4
Eton College (1546)[19]	5	£20.13.4	–	–	5	£21.6.8	–	–	10	–	–
Winchester College (1546)[20]	3	–	–	–	3	–	–	–	16	–	–
Thornton College (1548)[21]	0	–	–	–	5	£36.13.4	–	–	6	£16	–

political connections and investments in property in Boston and London,[25] Wendon soon became an affluent and powerful citizen in the town. When, in 1543, the unincorporated guilds of Boston were ordered to dispose of their jewels and ornamental plate, it was he who assumed the responsibility for their sale.[26] Two years later, at the incorporation of the town, Wendon was chosen one of the twelve aldermen to sit on the town council, and in 1548 he was elected mayor of Boston.[27] He died in 1554, having, among his possessions, "a pair of clavichords" valued at twenty shillings.[28]

Wendon's life resembles closely both what we know and what we conjecture about Taverner's. The two men were born within a few years of one another, and in the same vicinity. Both went to Oxford, then returned to Lincolnshire and lived in Boston. Both were professional musicians, working as clerks and organists in superb musical establishments. Both served Thomas Cromwell and sought his patronage. Both later rose to positions of high responsibility; their election as two of the original twelve aldermen of Boston in 1545 indicates their achievement of political success.

The lacuna in the documents of the Guild of the Blessed Virgin after 1525-26 prevents us from knowing how long after that year Wendon remained organist. We know only that by 1534 he was in touch with Cromwell and on the road to political activity, and in 1545, an alderman with Taverner. He had long since ceased being a professional musician (probably by 1535), but remained musically active, as suggested by the mention of a clavichord in his will.

The activities of Richard Gillmyn (1506-48) are equally interesting. During the late 1530s the guilds of Boston began to share in the general commercial decline of the town. They suffered, too, from legislative onslaughts against superstitious practices and devotions which they helped to perpetuate. One imagines that the Guild of the Blessed Virgin with its treasured relics and wealth was especially susceptible to these attacks, for by 1538 its income and membership were decreasing notably. Early in the following year, therefore, the masters of the guild wrote to Thomas Cromwell, asking permission to reduce the number of wages of its clerks. Richard Gillmyn decided to contest the matter. He went to London, contacted an agent of Cromwell's, one Master Turnor, and obtained Cromwell's signature on a letter of 28 April 1539 demanding that the guild *increase* his wages above their present level of £8.13.4. He then returned to Boston and personally handed the letter to the aldermen of the guild. Infuriated, they not only refused to increase his stipend but threatened to dismiss him, and, in a letter of 6 May to Cromwell, reiterated their inability to support the chapel at its present size, reminding him that Gillmyn was already receiving a salary far higher than the £6 paid the other clerks.[29] Undaunted, Gillmyn wrote to

Turnor asking for the stronger letter promised by Turnor in the event that the first note failed in its purpose. Surely, he added, from its income of £300 from property and £200 from "charges"--membership had declined sharply since 1525-26, when membership and entrance fees exeeded £1000--the guild had money enough to pay him and the others.[30]   According to the one later record of salaries extant, the Chantries Commission report of 1548, a compromise was reached wherein Gillmyn remained in his post, but was denied his request for an increase in his salary.[31]

Given the original aims of the two parties, it was a compromise in the musician's favor, against the corporate will of the guild. The clue to how Gillmyn accomplished this lies in the final passage of his letter to Turnor:

> I pray you show Master Vavysor that I have spoken with Dr. Porret, and he hath paid the money to one Dr. Brynkley, of the same religion, and have a fair quittance to show, which I did see, and he saith that the Bishop of Dover hath seen it, and is well contented, and Doctor Vavisar can tell well enough saith he.

Richard Ingworth, suffragan Bishop of Dover, had been appointed visitor to the four orders in friars in England in February 1538, and was charged with their suppression. Porret was one of his agents. Peter Bringley and William Vavasour were members of the Order of Grey Friars,[32] which had recently been suppressed. Porret, who was a colleague of Gillmyn's in this matter, apparently had taken possession of one of the friaries and paid Bringley for its value. Gillmyn was thus an agent in the suppression of the friaries, responsible directly to Ingworth and through him to Cromwell, and would look to Cromwell for his patronage. Here then was the source of his leverage in the altercation with the Guild of St. Mary. Here too is proof that an active musician could participate in the liturgy and ritual of the Catholic church at the same time that he was engaged in the suppression of her religious orders.

Taverner, as we shall discover, played a role in the suppression similar to Gillmyn's. The two men were friends, colleagues and agents of Cromwell. Gillmyn's life demonstrates what we should have known in the first place, namely, that a musician who contributed to the service of the church as a hired servant functioned as a musician and not as a cleric. His theological views had no bearing upon the execution of his duties, unless those views were radically heretical--and in Cromwell's England, even the most orthodox Lutheranism was not considered radical. Heretics were burned for holding Anabaptist beliefs, not Lutheran ones.

But we have no reason to assume radical beliefs on Gillmyn's part. He was simply serving the king's will as embodied in Cromwell's policies, and could expect Cromwell to intercede in return, when necessary, on his behalf. His activities as an agent of the crown had no more to do with his life as a musician than his religious views. This statement will hold true for Taverner as well.

The Guild of Corpus Christi was founded in 1335 by thirty prominent citizens, one of them a Taverner. Fifteen years later, it received royal letters patent stipulating that it maintain six chaplains to pray for the health of the royal family and of its members, and for their souls after death. The register (Lbl 4795)[33]--the only surviving Boston guild register--is our primary source of information concerning the guild documents, the heterogeneity of its membership, and the prestige which came to be associated with it. Among the brothers and sisters of the Corpus Christi were royalty and nobility, bishops and abbots, canons, priors, nuns and rectors, professors and lawyers, German and English merchants, drapers, mercers, ropers and tailors, bakers, fishmongers, spicers and vintners. Among the nobility recorded are the Cromwells of Tattershall, Henry Cardinal Beaufort, Humphrey Duke of Gloucester, and Queen Margaret Beaufort. Lincolnshire ecclesiastics traditionally associated with the guild were the bishop of Lincoln, the abbots of Bardney, Barlings, Kirkstead and Revesby, the prior of Spalding, the master of Tattershall College (John Gigur was alderman of the guild in 1472, Henry Hornby in 1517), and the rector of St. Botolph's. Two notable members were the Boston friar John Vynde (late fifteenth century), provincial of the Carmelite friars in England, and George Brown of Oxford (ca. 1530), provincial of the Austin Friars. Virtually every family of note in the area around Boston--Bourgchier, Esterling, Holland, Hussey, Paynell, Pulvertoft, Robertson, Spayne, Sutton, Tailboys, Tilney, Willoughby, and a host of others who made individual fortunes--is found in the register.

One had to have means in order to join the guild, for an ordinance of 1426 established an entrance fee of £2.4.4 to help support its functions. This stipulation colored the membership and character of the guild and insured substantial mercantile representation. Nevertheless, the register indicates that Corpus Christi was predominantly ecclesiastical, certainly at least by the late fifteenth century. Membership was often honorary: many brothers, notably almost all the famous men, were non-residents of Boston, while the wealthiest local merchants joined several guilds. Its membership, like that of the Guild of the Blessed Virgin, was diverse, as were its functions. Corpus Christi owned land and tenements throughout Boston and the surrounding countryside, and from its revenues supported twelve poor men in the town, and services at St. Botolph's. According to the report of the Chantries Commissioners of 1548--which established its income as £114.16.8, roughly a third that of St. Mary's--Corpus Christi supported seven chaplains[34] (one more than its statutory number) with a stipend of £5.13.4 each. A "keeper of the choir" in the Corpus Christi chapel in St. Botolph's received £3.2.11. Six clerks (*presbyteri*)--the report does not name them individually--were paid by the guild; at the time of the suppression of its chantry chapel at St. Botolph's a few years later, they were being paid £5.6.8 (including livery) each. The guild spent £3.17.4 for ceremonies in connection with the Feast of Corpus Christi that year, a rather larger sum in relation to its income than that (£5.1.9½) spent by St. Mary's. But the first declared purpose of the guild in its statutes was to honor this festival, and it is probable that Corpus Christi led the ceremonies of this day with a service in the nave and the choir of St. Botolph's, followed by a liveried procession through the streets of the town with players and musicians, and an annual dinner in the guildhall. This was a procedure followed by all English guilds on the feast day from which they took their name.[35] Year round, like the other guilds of the town, Corpus Christi kept obits and anniversaries for its members and patrons, at its chantry chapel in St. Botolph's.[36]

In contrast to the paucity of material on which the rest of Taverner's biography is based, there is such ample documentation of his involvement in the suppression of the Boston friaries--three letters by him and one concerning him have come down to us--that significance of this involvement has been thoroughly exaggerated. Furthermore, the contents of these documents have led to misleading interpretations of his character and peculiar hypotheses about how he spent his last years. To keep matters in balance, we must place the materials that deal with this involvement in a wider historical perspective than they have heretofore received from writers on Taverner.

The dissolution of the friars' orders constitutes only one relatively brief episode in the suppression of the religious orders in England, that enormous social upheaval and sweeping transfer of property which was carried out under the guidance of Thomas Cromwell during the last five years of his life.[37] Precedents for wholesale suppressions existed, as we have seen, in Wolsey's earlier actions in connection with the founding of his colleges at Oxford and Ipswich, an activity in which Cromwell played a major role as an agent of the cardinal. A layman and civil lawyer whose sympathies lay with the new learning and who saw in the monastic orders a vast and vulnerable source of potential wealth for the crown, Cromwell seems to have conceived his plan for their dissolution not long after the consolidation of his personal power. He implemented his first offical step towards it in 1534 with his compilation of the *Valor Ecclesiasticus,* as assessment of the income of every religious foundation in England. It remains to some extent an open question as to how far-reaching his plans were at the time, and even later on; there is much evidence throughout the next three years that Henry and Cromwell proceeded with some hesitation from one step to the next, and that as late as 1538 the fate of the monasteries was not sealed.

The government's central motives were financial and political: Henry's coffers were badly depleted, and the income that he stood to gain from the seized property far exceeded his own. The motives were not religious--the eagerness with which conservative men such as Bishop Longland worked on Henry's behalf in this matter attests to that--even though the monks stood to lose by the general attacks on popery, relics and superstitious practices. The religious orders were, however, the most exposed targets, the richest and easiest plums for an overextended royal treasury; they were depleted in numbers and spiritually depressed, and most of them simply collapsed under Cromwell's threats. As early as 1534, his intentions were so widely rumored and the abbots so fearful that they began to dispose of their capital and property. His first direct move was a lay visitation towards the end of 1535, superficially akin to the episcopal visitation on which it was based, but foreboding something quite new in its injunctions and in the attitudes of Cromwell's visitors. It was immediately followed in the spring of 1536 by the first Act of Suppression of the lesser monasteries, those with less than £200 income and fewer than twelve brothers. Although for more than a year afterwards the government took no official actions, and although the king dispensed a quarter of the smaller houses from the order to dissolve, even founding a few new houses, the spirit of the religious faltered and one by one the larger houses began to submit voluntarily to dissolution.

Late in 1537 Cromwell moved once more, this time on three fronts, with visitations of the greater abbeys to provoke their dissolution, attacks on shrines and removal of their jewels and precious metals to the royal treasury, and the suppression of the four orders of friars: Augustinian, Carmelite, Dominican and Franciscan (known, respectively as Austin, White, Black and Grey Friars). These orders had come to England 300 years earlier, built homes and churches with the aid of noblemen and townsfolk, and contributed immensely to learning in England. But recent years had seen their decline. Many of the brightest young friars were converted to Lutheran beliefs, others went to serve their king, and the small number who remained seemed to lack both distinction and ambition. It was their further misfortune that of all the religious orders the friars were most closely associated with the papacy, and though spared suppression at the beginning, they were placed under the direct supervision of Cromwell and his agents, men whose benefaction they might well doubt. Unlike many monastics, these men were poor and without political or social resources. When in February 1538 Cromwell commissioned Bishop Ingworth, a former Dominican provincial, to visit them and receive their surrender, his intention was not to enrich the royal coffers so much as to mop up an impoverished remnant of the old religion. Ingworth was an adherent of that religion, if not of its appurtenances, and at first he conducted his visitations with some hesitation and evident sympathy; but under Cromwell's prodding he soon developed an effective technique without directly suppressing the houses. He would note the miserable condition of the friaries, announce his intention to reform them, present them with injunctions that they could not accept, and then receive their house and property into the crown's possession. Ingworth's colleague in the visitations was the unpleasant Dr. London of New College, whose theology had remained constant in the ten years since the Oxford heresy (he maintained his staunch conservatism until his death in 1543 while in prison for having plotted against Archbishop Cranmer and his reformist circle). London was brutal towards the friars, dispatching their houses roughly and relieving them of their wood, iron, lead and glass before (as he claimed) the poor people could get their hands on them. By Easter of 1539 the tawdry job was done: the friars had disappeared entirely from the land.

The friars of Boston shared the melancholy history of their brothers, and when Taverner came to deal with them in 1538 he found them a pitiable lot giving bare evidence of their earlier status.[38] The four houses with their libraries, chapels and gardens had been landmarks in the town for over 200 years, attracting scholars, preachers and theologians from the very beginning until almost the last years of their existence. For most of that time they were patronized by the wealthy and noble, receiving gifts from the kings of England, the Cromwells of Tattershall and Boston merchants, and their cemeteries contained the remains of many local eminences.[39] The oldest house was the Franciscan (Grey) Friary, founded about the middle of the thirteenth century and supported by the merchants of the steelyard. Members of the Esterling, Mounteville and Witham families were buried here. John Porret, a Doctor of Theology from Oxford (1527), was warden of the house during its latter years. Upon its dissolution in 1539, its site was valued at only 44s annually. The foundation of the house of Dominican (Black) Friars during the latter half of the thirteenth century was associated with the Tilney family, and during its early years it seems to have been particularly favored by the royal family. Its lands and tenements were valued at 46s.8d in 1539. The Carmelite (White) Friars came to Boston shortly after the Dominicans, and the foundation of their house at the turn of the fourteenth century was supported by the de Orreby family. John Vynde came from this house, as did the chemist George Ripley (d. 1490). Its site and property were valued in 1539 at 80s. The Tilneys seem to have been instrumental in bringing the fourth order, the Austin Friars, to Boston early in the fourteenth century. At its dissolution this house had an annual income of 78s.8d. It seems to have been the largest of the friaries, its site of ten acres being double that of each of the others. How large the membership of these houses was when Taverner came to deal with them is not known; in 1328 Boston had twenty Austin Friars, twenty-two Carmelites and twenty-eight Dominicans (the number of Franciscans is not recorded), but by the late 1530s these figures had shrunk drastically. On his visit to Boston in 1538, Leland noted neither their size nor their condition. He was interested only in their libraries. The seven remaining volumes in the Dominican collection included histories of Greece, Rome and England, a biography of Charlemagne, and treatises of New Testament texts; the Carmelites had a large collection of printed books. Leland was kept from visiting the Franciscan library by the absence of the prior, and from the Austin Friars' library by an outbreak of the plague.

Taverner's involvement with the friars of Boston evolved not from any special concern with them but from his work as an agent of Thomas Cromwell, who as the king's chief minister had jurisdiction to guide the ecclesiastical and secular affairs of England in Henry's name. His work for Cromwell has been widely attributed to his supposed Lutheran learnings, from the Oxford heresy incident in 1528. But Taverner's work for Cromwell originated in all probability in a more recent and local event, the Lincolnshire Rising against Cromwell and his policies (and thus against the king) in 1536. The short-lived rebellion "cut through society like a knife,"[40] and its decisive resolution in favor of the king's minister led to an upheaval among the gentry: the loyal were rewarded, the disloyal and those of questionable sympathies were punished. Cromwell's drive against the major monasteries and the friars in the following year, which necessitated the appointment of local agents and deputies, allowed other men to rise in an unstable and rapidly changing political climate. What counted was not one's religion, but one's loyalty to the crown. Among those who rose among the lesser gentry we may count Taverner. In 1528 he had been "but a musician;" by 1545 he would be referred to as "gentleman."

The earliest of three extant letters from Taverner to Cromwell, "written at Boston this xj day of September 1538 by the hands of Your Lordship's poor servant,"[41] gives ample evidence of the scope of Taverner's affairs. It concerns three apparently unrelated matters. The first is Taverner's role in the continuing campaign against relics. The second concerns information about a Scottish physician, a former inmate at the Carthusian Priory of Mount Grace in Yorkshire who had eluded a servant sent by Taverner and had "gone abroad to excercise his practice in physic and surgery." The third matter is a case, to be tried before the Council of the North, involving the wardship of a young Bostonian named John Copley, scion of a once wealthy family who

> hath no lands but in reversion and is of the age of xxj years. If Your Lordship be good lord unto me in this I am bound to pray for Your Lordship during life, and I do not doubt but my Lord of Suffolk at your desire will be content that I or his mother have him and whatsoever Your Lordship shall award me to pay I shall bring it up at the next term.

The issues involving Copley reveal Taverner in a most sympathetic light, but Fellowes was blinded to it by the first part of Taverner's letter, which he interpreted as the writing of a "fierce fanatic . . . under pressure of religious conviction":

> According to Your Lordship's commandment the rood was burned the vij day of this month being also the market day and [there was] a sermon of the Black friar at the burning of him, who did express the cause of his burning and the idolatry committed by him, which sermon hath done much good and hath turned many men's hearts from it.

Taverner simply reports that the cross was burned as an idolatrous image--a relic of Roman "superstition"--and that its burning was accompanied by a sermon expounding the evils of that superstition. His account marks him as a local official who held to the Henrician *media via,* but not as a fanatic. The language of his report was conventional in its approval, and his attitude conformed to the policy of the man whom he served.[42]

The second letter to Cromwell, written on 20 January 1539, concerns the friaries.[43]

> Right honorable and my singular good Lord in most humble wise I recommend me unto Your good Lordship. It may please Your Honor to be advertised that the priors with their brethren of the friars Dominicans, White and Austins hath oft & divers times resorted unto me sore & piteously lamenting their great poverty knowing no manner of ways how to provide livings for them and their poor brethren till such time as their houses be surrendered. For why? the devotion of people is clean gone, their plate and other implements be sold and the money spent so that in manner there is nothing left to make sale of now but only lead which (if I had not

given them contrary commandment) they would likewise have plucked down and sold to have relieved therewith them and their poor brethren. But in avoiding such spoil I bade them come to me in meanwhile at all times when they lacked anything and they should have it of me. Wherefore I humbly beseech Your good Lordship that they may know your pleasure and commandment by my servant what they shall do. And your Lordship shall bind both them and me to be your daily bedesmen so long as we shall live. As God knows who ever preserve your honorable estate long to endure. At Boston this xxth day of the month of January by the hands of your poor servant to my little power.

John Taverner

This simple and moving letter makes clear that Taverner had become the patron and advocate of the friars, not their suppressor. In fact suppression was not the issue. The inmates did not fear the imminent dissolution of their houses; on the contrary, they seem to have looked forward to it as the solution to a long-standing problem, "their great poverty." The friars derived a meager income from their property, and, from the very beginning, had depended upon the people of the town for their support. That support had vanished in recent years as a result of the commercial decline of the city, and perhaps too because of the torrent of anti-clerical feeling unleashed by Cromwell's policies. Now, faced by the disappearance of their major source of income, yet still bound by their religious vows, the friars had sold all of their capital goods to defray daily expenses; they were left with nothing except the lead roofing of their houses which they would have "plucked down" but for Taverner's advice. Having helped them for a while, he now turned to Cromwell for aid, trusting that "Your Lorship shall bind both them and me to be your daily bedesmen." To have identified his personal welfare so closely with that of men who were desperately poor and despised by both his patrons and his fellow-townsmen seems a courageous and generous act, not one of a "fierce fanatic."

No answer to Taverner's letter is extant. Not long after he wrote it, Ingworth left London on his visitation of Lincolnshire and the north country. After passing through the town of Huntingdon, he arrived in Boston, suppressed the four friaries and went on to Lincoln. From there, on Sunday 14 February, he wrote to Cromwell that

according to my duty at your commandment I have received to the King's Highness use of iij houses of friars in Boston, very poor houses and poor persons, and according to your letter I have delivered the same houses to Master Taverner and Master Johnys, servants to the King's Grace, with all the poor implements for his money. In my way there I found a house of Austin friars in Huntingdon, very poor, the which also I received, and delivered the same to one Phelyp Clampe, one of the king's servants, according to the King's pleasure as Master Chancellor's letter of the augmentation signified to me. The houses be all meetly leaded; I think in Huntingdon about viij fother, and in Boston I think in the iiij houses about iiij score fother or more. I now am in Lincoln, where that also I have received iiij poor houses, nothing left but stones and poor glass, but meetly leaded. All the lead and bells I leave to the king's use; and as for plate also I save, the which is very little. . .[44]

The story was the same everywhere, as Ingworth "received" one house after another. Occasionally he found some valuables--chalices, brass pots, pans, pewter, cutlery, bells, vestments--but usually there was little left for the king's treasure. Most friars had sold everything they possessed and taken what money they could before the royal visitor could relieve them of their valuables. The only thing remarkable about the Boston friaries--and indicative of their substantial size--was their lead roofing: eighty fother is the equivalent of some eighty-seven tons of lead. This they kept on Taverner's advice until their suppression by Ingworth.

What happened afterwards is unclear. Ingworth asked Cromwell to give the friars their "capacities," that is, to dispense them from their vows, and his request must have been granted. As for the lead, Taverner and Jones, after receiving the houses from Ingworth, could either have claimed it for the king's use or sold it on the friars' behalf. The second action would have been more in keeping with Taverner's attitude towards the friars, and evidence that he took that action may possibly be found in a letter of 22 February from Thomas Paynell to Cromwell. Paynell, the man to whom Leland had spoken while on his sojourn in Boston, was a bailiff and leading citizen of the town, and now, as one of the king's officers, was responsible for the maintenance of the tenements and sea walls of the area. He therefore requested permission from Cromwell to keep for the town's use the iron, stone, tile and timber of the suppressed friaries--that is, the disassembled materials left from their demolition--so that these materials could be used for the necessary repairs. Otherwise, Paynell warned, the port and surrounding lands would be ruined, "and surely if these decays should still be suffered, it would be the very mean whereby His Grace's customs daily should decay."[45] He knew Cromwell well. Nowhere is mention made of substantial amount of lead, the one item which caught Ingworth's experienced eye.[46] Perhaps it had already been shipped to London. But that is improbable, for Paynell's letter was an attempt to mollify his fellow citizens, who had accused him of ignoring the interests of the town. Had there been valuable lead to save, he would have tried to save it. It is probable, therefore, that the friars had already sold their last marketable commodity with Taverner's aid.

So much, then, for the myth of Taverner as fanatical Protestant and persecutor of helpless friars. He exercised his responsibilities in a benign fashion and displayed courage in taking up the cause of victims of the prevailing religious chaos. The tone of his letters is occasionally neutral at worst, but usually compassionate. His statements betray absolutely no sign of religious conviction one way or the other; in the case of the friars, in whose suppression he played only a secondary role-- in effect, he and Jones received what was now crown property from Bishop Ingworth--religion seems to have played no role at all. The friars, after all, were concerned with one matter only, their miserable poverty, and they looked forward to their release from vows as the one hope of salvation. The very fact that they came to Taverner for aid again and again suggests their confidence in his concern for their welfare.

In one final matter relating to the suppression of the friaries, the transfer of their property, Taverner seems to have maintained a remarkably high moral standard. When in 1538 the Crown began to grant and sell the lands that it had gained through the dissolution of the religious houses, the men given the opportunity to obtain these properties were those who had worked for the crown or those on whom it depended for the administration of its new order: prominent townsmen, country gentry, yeoman farmers, lawyers, courtiers, and royal agents and officials. While some of them were outside speculators, most were prominent local citizens whose involvement in the great transfer was regarded as their proper due. Neither religion nor moral scruple seemed involved, and those who had the opportunity took it.[47] Yet when we examine the transfer of the friar's property in Boston and the names of its beneficiaries, we find no trace of Taverner.[48] The property of the Black Friars was granted to the Duke of Suffolk, who leased its tenements to John Bate, Thomas Crowe, John Neal and William Spynke; the other three friaries were held by the king, with portions of their property being leased to Thomas Browne, John Fawcote, William Heydon, John Noppye, John Tupholme and Thomas Waltehewe. In 1545 all four sites and their property were bought by the newly incorporated borough of Boston.[49] It seems, therefore, that Taverner took no advantage of the opportunity that presented itself upon the dissolution of the friaries. We may conclude that his involvement in that episode arose in the course of his work as Cromwell's agent--it was not something he sought for reasons of personal gain or religious conviction-- and that in itself his was a disinterested act shedding no light on his personal beliefs.

The third and last surviving letter from Taverner to Cromwell, dated 2 May 1540,[50] pleads the cause of "my near kinsman and singular friend Charles Yerburgh a man both aged impotent and blind," the plaintiff in a dispute with one Arthur Key over title to the manor of

Sleightwayte in Yorkshire. At Taverner's request Cromwell had written to the Council of the North, which was hearing the case, but the matter remained unresolved. This kinsman had "good manifest & apparent right" to the manor, Taverner argued, while Key had only a continued illegitimate possession prolonged by a lease made to one John Merkynfeyld "for term of his life natural" by John Tyas, an ancestor of Yerburgh's. Tyas died eight years after the transaction, and Merkynfeyld survived him by a hundred years (!), "which was time out of memory." Taverner added pointedly that Key's illegal possession of the manor was supported by the late Lord Darcy, a personal enemy of Cromwell's, whom Key and his ancestors had served. Since Yerburgh was unable to win his suit through the common law or "to contend long in suit before the said Council" (probably because of his ill health), Taverner asked Cromwell to order the president of the Council to settle the case quickly "according to conscience & justice." In return, he promised,

> my said kinsman for Your good Lordship's pain therein upon the obtaining of the said manor according to his right will beseech Your good Lordship to rescue unto yourself during Your Lordship's life natural an annuity of x pounds sterling out of the same manor, which although it be not correspondent to Your good Lordship's gratitude and kindness in this behalf yet with most hearty good will he is contented to grant Your good Lordship the same as knows God whom I beseech to preserve your honorable estate long to endure.

Taverner's argument rested not only on his delicately phrased bribery, but also on the relationship between Key and Lord Darcy, a powerful northern magnate who had been the most prominent supporter of the Pilgrimage of Grace in 1536; when that rebellion against Cromwell and his policies was quashed, he was accused of high treason and beheaded, and his lands and property were forfeited to the crown. If Key stood to lose by Darcy's fall, Yerburgh stood to gain from it. There is evidence that Yerburgh was considered for, or impaneled to sit on, a Lincolnshire jury in the indictment against Darcy (and Lord Hussey, another supporter of the rebellion) in May 1537, placing him unequivocally among the supporters of Cromwell--a fact to which Taverner, surprisingly, does not allude in this letter.[51] The Council of the North was a bureaucratic body established recently (1537) by Cromwell to bring the northern countries under the direct jurisdiction of the crown, and its officers owed their positions to Cromwell. Whatever the merits of Key vs. Yerburgh, therefore, we may assume that Yerburgh won his suit. If so, he won it cheaply, for Cromwell's "life natural" ended abruptly less than two months later.

Taverner's political awareness and his willingness to bend with the prevailing political winds (which we have seen earlier in connection with his departure from Cardinal College) is one notable facet of this letter. Another is the indication of a close relationship between him and Cromwell dating back to Oxford days; for this third letter does not touch on public events or situations in which Cromwell was involved, but simply requests--for the second time--a personal favor in a case in which Cromwell could have little interest. Third, this letter pleads a cause on behalf of a distressed party and one which could not have benefited the composer personally. Finally, it adds evidence concerning Taverner's Lincolnshire origins. Yerburgh is a variant of the name Yarborough found commonly in Lindsey, the northern division of Lincolnshire (where there is a town called Yerburgh), and it is found there in guises such as Yerdeburc and de Yerdeburch from the thirteenth century on.[52] Probably members of the local gentry, the family continued down into the sixteenth century, when Charles Yerburgh, the relative of our composer, was appointed a commissioner to collect the royal subsidy in the division of Lindsey in 1523 and again in the following year.[53] His name is found there with such familiar Lincolnshire gentry names as Hennege, Holland, Hussey, Meere, Paynell and Robertson, suggesting that he owned substantial lands and was well known locally. In 1542, Yerburgh, who lived in the town of Kelstern (near Louth) was one of the local men charged to provide harness for the king's army in the muster for the war against Scotland.[54] He died in 1544.[55]

Cromwell's execution in July 1540 deprived Taverner of political patronage and, we may assume, brought to an end his activity as a crown agent. But in no way did it taint him. His political and religious convictions were sufficiently moderate so that with the fall of Cromwell and the subsequent entrenchment of the conservative reaction, he did not suffer from the association with his late patron. Quite the contrary: he was elected treasurer of the Guild of Corpus Christi in 1541 and remained in that post until at least 1543 (when the register of that fraternity ceases) and perhaps longer. In February 1545 Boston was incorporated a free borough, and four months later one last token of recognition was bestowed on him:

> The first day of June in the xxxcij year of the reign of our
> Sovereign Lord Henry the viijth by the grace of God King of
> England, France and Ireland, Defender of the Faith and of the
> Church of England and also of Ireland, in earth the Supreme Head.
> Nyclas Robartson esquire, mayor of the borough of Boston, by the
> authority of the King's Majesty's Charter, did take his corporal oath

in the Guildhall of the said borough, in the presence of the recorder, the xij aldermen and the inhabitants of the said borough.

The same day the xij aldermen of the said borough, that is to wit, Nyclas Felde, John Tupholme, John Wendon, John Taverner, William Spynke, William Kyd, Thomas Soresby, Harrye Foxe, William Bollys, John Margarie, William Ysott, and Harry Hoode, by the authority of the said Charter, did take these corporal oaths.[56]

Election to the executive council of the town was the last honor Taverner was to enjoy. That summer, apparently, his health deteriorated rapidly. Having no children, he transferred land that he had acquired in and around Boston to joint ownership with his wife Rose. The transaction is recorded in an *Inquisition post mortem*, a posthumous investigation of his landed property taken at Donington, Lincolnshire, on 5 October 1546.[57]

It is through the posthumous record of the land transfer, and through the will in 1553 of his widow, that we learn of Taverner's family. Some time after leaving Oxford (and probably after his arrival in Boston), he married Rose Parrowe of Boston, a widowed mother of two daughters, Emma and Isabell.[58] Nothing is known of her first husband, but we know that her own family were local gentry. Her father, Thomas Parrowe, was a member of the Blessed Virgin and Corpus Christi guilds, and alderman of the former fraternity in 1519.[59] He held lands in the town as early as 1498.[60] Her brother John also held lands in Boston.[61] During the 1550s he was a member of the town council, from which he was dismissed in 1561.[62] He died eleven years later.[63]

The major portion of the *Inquisition post mortem* concerns a parcel of seventeen acres of arable land and eleven acres of pasture in Skirbeck, adjoining Boston, which Taverner held in freehold tenure. On 8 August 1545, "John Tavernor of Boston in the county of Lincoln, gentleman," gave this property to Richard Goche [Goge] and Richard Gillmyn, on condition that, within ten days, Goche and Gillmyn

make or cause be made . . . to the aforesaid John Taverner and the aforesaid Rose [Taverner] a good and lawful estate in law of and in the aforesaid seventeen acres of land and eleven acres of pasture with appurtenances, to have and hold to the aforesaid John and Rose and the heirs of the body of John lawfully begotten, and for default of such issue to remain to the aforesaid Rose, her heirs and assigns, to the proper use and behoof of Rose, her heirs and assigns, forever.
. . .

On 10 August, Goche and Gillmyn fulfilled the condition, with the result that John and Rose Taverner received the property together, "and were seised thereof in their demesne as of fee tail." This cumbersome instrument was necessary because Taverner had no children (as its long-winded legal formulas indicate), and because no legal instrument existed enabling land to be transferred directly from husband to wife. Rose's right to the property was now secure. At her own death, it would pass to her children by a previous marriage.

The *Inquisition* went on to state that

> the aforesaid John Taverner died seised thereof of such estate, and the aforesaid Rose survived him and held herself within by right of survivorship, and is still in full life, namely at Boston.

Six acres of the property were owned by the heirs of Charles Brandon, Duke of Suffolk, the rest by the College of St. Peter, Westminster. The freehold of the whole property cost Taverner 22d each year. According to the *Inquisition*, the net annual value of the land was £4.8.4. The original purchase of the land to Taverner, calculated at twenty times' rent, if we accept that valuation, was almost £90.

Less than five months after being elected alderman, and barely two months after effecting the transfer of his landed property, Taverner died at Boston on 18 October 1545.[64] He was given the singular honor of burial under the great bell tower of the parish church of St. Botolph's.[65] One other person had been so honored: Maud Tilney, a member of one of the wealthiest families in the town, who had "laid the first stone of the goodly steeple of the parish church of Boston."[66] Taverner's honor, however, was the result of neither high birth nor great wealth. It came from some other source, and that source was surely the service he had rendered to the music of St. Botolph's.

After giving the date of Taverner's death, the *Inquisition* named William Taverner, "aged forty years and more," as John's "kinsman and next heir." This man must be identified as the William Taverner of Tattershall who died in 1556.[67] Since the *Inquisition* was taken in 1546, his birthdate was ca. 1505 at the very latest, but probably ("forty years and more") some years before that. As John's "kinsman and next heir," William was in all probability his younger brother. The identification of Tattershall as his home is of special interest. We can safely assume that one did not move to that remote village except to be connected with the little collegiate community, and there is no sign whatever that William was ever connected with that community. We must conclude that Tattershall was his birthplace, and therefore, too, the birthplace of the composer. William Taverner died in 1556; his will identifies him as a yeoman farmer.[68]

The *Inquisition* concluded with the statement that John held no other lands "of the said Lord King" in the county. The statement did not cover property that Taverner held in the city of Boston under the system of burgage tenure, property mentioned later in his widow's will.

Rose survived her husband by eight years, dying in May 1553. Her will, written on the first day of that month and probated seventeen days later,[69] was witnessed by Robert Richardson and Steven Mychell, chaplain and clerk, respectively, named among the men in the pay of the Guild of the Blessed Virgin in 1548; Christopher Ratclif, probably the clerk "Christopher" noted without surname in the same list; and John Parrowe. She requested that her body "be buried in the parish church of Saint Botolph in the said Boston in the bell house next my husband." She left several articles of clothing and furnishings to her brother John Parrowe, her sisters Agnes Dyan and Alice, a maid-servant and two other women. To Jeffrey Parrowe, John's son,[70] she left "vj silver spoons and all the hangings about my parlor, one table of wainscot square." The rest of her property, including the land left by Taverner, went to her two married daughters, Emma Salmon and Isabell Hodge, and their families:

> I give and bequeath all my lands within the town and fields of Skirbeck and also one tenement lying in Boston in Wormgate in the tenure of William Lynam, all which lands & tenement I had of the late gift and fiefment of John Taverner my late husband deceased as by the deeds thereof made more plainly it doth appear, unto my ij daughters, that is to say, to Isabell Hodge wife of Roger Hodge and the heirs of her body lawfully begotten and to Eme Salmon the wife of Steven Salmon and to the heirs of her body lawfully begotten forever, and for lack of such issue it to be sold and disposed in deeds of charity at the discretion of mine executors. Item to Eme Salmon my silver salt gilt. The residue of my goods not given nor bequeathed my legacies and funerals deducted I give them to my ij daughters' children to be equally divided betwixt them at the discretion of Roger Hodge and Steven Salmon, whom I make mine executors of this my last will, and either of them to have for their pains xl[s].

The Boston property that Taverner had left to his widow consisted, at least in part, of one and a half acres of land in Wormgate and two acres of arable land and pasture, in the title of the Guild of the Blessed Virgin. In January 1555, it was granted to the borough of Boston.[71]

The reference to "my ij daughters' children" must date the birth of these two daughters to the early 1530s at the latest, and perhaps into the 1520s. We learn, therefore, that Rose was a widow when she married John Taverner.

The last extant document dealing with Taverner's family dates from some time between the death of Stephen Salmon, Rose Taverner's son-in-law, in 1569 and 1579.[72] It consists of a suit brought by her other son-in-law, Roger Hodge, against Emma Salmon, Emma's answer, and

Hodge's reply to Emma.[73]   Hodge and Stephen Salmon were the executors of Rose Taverner's will, under which they were to divide her good and chattels equally among her daughters' children. A fulling mill in Spilsby in her lease rented by "Stephen or his farmer or occupier," was part of the inheritance; the annual rent of £4.10.0 that it brought to the estate was to be divided equally so that Stephen's children received one half of the income (45s), Roger's, the other. Upon Stephen's death, his wife and executrix, Emma, "casually" took over the lease of the mill. Her late husband before his death ("what is the lifetime of the said Stephen Salmon") and Emma after it ("and sin[ce] his [death]") had not paid the rent for eleven years. Roger Hodge, the sole surviving executor of Rose Taverner's will, now demanded the full sum in arrears £4.10.0), in order to pay his and Stephen's "poor infants," when they came "unto their full and lawful age," the "legacies and bequests" of the will. Furthermore, he demanded the return of the lease of the mill. "And for that the said Eme hath goods and chattels sufficient of her said husband's to pay and discharge . . . [the] arrearages of the said mill over and besides wherewith to pay and discharge his [Stephen's] debts and legacies."

   Emma Salmon answered that she was never in possession of the mill. Her husband Stephen had occupied the mill for three years during the lifetime of Rose Taverner (apparently on a second lease or sublease). He made his son George, not Emma, his only executor, and George succeeded to the lease. Emma denied the arrangement concerning the 90s annual income and the eleven-year arrears, and insisted that she had taken no profit from the mill. Roger Hodge, in turn, repeated that his charge was true, and that although Emma may not have been Stephen's executrix she had received the profits.

   With these documents we come to the end of the Taverner biography with a comparative wealth of suggestive evidence. Through their testimony, we can identify Taverner's birthplace almost without question as Tattershall. His immediate family were yeoman farmers, but they were related to landed gentry, the Yerburghs, in northern Lincolnshire. Taverner rose through education, service in the church, the political connections with Wolsey and Cromwell, professional and family associations in Boston, and his own undoubted gifts, from son in a yeoman family to lay clerk, then to *informator* and organist of a great musical establishment, and finally to "gentlemen" and alderman on a town council. He had acquired enough money to purchase farming and pasture land at a cost of approximately £90. This was land acquired not by his marriage to Rose Parrowe, nor by any dubious transactions arising from the tranfer of suppressed religious properties, but through his own means. By the time of his death, Taverner had acquired at least three and a half acres of land within Boston itself--probably the land on which he lived--and he left his widow with enough cash to purchase the lease, at a cost of around £90, of a fulling mill in a neighboring town. The value of these purchases marks Taverner as a moderately well-to-do, though certainly not leading member of the local gentry.[74] He was able to provide his family with security and comfort, as well as a few luxuries (such as the six silver spoons, perhaps, willed by Rose Taverner to her nephew).

The documents tell us about Taverner's family and allow us to speculate about the time of his marriage. He left no children. His wife Rose had two daughters by a previous marriage. At the time of her death in 1553, both daughters were married and had children. Isabell and Roger Hodge moved to London; the Salmons remained in Lincolnshire. Emma's son George was executor of his father Stephen's will in 1569, and succeeded to Stephen's lease of the mill. He was the Salmon's oldest son, therefore, and was born in the late 1540s at the latest. In his suit, Roger Hodge identified his own children, as well as Stephen's and Emma's, as not yet having reached legal age, calling them "poor infants." That suit, as we have noted, was brought at some time after Stephen's death in 1569, and by 1579 at the latest. Since Hodge seems to have included the Salmon children among the "poor infants," the suit cannot be dated more than two or three years after Stephen's death; but since he noted that Emma has had the lease for some time since his brother-in-law's death, it cannot be dated much earlier than two or three years after 1569. We may assign a date, then, of ca. 1571 to the suit. Emma would have had to be of child-bearing age from the 1540s until the late 1560s; we may ascribe a birth date of ca. 1530 to her. She died in 1599.

It is unclear whether Isabell Hodge was older or younger than Emma. The wording of Rose Taverner's will has Isabell's name precede Emma's, and her husband's name precede Stephen Salmon's, suggesting that Isabell was the elder sister. But the one gift specified by Rose in her will, "my silver salt gilt," went to Emma. It does not matter much who was the elder. Since Isabell, like Emma, was married at the time of Rose's death in 1553 and had "poor infants" at the time of the suit, we may assign to her the same approximate birth date as Emma's, ca. 1530.

The information we have culled from these last documents enables us to settle one more point that has remained unresolved: the prospect "of a good marriage" that Taverner cited to Bishop Longland as a reason for not wishing to leave Tattershall in 1526. We now can assume safely that this prospect involved a woman unknown to us, that

Rose Parrowe was married at the time, and that she was not widowed until ca. 1530 or sometime thereafter.

The Boston documents tell us nothing directly about Taverner's musical activities, but collectively they present us with sufficient information to allow the construction of a hypothesis connecting the documentary evidence that we do have. Taverner, having been born into a yeoman family in Tattershall, educated at the collegiate church, and employed there before his reluctant departure for Oxford in late 1526, left Oxford in the spring of 1530 with the collapse of Wolsey's protection and patronage, and returned to his native shire. Tattershall was out of the question now. He assumed a musical position in Boston. Perhaps that position was a lay clerkship at St. Botolph's. More likely, in view of the status of his former post, he became *informator* or organist. His salary was paid by the Guild of the Blessed Virgin. At St. Botolph's he met two men who would become trusted friends, Gillmyn and Goche. Undoubtedly, too, he came to know John Wendon. Through the guild he met the Parrowe family. He married the widow Rose Parrowe, whose father Thomas was a member and alderman of the guild, and a member of the Corpus Christi Guild as well. Perhaps through his father-in-law's aid, he prospered sufficiently to buy land and gain membership by 1537 in the Corpus Christi Guild. He may have joined the Guild of the Blessed Virgin as well.

How long Taverner may have continued as a professional musician is unknown. Wendon had probably quit his post by 1534 at the latest, at about the time the Guild of the Blessed Virgin began to experience financial difficulties as a result of the reformation under Cromwell, and began to rise politically through his association with Cromwell. Gillmyn, though he too associated himself with the new politics, remained a church musician; his battle with the guild over salary in 1539 is evidence of the decline of support for music at St. Botolph's. In 1538 Taverner became involved with Cromwell, whether through their possible acquaintanceship ten years earlier at Cardinal College, or through Taverner's more recent friendship with Gillmyn or perhaps Wendon. He oversaw the dissolution of the Boston friaries, as benignly and generously as possible. Gillmyn's activities demonstrate that it is not impossible that Taverner was still at St. Botolph's while he acted as Cromwell's agent; but given his membership in the Guild of Corpus Christi, it is unlikely. He remained an orthodox Catholic but not a "papist," his religious views being conservative enough for him to participate in the affairs of the guild, but liberal enough for him to be associated with Cromwell until the minister's sudden fall in 1540.[75] He became an officer of the guild in 1541, and town alderman in 1545. He died a "gentleman" of reasonable means, and was buried under the tower of St. Botolph's, a sign of the esteem of his fellow citizens for some extraordinary service--surely a musical one--to the town of Boston.

CHAPTER 7

SOURCES OF THE CHURCH MUSIC

Virtually the entire extant body of Taverner's church music is collected in the first and third volumes of *Tudor Church Music*. It is a not entirely satisfactory edition. The editors barred their transcriptions irregularly, failed to correct several corrupt readings, and made many dubious decisions on others, usually with regard to accidentals.[1] Furthermore, they neglected to supply the plainsong sections necessary for a liturgically complete rendering of the music--notably the *alternatim* settings of the *Magnificats, Te Deum, Alleluias,* the responds, and the prose *Sospitati dedit aegros*. Examination of the volumes should be accompanied by a reading of H. B. Collins's two critical essays,[2] and performers using them should feel free to consider the alternate readings offered in their footnotes.

Almost all of the known extant sources of Tavener's music were consulted for the edition, and they are identified and described in it. CHe 1, Tsm 1464, 1469-71 and 1486 and WOw were found later by Fellowes, who described and catalogued them, and listed their alternate readings, in the *Tudor Church Music Appendix* of 1948.

Several items attributed to Taverner in the manuscripts and printed in *Tudor Church Music* are not by him. *Esto nobis* (3:133,[3] from Lcm 2035) is a section of Tallis's *Ave Dei patris filia*. *Rex amabilis* (3:125, from John Baldwin's Lbl 24 d.2) is taken from Fayrfax's *Maria plena virtute*. *Tu ad liberandum* and *Tu angelorum domina* (3:127, 129, respectively, from Lbl 24 d.2) are from Aston's *Te Deum*.[4] *Ave regina caelorum* (*Appendix*, from Tsm 1486 and WOw) has been misattributed to both Taverner and Byrd.[5]

Some other attributions of works to Taverner are questionable on stylistic grounds, although no attributions to other composers have been found for them. In 1597, Thomas Morley printed "a piece of composition of four parts of Master Taverner in one of his Kyries."[6] It is found in no other source and is certainly not authentic. The editors of *Tudor Church Music* have not included it in their edition, but they have accepted an *Agnus Dei* (3:60) that seems of dubious authenticity, attributed to Taverner in Lcm 2035. His authorship of the five-part *Te Deum* inscribed by Baldwin in Och 979-83 (3:26) has also been questioned.[7]

The untexted *Sanctus* and *Benedictus* (3:58, 59, respectively, from Lbl 18936-37, 18939) are taken from his own *Gaude plurimum* ("Gaude Maria virgo," 3:79-80) and *Traditur militibus* (3:132).

The remains of two other works have come to light since the publication of the *Tudor Church Music Appendix*.   One is the countertenor part of a five-part setting of the respond *Dum transisset Sabbatum*, found in Lbl 47844 but not known from any other source. It is reproduced on Plate 19.   The other is a second countertenor ("secundus contratenor") part of a *Kyrie* found on the flyleaf of a printed Sarum processional, Lbl 1545.c.35, f. 14:[8]

This fragment may be part of one of the works mentioned in an inventory at King's College, Cambridge, in 1529, and now missing: "Taverner's Kyries," "a Mass of Taverner's for children," and "Taverner's Kyries with the Sequences."[9]

Taverner's extant church music is found in some thirty manuscript collections of the sixteenth and seventeenth centuries, located now in Cambridge, Chelmsford, London, Oxford, Tenbury and Worcester. The following list of these manuscripts is divided into four sections according to their approximate date of compilation: the early, middle and late years of the sixteenth century, and the early years of the seventeenth.[10] The first two sections are listed in probable chronological order, while the last two are listed alphabetically by their present location, because of the difficulty of dating most of the later sources accurately.[11]   Many of the manuscripts contain excerpts from longer works. These are identified in the appropriate manuscript references in *Tudor Church Music*.

Taverner: Liturgical Music

		TCM	PTS	NOTES
Mass:	Corona spinea	1:158	6	
	Gloria tibi Trinitas[12]	1:126	6	
	Mater Christi	1:99	5	1 part lacking
	Mean	1:50	5	*TCM: Sine nomine*
	O Michael	1:194	6	

		TCM	PTS	NOTES
	Plainsong	1:30	4	
	Sancti Willelmi devotio	1:70	5	*TCM: Small devotion;* 1 part lacking
	Western wind[13]	1:30	4	
Mass Movement:	*Agnus Dei*[14]	3:60	3	fragment
	Christe eleison[15]	3:57	3	3 settings
	Kyrie eleison[16]	3:54	4	
	Kyrie eleison	-	?	fragment
Mass Proper:	*Alleluia*	3:52	4	
	Alleluia Veni electa mea	3:53	4	
	Ecce Mater Jerusalem	3:122	2	verse of processional antiphon *Ecce carissimi*
	Jesu spes penitentibus	3:123	3	v. 3 of sequence *Dulcis Jesu memoria*
	Tam peccatum	3:126	3	v. 4 of tract *Dulce nomen Jesu Christe*
	Traditur militibus[17]	3:132	3	v. 6 of sequence *Coenam cum discipulis*
Votive Antiphon:	*Ave Dei patris filia*	3:61		
	Ave Maria	3:34	5	2 parts lacking
	Christe Jesu pastor bone[18]	3:73	5	1 part lacking
	Fac nobis	3:135	5	2 parts lacking
	Gaude plurimum	3:78	5	
	Mater Christi[19]	3:92	5	
	O splendor gloriae	3:99	5	
	Prudens virgo	3:124	3	fragment (verse?)
	Sancte Deus, sancte fortis	3:139	5	2 parts lacking
	Sub tuum praesidium	3:141	5	2 parts lacking
	Virgo pura	3:131	3	fragment (verse?)
Magnificat and *Te Deum*:	*Magnificat*[20]	3:3	4	
	Magnificat	3:9	5	1 part lacking
	Magnificat	3:17	6	1 part lacking
	Te Deum	3:26	5	1 part lacking

		TCM	PTS	NOTES
Respond:	*Audivi vocem de caelo*[21]	3:35	4	
	Dum transisset Sabbatum[22]	3:37	5	
	Dum transisset Sabbatum	3:40	4	alternate version of *TCM* 3:37 setting
	Dum transisset Sabbatum	3:43	5	
	Dum transisset Sabbatum	--	5	4 parts lacking
	Gloria in excelsis[23]	3:46	4	verse of *Hodie nobis caelorum rex*
	In pace in idipsum[24]	3:48	4	
Prose:	*Sospitati dedit aegros*	3:110	5	
Psalm-motet:	*Quemadmodum*	3:117	6	

Early Sixteenth-Century MSS

1a.   Cjc K.31 (James 234), ca. 1520. Bass partbook of an original set of five. Two works by Taverner: *Ave Dei patris filia* and *Gaude plurimum*. See pp. 38-39, and Plate 4.

1b.   Cu Dd.13.27, ca. 1520. Countertenor partbook of the same set.

2.   Lbl 1709, ca. 1525-35. Mean partbook of an original set of five. Two works by Taverner: *Ave Dei patris filia* and *Gaude plurimum*. See pp. 39-40.

3.   Lbl 34191, ca. 1525-47. Tenor/bass partbook of an original set of five containing Masses and other Latin settings, as well as English service items. One work by Taverner: *Gaude plurimum*.[25] See p. 40.

4.   Ob 376-81, ca. 1527-85. Temporarily reclassified as Arch. F.e. 19-24. The Forrest-Heyther partbooks. Six books containing eighteen Masses, begun by or under the supervision of Taverner at Cardinal College, to provide his chapel choir with a repertory of festal Masses. In five of the partbooks, the *initium* of the Mass *Gloria tibi Trinitas* (which opens the MSS) is decorated with a portrait assumed to be Taverner's, for in three books it is accompanied by a ribbon bearing

his name (see Plates 5-10). The first hand ends with the eleventh Mass, John Norman's *Resurrexit Dominus* (see Plate 11). In 1530 the set came into the possession of William Forrest, a petty canon at Cardinal College. The date may be significant: that was the year Taverner left the college. Perhaps he gave the set to Forrest upon his departure, or simply left them for Forrest to claim in the confusion of that unsettled time in the college chapel. The manner of exchange is unimportant: what is of interest is the suggested confirmation of our assumption that the set was in Taverner's possession during his tenure at Cardinal College.

During the 1530s, Forrest was chaplain to Queen Mary. It was probably at this time that he added seven more Masses: Taverner's *Corona spinea* (no. 12) and *O Michael* (no. 15), Ashewell's *Ave Maria*, Aston's *Videte manus meas*, Sheppard's *Cantate*, Tye's *Euge bone*, and Richard Alwood's *Praise Him praiseworthy*. He died in ca. 1581, leaving the sixth partbook (Ob 381) incomplete. The set came into the hands of the Windsor scribe John Baldwin who, beginning in the middle of the Agnus Dei of the Mass *O Michael* (see Plate 15), completed it from a source now lost.[26] See pp. 61-62.

5.   Lbl 56, ca. 1530-45. Musical commonplace book. One work by Taverner: keyboard arrangement of an extract from the Mass *Western wind.* See p. 44.

Mid-Sixteenth-Century MSS

6.   Cp 471-74 (*olim* 40, 41, 31, 32), ca. 1539-41.   The Henrician set. Four partbooks of an original set of five (tenor lacking, treble incomplete) containing Masses and settings for the Sarum liturgy.[27] *Unicum* source of six Taverner settings: *Ave Maria, Fac nobis,* the five-part *Magnificat,* the Mass *Mater Christi, Sancte Deus, sancte fortis,* and *Sub tuum praesidium.* Six other Taverner works: *Ave Dei patris filia, Gaude plurimum,* the antiphon *Mater Christi, (O) Christe Jesu pastor bone* (see Plate 16), and the *Mean* and *Sancti Willelmi devotio* Masses.

7.   Ob 420-22, ca. 1547-50. The Wanley partbooks. Three books of an original set of four (lacking tenor) containing music for the English liturgy. English adapations of three Taverner works: *Mater Christi* (as *God be merciful unto us*) and the *Mean* and *Sancti Willelmi devotio* Masses.[28]

8.   Lbl 17802-805, ca. 1553-80. The Gyffard partbooks. Four partbooks of an original set of five (lacking tenor) containing Masses, a Passion setting, and other music for the Sarum rite. *Unicum* source of eight Taverner works: *Alleluia, Audivi vocem de caelo (pars ad*

placitum by Whytbroke), the four-part *Dum transisset Sabbatum, Gloria in excelsis, In pace in idipsum* ("for iij men and a child;" see Plate 17). *Kyrie Le Roy*, the four-part *Magnificat*, and the *Plainsong* Mass. Earliest source of *Alleluia Veni electa mea*. Also contains the *Western wind* Mass.[29]

Late Sixteenth-Century MSS

9. Ckc 316, ca. 1570. Mean partbook (labelled "contratenor") of an original set of probably five containing Latin motets, English anthems (most of them adaptations of motets), partsongs and instrumental music. Two works by Taverner: *Gaude plurimum* (*I will magnify Thee*) and *Mater Christi* (*O most holy and mighty Lord*).

10. Tsm 1464, ca. 1575. Bass partbook of an original set of probably five containing Latin church music and a few anthems, partsongs and instrumental compositions. Three Masses by Taverner *Gloria tibi Trinitas*, the *Mean* Mass, and *Sancti Willelmi devotio*.

11. Lbl 31390, ca. 1578. A book of "sol-faing songs" and instrumental compositions and transcriptions of Latin settings of from five to eight parts.[30] Two works by Taverner, both without text: a five-part *Dum transisset Sabbatum* (see Plate 19), and *Quemadmodum* (unattributed; see Plate 18).

12. Och 979-83, ca. 1580-1605. Sixteenth century, five partbooks of an original set of six (tenor lacking) in the hand of John Baldwin, containing Latin church music and some instrumental compositions. *Unicum* source of Taverner's *Ecce mater Jerusalem* and Te Deum. Contains nine other settings by Taverner: *Ave Dei patris filia, Christe Jesu pastor bone, Dum transisset Sabbatum a5* (two settings), *Gaude plurimum*, the Mass *Gloria tibi Trinitas, Mater Christi, O splendor gloriae* (attributed to Taverner and Tye), and *Quemadmodum* (untexted).[31]

13. Lbl 47844, dated 1581. Countertenor partbook of an original set of five containing textless versions of Latin settings. *Unicum* source for a lost five-part setting by Taverner of *Dum transisset Sabbatum* (See Plate 20).

14. Och 984-88, dated 1581. The (Robert) Dow partbooks. Five books containing motets, partsongs, and a few anthems and instrumental pieces.[32] The only complete source of one of Taverner's five-part settings of *Dum transisset Sabbatum* (*TCM* 3:37).

15.   Ob 1-5, dated 1585. The (John) Sadler partbooks. Set of five books containing mostly Latin church music. Only complete source of four Taverner settings: *Ave Dei patris filia, Gaude plurimum, Mater Christi* and *O splendor gloriae*; also has the *Western wind* Mass.

16.   Lb1 24 d.2, ca. 1590-1610. Musical commonplace book inscribed by John Baldwin. *Unicum* source of four Taverner settings: *Jesu spes penitentibus, Prudens virgo, Tam peccatum* and *Virgo pura*, as well as *In women is rest/No season* (see Plate 22). Also by Taverner are *Traditur militibus* (untexted), and excerpts from *Gaude plurimum, O splendor gloriae*, the Mass *Gloria tibi Trinitas* (untexted). *Tu ad liberandum* and *Tu angelorum domina*, misattributed by Baldwin to Taverner, are taken from Hugh Aston's *Te Deum*. A third misattribution by Baldwin to Taverner, *Rex amabilis*, is an excerpt from Fayrfax's antiphon *Maria plena virtute*.[33]

17a.   Tsm 1486, dated 1591. The Braikenridge MS. Tenor partbook of an original set of five containing motets, in the hand of John Sadler. One composition by Taverner, *Gaude plurimum*, as well as the unauthentic *Ave regina caelorum*.

17b.   WOw, dated 1591. The Willmott MS. Mean partbook belonging to the same set as Tenbury 1486.

18.   CHe 1, late sixteenth century. Bass partbook of an original set of five containing mostly Latin music. Six works by Taverner: *Gaude plurimum, Mater Christi, Mean* Mass, *O splendor gloriae, Quemadmodum* (untexted) and *Sospitati dedit aegros* (untexted).

19.   Lcm 2035, late sixteenth century. Full set of three partbooks (treble, mean, countertenor) containing mostly excerpts from Latin settings. Seven works by Taverner: an isolated *Agnus Dei* (*unicum*), and excerpts from *Ave Dei patris filia, Gaude plurimum, Sospitati dedit aegros*, and the *Corona spinea, Gloria tibi Trinitas*, and *Mean* Masses. *Esto nobis*, misattributed in this source to Taverner, is an excerpt from Tallis's *Ave Dei patris filia*.

20.   Ob 423, late sixteenth century. Countertenor partbook of an original set of five containing motets, anthems, partsongs and instrumental music. Four works by Taverner: *Ave Dei patris filia, Gaude plurimum*, the six-part *Magnificat* and *Mater Christi*.

21.   Tsm 341-44, late sixteenth century. Four partbooks of an original set of five (bass lacking) containing Latin church music. Two

compositions by Taverner: *Mater Christi* and *Sospitati dedit aegros.* Tsm 342 contains three- and four-part excerpts from Taverner's *Gaude plurimum* and his Masses *Corona spinea, Gloria tibi Trinitas* and *Sancti Willelmi devotio.*

22. Tsm 354-58, late sixteenth century. Full set of five partbooks containing Latin church music. Seven settings by Taverner: *Gaude plurimum, Mater Christi,* and excerpts from *Ave Dei patris filia,* the six-part *Magnificat,* the *Gloria tibi Trinitas* and *Mean* Masses, and *Sospitati dedit aegros.*

23. Tsm 1469-71, late sixteenth century. Three partbooks (treble, countertenor, bass) of an original set of five containing Latin church music and a few anthems and partsongs, in the same hand as Tsm 354-58. Three compositions by Taverner: *Gaude plurimum,* the Gloria of the Mass *Gloria tibi Trinitas,* and *Sospitati dedit aegros.* An *Ave regina caelorum* ascribed to Taverner here and in Tsm 1486 and WOw is almost certainly misattributed.[34]

Early Seventeenth-Century MSS

24. Lbl 29246, ca. 1611. Lute book with excerpts from five Taverner settings: *Gaude plurimum, Sospitati dedit aegros,* and the *Corona spinea, Gloria tibi Trinitas* and *Mean* Masses. An excerpt from Tallis's *Ave rosa sine spinis* is misattributed to Taverner.

25. Lbl 18936-39, after 1612. Four partbooks of an original set of five, a commonplace collection containing mostly sacred and secular vocal music, often without text. Seven three-part settings by Taverner, all untexted: three settings of *Christe eleison* (*unicum*), two excerpts from *Gaude plurimum* (one of them, taken from the passage beginning "Gaude Maria virgo," mistitled "Sanctus") and one from the six-part *Magnificat,* and *Traditur militibus* (mistitled "Benedictus"). A seventh brief work attributed in the MS to Taverner, *Osanna in excelsis,* was rejected properly by the editors of *Tudor Church Music* as unauthentic; it is probably from an early Anglican Communion setting.

26. Cp 485-91 (*olim* 44, 42, 43, 37, 45, 35, 36), ca. 1635. The Caroline Books, second set. *Decani*: mean, countertenor, tenor, bass; *cantoris*: mean, tenor, bass. Incomplete set of partbooks containing mostly Anglican music. One work by Taverner: the *Mean* Mass (with Latin text).

27.	Lb1 4900, early seventeenth century. Songbook with lute accompaniment. One work by Taverner: *Alleluia Veni electa mea.*

28.	Lb1 34049, early seventeenth century. Treble partbook of an original set of five containing mostly Marian compositions, all unattributed. Three works by Taverner: *Gaude plurimum, Mater Christi,* and *Sospitati dedit aegros.*

29.	Lb1 41156-58, early seventeenth century. Three partbooks (treble, mean, countertenor) of an original set of five containing mostly instrumental compositions, many of them adaptations. Two works by Taverner, untexted (except for an *incipit*) and unattributed: *Gaude plurimum* and *Sospitati dedit aegros.*

30.	Och 45, early seventeenth century. A book of Latin church music, mostly excerpts from longer works, of from two to four parts. Taverner is represented by *Traditur militibus* and excerpts from the six-part *Magnificat.*

31.	Tsm 807-811, early seventeenth century. Five partbooks of an original set of six (treble lacking) containing Latin church music, anthems and a partsong. One composition by Taverner: the six-part *Magnificat.*

The foregoing summary list of the sources containing Taverner's extant church music[35] prompts several observations. Cjc K.31, Cu Dd.13.27, Lb1 1709 and Lb1 34191, compiled in London, indicate a date of ca. 1520 for two of his three large-scale antiphons. Ob 376-81 places the Mass *Gloria tibi Trinitas* in Oxford in ca. 1527-28 at the latest; *O Michael* and probably *Corona spinea* were composed by then as well. That these sources account for only five Taverner settings leads to the conclusion that virtually all of the manuscripts in which his music first appeared have been lost or destroyed. Cp 471-74, copied late during his lifetime and almost certainly without his knowledge, is the earliest source for ten more settings by him. Cp 471-74, Ob 420-22 and Lb1 17802-805, dating from the middle of the century, constitute a second generation of manuscripts; that is, they are probably one or two steps removed from the original sources. Cp 471-74 and Lb1 17802-805 probably represent with reasonable fidelity the intentions of the composer, notwithstanding their many minor scribal errors. Together with the earlier manuscripts, this middle group accounts for twenty-five Latin settings by Taverner. For the nineteen other extant settings, we must rely on what are probably third and fourth generation manuscripts, for the most part, from the later Tudor and Stuart periods.

Twenty-three of Taverner's surviving Latin settings appear only once in the sources; four of the *unicum* sources, containing nine of these compositions, were copied long after his death. With so large a number of works owing their survival to one manuscript (six of them, in fact, to one scribe, John Baldwin), we can only wonder how many have disappeared with the loss of the other sources.

On the other hand, certain compositions, or excerpts from them, appear in several manuscripts. Among the Masses, *Gloria tibi Trinitas* and the *Mean* Mass are found in eight, *Corona spinea* in five and *Sancti Willelmi devotio* in four. Of the other works, *Ave Dei patris filia* and *Sospitati dedit aegros* are found in eight sources, and *Gaude plurimum*, the most frequently copied of Taverner's settings, in nineteen. Uncritical acceptance of such numbers may lead us, however, to incorrect assumptions about the circulation and popularity of certain compositions. Thanks to a brilliant piece of scholarship, for instance, we know that seven sources--CHe 1, Lcm 2035, Tsm 354-58 and 1469-71, and Lbl 29246, 34049 and 41156-58-- are connected with the Catholic household of Edward Paston of Norfolk around the turn of the century.[36] In this collection of manuscripts, several compositions of Taverner's appear seven times each. Thus, the presence of *Sospitati dedit aegros* in eight sources, which would point at first glance to its popularity, seems to indicate the opposite: aside from the Paston collection, it appears only once, in the manuscripts Tsm 341-44. What remains indisputable from a straightforward enumeration of works and sources, however, is Taverner's preeminence among early Tudor composers in the eyes of the scribes and musicians who inherited their legacy.

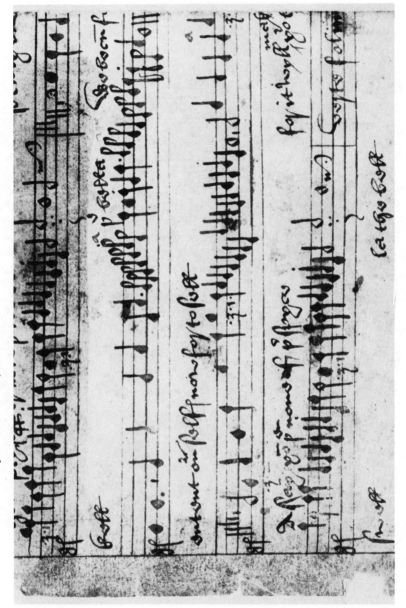

Plate 1.   Fragment of *The bella, the bella* (right margin slightly cropped in photograph)
NYpl 4183, front flyleaf

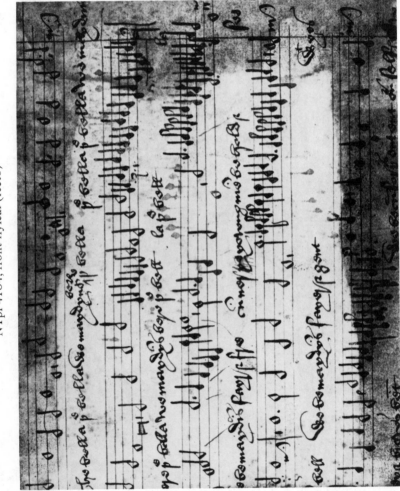

Plate 2. Fragment of *The bella, the bella*
NYpl 4184, front flyleaf (recto)

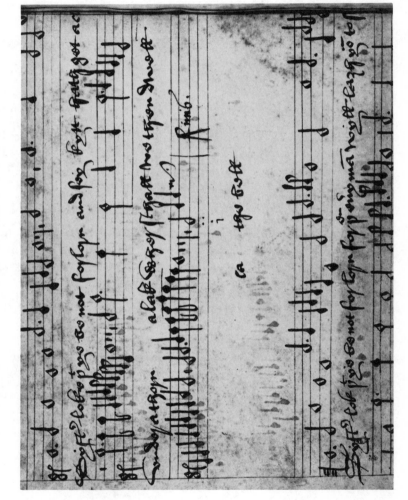

Plate 3. Fragment of *The bella, the bella*
NYpl 4184, front flyleaf (verso)

Plate 4. Beginning of *Ave Dei patris filia,* bass part
Cjc k.31, f. 11

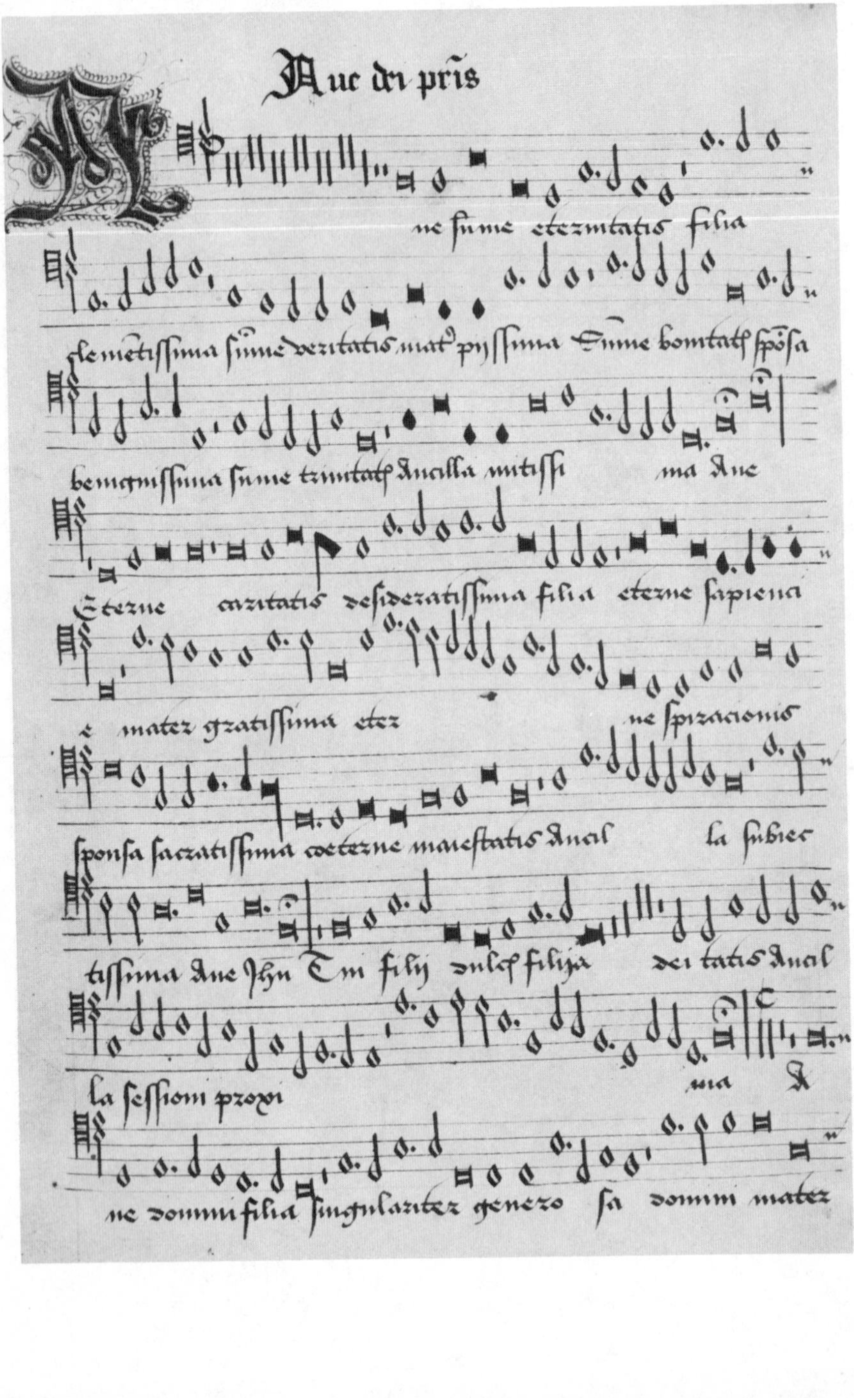

Plate 5. Beginning of the Mass *Gloria tibi trinitas*, treble part
Ob 376, f. 5

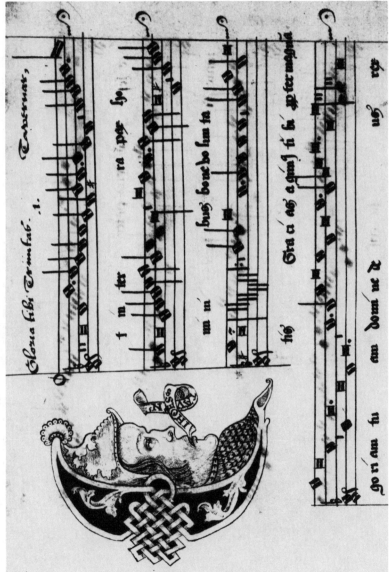

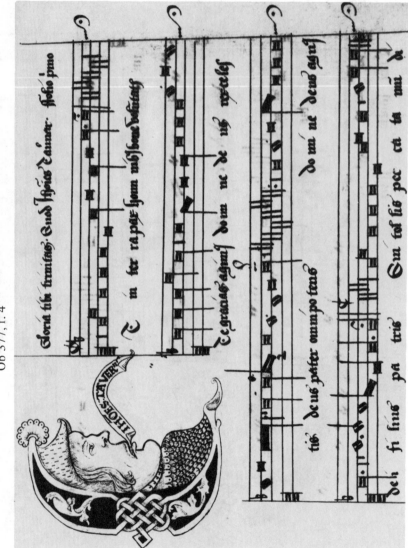

Plate 6. Beginning of the Mass *Gloria tibi Trinitas*, mean part Ob 377, f. 4

Plate 7. Beginning of the Mass *Gloria tibi Trinitas*, first countertenor part Ob 378, f. 4

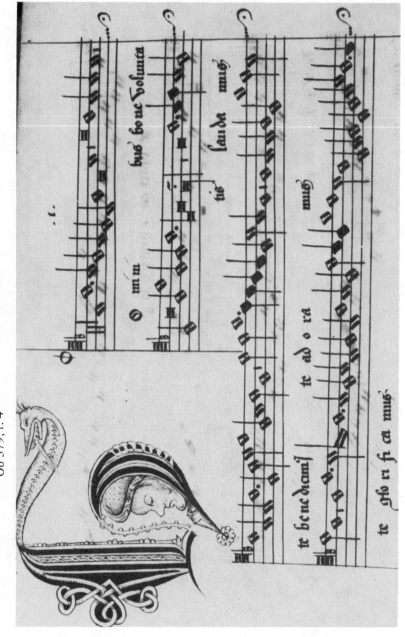

Plate 8. Beginning of the Mass *Gloria tibi Trinitas*, second countertenor part
Ob 379, f. 4

Plate 9. Beginning of the Mass *Gloria tibi Trinitas*, bass part
Ob 380, f. 4

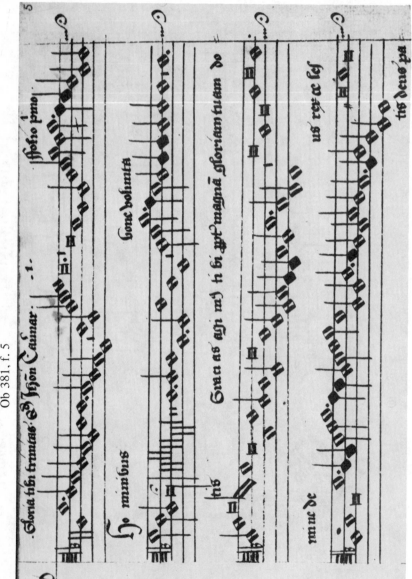

Plate 10. Beginning of the Mass *Gloria tibi Trinitas*, tenor part
Ob 381.f. 5

Plate 11. Beginning of the Mass *Corona spinea,* treble part:
William Forrest's hand replaces first scribe (Taverner?)
Ob 376, f. 93v

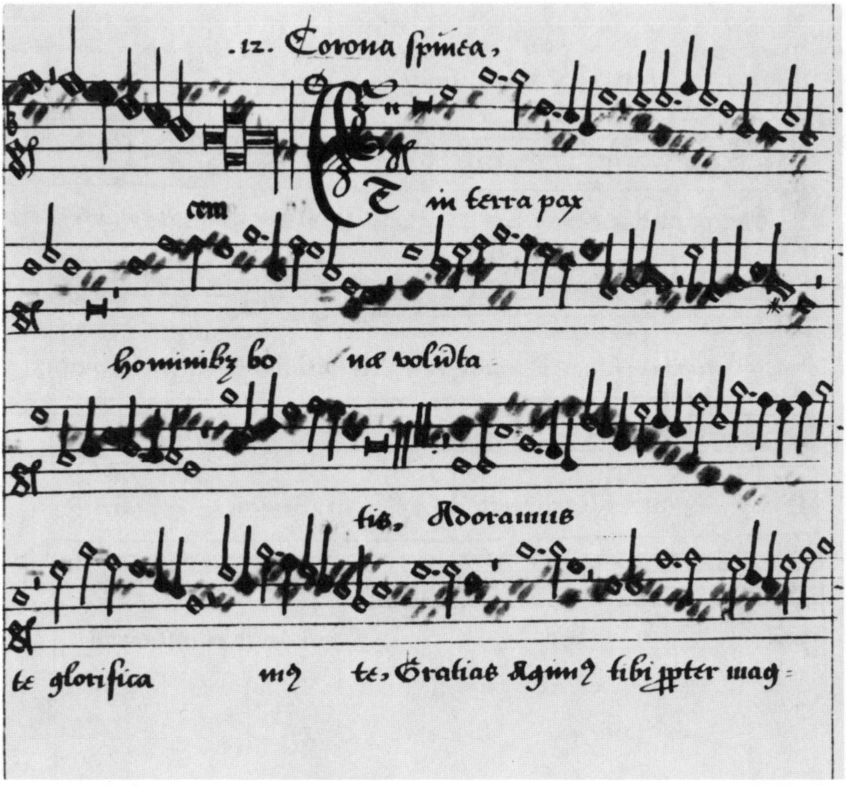

Plate 12. Beginning of the Mass *Corona spinea,* second countertenor part
Ob 379, ff. 83v-84

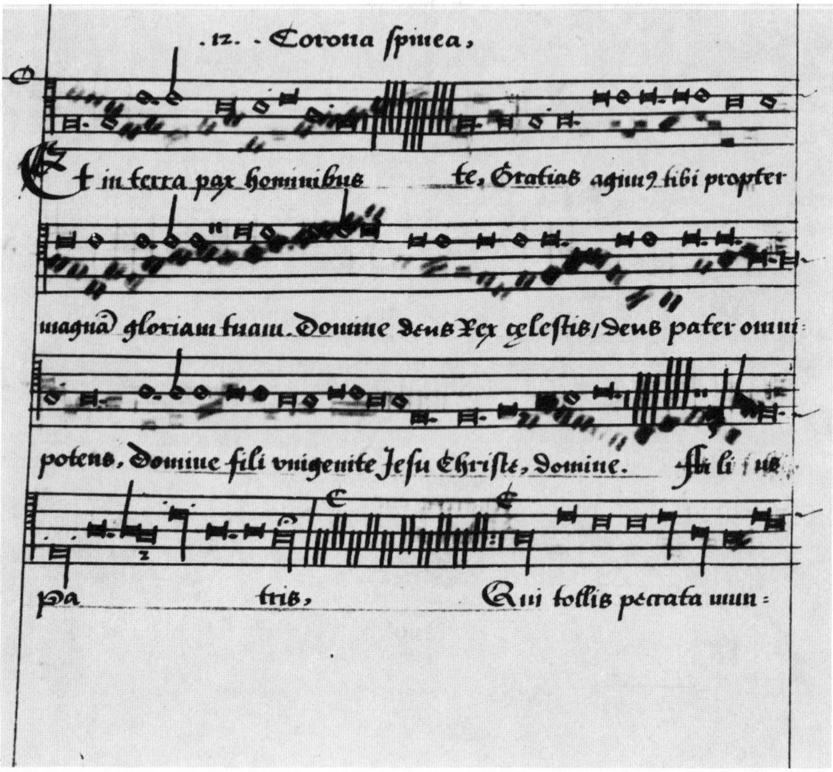

·12·
di: suscipe deprecationē no strā, Qui sedes ad dexterā
patris: miserere no bis. Qm̄ tu solus. Tu solus dominus. Jesu
Christe, Cum sancto spiritu: in gloria dei pa tris. A
men, Patrem, Et ex patre natū ante

Plate 13. Beginning of the Mass *O Michael,* tenor part
Ob 379, ff. 83v-84

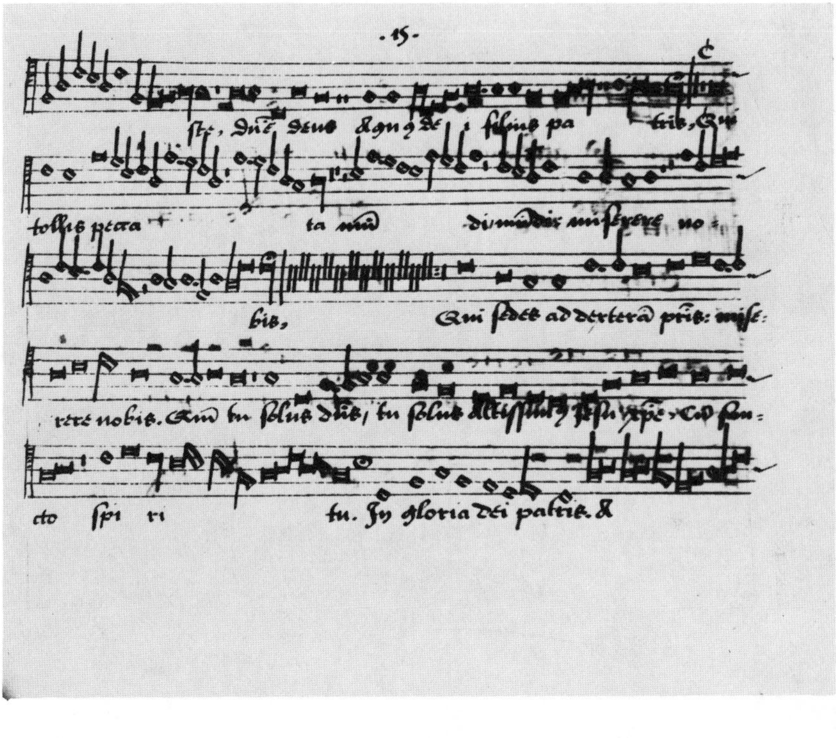

Plate 14. Canon at "filium Dei unigenitum" in the Mass *O Michael,*
treble part in gimel
Ob 376, f. 114v

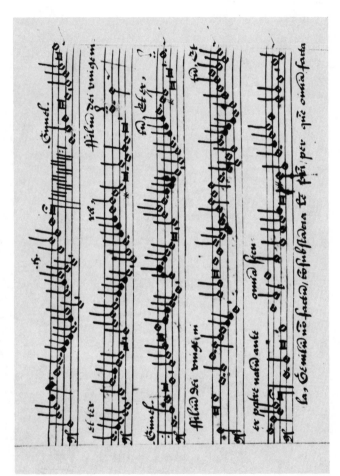

Plate 15. Portion of Agnus Dei from the Mass *O Michael*, second countertenor part:
John Baldwin's hand replaces William Forrest's
Ob 381, ff. 42v-43

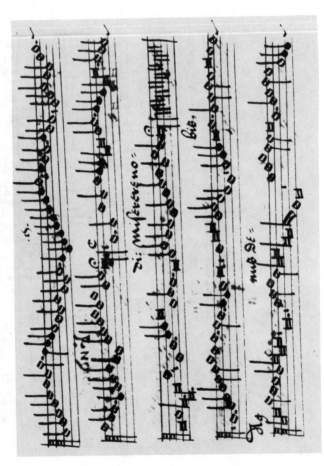

Plate 16. *O Christe Jesu pastor bone,* treble part
Cp 471, f. 71

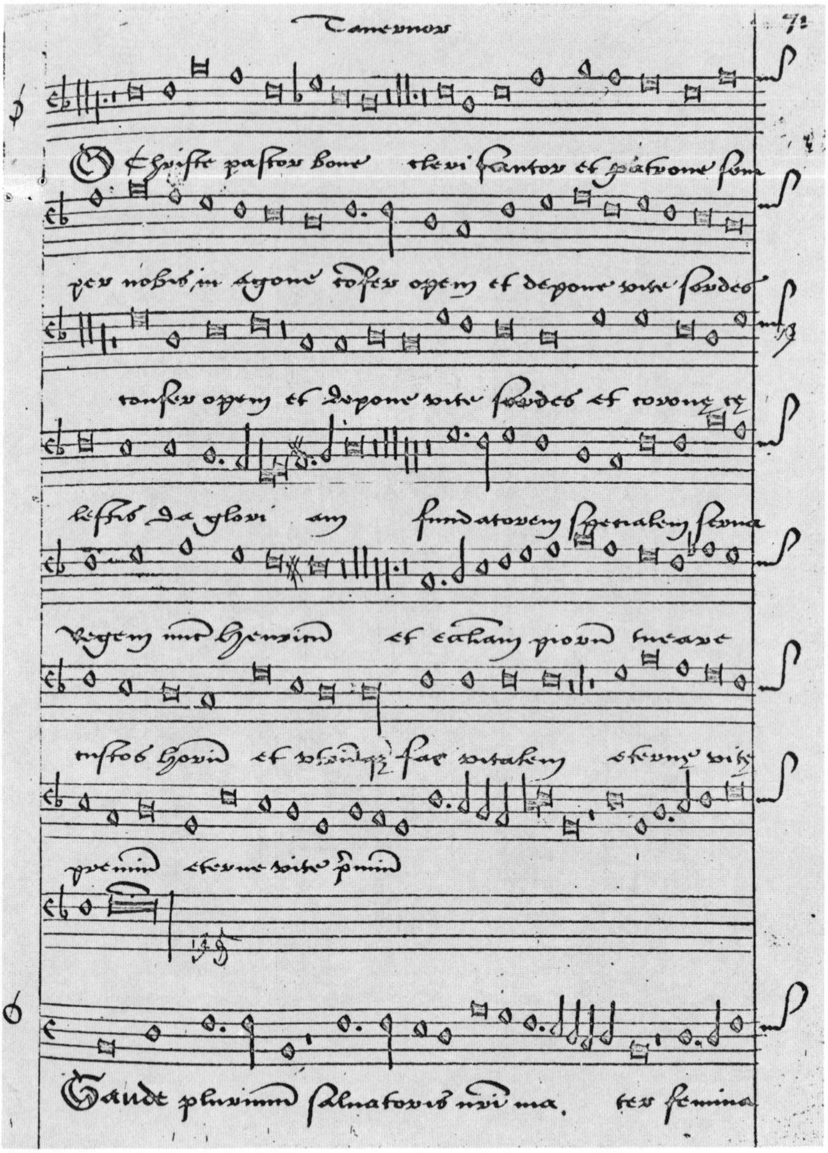

Plate 17. Beginning of *In pace in idipsum*
Lbl 17803, f. 107

Plate 18. *Quemadmodum*
Lbl 31390, ff. 11v-12

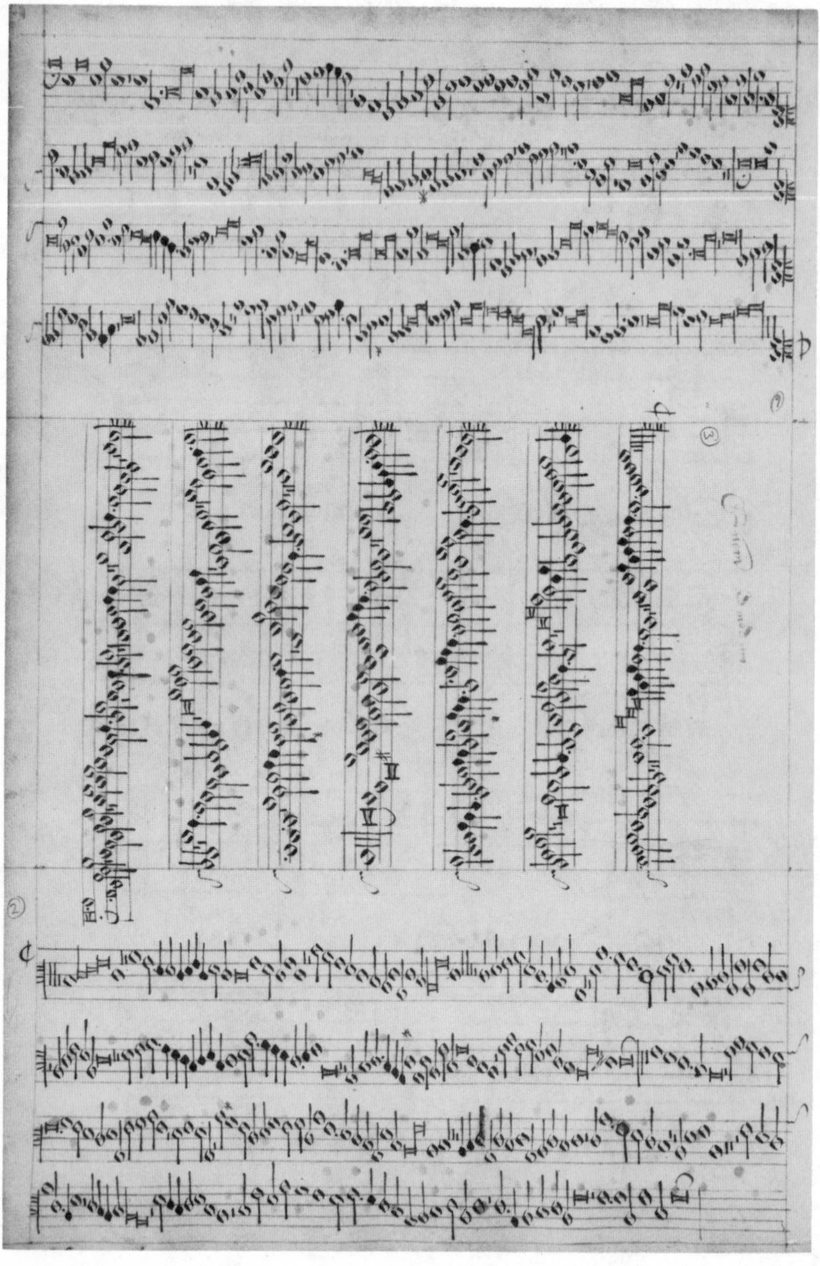

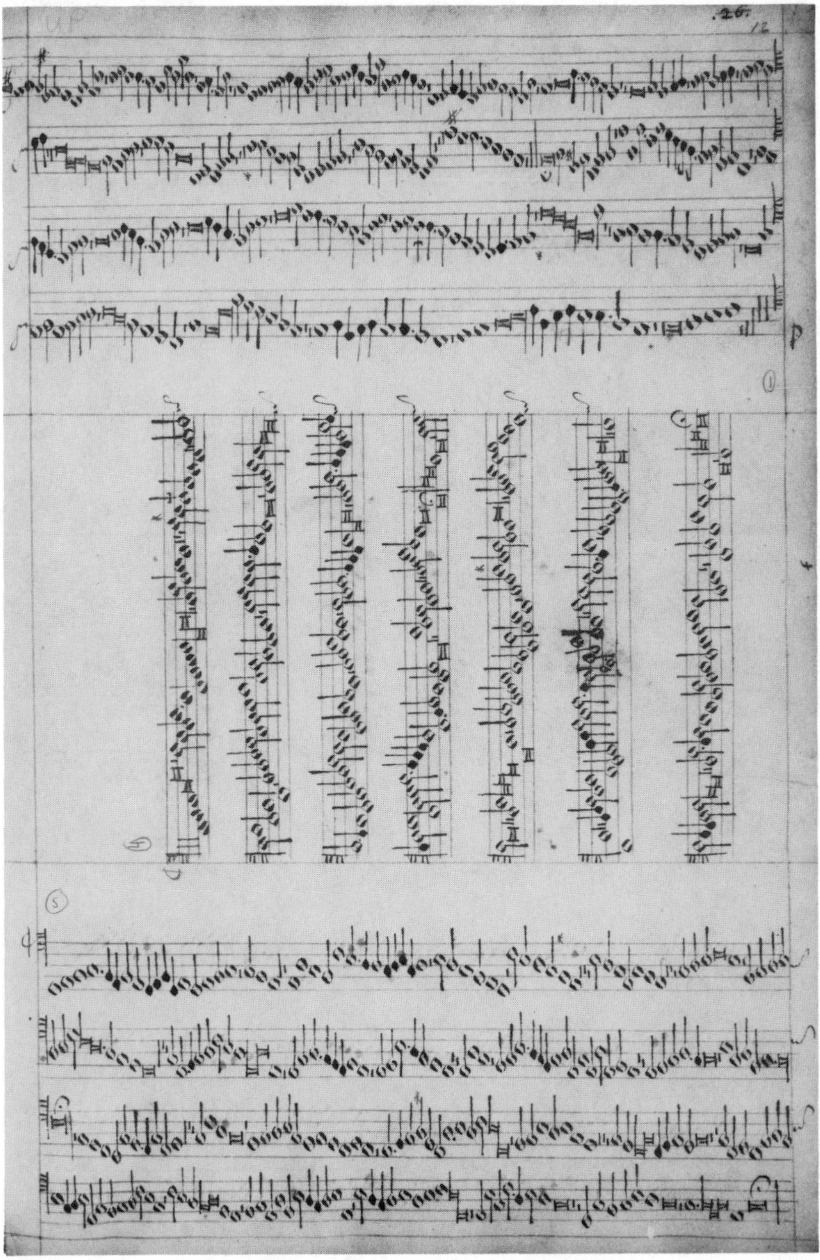

Plate 19. *Dum transisset Sabbatum*
Lbl 31390, ff. 106v-107

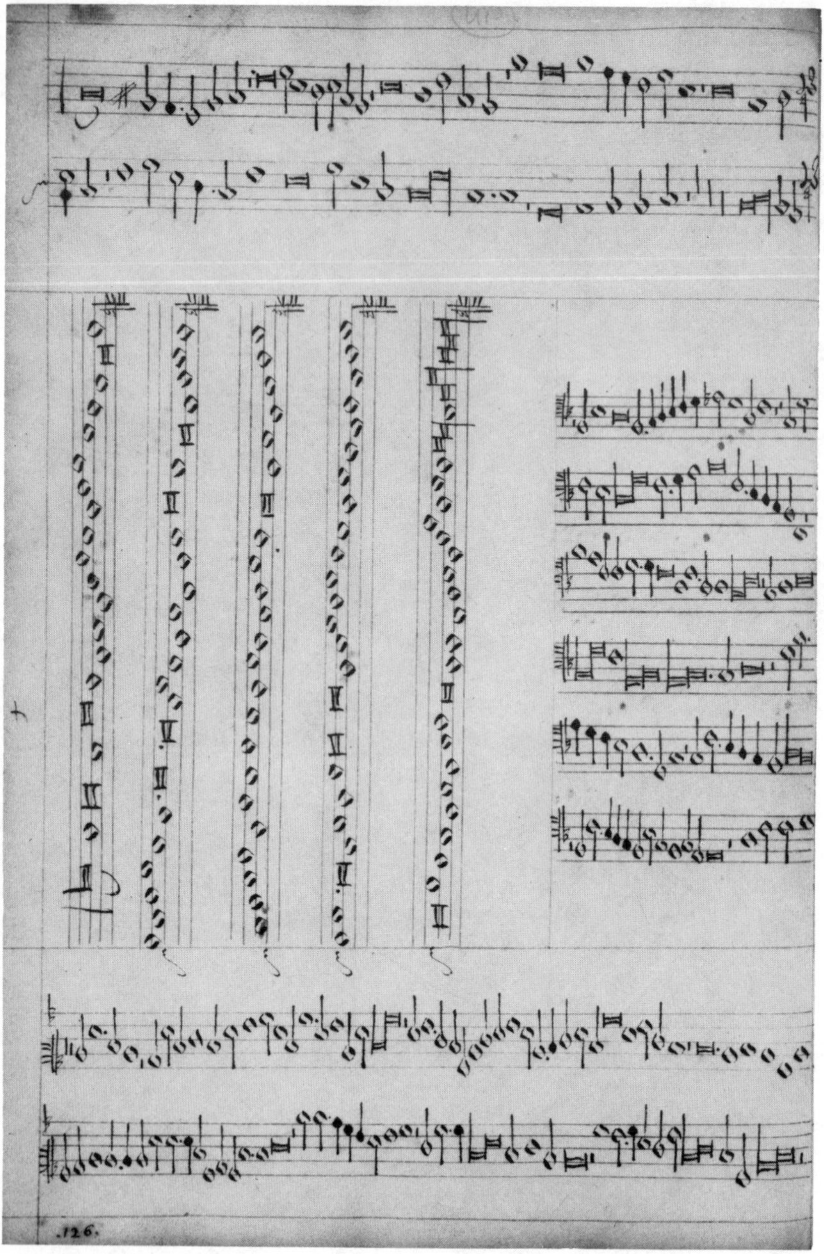

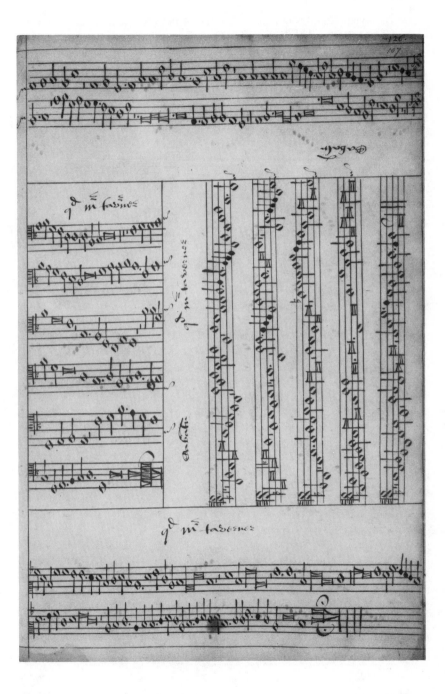

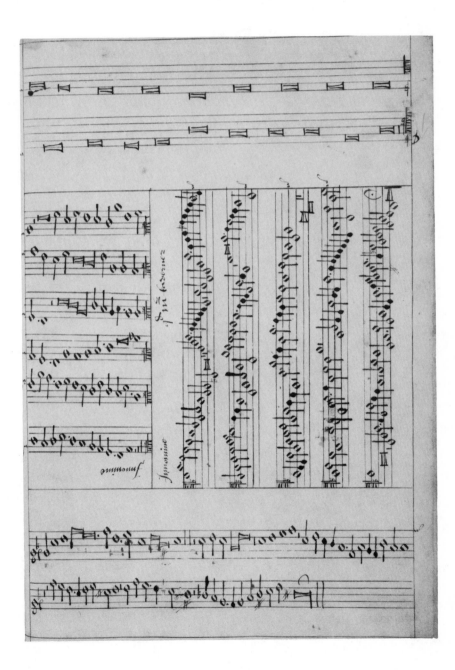

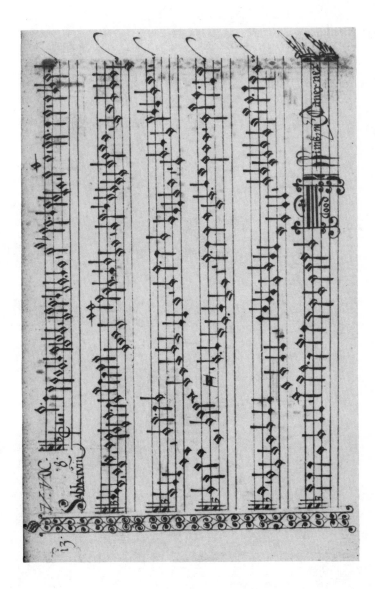

Plate 21. *Dum transisset Sabbatum*, countertenor part of a lost setting
Lbl 47844, f. 8v

Plate 22. *In women is rest/No season*
Lbl 24.d.2, ff. 99v-100

In wome~ is rest & pacience :—.   for sooth out of charitie they be, both by night

no season   for sooth out of charitie they be, both by night

& day   they gane confidence

mutabilitie   they

gane wt out naye, But stedfastnes

in them may ye ne{u} fynde I gesse   cruelltie

such coditions they gane both more   er

lesse :—.   alway of treason

out of blame they be

no tyme as men say

CHAPTER 8

THE CHURCH MUSIC

The major institutions supporting the church music of medieval England were colleges, collegiate chapels, royal and aristocratic household chapels, and to a lesser degree, secular cathedrals, monasteries and parish churches. In these institutions, which spent generously to have their major services adorned with polyphony, one heard the festal Masses, Magnificats and votive antiphons that are the central masterpieces of pre-Reformation polyphony. Much music was written as well for churches and chapels having fewer resources and smaller, less skilled choirs, and for the larger foundations on lesser holidays. It is a less elaborate music, smaller in scale and more modest in its demands on singers.

Taverner wrote for several of these institutions: a college chapel, a collegiate church, one or more parochial or other establishments in London and very probably the wealthy parish church of St. Botolph's. In scale, style and formal principles, his music grew out of an English tradition that developed during the second half of the fifteenth century and continued to evolve under the aegis of the ancient Church it served. His last years witnessed a period of political and religious reform in England, and he played a local role in an institutional upheaval that augured the Anglican reformation. But at his death in 1545, the Church in England remained Catholic, its liturgy the medieval *Use of Sarum*. Taverner was the last major composer whose church music was concerned exclusively with the Sarum liturgy. His contribution--along with those of Sheppard, Tallis and Tye, who all lived to see the establishment of an Anglican Church--represents a final link in that musico-liturgical tradition.

The festal compositions are large in scale, complex in structure and florid in style. The settings of mass ordinaries run to three-quarters of an hour, and these on texts with no Kyrie and a substantially abbreviated Credo. The antiphon *Ave Dei patris filia*, perhaps the longest single-movement work written by Taverner, runs about fifteen minutes. The usual scoring is in five parts--the characteristic English treble, the mean, and three men's voices--spanning a range of three octaves and more; occasionally a fourth man's voice is added.

The melodic style is based on the progression of a line that begins with a simply stated, triadically oriented point, and opens out into an exploration of motivic possibilities or a swirl of free melismatic activity, often based on powerful scale passages. The forward motion is irregular, the phrasing asymmetrical. Movement is tied to the strong beat; while there is liberal use of syncopation, it is not harnessed by the point as a significant generator of motion. The contrapuntal girding of voices is seemingly free. True, many passages are grounded in ostinatos, shaped by sequences (that may be carried by one voice or shared by several), or elucidated by the application of imitation to the point entries. But usually the counterpoint is governed only, it would appear, by the rules of consonance, and its forward motion, by increased rhythmic activity towards internal and final cadences.   A rich and pulsating sonority is created through the differentiation of pitch, rhythm, melody, phrase and vocal color, all underpinned by a leisurely harmonic rhythmic that endows it with a sense of vast space and time. The dense machinery of this massive and elaborate music absorbs the contrapuntal integrative techniques of imitation, sequence and ostinato without undergoing serious transformation of character, for it remains bound to an aesthetic in which polyphony is considered an enrichmment of the liturgical chant.

Music in this festal style does not elicit the understanding, much less invite the participation, of the congregant. It is music of the High Church. It awes, overwhelms and, perhaps oddly, comforts, as did the ritual to which it was attached, and the buildings in which it was sung. A Mass setting like *Corona spinea* is seen properly not as an early expression of European humanism, but as a last flowering of the Middle Ages.   It is also one of the great glories of English culture.   But humanism was increasingly part of the intellectual and cultural landscape of Henrician England, through its scholars and teachers, its books, and also its music. Its spirit is unmistakable in compact compositions such as the antiphons *Christe Jesu pastor bone* and *Sancte Deus, sancte fortis*, the responds, the four-part *Magnificat* and the *Te Deum*, the psalm-motet *Quemadmodum* and the *Mean* Mass. In these and other works, syllabic presentation of the text allows its easy comprehension, the point is reined in by clear cut motives and regular phrasing, the counterpoint is integrated by structurally significant imitation, the sonority is articulated by antiphony and homophony, the pulse and expression are restrained.

Except in the last works, where it is harnessed by accented suspensions to create clearly directed harmonic motion, dissonance is limited to a minor role, in the form of auxiliary and passing notes and occasional suspensions at cadences. The harmony consists almost entirely of root position or (to a far smaller extent) first inversion triads, moving usually by fourths; a predilection for thirds, often doubled and always present in final chords, accounts in good part for the rich sonority characteristic of Tudor polyphony. Cadence patterns are varied. The common usage is VII^b-I in duets, V-I in sections for four or more voices, and either in vocal trios. Interior sections may end on IV or V. One sometimes finds at the cadence the descent from supertonic to tonic, or the early arrival of the tonic, in one of the lower voices, and, in the Mass *O Michael*, the archaic leap of an octave. Taverner uses all the modes, though Phrygian is uncommon. The frequent B flat key signature in Dorian and Lydian produces transposed Aeolian and Ionian, virtually the equivalents of minor and major works; in final cadences of transposed Aeolian, as in *Gaude plurimum*, the third is sharpened invariably.

Structural articulation is of two kinds: that derived from ritual practice, and that imposed by the composer. In the former category are those items sung in alternating plainsong and polyphony: the *Alleluias* of the Lady mass, and the responds, *Magnificat*, *Te Deum* and the prose *Sospitati dedit aegros* associated with various offices. The second, entirely compositional mode of articulating structure, is found in the through-composed works--notably the large votive antiphons and Mass cycles-- and a variant of it as well in the larger *alternatim* settings.

The basic articulating device in a long polyphonic movement is its division into two major sections, divided by a double bar. The first section is usually in triple meter, the second in duple. Each begins with one or usually two passages for reduced scoring, then builds into a long passage for full scoring, with which the section (or movement) ends. Occasionally a movement will begin with a brief introductory passage in full scoring, or end with a coda-like section in triple meter. The use of various vocal groupings is a means not only of assuring structural articulation and contrast, but also of orchestrating the choral sonority. The trio, and after it the duo, are the most commonly used chamber scorings; quartets are found in the larger six-part works and the *Mean* Mass. One variation on the pattern is the division of a single part, usually the trebles, into two, called "gimel" (from the Latin *gemellus*, or twin), and set against a third voice. Taverner extended this practice to double gimel in the second Agnus Dei of the *Corona spinea* Mass. He used gimel for the setting of all five canons in the *O Michael* Mass, associating the twinning of voices with that of contrapuntal lines; and extended the practice to double gimel in the Agnus Dei of the *Corona spinea* Mass. His vocal combinations and juxtapositions are perhaps the most sensitive, varied and imaginative in the repertory of Tudor church music. But in his apparently later works, Taverner began to abandon selectively the practice of frequent sectioning and varied scoring. In the responds, contrast was achieved by the alternation of plainsong and polyphony; in some of the shorter antiphons, by the antiphonal division of the choir. In the *Plainsong* and *Mean* Masses, his attention shifted to entirely new means of articulation, while in a few short antiphons and *Quemadmodum* he embraced the practice of continuous full scoring.[1]

The various divisions within movements often have approximate relationships of length. Hugh Benham has focussed on this facet of structure; his results seem to indicate that only rarely did Taverner and his contemporaries consciously seek precise equality of length between these divisions, but that they did achieve some general proportionality.[2] The obvious place to find equal division of a movement would be between its first and second major sections, but Benham has found "no more than a broad similarity" of length between them.[3]   The same broadly balanced but not equal length relationships are found often, though far from invariably, among the four movements of the Mass Ordinary. The assumed intention on the part of Tudor composers to achieve such balanced relationships is often posited as the explanation for the puzzling practice by Tudor composers of abbreviating the Credo text and extending the Sanctus and Agnus Dei movements through the liberal use of melismas. The *Western wind* Mass is cited as "the only Mass in which all four movements balance (with 100 bars each in the Gloria, Credo and Agnus, and 97 in the Sanctus)."[4] But this Mass is exceptional in its construction among Taverner's Masses, and the equal lengths of its movements follow from that construction.

Oddly, there do seem to be close length relationships where we might not expect them. Benham has ascertained, for instance, an exact correspondence of semibreves (376) between the first four (of six) polyphonic verses and the reduced scoring, and (261) between the last two polyphonic verses and full scoring, in Taverner's five-part Magnificat; "and a somewhat similar arrangement in the six-part one with the first and second polyphonic verses balancing the full sections."[5] On the larger scale of the Mass Ordinary, he cites the near-equality between the four first and second major sections taken together, in the Masses *Corona spinea* (381 and 386 measures, respectively) and *Sancti Willelmi devotio* (150 and 152 measures). He then notes the relationship in the Mass *Mater Christi* between the four first major sections and full scored passages (143 and 145 measures), and, conversely, between the four second major sections and reduced scoring (196 and 194 measures). These are exceptional figures, however, not normative ones. If Tudor composers planned length relationships among textures, sections and movements as an integral part of the structure of their music, they were entirely inconsistent in the execution of that goal. Exact or near-exact proportions were either accidental, or the result of the properties of a given cantus firmus construction. We can conclude only that a general balance was important in length as it was in scoring procedures, an established goal rather than a finely calculated scheme.

Taverner's choral music, like that of his contemporaries, was performed by chorus alone. With the rarest of exceptions, no sanction is given in the musical manuscripts or in documentary entries concerning music and musical performances for instrumental accompaniment of the singers. The organ was used in certain *alternatim* works; it is no accident that the *Magnificat* is mentioned in our one extant reference to Taverner's organ playing: "they were almost at Magnificat before I came thither, I stood at the choir door and heard Mr. Taverner play, and others of the chapel there sing."[6]

The size of the choral forces was variable, but their balance was probably not. At Tattershall polyphony was sung by ten boy choristers and six clerks, at Cardinal College by sixteen boys and twelve clerks, and at St. Botolph's by probably eight boys and ten clerks in 1525-26 and, we may assume, when Taverner was there in the 1530s as well. (The lower 1548 figures are representative not of the earlier years, but of the decline of the status of the Catholic guilds as a result of the Edwardine reformation.) At full strength, then, the Oxford choir would have had up to eight boys on each of the top two parts and four men on each of the three bottom parts (or three men on each of the four bottom ones in the six-part Masses); at Tattershall five boys and two men; and at Boston, probably four boys and three men. The full chorus would have sung in all full sections. In passages and sections for reduced scoring, the number of singers on each part was probably reduced; given the frequent splitting of final chords and the practice of gimel, that number was in all likelihood two.

The pitch at which Tudor polyphony was sung has been the subject of speculation and disagreement. David Wulstan has worked out an elaborate system of transpositions based on the various clef configurations in sixteenth-century manuscripts, explaining the discrepancies of pitch placement of the same work in different sources and providing a standard series of voice ranges. Works in "normal" clefs (bass clef in the lowest part, a C clef in the highest) call for upward transposition by a minor third; in "high" clefs (baritone and usually treble clefs, respectively), downward transposition by a tone; in "highest" clefs (tenor and usually treble clefs, respectively), downward transposition by a major third. The presence of an F in the bass signals upward transposition, and a contrabass clef in the bottom part indicates upward transposition by a fourth.[7]

Most of Taverner's compositions are found in "normal" clefs, their voice parts having roughly the following (written) ranges: bass, F-b♭; tenor, A-d′; countertenor, c-f′; mean, g-c″; and treble, d′-g″. Four compositions in "abnormal" clefs require transposition to bring them into conformity with these general ranges: *Ave Dei patris filia* and *Quemadmodum*, by an upward half-step; *Gaude plurimum*, by a downward major third; and *O splendor gloriae*, by a downward fourth. It is from this standard that Wulstan recommends upward transposition of a minor third.

We have no way of knowing, of course, whether pitch around 1500 was consistent with pitch fifty or a hundred years later, let alone with pitch today. While it is agreed generally that transposition of some sort was used in Tudor choral music, the degree of transposition to be applied today remains uncertain. Wulstan's argument has not won universal acceptance, and the subject is far from settled, as a reading of the editorial matter in recent editions of Early English Church Music and related reviews and correspondence demonstrates clearly enough. The questions of tempo and tempo relationships, pronunciation and underlaying of words, and application of accidentals (these latter conveniently if inaccurately grouped together as musica ficta) are equally problematic, obviously vital to the proper performance practice of this music, and far from resolved. The recent bibliography on these issues is large and still growing, and the student of Tudor polyphony is advised to consult it.[8]

The subject of musica ficta is of especial importance, since the application of sharps and flats affects at the root our perception of mode, melody, harmony and cadence and dissonance treatment in this music.[9] In the absence of its resolution, we lack a commonly accepted foundation for the accurate analysis and proper performance of Tudor choral music; yet the achievement and broad acceptance among the scholarly community of its resolution remains a distant hope. Hardly a rule that is not broken can be found to govern the application of accidentals. Thomas Morley insisted in 1597 only on the sharping of the leading notes of final cadences,[10] but the evidence of the Eton choirbook of ca. 1500 holds even that application in doubt for early sixteenth-century music. The only near-universal sharping in that period is of the minor third in final chords.[11]   Furthermore, no manuscript of Henrician polyphony is to be trusted uncritically in its use of sharps and flats, no matter what its date and provenance. Ob 376-81, for instance, begun at Cardinal College when Taverner was there and continued some years later by his Oxford colleague William Forrest, should be considered as a trustworthy representation of Taverner's intentions.   But many of its accidentals were added apparently by a later hand whose judgment was unreliable at best; their absorption into its version of Corona spinea, for one, compromises that reading hopelessly.

The religious and political nature of the Henrician settlement of the 1530s has been brought to bear on the matter of musical style from time to time. This argument asserts that the reformation in general, and Archbishop Cranmer's contacts with the German Lutherans in particular, had some effect upon the polyphonic settings of the liturgy during the last fifteen years of Henry's reign.   Erasmus's fulminations against "ornamental neighings and agile throats"[12] are cited, followed by references to Luther's encouragement of congregational participation in simple four-part polyphony, to a few isolated liturgical experiments in

London, and finally to Cranmer's publication in 1544 of an English processional litany to be sung, in his words, not "full of notes, but, as near as may be, for every syllable a note; so that it may be sung distinctly and devoutly...."[13]

But this argument is altogether facile and lacks solid musical documentary support. One follows the unfolding of the Henrician settlement, first as it curtails the rights and privileges of the English church, then as it brings forth a series of theological documents (quasi-Lutheran at first, then ever more conservative) and practical reforms during the late 1530s and the 1540s. One notes the curtailment in 1536 of virtually all saints' days falling during the summer, the injunctions of 1538 ordering the destruction of images that were the objects of worship (in conformity with which Taverner supervised the burning of the rood at Boston), and the suppression in 1541 of pilgrimages, shrines and popular observances associated with feasts such as Holy Innocents and St. Nicholas. Yet the connection between these reforms and stylistic changes in music in the 1530s remains insecurely grounded. Nothing in this ferment of legislative activity impinged in any substantial way, as far as we know, on the work of Tudor musicians before the mid-1540s. The liturgy, the festivals and the devotion to Jesus and Mary--that is, virtually all occasions for which early Tudor church composers wrote polyphony--remained intact, for the time being at least.[14] References to musical experiments growing out of the reformation in the 1530s are conspicuous in their rarity.[15] In the absence of further evidence, we cannot look to the Henrician reformation for aid in establishing a stylistic chronology of Taverner's music.

Masses

Taverner's eight Masses display a diversity of style and structure not found in those of his English predecessors or contemporaries. The three six-part Masses--*Corona spinea*, *Gloria tibi Trinitas*, and *O Michael*--are based on a liturgical cantus firmus; the four-part *Western wind* is a variation Mass; *Mater Christi* and *Sancti Willelmi devotio*, both in five parts, are derived from votive antiphons; the five-part *Mean* Mass and four-part *Plainsong* Mass are freely composed, that is, not based on pre-existing material of any kind. All but the latter range in compass from bass to treble; the *Mean* Mass is for low boys' and men's voices, the *Plainsong* Mass for men alone. All of them but *Sancti Willelmi devotio* use a common motive, with varying degrees of strictness, at the head of each movement (though the peculiar structural properties of *Western wind* render this statement meaningless in its case). The *Mater Christi*, *Mean* and *Plainsong* Masses also use a common motive at the end of each movement. All eight Masses lack a Kyrie, and in each one a portion of the Credo is omitted, although that portion is not always the same.

Concerning the Kyrie omission, it has been suggested that Kyries were sung on major festivals with their appropriate trope (following the Sarum Ordinal), a usage rendering them to some degree a part of the proper rather than of the ordinary of the mass.[16] Furthermore, it is quite obvious that the presence of a Kyrie with its particular trope would confine the performance of a Mass to the festival to which it was appropriate--a limitation that composers would have not welcomed, given the work that went into the composition of a large-scale mass setting. But Lady Masses and Masses for lesser festivals called for untroped Kyries. The extant Lady mass settings do include polyphonic Kyries;[17] the mass settings for lesser festivals, oddly, do not. A possible answer lies in the historical development of the polyphonic Mass Ordinary in England. These Masses were distinguished from the festal Masses in being not tied to a liturgically specific cantus firmus. In the fifteenth century, they used the chants of the ordinary itself; and not as a structural scaffolding in elongated note values, but instead paraphrased or elaborated. The chant, that is, served not as a foundation but as the basis of melodic points. So few of these shorter Masses survive from the early Tudor years that one is tempted to assume that the genre went into eclipse.[18] When it reappeared with Taverner's settings, the connection with plainchant was severed, and, following the dominant tradition of the festal Masses, the Kyrie was dispensed with.

A large body of opinion has arisen concerning the Credo omissions. The argument put forward by Ruth Hannas that these omissions reflect theological and political stances is vitiated by the variety of passages omitted in the Masses of individual composers. Jeremy Noble has suggested that the omissions were a practical expedient: Henrician composers, bound apparently to a tradition of Mass movements of equal length, had not yet developed a style permitting them to shorten the Credo (with its long text) through musical means, and so they cut that text.[19] But the assumption of equal lengths among movements must be modified substantially: if the tradition existed, it functioned within wide tolerances. In the *Plainsong* Mass, the Credo and Sanctus are each half again longer than the Gloria and Agnus Dei; in *Gloria tibi Trinitas*, the Gloria and Credo are half again longer than the Sanctus and Agnus; in *Mater Christi*, the Sanctus is considerably longer than either the Gloria or the Credo, and about twice as long as the Agnus Dei. Furthermore, most of Taverner's Credo settings have melismas that would not be there had he been determined to abbreviate the Credo at all costs. A more recent argument argues that Credo omissions had their genesis in the suppression of certain text passages in

English Credo settings of the mid-fifteenth century. But these suppressions are found only in Continental sources of English works, not in English sources;[20] that evidence undermines the argument at its base.

One finds the passage "Deum de Deo, lumen de lumine, Deum verum de Deo vero" deleted from the first half of the Credo only in the *O Michael* Mass.[21] The major omissions are found towards the end. They begin commonly at "Et in spiritum sanctum" and continue through "in remissionem peccatorum" in the Masses *Corona spinea, Gloria tibi Trinitas, Mater Christi, Plainsong, Sancti Willelmi devotio,* and *Western wind*;[22] the omission continues until "resurrectionem mortuorum" in *O Michael.*[23] In the *Mean* Mass the deletion occurs from "Et iterum venturus est" until "in remissionem peccatorum."[24]

The principle of division of each movement into two major sections, each ending with a passage in full scoring and the second opening with one in reduced scoring, is found in all eight Masses. In the three six-part Masses, the division is marked by a change from $\emptyset$ to C; in the others, the first major section is in C as well. Several movements end with coda-like sections in variants of triple time--$\emptyset$, $\overset{\emptyset}{3}$, $3\overset{0}{:}1$ and C--in tripla or sesquialtera relationship to the preceding duple time: the four movements of the *Mean* and *Sancti Willelmi devotio* Masses; the Gloria, Credo and Agnus Dei of *Corona spinea* and *Western wind*; the Sanctus and Agnus Dei of *Mater Christi*; and the Agnus Dei of *Gloria tibi Trinitas.* Only the *Plainsong* Mass is in imperfect time (C) throughout.

The execution of the principle of bisectional division is so free that no two movements are exactly alike in their construction. All four movements of the *Western wind* Mass, the Sanctus and Agnus Dei of *Gloria tibi Trinitas, O Michael* and *Plainsong,* and the Sanctus of the *Mean* Mass, begin with fully scored passages; all the other Mass movements open with reduced choir. The number of reduced-to-full sequences in major sections is usually one or two; the first major sections of the Gloria and Credo in *O Michael* and the Gloria in *Gloria tibi Trinitas* are exceptional in having three such sequences. The first full passage following reduced scoring in the Gloria is found at "hominibus" in *Gloria tibi Trinitas, O Michael* and *Plainsong*; at "gratias agimus" in *Corona spinea, Mater Christi,* and *Mean* (it is the second full passage in *Gloria tibi Trinitas* and *O Michael*); and at "Domine Deus, rex caelestis" in *Sancti Willelmi devotio* and *Western wind.* The second major section begins with reduced scoring at the first "Qui tollis" (the second "Qui tollis" in *Plainsong*), followed by full scoring at "Qui sedes" ("miserere nobis" in *Plainsong*). In the Credo, the pattern of these three defining sections is usually "factorem caeli" (*Gloria tibi trinitas, O Michael*) or "et ex patre" (*Corona spinea, Mater Christi, Mean* and *Sancti Willelmi devotio*; this full section begins at "visibilium" in *Plainsong* and at

"Deum de Deo" in *Western wind*), "et incarnatus est," and "et resurrexit," respectively. In the Sanctus, it is "Dominus Deus sabaoth" (except in *Plainsong*, where the preceding threefold "Sanctus" is set for full chorus), "Benedictus" (the *Mean* and *Plainsong* Masses are exceptional in opening this second section with full scoring) and "Osanna." In the Agnus Dei, the pattern is usually "miserere nobis" of the first Agnus Dei ("qui tollis" in *Mean*; the entire first Agnus statement is fully scored in *Plainsong*), the second Agnus Dei, and the third Agnus Dei (but "dona nobis pacem" in *Gloria tibi Trinitas* and *O Michael*), respectively.

The characteristic sonority of each Mass is determined largely by two factors: the composition of its choir, and the disposition of vocal combinations among its passages and sections for reduced forces. Only two Masses, *Mater Christi* and *Sancti Willelmi devotio*, are scored in the normal early Tudor fashion, for treble, mean, countertenor, tenor and bass. The third five-part Mass, the *Mean* Mass, substitutes a second countertenor for the treble. Of the two four-part Masses, *Western wind* lacks a countertenor, while *Plainsong*, dispensing with boys' voices altogether, is scored for two countertenors, tenor and bass. The three six-part Masses have an added countertenor.

The reduced scoring is fairly straightforward in four Masses. In *Mater Christi* and *Sancti Willelmi devotio*, it is based upon the division of the choir into the two boys' and three men's parts. In the *Mean* Mass, it consists of quartets; in the *Plainsong* Mass, of trios. In a fifth Mass, *Western wind*, we find duos and trios for a number of combinations, including one of only two passages in Taverner's Masses for boys' voices alone (at "Benedictus"); but the variety of sonorities is mitigated somewhat by the preponderance of passages in which the treble voice dominates the scoring.

In contrast, the festal six-part Masses are superbly imaginative and varied in their vocal orchestration of reduced passages and sections. Among the duos in these Masses, we find eight combinations for the five voice ranges (two of the six voices share the countertenor range): treble with countertenor or bass, and every combination among the four lower ranges. There are fourteen combinations among the trios, nine among the quartets, and three among the quintets. The favored grouping is the trio, usually for mixed voices; *Gloria tibi Trinitas* has several, and *O Michael* one, for men alone. Most of the duos are also for mixed voices; each Mass has one for men alone. Among the quartets, *O Michael* has five, and *Corona spinea* one, for men; in *Corona spinea* there is an ethereal quartet for boys alone, at "qui tollis" in the second Agnus Dei (1:188).[25] Quintets are rare: two in *O Michael*, one each in *Corona spinea* and *Gloria tibi Trinitas*. Notable among these chamber sections are groupings at the extremities of the full choral compass: the duo for treble and bass at "gloria tua" in *Corona spinea* (1:178); the trios for paired trebles and bass at the second "Qui tollis" of the Gloria (1:199), "gloria tua" (1:214) and Benedictus (1:216) in *O Michael*, and "Crucifixus" in *Gloria tibi Trinitas* (1:141); the quartet for paired trebles, tenor and bass at "in nomine" in *Corona spinea* (1:181); and the quintet for paired trebles and means with bass at the second "miserere" of Agnus Dei in *Corona spinea* (1:190), a continuation of the boys' quartet noted above.

Among the six-part Masses, chamber scoring is most widely used and most varied in *Corona spinea*: its thirty-two reduced passages and sections make use of eighteen vocal combinations. In *Gloria tibi Trinitas* there are twenty-one such passages with sixteen vocal combinations; in *O Michael*, twenty-two with thirteen. The number of these passages using boys' voices is thirty in *Corona spinea*, fifteen each in *Gloria tibi Trinitas* and *O Michael*; using treble voices specifically, nineteen, ten and thirteen, respectively. Its relatively light scoring (in terms of the total number of chamber passages and the number of them using boys' and specifically treble voices) and its Mixolydian modality give *Corona spinea* the most translucent and brightest sonority among the festal Masses. The relatively small number of chamber sections for boys (trebles in particular) and its Dorian modality render *Gloria tibi Trinitas* the darkest of the festal Masses in sound.

The Mass *O Michael* is constructed on *Archangeli Michaelis interventione*, the ninth respond at Matins of the Feast of St. Michael in Monte Tumba (16 October) and the third respond at first vespers and matins at the Feast of the Apparition of St. Michael.[26] The Mixolydian cantus firmus (Plate 13), placed in the tenor voice, is stated seven times: twice in the Gloria, Credo and Sanctus, and once in the Agnus Dei. Only in the Credo do its statements correspond to the bisectional division of the movement. In the Gloria and Sanctus, its second statement begins towards the end of the first major section, at "Domine Deus, agnus Dei" and "pleni sunt caeli," respectively. Its one statement in the Agnus Dei is stretched through both major sections. Perhaps because of its length (it has more than twice as many notes as the cantus firmus in *Gloria tibi Trinitas*, and almost three times the number in *Corona spinea*), the cantus firmus is disposed occasionally in the semibreve pulse of the other voices; at other times its generally breve-dominated pulse is shared by the bass. Its pattern of breaks is irregular, as is its placement: it is found occasionally in reduced sections[27] as well as fully scored ones, and is placed twice in the bass voice (its higher passages transposed down an octave) rather than in the tenor.[28] On occasion a few leaps of thirds are filled in, and repeated pairs of notes are omitted. In a few instances the tenor part is freely composed; at "Domine fili unigenite" (1:197) it begins as a free voice, then without break returns to quoting the chant. Such usage tends to integrate the cantus firmus thoroughly with the other voices; in no other composition of Taverner's is the foundation voice so hidden.

The use of a common opening motto for the four movements is worked out rather freely. The same countertenor figure opens each movement, followed after three or four breves by the cantus firmus. A common treble figure is found in the Gloria, Sanctus and Agnus Dei, while a common mean figure opens the last two movements.

The text of *O Michael*, whose only surviving sixteenth-century source is Ob 376-81, is beset with parallel fifths and octaves and awkward dissonances at "Deus Pater" (1:196), the closing passages of the Gloria (1:202) and Credo (1:211), and the beginning of the Sanctus (1:212). Benham has attributed these to Taverner,[29] the editors of *Tudor Church Music* and H. B. Collins, to the copyist whose text "cannot possibly be correct."[30] Surely the latter view is correct. *O Michael* is found in the second layer of Ob 376-81, copied by William Forrest probably in the mid-1550s from a source now lost. There are mistakes in the other Masses he inscribed in Ob 376-81, (all for six parts and perhaps, though not necessarily, from the same lost source), if not as great a number as are found in *O Michael*.[31] Those errors could be the responsibility of Forrest or of the scribe of the lost manuscript; it is not necessary to ascribe them to Taverner, nor impossible to correct them.[32]

For other reasons, nevertheless, we may consider *O Michael* an early work. The vocal groupings of its reduced sections are less varied than those in the other six-part Masses, and their figuration is uncommonly busy. Its counterpoint is conservative in its limited use of imitation, sequence and ostinato, and occasionally clumsy at cadences, as at the octave leap downward at the full stops at "[volun]tatis" (1:194) and "patris" (1:198). Another sign of early composition may be the unmotivated cross rhythms in the duo on "Dei" in the second Agnus Dei (1:221). But this same passage exemplifies in its bold figuration and playful exchanges (three times the voices race up from c to f', or c' to f'') the bracing audacity and spirit of experiment that characterizes *O Michael*. Note, for instance, the exuberant lines in the quartet on "terra" in the Sanctus (1:214), and the grinding eightfold sequence in the duo on "[sepul]tus" in the Credo (1:208).[33] Most remarkable, however, are the five canons that set *O Michael* apart from every other Tudor composition. The isolated canons in the older works of the Eton choirbook (by William Horwood and J[ohn?] Nesbett) are brief and tentative. Taverner's, on the other hand, are extended and assured. His placement of them at the extremities of the pitch range, moreover, leaves little doubt that he chose deliberately to draw attention to them. The

first four are sung by trebles in gimel: at the unison over a free bass, at
the second "Qui tollis" of the Gloria (1:199-200);[34] at the second above,
over the mean, at "filium Dei" of the Credo (1:204); at the unison over
the bass, at "gloria tua" of the Sanctus (1:214); and again at the unison
over the bass, at the Benedictus (1:216). The fifth canon is for the basses
in gimel, again at the unison, with the two countertenor parts free,
opening the last Agnus Dei (1:222-23). This final canon, the longest of
the series, is part of a larger scheme leading to a climactic intensification
of the part writing. It is followed immediately by a trio on "qui tollis"
animated by an accumulating rhythmic tension and velocity, then by the
full scoring in which the bass part remains split; and so, for the first
time since the music of the Eton choirbook, we find at "dona nobis
pacem" choral writing in seven parts.

The Mass *Corona spinea* is based on an unidentified cantus
firmus placed in the second countertenor[35] (Plate 12) and stated ten
times: three times in the Gloria (twice in the second major section) and
Sanctus (twice in the first major section), and twice in the Credo and
Agnus Dei.

The chant is disposed unornamented in long note-values but not
monorhythmically, with longs, breves, and occasional semibreves to fit in
syllables and words of the Mass text. Its second, seventh and eighth
statements are set straight through; the others are broken up, but as in *O
Michael*, there is no consistent pattern to the breaks. The disposition of
its two Agnus Dei statements is particularly free: the first major section
ends with the twenty-first note of the first statement, which then resumes
with the fully-scored passage in the second major section, ending at the
sixth note of the second statement; the remainder is set in the coda at
"dona nobis pacem." The chant is used during all full sections, as well
as some passages for reduced choir where the second countertenor voice
is present.[36] In other reduced-scoring sections, this part is freely
composed.[37]

Denis Stevens has suggested that the Mass was written for the
Feast of the Crown of Our Lord.[38] But we know neither where Taverner
found his Mixolydian cantus firmus, nor why he chose to use it. Perhaps
the reason lies in its melody. The opening three-note configuration is
found often enough in Taverner's works to be considered a melodic
commonplace. In this Mass, however, its frequent use at the start of
points and interior phrases can be seen as not only a matter of style but
also a procedure justified by the cantus firmus. The same may be said for
the figures marked *b* and *c* in the example above. Figure *a*, however, is

not a commonplace, and its frequent use in *Corona spinea* must be attributed strictly to the cantus firmus.[39]   This network of chant-related motivic recurrences, rather than the cantus firmus itself (whose disposition is unpredictable and whose varying note-values deprive it of recognizable melodic shape), supplies the primary aural means of chant-derived unification in this long and elaborate Mass.

The use of a motto entirely free of the chant is as idiosyncratic as is that of the cantus firmus. It engages only the treble point, not the counterpoints of the other voices. As found in its first statement in the Gloria, it is brevity itself, with the outline (g)-d''-e''-g''-e''. In its later appearances, which embrace the openings of the other three movements as well as the second "Osanna" (1:183) and "dona" (1:192), the outline is expanded to g'-b'-d''-e''-g''-e'' and undergoes a series of subtle variations. From it are extracted two briefer motives, g'-b'-d'' and d''-e''-g'', which are used as the basis of many points throughout the Mass. Of course they are commonplace, but their firm Mixolydian configuration (i.e., beginning on g and d, respectively) fixes them firmly in our ears as unifying motives.

Thus *Corona spinea*, while lacking both a coherent cantus firmus structure and a strictly employed contrapuntal motto, is heard paradoxically as a work of subtly controlled organization, melos and sonority: this is the one six-part Mass of Taverner's most given to varied "chamber music" passages of reduced scoring, and least bound by the techniques commonly used to integrate the contrapuntal texture. Imitation at the head of points is generally brief and loose, of rhythmic rather than melodic configuration. Strict imitation, such as that among three voices over a bass sequence with the same figure at "de Deo vero" in the Credo (1:169), or the anticipation of the cantus firmus at the second "Osanna" (1:183), is rare. There are many wonderful passages using sequence, however: the end of one melisma on "[visibi]lium" (1:167) as a four-note group tightens to three notes towards the cadence, another on "[gloria] tua" (1:178), and a third at the opening of the first "[Agnus] Dei" (1:185). These all involve one voice, the treble. In other passages the sequence cuts through the scoring: between tenor and bass at "Amen" in the Gloria (1:166) and "excelsis" in the Sanctus (1:179); among three voices at "[miserere] nobis" in the first Agnus Dei (1:187), and among four at "nobis pacem" in the last (1:193). In contrast, a notable example of layered sonority is the passage at "salutem descendit de caelis" in the Credo (1:170): here a trio of high voices weaves rapid free counterpoints over a moderately paced ostinato split between the two lowest voices (whose entries are spaced progressively closer as they approach the cadence), the two sonorities separated by the almost static cantus firmus in the tenor. Perhaps the most striking example of scoring, both for its inherent beauty and its elucidation of texture, is the double

(1:188-190). Here one voice in each pair begins its own point, then at length the corresponding second voices enter in respective imitation. A second extended point is begun at "miserere nobis", this one shared by all four voices. Quite unexpectedly it is taken up by the bass voice, which then proceeds to act as a pseudo-cantus firmus supporting the boys' voices as they move with increasing animation towards the cadence.

The Mass *Gloria tibi Trinitas* is based on the antiphon of the same name at lauds and second vespers of the Feast of the Holy Trinity, the first Sunday after Pentecost.[40] The Dorian chant is placed in the mean voice (Plate 6), not in the usual tenor,[41] and presented eleven times: three times each in the first three movements, and twice in the Agnus Dei. The relationship between chant statements and sectional divisions of the four Mass movements is clear and straightforward, uniquely so among Taverner's three cantus firmus Masses. The chant is presented once in the first major section of each movement, once in the main body of the second major section of each movement except the Agnus Dei, and once in diminution in the fully-scored coda of each movement. It falls into four phrases

whose divisions Taverner observes in the following dispositions:

Gloria:	Et in terra (trio)	1a
	Gratias agimus (full)	1bc
	Domine Deus, agnus (full)	1d
	Qui tollis 1 (trio)	2ab
	Qui sedes (full)	2cd
	Cum sancto spiritu (full)	3abcd
Credo:	Patrem (trio/full)	1a
	Et ex patre (full)	1bcd
	Et incarnatus (quartet)	2ab
	Et resurrexit (full)	2cd
	Et exspecto (full)	3abcd

Sanctus:	Sanctus (full)	1a
	Dominus Deus (full)	1bc
	Osanna (full)	1d
	In nomine (quartet)	2abcd
	Osanna (full)	3abcd
Agnus Dei:	Agnus Dei 1 (full)	1a
	Qui tollis 1 (quintet/full)	1bcd
	Dona nobis pacem (full)	2abcd

The chant is disposed generally in longs and breves, though not monorhythmically; however, in its last statement in each movement, it is usually in semibreves and virtually monorhythmic in the last three movements. Occasionally it is ornamented by the filling in of skips of a third. It is absent, of course, when the mean voice is not being used, and in some passages even when that voice is present.[42]

In every characteristic--its placement near the top of the vocal compass, its several unbroken statements, the predictable breaks at phrase endings in its other statements, and the coincidence of its statements with the major sections of the Mass movements--the cantus firmus in *Gloria tibi Trinitas* acts in a more audible and regular manner than those underpinning the *O Michael* and *Corona spinea* Masses. It is heard as an organizing force that both articulates and unifies the four movements. But Taverner also finds other, subtler ways of using it. One way--we have seen it in *Corona spinea* as well--is the borrowing of brief chant-derived motives by other voices at the beginning of their parts: either anticipating the cantus firmus itself, as in the opening points of the four movements of "Cum sancto" in the Gloria (1:134) and of the well known "in nomine" (1:148); or growing from it, as at "rex caelestis," where the second countertenor anticipates the cantus firmus and the other four voices follow it (1:128).[43] Another technique, this one not found in the other cantus firmus Masses, is the use of a phrase of the chant in a voice other than the one carrying it, which then acts as a pseudo-cantus firmus temporarily. An example of this technique is found at "qui tollis" in the Gloria. After an anticipatory entry by the second countertenor, the bass presents the first phrase of the cantus firmus in breves until it is supplanted by the mean. The second phrase (*b*) is handled "correctly." The third is begun by the first countertenor and then by the treble in long notes, but both wander off into a trio with the tenor. When the six voices enter on a fresh point at "Qui sedes," the mean finally presents that third phrase "correctly" (1:132). Another use of pseudo-cantus firmus technique occurs at the opening of the Benedictus. First the bass has it in monorhythmic breves, then the tenor; finally the mean takes it, anticipated by the treble and followed by two other voices, to begin the well-known "in nomine" quartet.[44] The cantus firmus plays yet another role in the Mass: its third phrase (c) is closely related to (and probably the basis of) the motto of the Mass, stated at the beginning of the Gloria, and recurring contrapuntally at the opening of the other three movements and melodically at the start of the final statement of the Agnus Dei.

While the cantus firmus acts with unusual force to unify the Mass cycle, imitation technique acts to integrate its contrapuntal texture. It is found commonly at opening and interior motives of points, both of the strict (melodic and rhythmic) and loose (rhythmic) varieties, usually at the unison or octave. In full sections it may engage anywhere from two voices, as at "Qui sedes" in the Gloria (1:132) to all six, as at "filius patris" in the same movement (1:130); usually all voices but the cantus firmus are involved, and only to short points or the opening motives of longer ones. The spacing of entries in pitch and length, and the order of entering parts, are free. A notable instance occurs at "Amen" in the Gloria, the imitation on a rising rapid scale passage, accompanied by a leisurely counterpoint heard first in the tenor at "patris" and then in the mean, and anchored in its fourth and fifth entries by a bass motive that drives the passage through a fourfold sequence to its cadence (1:135). Another is the long and powerful full passage beginning at "Deum de Deo," which drives through a concentrated series of imitative points to "descendit" in the Credo (1:137-39); the entries at the beginning of this superb passage are so written and disposed that we hear the first four of them ("Deum de Deo/lumen de lumine/Deum verum/de Deo vero") as a fourfold sequence. In fact, sequence is found in many passages as a means of defining phrase motion and clarifying the contrapuntal texture: in the bass at "mundi" (1:131), in the treble at "[unige]nitum: (1:137), contrapuntally in the bold ascent of "et ascendit" from F to g" (1:142), and in the bass at "Osanna in excelsis" (1:148). In "miserere nobis" of the first Agnus Dei, sequence is deployed with such persistence that it becomes the dominant element of the entire passage (1:151-52).

Aside from three six-part Masses girded by a liturgical cantus firmus, Taverner wrote five others that are shorter, smaller in scope, scored for fewer voices and free of a ritual plainsong base. These differ considerably from one another in structure, idiom, length and scoring. For the most part, however, they are more often homophonic than their festal counterparts, their melodic lines are less ornate, and their contrapuntal resources appear more clearly articulated, more audible, more lucid in definition.

The *Western wind* Mass[45] was the earliest known English Mass built upon a secular cantus firmus. It is based upon a charming courtly song stated thirty-six times, in every voice but the countertenor, imbuing the other lines with its rhythms and pulse. The result is not a structure based in the traditional manner on a cantus firmus, but rather a series of variations upon a tune.   Nine variations--more precisely, contrapuntal elaborations of the melody--occur in each movement, in two groups of four with a final variation in triple mensuration in the Gloria and Credo, and in three groups of three in the Sanctus and Agnus Dei.   The tune, ornamented occasionally at the cadence, is varied only to the extent that once in each movement the last of its three phrases is omitted.   An exact correspondence of positions of full four-part sections in the Gloria, Credo and Sanctus (the first, third, fourth, sixth, seventh and ninth variations) and an approximate one in the Agnus Dei (the first, third, seventh and ninth), further tightens the structure of the Mass.

Western wind stands midway stylistically between the festal cantus firmus Masses and the others.   While much of the writing is exuberant and long-breathed, the use of only four voices produces a leaner sonority than that found in the festal Masses, allowing the techniques of repetition and imitation to be grasped by the ear with ease. There is an occasional ostinato figure, though the one extended use of the technique occurs at the opening variation of the Sanctus, where the bass delivers a stepwise phrase rising a tenth from G five times before falling back to g, shaping the full statement of the tune with wonderful authority (1:16).   Imitation is used mostly to define the opening notes of a given point or phrase, as at "in gloria Dei patris" in the Gloria (1:8) and "Domini" in the Benedictus (1:21).   Usually it is brief and loose, aiding the integration of the contrapuntal texture rather than motivating its gestures.   On the other hand, chains of sequences are found frequently as articulating devices; the most extended of these is the tenfold sequence in the tenor underpinning the fourth variation of the Gloria, at "Domine Deus, Agnus Dei" (1:5).

The four-part scoring of the Western wind Mass has been cited as unusual for a Henrician Mass, which it is, and indicative of a possible Lutheran influence on Taverner during the 1530s, which it is not.[46]   We have good reason to believe that Taverner wrote it in London during the second decade of the sixteenth century.[47]   During these years there was a growing body of Franco-Flemish music in London, music that Taverner probably saw and heard, most of it written in four parts.[48]   This music had a narrower compass than that of Taverner's Mass, for it did not embrace the high treble pitch area.   Taverner may have adopted the Continental scoring model, adapting it by keeping the characteristic English treble.   But he had English precedents as well.   Twenty-two of the ninety-three compositions originally copied into the Eton choirbook were in four parts, and apparently included in their three-octave compass the treble voice.   The majority of the Masses from the turn of the century found in the York manuscript[49] are in four parts, as are a few other early Tudor works such as Fayrfax's Mass Sponsus amat sponsam and songs and instrumental works in the early Tudor songbooks.[50]

A few stylistic traits would seem to confirm an early date for the *Western wind* Mass. Like *O Michael*, it has unusual uninterrupted stepwise figures encompassing a tenth, ascending in the tenor at "no[bis]" in the Agnus Dei (1:27) and five successive times in the bass in the opening Sanctus ostinato variations mentioned above; there is even a stepwise eleventh on the "Amen" ending the Credo (1:15), a figure found nowhere in the later festal Masses. The disposition of the words through the four voices shows little concern for textual clarity, or for their just accent, as on "invis*i*bilium" (1:9) or "*ven*turi" (1:15). Melismas prevail throughout the last two movements, and in much of the first two. (In his later works, Taverner would tame them through text repetition at appropriate places.) The great number of florid duos and trios of this Mass relate it to the festal Masses rather than to the smaller-scale works, or for that matter to Continental Masses, which maintain full scoring in longer sections. Perhaps also indicative of an early date are the passages in the Sanctus and Agnus Dei built on rhythmic proportions (1:17, 23, 25), reminiscent of the songs found in Lbl 5465 and Lbl 24 d.2.

The *Western wind* Mass has the extrovert charm of the tune on which it is based, and the thirty-six statements of that tune endow it with an audible structure unique in Taverner's music. It is technically accomplished and undeniably attractive. But I find it the least interesting of Taverner's major works, in good part because of its unbalanced choral sonority. Four of the five duos and ten of the twelve trios--a total of fourteen of the seventeen variations for reduced voices--involve the treble voice, whose high register tends in many cases to make it the dominant part. In comparison, the tenor is used twelve times in these variations, the mean and bass, only ten times each. The problem is compounded by Taverner's distribution of the statements of the tune: the treble carries it in all four of its duets, and in five trios--that is, in nine of the seventeen chamber variations. In full sections, it dominates still more, carrying the tune in thirteen of nineteen full variations. In the thirty-six statements of the complete Mass, then, the treble carries the tune twenty-two times, the tenor only nine, the bass five. (The treble domination is concentrated towards the middle of the Mass: from the last variations of the Gloria through the third one of the Sanctus, the high voice carries the tune ten times, the tenor and bass only once each.) Changes of meter, skillful fresh counterpoints, and imaginatively varied accompaniments do not mask the rigidity of the scoring scheme. The reworked tune is no help: its three phrases of four measures each, its insistence on transposed Dorian G, from which the first phrase rises and to which the second and third fall, and its direct melody are pleasant enough in themselves; but such easy grace and regularity work against the needs of a massive structure. Something more neutral, malleable and susceptible of reinterpretation is needed to bear the burden of thirty-six iterations encompassing a half hour's time in performance.

The *Western wind* Mass can hardly be judged a failure. Each variation is masterly in its own right, part-writing could not be more elegant, and the variety of colorings within the dominant transposed Dorian mode are wonderfully imagined. The pacing of the Mass, from smallest rhythmic detail to its consideration as a four-movement cycle, is beautifully judged. But there remains above all a discrepancy between the material chosen and the structure built upon it.[51]

The Mass traditionally referred to as *Small devotion* is one of two by Taverner derived from an antiphon. The argument proposed by Harrison that its original title was *Sancti Willelmi devotio* (the abbreviation of which, *S Will devotio*, was corrupted to the English title) is entirely convincing, and that name should be restored.[52] The Mass is derived from an antiphon in Cp 471-74 (compiled ca. 1540-47) whose text begins with the words "O Christe Jesu pastor bone" and ends with a prayer for the king, "fundatorem specialem serva regem nunc Henricum" (Plate 16). In a later source, Och 979-83, the closing prayer has been altered to honor the monarch reigning at the time of its compilation (ca. 1580-1600): "et Elizabetham nostram Angliae reginam serva." But the prayer for Henry may have been an alteration as well. The original text was an antiphon for St. William of York, "O Willelme pastor bone,"[53] sung daily at Cardinal College,[54] and may have closed with a prayer for the founder (*fundator*) of that college: "Fundatorem specialem serva Thomam Cardinalem."[55] (With Wolsey's disgrace and death, and the refounding of the college by King Henry in 1532, the words would have had to be changed, a condition reflected in Cp 471-74). The derived Mass would then have been, like its parent antiphon, a devotion to St. William: *S(ancti) Will(elmi) devotio.*

The loss of the original tenor part of the Mass has deprived us of a superb work, as the remaining four parts attest.[56] It was written between 1526 and 1530, when Taverner was at Cardinal College: possibly, more specifically, in 1527.[57] While the parent antiphon *Christe Jesu pastor bone* embraces the new stylistic elements--antiphony, homophony, imitation, the use of short, characteristic points, text repetition and syllabic setting--unreservedly, Taverner had not yet found a way to deploy these elements consistently through the larger structure and scale of the Mass. The first two movements are in the newer idiom, with only a few decorative melismas reminiscent of earlier works; but the Sanctus and Agnus Dei revert to the diffuse ornamental patterns of the old style. We find text repetition in a couple of places where formerly Taverner might have placed a melisma: at "Domine fili unigenite" (1:71-72) and "in gloria Dei patris" (1:76) of the Gloria. In the first two movements, chordal sonority is found not only in antiphonal but also in full sections, briefly at "genitum non factum" (1:79) and "cum gloria" (1:83) of the Credo and at the imprecations on "Jesu" (twice) and "et homo factus est" (1:72, 75, 81), and in one extended passage, "et resurrexit tertia dies secundum scripturas" (1:82). Throughout the Mass there is frequent use of imitation, in both reduced and full sections. In many of the latter, furthermore--notably in the triple-time sections ending each of the four movements--it is far from incidental, but rather, extended and decisive to the course of the point.

The Mass *Sancti Willelmi devotio* borrows only three major passages from its parent antiphon: the opening phrase, quoted at the beginning of the Gloria and "miserere nobis" of the first Agnus Dei (1: 70, 94); the second phrase ("cleri fautor . . . "), at "Domine fili unigenite" (1: 71-72) and, briefly, at "miserere [nobis]" of the second Agnus Dei (1:96); and the closing passage ("aeternae vitae"), at the end of the Gloria (1:76) and of the Agnus Dei (1:98). If specific borrowings are few, however, the general influence of the antiphon is enormous, notably in its antiphonal division of the two boys' and three men's parts, and the prevailing chordal treatment of these two sub-choirs. They, and the sections for full five-part choir, provide the three sonority units of the entire Mass, with the exception only of a duet for countertenor (and tenor) at "tu solus altissimus" (1:75), and the trio for treble, mean and bass (possibly a quartet with the lost tenor, though there is no other quartet in the Mass) at "Crucifixus" (1:81).

The Gloria is exceptional. Its borrowed opening phrase, sung antiphonally first by the boys, then by the men--that is the common antiphonal sequence throughout--acts as a generating cell of the entire movement. Its opening and closing dotted rhythms, syncopation, suspension, cross rhythm, and distinctive melodic contour provide the elements that motivate and integrate the subsequent points in a manner unusual in English music of the period. Note, for instance, the dotted rhythm of the little three-note cadential figure at "hominibus" (1:70). Seemingly innocent of any interest--indeed, a makeshift adaptation of the antiphon's "bone" to accommodate the three syllables "[ho]minibus"--it soon reappears in twofold expansion at the head of the point on "gratias agimus," then again at the three succeeding points, as well as at several thereafter (the third "Domine Deus," "filius patris," and "suscipe"). The pitch series of the "gratias agimus" figure (c-a-d-c) recurs in turn at "Agnus Dei" (1:72), "et in unum" (1:77), and "Deum de Deo" (1:79). One can follow the more obvious course of the opening four-note element and find in its pitch series (c-c-f-e) or rhythmic cast the seed of almost every point in the movement. Only one point in the movement is free of the generating cell: the neutral little ascending figure immediately following that cell on "Laudamus te" (1:70) that reappears unexpectedly at the closing "cum sancto spiritu" (1:76). But it turns out to be borrowed from the bass which is replaced in the Mass by a counterpoint derived from the newly-composed mean counterpoint at "Et in terra" (1:70). The latter, for its part, provides the pitch series of the important point at the first full five-part passage, at the second "Domine Deus" (1:71).

None of the following movements matches the Gloria in its economy of means, the force of its argument, or the beauty of its lines. (Significantly, none of them owes so much to the lovely parent antiphon.) But none, either, is less than masterly. The Credo is notable for its lucid textures and vigorous chordal passages, and its striking setting of "et homo factus est" (1:82). The melismatic lines of the Sanctus and Agnus Dei are old-fashioned in their length, their freedom from the restrictions of text, and the apparent differentiation (rather than integration) of their counterpoint; but their chaste melodic patterns and quiet pulse bestow on them a serenity quite removed from the earlier style. And each movement has its demonstrations of technical skill: the rising sevenfold sequence in the countertenor at the first "Osanna" (1:89), the canon at a seventh below at "in nomine" (1:91),[58] and the descending ostinato at "miserere nobis" of the first Agnus Dei (1:94), handled with particular imagination as it crosses over from one voice to the next.

The Mass *Mater Christi* is strikingly similar to *Sancti Willelmi devotio*, and probably dates from the same period. Both are derived Masses, and much of their shared character is owed to the similarity of the parent antiphons: their duple meter, their scoring for the same five parts, a sonority arising from antiphonal groupings of two boys' and three men's parts, similar opening subjects, the use of homophony and strongly articulated imitation, and a chaste melodic and rhythmic idiom. The kinship of the two Masses goes beyond their derivations. They are about the same length, the major sectional structures are similar (their antiphonal and full choral sections disposed in equivalent places in each movement), and they have the same Credo omission. The Mass *Mater Christi* is replete with close points of imitation, some so exact and extended that one perceives them as canons, as at "Amen" in the Gloria (treble and countertenor, 1:105), and "et exspecto resurrexionem mortu[orum]" in the Credo (countertenor and bass, 1:113). While the Gloria and Credo are set syllabically, and there are two brief instances of text repetition at "rex caelestis" in the Gloria (1:100) and "miserere" in the second Agnus Dei (1:123-24), the Sanctus and Agnus Dei are overwhelmingly melismatic, though not old-fashioned in their melodic lines. Noteworthy in the latter movements are an ostinato at "dona nobis pacem" (1:125) and a sequential passage at "[De]us sabaoth" (1:115), the latter being a long twofold sequence, each statement consisting in turn of a fourfold sequence.

There are differences, of course, between the two Masses. The small one comes at the closing sections of the four movements: while those of *Sancti Willelmi devotio* are in triple time, *Mater Christi* maintains its duple meter throughout. But the major difference lies in the extent of their derivation. Whereas *Sancti Willelmi devotio* quotes only a few passages from its parent antiphon, the parody technique in the Mass *Mater Christi* is thoroughgoing and structurally decisive.[59] Taverner quotes the opening section ("Mater Christi sanctissima . . . benignum redde filium") with only incidental variation at the opening sections of the four Mass movements, and the closing section ("vescamur in palatio") at all the closing sections but that of the Sanctus, whose final phrase, however, is adapted from the final phrase of the antiphon as well. Virtually every other passage of the antiphon is quoted once in the Mass, while many are used again, with varying degrees of freedom. One passage in particular, on "vitalis cibus" (3:94), is reworked with subtlety and imagination to provide the material for so many passages, that it, rather than the more obvious head- and tail-motives noted above, is the dominant parody element in the Mass.[60]

The Mass *Mater Christi*, like its sister Mass, has come down to us from Cp 471-74 without its tenor part.[61] The loss is lamentable, for the parody technique here represents a palpable advance over that of *Sancti Willelmi devotio*. The use of a common head- and tail-motive, providing a frame for the four movements, and the transfer of sections of the antiphon throughout them, creates a unity of structure, idiom and sonority maintained in the newly composed as well as the derived sections. We have, then, a true Mass cycle here, an integration of form and sound more varied and subtle than that in the Mass *Western wind* and more fully developed than that in *Sancti Willelmi devotio*.

The *Plainsong* Mass in four parts (divided tenors and basses) is the most austere of all Taverner's works. Its title--bestowed on it probably not by Taverner, but by a scribe working several years after Taverner's death[62]--refers not to any chant, but to the pulse of the music, which moves almost entirely by the breve and semibreve, suggesting a mensural version of plainsong rhythm.[63] It shares several forms and structural facets with the Masses *Sancti Willelmi devotio* and *Mater Christi*. Like them, it adheres to the traditional formal division of its movements into two major sections, and of all four movements into many passages for reduced choir. It has the same Credo omission. The text is set syllabically in the two first movements, melismatically in the Sanctus and Agnus Dei. Like the Mass *Mater Christi*, it is entirely in duple meter; and the opening and closing motives of its Gloria are repeated, though here the repetitions are varied contrapuntally. Internal subjects as well are transferred from the Gloria to other movements, mostly to the Credo (unless noted otherwise in the following list):

"glorificamus te" to "et ascendit" (1:32), the second "sanctus" (1:40), and "peccata mundi" in the first Agnus Dei (1:46); "Gratias agimus" to "Domine Deus" (1:40) and "miserere nobis" in the first Agnus Dei (1:46); the first "Domine Deus" to "sedet ad dexteram" (1:38) and "non erit finis" (1:39); the second "Domine Deus" to "filium Dei" (1:34); the second "Qui tollis" to "Crucifixus" (1:37); "cum sancto" to "et exspecto" (1:39); and the "Amen" to "et ascendit" (1:38) and "qui tollis" in the first Agnus Dei (1:47), as well as to the three other closing sections. The cycle is unified not only by these specific thematic correspondences, but also by the stylistic kinship of the general motivic material. Indeed, given the severely restricted pitch-range and rhythmic configurations imposed by the "plainsong" idiom in general, the challenge for Taverner must have been the creation not of thematic relationships but rather of thematic variety and differentiation.

Noteworthy among the instances of contrapuntal and textural integration are the imitation at the brief four-note descending figure on "consubstantialem" (1:35) and at the long descending scale passage at "mundi, dona nobis" (1:49); the long descending sequences at "et propter nostram salutem . . ." (1:36) and "[sa]baoth" (1:40), and the superb ascending one at "nobis" in the first Agnus Dei (1:46); the ostinato in the trio at "et terra" (1:41), and the two near-canons at "cum sancto spiritu . . ." (1:33) and "judicare vivos" (1:38-39). The Mass is divided about evenly into chordal and contrapuntal textures, corresponding generally to syllabic and melismatic text-settings. But even the latter are made to sound homophonic by the restricted use of breve and semibreve: whatever the underlying compositional technique, the voices are heard to move together. This dominant chordal quality sets the *Plainsong* Mass apart from everything else Taverner wrote; denied recourse to the creation and resolution of motion and tension through his usual manipulations and adjustments of contrapuntal rhythm, he here lavishes accented nonharmonic tones and suspensions upon a triadic fabric rich in thirds. This chastened dissonance treatment is entirely new to Taverner's music, creating a quiet but firm pulse and, harnessed to the contrapuntal techniques discussed above, a sonority of deceptive simplicity and great beauty.

The *Mean* Mass, like the *Plainsong* Mass, is based neither on a cantus firmus nor on a known motet. It is another *Missa sine nomine*, found without any title in its two earliest surviving sources.[64] The present title appeared first in manuscripts compiled thirty or more years after Taverner's death, apparently a makeshift describing the compass of its highest voice.[65] As in the *Plainsong* Mass, a unified cycle is created by the transferral of a network of passages and sections from the Gloria to the other movements. The opening and closing passages of the Gloria are restated, in subtly varied form, at the start and end of the Credo,

Sanctus and Agnus Dei. The following internal passages are repeated or reworked: "Domine Deus, agnus Dei . . .," at "Domine Deus sabaoth" in the Sanctus (1:61); the second "Qui tollis," at "Et incarnatus est" in the Credo (1:57); the chordal "gratias agimus . . .," at "et ex patre natum . . ." in the Credo (1:56) and the opening of the third Agnus Dei (1:68). These three last-named chordal sections, as well as several others, are in triple time; providing points of textural and metrical contrast, they act as articulating devices within a basically contrapuntal duple-meter scheme in a manner reminiscent of contemporary Continental Masses.

Such transferrals and cross-references create an "exterior" unity, a frame. In the *Plainsong* Mass, Taverner creates an "interior" unity of style through the bold adoption of chordal (mensural "plainsong") style; in the *Mean* Mass, he does so through the domination of imitative technique. In this Mass, he refashions singlehandedly the vocabulary of Tudor polyphony, composing compact points of narrow compass and clear melodic definition driven by terse rhythmic cells, and introducing the imitating counterpoints at various spacings of pitch[66] and beat. Suspensions and nonharmonic tones create the requisite harmonic tension to press the points and phrases to their appointed goals. Their pulse terse and direction explicit, these points and phrases are punctuated by rests in one or another voice, so that the overlapping voice entries articulate the larger rhythm and shape of phrase or section, with a clarity and consistency not found previously in Tudor music. Note, for instance, the closely argued four-part section at "visibilium et invisibilium . . ." in the Credo (1:55-56) with its stretto-like entries, the entire passage composed of two points, each repeated, and built on a clear I-III-I of its transposed Dorian mode; and the even more concisely built "dona nobis pacem" (1:68-69), with its dramatic shift at the last possible moment from Lydian back to its home mode.

This extension of imitation and its pervasive role in defining the sonority, pace and structure of the work can be seen to flow naturally from the evolution of Taverner's contrapuntal technique. But one species of it, the pairing of imitative entries appearing in the head-motive and in other passages--notably "suscipe deprecationem nostram" (1:53), "Quoniam tu solus sanctus" (1:54), and "qui tollis" in the first Agnus Dei (1:66)--signals the unmistakable influence of Franco-Flemish composers, and probably Josquin in particular. While a considerable amount of Continental music circulated in London while Taverner was there (and later), there is little or nothing in his music from those years, or indeed from anything before this Mass, to indicate that he studied and absorbed it. If this Mass dates from the years of his residence in Boston (i.e., after 1530), as its style strongly indicates, we may assume that he had access during this period to other manuscripts containing Franco-

Flemish music, or to Continental prints; and that these, unlike any known surviving Continental manuscripts in England, contained Mass cycles.

There are other signs in the *Mean* Mass that may suggest Continental models. One is the interjection of triple-meter chordal sections noted above. Another is the unusual frequency of four-part writing in the reduced-scoring sections; in contrast, there is only one passage for vocal trio--"Et incarnatus est . . ."(1:57-58), which begins a splendid section moving to antiphony at "Crucifixus," then double counterpoint at "sub Pontio Pilato," and finally to a powerful climax at the repeated ascending figure on "et ascendit"--and none for vocal duet.[67] A third sign is the extension of syllabic text-setting to the Sanctus and Agnus Dei, and the abbreviated length of the Agnus Dei. A last sign may be found in the five-part scoring. While that number is conventional enough, the disposition of the voices is unique among Taverner's Masses, and found only in one other work, the five-part Magnificat: mean, two tenors and two basses. Taverner dispensed with the characteristic English treble in one other Mass, the *Plainsong* Mass, and there he avoided boys' voices altogether, probably intending the Mass for performance at a service where boy choristers were unavailable. (We need only remember the purpose of Taverner's visit to Hampton Court in 1528 to remind ourselves of the premium placed on the treble voice.) But if such scoring was unprecedented among Tudor Masses it is common enough on the Continent.

We must be cautious, however; there is precedence in Taverner's Masses for triple-time homophony, text repetition, unequal length among the movements, and unusual scoring procedures (these last, notably, in the six-part Masses). The extension and intensification of these procedures may have come about through the evolution of a personal style rather than through the illuminating influence of Continental Mass style. But the pairing of imitative entries seems undeniably indebted to foreign models.

The *Mean* Mass represents the end of the development of Taverner's Mass composition. In *Western wind* and the three six-part Masses, he had begun with the traditional unifying foundation of a *cantus prius factus*, and built upon it edifices remarkable for their differentiation and variety. With the two derived Masses, he abandoned the use of a unifying cantus firmus in favor of an integration of the voice-parts and the use of framing devices and thematic recurrences. In the *Plainsong* Mass, he created a new unity of style through the exploitation of chordal motion and sonority. In the *Mean* Mass, he achieved that unity through the exploration of the structural potential of imitative counterpoint, the use of homophony for contrast and articulation of structure, and the harnessing of text and music for clarity of expression. The *Mean* Mass did not go unrecognized: it was one of two Taverner Masses (*Sancti Willelmi devotio* was the other) translated and adapted for the early Anglican liturgy,[68] and it provided a model for Sheppard's *Frences* Mass, Tallis's four-part Mass, and Tye's "Peterhouse" Mass.[69] It may be considered one of a handful of seminal works of Henrician polyphony.

Aside from a three-part excerpt from an *Agnus Dei* (3:60) attributed to Taverner in the late sixteenth-century manuscript Lcm 2035, whose authenticity seems open to doubt on stylistic grounds, several short compositions for the daily Lady mass have come down to us from Taverner's hand, survivors perhaps of larger cycles of Lady mass settings. The *Kyrie Le Roy* (3:54-55)--referring possibly to Henry IV or V, the Roy Henry of the Old Hall Manuscript--and three settings of *Christe eleison* (3:56-67) are based on non-liturgical cantus firmi drawn from a collection of mensural tunes known as squares, written in the fifteenth century and associated with the daily Lady mass.[70] The *Kyrie Le Roy*, an exquisite four-part setting in the florid style, is based on the square for the Sunday Lady mass, here ornamented, transposed up an octave, and placed in the treble voice. For the three-part *Christe eleison* settings, Taverner uses the square for the Tuesday Lady mass, transposing it up a twelfth and placing it in the middle voice in the first two settings (as printed in *Tudor Church Music*) and in the treble in the third.

Taverner's two surviving four-part *Alleluias* for the daily Lady mass are polyphonic settings of the choral portions of the responsorial chant. The relationship between plainsong and polyphony is similar to that found in the choral respond *Dum transisset Sabbatum* discussed below. That chant begins with a brief phrase on the word "Alleluia," followed by the choir who repeat that phrase and add a jubilus on the last syllable. A verse is sung by the soloist(s), but its last words are sung by the choir to the plainsong melody of the "Alleluia" with its jubilus. The "Alleluia" with its jubilus (or occasionally with a sequence) is repeated. Thus the music found in *Tudor Church Music* is sung two or three times in the full ritual performance with plainsong. In both settings the chant is disposed monorhythmically in semibreves.

One of the two settings (3:53) has been identified as the *Alleluia* with verse *Veni electa mea*, for the Thursday Lady mass.[71] The cantus firmus is transposed up a fourth and placed in the treble voice, where it floats serenely over a florid contrapuntal texture using points in imitation (the first of them based on and twice anticipating the cantus firmus), ostinato and sequence. The setting ends with an imbrication of rapid scale passages.[72]

The *Alleluia* in the Mixolydian mode (3:52), identified tentatively by Harrison as the Alleluia with verse *Salve virgo* for the Friday Lady mass,[73] has the cantus firmus in the tenor. Its construction is particularly cogent and economical. It is built on a stepwise figure descending a tenth from g", found first in the treble part; different segments of that figure, always beginning on g, recur so often that they constitute a quasi-ostinato for the entire composition. Towards the cadence, the figure is reduced to five notes and transposed to the bass
and then mean voices, where it becomes a strict ostinato.

Ecce mater Jerusalem is the verse of the processional antiphon *Ecce carissimi* at high mass on the three Sundays before Lent.[74] Since the rubrics call for it to be sung by two clerks, Taverner has set it, appropriately, for two voices, and without cantus firmus. It is an attractive little exercise in florid counterpoint, its opening point of imitation bearing a passing resemblance to the opening notes of the "Western wind" tune.

Two three-part sequence verses copied by John Baldwin may well be the surviving excerpts from a cycle of four-part *alternatim* settings.[75] *Jesu spes penitentibus*, the third verse of the sequence *Dulcis Jesu memoria* for the mass of the name of Jesus,[76] is set for treble, mean and tenor; the monorhythmic cantus firmus, embellished briefly at the cadence, is in the mean part. *Traditur militibus*, the sixth verse of the sequence *Coenam cum discipulis* for the mass of the five wounds of Jesus,[77] is set for mean, tenor and bass; the monorhythmic cantus firmus, disposed in semibreves rather than the usual breves, is placed in the tenor.

Another trio copied by Baldwin, *Tam peccatum*, is the fourth verse of the tract *Dulce nomen Jesu Christe* for the Jesus mass from Septuagesima to Easter.[78] Set freely, (i.e., without cantus firmus) for treble, tenor and bass, it is based on an ostinato figure stated three times in proportionally diminishing note-values (first in breves, next in semi-breves, and finally in minims) in the treble part; each statement consists of a four-note descending figure stated four times in ascending sequence.[79] This is the only tract verse known to have been set by a Tudor composer.

Antiphons

Three five-part votive antiphons are comparable in scale and structure to the movements of the festal six-part Masses. *Ave Dei patris filia*, set in the Phrygian mode, is the longest of them, and the only one based on a cantus firmus. Its extravagant and ponderous Marian text, a popular one among Tudor composers,[80] is composed of eight stanzas: seven quatrains followed by a final three-line stanza and an "Amen" that is treated as a fourth line of that stanza.[81]   Taverner observes its form scrupulously.   Setting each line or phrase to a fresh point, he devises his setting into the customary two major sections, the first in triple meter and the second in duple, each one on four stanzas.   The scoring is carefully symmetrical in its apportioning of reduced and full choir: the first two stanzas of each major section are for vocal trio, the last of them at "Ave plena gratia," a lovely gimel section ending on an extended melisma replete with imitation and sequence (3:67-69); the last two stanzas of each are for full chorus.   The final quatrain acts as a coda, beginning as a duo on "Esto nobis," continuing as an ostinato-based trio on "ubi pax," and concluding on a fully scored "Amen" built on an ostinato shared by the treble and bass whose opening notes permeate the mean and countertenor voices as well (3:70-72).

The cantus firmus, disposed in long notes in the tenor and present only in the full sections, is taken from five verses of the Te Deum[82] and the neuma of the fourth mode.   The design is carefully worked out: as Harrison has noted, "the lay-out, both of the cantus and of the complete piece, seems to be an example of calculated proportions.   The cantus firmus is disposed thus: $(60 \times ♪) + (30 \times o) + (48 \times ♩)$; the complete piece has $(113 \times ♪) + (113 \times o) + (48 \times ♩)$."[83]   The cantus firmus provides most of the material for what limited imitation there is in the full sections of the work: the opening notes of its first entry are anticipated at the very start of the antiphon by the treble and tenor (3:61), and just before that same entry by the bass (3:63); and its entries at "Jesu" and "Deitatis" are loosely and briefly followed by the bass and treble, and bass alone, respectively (3:65).   There is a good deal of imitation in the trios, for example, at "et trini ancilla subjectissima" (3:62), on the long point at "summae bonitatis" (3:62-63), and on the musical pun at "ut sol" (3:69).[84]   *Ave Dei patris filia* is impressive evidence of Taverner's mastery by ca. 1520, then, but it is somewhat conservative in its musical language.   There is nothing in it that might not have come from the pen of Robert Fayrfax.   The rapid scale passages, ornamental melodic filigree, dramatic accumulation of sonority in full sections, bold points, and technical virtuosity demanded of the singers so characteristic of his high festal style are not to be found here.

The text of *Gaude plurimum*, while unencumbered by the weight of superlatives that oppress *Ave Dei patris filia*, does not have that text's compensating clear poetic form.   It is a piece of indigestible prose in honor of the Blessed Virgin, divided into six long sentences, each of these composed in turn of phrases of varying length.   Taverner again observes the available divisions: a point for each phrase, a minor section for each sentence, and a major section for each group of three sentences.   The form of the Dorian mode setting is conventional: two major sections, the first in triple meter and the second in duple, each beginning with reduced scoring and ending with full five-part choir. But this time the relationship of the sentence to scoring is asymmetrical. In the first major section, the first two sentences are set to trios, the third to a full chorus. In the second major section, the first sentence is divided into two, the halves set respectively to trio and duo; the second sentence is fully scored; the coda-like third sentence opens with an antiphonal division of the choir into boys and men at "Eundem igitur" (3:88), the entry of full chorus being delayed until the dramatic chordal assertion on "assequi non valemus" (3:89).

The technique of imitation in *Gaude plurimum* marks a noticeable advance over that in *Ave Dei patris filia*. Not only are imitative entries more frequent, they are also more varied in length, spacing of pitch, beat, and number of voices involved in the point. The longest points are treated most cautiously: those at "sempiternum fili[um]" (countertenor and bass, 3:79), "benignius hominem" (bass and mean, 3:79), and "eandem tecum caelestem gloriam" (treble and tenor, 3:90-91) are at the octave or double octave and do not overlap. Most, however, do overlap, and are spaced flexibly: compare, for instance, "quae Christum Jesum" (treble, countertenor, tenor, 3:80), "perpetuam restituit" (mean, treble, 3:83) "qui caelica sua potestate" (all but countertenor, 3:82), and "vitámque humano generi" (all voices, 3:83), as well as the hollowly spaced entry (two octaves and a major second) at "gratias habentes" (treble, bass, preceded by a non-overlapping tenor entry, 3:86-87). Note, too, the ascending sixfold sequence at "[tra]didit" (treble, 3:84) that drives its section to a close, and the ostinato woven into four of the five voices at "assumpta" towards the end of the fifth sentence (3:87-88).

Taverner treats the long prose text of the Jesus antiphon *O splendor gloriae* rather more succinctly than he does those of *Ave Dei patris filia* and *Gaude plurimum*. Aside from some phrase-ending melismas—decidedly briefer than the ones in those other two antiphons—and the long one on the concluding "Amen," his setting is syllabic, and there is some repetition of text, notably the triplet statement of the last phrase, "te prece precamur humili" (3:108-109).[85] The prayer is divided into eight statements. The first five are gathered into a triple-meter major section, the last three into a duple-meter section, each half moving from reduced to full five-part scoring. But the treatment of individual sentences is more flexible than that found in the other two large votive antiphons. The schemas of the three antiphons according to their stanza or sentence division may be compared in the following table:[86]

Ave Dei patris filia

Verse or Sentence:	Time signature:	Voices/Double bar:
1	Ø	TrMT
2		CTB
3		F
4		F‖F‖
5	¢	CTB
6		TrTrM
7		F
8		TrC/TrCB/F‖

Gaude plurimum

Verse or Sentence:	Time signature	Voices/Double bar:
1	Ø	MC/MCB
2		TrCT
3		F‖
4	¢	TrMT‖CB
5		F‖
6		F‖

O splendor gloriae

Verse or Sentence:	Time signature:	Voices/Double bar:
1	Ø	MT/TrMT/F‖
2		CTB
3		TrMB
4		F
5		F‖
6	¢	TrCB
7		MCTB/F/MTB/F
8		F‖

O splendor gloriae is without doubt the latest of the three major antiphons. Its points are generally terse, based on syncopated or dotted rhythms, and on larger recurring rhythmic and melodic patterns that clarify the cadential goals. Accented suspensions rather than rapid ornamental figures generally provide the momentum from one beat to the next. The counterpoint is integrated by at least quasi-imitation at almost every entry, and there are many extended passages in which the imitation pervades the entire texture. Note, for instance, the fine trio at "duram vitam . . . laceratus" (3:103-104) and others at "in corpore tuo scelera," "passus et crudelissimam" and--to an appropriately rising scale passage--"summa es elevatus" (3:103-106). Similar, but extended to the full five-part scoring are "pro nobis miseris" (3:105-106) and "te prece precamur humili" (3:108-109). The last-named passage has been noted by every student of Taverner for its striking technique: no voice escapes the imitative action of its subtly varied threefold point. It is also remarkably modern in its articulation of the five-part sonority, its sustained use of suspended dissonance, and its strong assertion of the F major tonality (transposed Ionian, we may call it) that governs the entire antiphon.[87]

The manuscript evidence we have studied indicates that *Ave Dei patris filia* and *Gaude plurimum* were composed (or at least known) in London by ca. 1520. *O splendor gloriae* probably dates from the Oxford years, or later. It certainly seems a more advanced work than any of the six-part Masses, at least one of which, *Gloria tibi Trinitas*, is associated firmly with Cardinal College.

The association with Oxford is certain in the case of the antiphon *Christe Jesu pastor bone*, a beautiful five-part work in transposed Ionian mode (F major) whose tenor part is lost,[88] and whose text has come down to us in apparently altered form.[89]   Its pulse, like that of the *Plainsong* Mass, is based on the breve, not the usual semibreve. A second short five-part antiphon, *Mater Christi*, is a Mixolydian setting of another problematic text, opening with an invocation to the Blessed Virgin and continuing with a prayer to Jesus. These two compositions, which are remarkably similar (their very opening statements betray a kinship), illustrate Taverner's newer style in perhaps its purest form. In both, the texture is generally chordal, with occasional short points of imitation; phrases move with a quiet pulse--the breve and semibreve predominate until almost the very end--and within a limited pitch range. Their characteristic sonority arises from a smooth succession of thirds and sixths, and is given definition by the antiphonal division of the five-part choir into two boys' and three men's voices. In *Mater Christi*, this restrained, syllabic style gives way at the cadences to melismatic embellishments; in *Christe Jesu pastor bone*, it is dominant throughout.

The connection with Cardinal College is also certain in the case of the short antiphons, *Ave Maria* and *Sancte Deus, sancte fortis*, which were sung daily there.[90] In the former, Taverner has made provision for the two interruptions stipulated for the ringing of bells. These two settings, as well as the Jesus antiphon *Fac nobis* and Marian antiphon *Sub tuum praesidium*, have come to us in an incomplete state, only three of their five original voice-parts surviving.[91] They are skeletons of what must have been lovely little works, their texts clearly projected through syllabic settings and pellucid textures. *Ave Maria* and *Sancte Deus, sancte fortis* are particularly restrained, their rich chordal fabric interrupted only briefly by simple points of imitation. *Fac nobis*, its second section graced by effortless florid lines, is a more ambitious work.

Two brief fragments of antiphons have survived: *Prudens virgo* and *Virgo pura*. These three-part settings for two tenors and bass, found among the many trios Baldwin copied in his common-place book Lbl 24 d.2, are almost certainly extracts from lost five-part antiphons of the Blessed Virgin. They are closer in style to the "London" antiphons-- *Prudens virgo* to *Ave Dei patris filia, Virgo pura* to *Gaude plurimum*--than to the later *O splendor gloriae.*

Magnificats

Taverner's three *alternatim Magnificat* settings follow the general practice from the late fifteenth century on of leaving the odd-numbered verses in plainchant and setting only the even verses. In the setting for five parts, he also followed English tradition by basing the polyphony of the full sections on an elaborated faburden of the plainchant in the tenor voice. In the settings for four and six parts, however, he used the chant itself in the tenor: the first tone somewhat ornamented in the six-part work, the sixth tone unembellished (except occasionally towards the cadence) in the four-part work.

The traditional English *Magnificat* structure was founded not only on the decision to set it in alternating plainsong and polyphony, but also to treat each pair of polyphonic verses as a "major section." Of the three pairs of verses that resulted, the first and third (verses two, four, ten and twelve) were in triple mensuration, the middle pair (verses six and eight) in duple. The first two pairs begin with full and end with reduced scoring, the last pair ends with full scoring. Furthermore, the caesura in the middle of each verse was commonly observed with a cadence and double bar. Taverner's settings follow this model closely:[92]

Magnificats

Verse:	Time Signature	a4 Voices/ double bar:	a5 Voices/ double bar:	a6 Voices/ double bar:
2 Et exultavit	Ø	F‖T	F‖	F‖
in Deo salutari		F‖T	F‖	F‖
4 Quia fecit		234‖	345	3456‖
et sanctam nomen		F‖T	125‖T	124‖
6 Fecit potentiam	¢	F‖T	F	F
dispersit superbos		F‖T	F‖	F‖
8 Esurientes		234‖	134‖	1345‖
et divites dimisit		123‖	2345‖	245‖
10 Sicut locutus est	Ø	F‖T	35‖	346‖
Abraham/et		F‖ ‖T	F‖	3456‖ ‖
semini				
12 Sicut erat		24‖	35	123
et nunc et semper		13	35	456
et in saecula		124	35	125
saeculorum Amen		F‖T	F‖	F‖

The *Magnificat* for four men's parts, the only one of the three settings that has come down to us intact, is perhaps the most advanced of them in its integration of the contrapuntal texture by imitation. Most of the points are free of the repeated cantus firmus, although those at "[in Deo] salutari" (3:3) and "Sicut locutus" (3:7) anticipate the plainchant, and the opening one at "Et exsultavit" both anticipates and follows it.

The five-part setting found in Cp 471-74 lacks its tenor part. But following the clue given by the treble points at "et sanctum nomen" (3:10) and "eius in saecula" (3:15), each of which begins with the same part of the faburden of the second tone (first ending), the editors of *Tudor Church Music* have supplied one based on a faburden of that tone. It is a lovely work, its florid duos harnessed by strong motives in sequence treatment, its full sections rather more restrained and only occasionally integrated by imitation. Exceptional in this respect is the section at "Abraham et semini eius in saecula," whose two extended points are treated in strict imitation and placed conterminously, so that the effect is of a pair of ostinati providing the foundation for virtually the entire section.

The six-part setting is the longest and most elaborate of the three. The treble part survives for only two sections, "Esurientes" and "Sicut erat," among the excerpts found in Och 45. The choice of scoring of the other sections as found in *Tudor Church Music* is therefore conjectural: a great pity, as the surviving bulk of the work is a superb example of Taverner's festal style, with magnificently arching lines, audacious vocal acrobatics in the reduced sections, and rich sonorities in the full ones. Its frequent and canny use of imitation and sequence, and evidence of text repetition, mark it as a mature work. The two sections for which we have all of Taverner's scoring are stunning; note the melismatic cadence preparation on "bonis," where the treble descends an eleventh gracefully in a subtly gauged rhythmic acceleration while the two countertenors race up in contrary motion (3:21); and the "Sicut erat," a passage as playful and exuberant as any Taverner wrote.

In one respect the six-part *Magnificat* is the largest of all Taverner's works: the compass of its voices. Its total range is three octaves and a fourth, from D to g". Only the *Gloria tibi Trinitas* Mass has so extended a pitch field. But whereas the individual voices of the Mass have the ranges of 11, 10, 12, 11, 11 and 13 notes (working down from the treble, respectively), those of this *Magnificat* have ranges of 11, 11, 12, 12, 14 and 13 notes, respectively.

Te Deum

The *Te Deum* for five men's voices survives in only one source, Och 979-83. Like the three other extant settings by Tudor composers[93] it is an *alternatim* setting, with only the even-numbered verses in polyphony. There are fifteen such verses. The tenor part is lacking; but the editors of *Tudor Church Music*, noting the presence of a monorhythmic cantus firmus in the bass part of the eleventh set verse ("Aeterna fac"), have assumed that it was originally present in the tenor part in the other verses, and so reconstructed it.[94] Apparently Taverner handled the chant quite liberally: his setting requires its transposition down a tone, as well as the alternation of several cadences.[95] In the eleventh and fifteenth verses, the transposition is at a fourth below, resulting in cadences on a, so that, as Harrison has noted, "the music from *Tu patris* [verse eight] to the end is kept in the fourth mode with the final A."[96]

The setting is one of Taverner's latest. It is set in duple meter and scored fully and transparently throughout. The points are generally terse, square, and narrow in range, and rarely allowed to run off in long melismas. Text repetition occurs at the end of phrases; the final words "in aeternum" are stated five times. Imitation, while not systematic, pervades the four free voices, and occurs at most of the available pitch intervals. The harmonic language is particularly modern. Especially at the cadences, we find accented dissonant anticipations and suspensions, and simultaneous cross relations, such as that on "Sanctus" (3:27).[97] The 6-5 suspensions over the "dominant function" cadences on A in the later verses are also unusual.[98]

Responds

Responds were chants sung, as the term suggests, responsorially by one or more soloists and the choir following the lessons at matins (three on ferial days, nine on important feasts), the lesson at vespers on most double feasts and weekdays in Advent and Lent, and the lesson at compline in Lent. In the most common responsorial pattern, the main prayer or "response" was begun by the soloist(s) and completed by the choir; a verse was sung by the soloist(s); and the choir repeated the latter portion of the response. Thus in *Audivi vocem de caelo*, set by Taverner and many other Tudor composers:

Response:	Audivi	soloist(s)
	vocem de caelo. . .sapientissimae. Oleum recondite. . .advenerit.	choir
Verse:	Media nocte clamor factus est. Ecce sponsus venit.	soloist(s)
Response:	Oleum recondite. . .advenerit	choir

In responds following the lesson at vespers and the third, sixth and ninth lessons at festal matins, this pattern was expanded by the solo singing of the first part of the Gloria patri to the music of the verse, and the repetition either of a still briefer concluding part of the response, or of the entire response. The former pattern appears in *Dum transisset Sabbatum*, the latter in *In pace in idipsum*:

Response:	In pace	soloist(s)
	in idipsum. Dormiam et requiescam.	choir

Verse:	Si dedero somnum oculis meis. Et palpebris meis dormitationem.	soloist(s)
Response:	Dormiam et requiescam.	choir
[Verse:]	Gloria patri et filio et spiritui sancto.	soloist(s)
Response:	In pace in idipsum. Dormiam et requiescam.	

Only four responds were commonly set to polyphony in late medieval England, and only the solo portions were set, the choral parts of the chant being left in plainsong. Each of these responds had a special ceremonial or liturgical significance. *Audivi vocem de caelo* was the eighth respond at matins on the Feast of All Saints.[99] The preceding lesson, read by a boy, was on the parable of the five wise virgins. The response was begun at the choirstep by five boys facing the altar and holding candles to represent the virgins with their oil lamps. In polyphonic settings there was usually a break at the words "Ecce sponsus," where the choristers turned to face the choir.[100]

Taverner's setting[101] follows the ritual scrupulously. The first word of the response is set for boys, with the cantus firmus in the first treble; the rest follows in plainchant. The verse "Media nocte" is again set, the plainsong in the second treble for the first phrase, in the first treble for the second, with a double bar before "[Ec]ce."[102] The polyphony is in four parts; but one clue tells us that it was to be sung by five boys as prescribed in the ritual: the splitting of the second treble part at "Ecce." We may conclude from this one chord that two boys were put on the cantus firmus, disposed in monorhythmic longs (except for the brief melisma), bringing it out above the florid counterpoint surrounding it.[103]

In pace in idipsum was special because it was one of only two responds sung at compline, both during Lent. It was sung from the first Sunday in Lent until Passion Sunday.[104] Set "for iij men and a child,"[105] it is the longest of the solo responds, with the cantus firmus disposed accordingly in longs and placed in the treble (Plate 17).[106] It is also the one most tightly controlled by imitation--both based on the chant, as at "In pace" (3:48) and "et palpebris" (3:49), and freely composed--and sequence. *In pace in idipsum* is one of the responds with the Gloria patri sung as a second verse: while the cantus firmus here is identical to that of the verse "Si dedero," Taverner invents a fresh series of counterpoints for it.[107]

A special ceremony was prescribed as well for *Hodie nobis caelorum rex*, the first respond of matins on Christmas Day. While the response was begun by two men and completed by the choir in normal fashion, the verse *Gloria in excelsis* was sung by five boys standing in a place high above the altar and holding lit candles, who represented the angels bringing word of Christ's nativity to the shepherds.[108]   As in *Audivi vocem de caelo*, the setting is in four high parts;[109] the cantus firmus, disposed in dotted breves in the second treble part, was sung probably by two boys, bringing the number of choristers to five as prescribed in the Sarum Ordinal. Following tradition, Taverner set only the verse, ignoring the soloists' words at the opening of the response, and brought out the plainchant at the words "et in terra pax" by having the surrounding voices use it as the basis of an imitative point.[110]

Taverner was the first known English composer to set *Dum transisset Sabbatum*, the third respond at matins on Easter Sunday, during the following week, and on Sundays until Ascension.[111] Perhaps because no tradition existed for the polyphonic treatment of the respond, Taverner set it in an entirely new manner, its *alternatim* structure the exact opposite of that used in the solo responds.[112]   Here the *incipit* ("Dum transisset') is left in chant, followed by the body of the response and Alleluia (for Easter season) in polyphony; the verse is then chanted, followed by polyphonic repetition of the latter part of the response (from "Ut venientes") and Alleluia; finally the Gloria patri is chanted, followed in turn by a repetition of the polyphonic Alleluia. Harrison explains this choral setting of the respond

> as a recognition of the accomplished fact that the choir of a secular foundation such as Cardinal College was now a polyphonic choir, and therefore ritual polyphony, which had been for centuries the preserve of soloists, was now given to the choir, and replaced its plainsong, as it had previously replaced the plainsong of the soloists.[113]

In this new type of setting, Taverner had to alter. his usual practice of setting the cantus firmus in long note-values, for the chant of the response was far longer than that of the *incipit* and verse together. His extant settings therefore dispose the tenor cantus firmus in semibreves, with a resulting faster harmonic rhythm and greater integration of the voices.

One of Taverner's settings exists in two versions: one for four men, in Lbl 17802-805[114] (3:40-42); another in five parts, in Och 979-83 (lacking the tenor part) and Och 984-88 (3:37-40). Although the four-part version is found in the earlier source, it has been assumed to be an arrangement of the five-part setting. It differs from the larger setting mainly in its rearrangement of the parts[115] and revision of some of the interior passages of the points. While both versions are attractive, the five-part setting uses its extra voice to achieve an added spaciousness and clarity in the entries of the points and in the sonority of its two boys' parts. Imitation is used to a degree not found in the solo responds; the point on "ungerent" is derived from the cantus firmus, while the others are freely composed. Particularly beautiful in the five-part version are the passage at "aromata"[116] (3:38) and the "Alleluia," whose opening point in the countertenor and treble is recalled with magical effect at the final cadence (3:39-40).

In the second five-part setting, the handling of sequence, ostinato and imitation is thoroughly accomplished, and long arched melodies produce a translucent contrapuntal sonority. But the text as presented in *Tudor Church Music* (3:43-45) is undoubtedly corrupt. It is based on two sources. One is Lbl 31390, compiled in ca. 1578, where the piece is entitled *Sabatum* and copied without words, intended as it was for solfaing or instrumental performance (see Plate 19). The other source is Och 979-83, compiled perhaps a few years later and now lacking its tenor partbook. The editors of *Tudor Church Music* have underlaid the words of the tenor cantus firmus reasonably enough. But the underlaying of the words in the other voices was bungled apparently by John Baldwin, the scribe of Och 979-83, in several places, notably at "ungerent Jesum. Alleluia" (3:45). More disturbing still is the seeming lack of breaks at that place and earlier at "aromata, ut venientes" (3:44); without these breaks, the respond cannot be performed liturgically. Given Taverner's usual care in providing for the proper ritual performance of his settings (always excepting those puzzling if traditionally sanctioned Credo omissions in the Masses), it is inconceivable that this text represents his original aims accurately.

There are eleven concordances between Lbl 31390 and Och 979-83, and it is almost certain either that Och 979-83 was copied from Lbl 31390 in the case of these works, or that both were copied from a common source that is now lost. In the first instance, we may assume that the copyist of Lbl 31390 transcribed the setting from an earlier manuscript, removing the words and altering the musical text slightly at "aromata, ut venientes"; and that when Baldwin came upon the piece, he realized (from its title *Sabatum*) what the original text had been, and set it down as best he could. (After all, it was a frequently set text, and he copied texted versions by Taverner and Tallis into this same manuscript.) In the second instance, both sources would have been taken from a corrupt earlier manuscript, and handed down its errors to posterity.[117] It is also possible that Baldwin copied some of these concordant pieces from Lbl 31390, and others from a third manuscript.

The misalignment at "aromata, ut venietes" is perplexing: to end "aromata" at the chord over the bass A leaves the following d (bass) and d" (treble) stranded, though we would have a well-managed break if we could bring ourselves to eliminate these two notes. The problem at

"Alleluia" can be resolved simply by setting the words of the countertenor and bass parts thus:

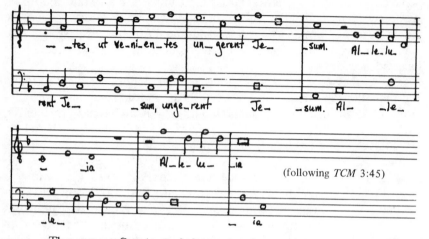

(following *TCM* 3:45)

The prose *Sospitati dedit aegros* is an insertion into *Ex eius tumba*, the ninth respond at matins on the Feast of St. Nicholas (6 December).[118] A summary description of the ritual performance of the respond aids in understanding the structure of Taverner's setting.[119] The opening words are intoned by the soloist, followed by the choir, who complete the respond. The verse "Catervatim ruunt populi" follows, sung not by the customary soloist, but by the choir. The respond is then repeated until the words "et debilis quisque." At that point comes the prose insertion--a trope of words and music replacing the original neuma--sung by the choir *alternatim*; its last verse is followed immediately and its meaning completed, by the remainder of the interrupted respond, "sospes regreditur."

As earlier English composers had done, Taverner set the entire prose, not merely its alternate verses (as the plainsong practice might suggest), as well as "sospes regreditur." In doing so, he took account of both the original *alternatim* practice of the prose and the importance of the final words of the respond. The scoring is for the usual five voices: treble, mean, countertenor, tenor and bass.[120]

The prose is made up of eight verses, and its Sarum plainsong has the double-versicle structure characteristic of a sequence: AABBCCDD. Taverner correspondingly divides his setting into eight sections, adding at the end a ninth section for "sospes regreditur." He recalls the *alternatim* plainsong practice by moving the cantus firmus, when it is present, back and forth in successive double versicles between the mean and tenor voices. (It is not present in the last double versicle for reasons which will become clear in a moment.) On top of this structure he superimposes the traditional structure of a polyphonic work of festal proportions: that is, he creates a large bisectional form, a large triple-meter section followed by an equivalent duple meter section, each with its progression from reduced to full scoring, with one significant exception. The following summary table will make his procedure clear:

Verse or sentence:	Voices:	Cantus firmus voice:	Time signature:	Double bar:
1	TrMC	M	$\emptyset$	
2	F	M		‖
3	MT	T		‖
4	F	T		‖
5	TrMC	M	¢	‖
6	F	M		‖
7	TrCB	-		‖
8	MCTB	-		‖

This would be a most odd structure, if the setting were to end here. The phrase "sospes regreditur," however, follows immediately (as in the original plainsong version). It must be heard to grow out of what follows, providing a fitting conclusion to the prose, even as it preserves its identity as the end of the respond.   Taverner achieves these apparently contradictory goals deftly. Having withheld both full scoring and a cantus firmus from the last verse of the prose, where we might expect it, he now presents both in the ninth section, emphasizing the cantus firmus of the respond by setting it in strict monorhythm for the only time in the entire work. He places it in the mean, keeping to the *alternatim* scheme not in the obvious manner (it would have been in the tenor in that case) but more subtly, suggesting that the *alternatim* principle remains firm, whether or not the chant is heard in one of its statements.   Finally, he distinguishes this ninth "respond" section from the prose, and provides a fine climax to the entire setting, by returning at last to triple meter. In doing so, he converts a conventional procedure into an imaginative clarification of the ritual forms through musical structure. Now we can complete our table:

Verse or sentence:	Voices:	Cantus firmus voice:	Time signature:	Double bar:
9	F	M	$\emptyset$	‖

The cantus firmus technique in the first six verses of the prose has been noted for its unusual freedom. In the first and second verses, the chant is quoted closely until the penultimate syllable of the last word of each, where it gives way to melismas. In the third verse, there are long melismas preceding both the caesura and the end ("Relevavit de*func*tis / defunctum in bi*vio*"). In the fourth, it is set strictly, and brought out by canonic imitation at the (octave and) fifth above, in the treble. Such special treatment of this fourth verse is surely no accident: it marks the verse as the final statement of the first major section of the composition. In the fifth verse the chant is treated again very freely; in the sixth, strictly. But the term "strict" refers so far only to pitch treatment. Not until the final "respond" section does it embrace rhythmic treatment as well: there it moves steadily in dotted breves (except for a little flourish preceding the final cadence), recalling the tread of the original plainsong as well as its melody.

A Probable Psalm-Motet

"Quemadmodum desiderat cervus" are the opening words of the forty-first psalm. Taverner's *Quemadmodum* in the Phrygian mode is very probably a psalm-motet setting the first two verses of the long text.[121] It must be the last of Taverner's compositions, for in every respect it is the most modern of them. Continuously scored for its full six-part complement and set throughout in duple meter, it is the only work by Taverner of significant scale that is divided into two uninterrupted parts, these being of virtually identical length. It is one of only two works of his (the other is *Christe Jesu pastor bone*) in which no voice has a compass greater than a ninth. It is the most thorough demonstration in all of Taverner's music of imitation technique, its steady pulse maintained by the liberal application of dissonant suspensions and syncopation to a succession of imitative points moving stepwise within a narrowly circumscribed pitch range. The points are related closely, each one developed from its predecessor, and all of them generated by the opening four-note rising motive and its inversion. It is all enormously skillful: note, for instance, the connection of the two first points by the entry of the mean voice, where the second point literally grows out of the first (3:117).

Withal, *Quemadmodum* is a severe and dark composition,[122] worlds away from the spectacular displays of the Mass *Corona spinea* or the chaste beauty of *Christe Jesu pastor bone*. The Phrygian modality, the restrained melodic and rhythmic gestures of the voices, and the close integration of counterpoint, sonority and pulse all contribute to the impression of austerity. It is not the work of the young Taverner.

Harrison has pointed out that psalm settings first appeared in England during the 1540s,[123] and it would not be unreasonable to date *Quemadmodum* from ca. 1540, given its advanced idiom. Yet scholars of Tudor music have hesitated to accept it as a psalm-motet.[124] The reason lies in the manuscript evidence. *Quemadmodum* appears in three sources--Lbl 31390 (Plate 18), Och 979-83 and CHe 1--each time with its title but with no text. It would seem, therefore, to be a sol-faing or instrumental piece, despite the fact that Taverner wrote no other such composition known to us, and that the title remains obscure. Filiation of the manuscripts provides an explanation. We may ignore CHe for the moment, for it is the latest of the manuscripts in question. The other two--Lbl 31390, compiled in ca. 1578, and Och 979-83, begun by Baldwin in ca. 1580 and continued over a number of years--are the important sources. We have noted that these were the manuscripts responsible for the puzzling text of one of the five-part *Dum transisset Sabbatum* settings. In the case of that composition, I suggested that Baldwin probably copied the textless version from Lbl 31390 and, on the basis of its title, added the rest of the text which he knew well. But the title *Quemadmodum* meant nothing to him--there is no other known setting of these psalm verses--and so he copied the composition as he found it, without a text. We must assume that the scribe of CHe 1 made his copy from one of these two Elizabethan sources, and that he had no choice but to inscribe it as a textless work. But it would be irresponsible of us, 400 years later, to attribute to Taverner the intentions of the scribe of Lbl 31390, who was assembling a collection of household *Gebrauchsmusik*, and accept the textless version of *Quemadmodum* as its authentic representation. Like the famous "In nomine" of Taverner's found in LB1 31390 (Plate 20), the *Quemadmodum* that has come down to us is nothing more than a transcription of a lost original made for the pleasure of musical Elizabethans.

CHAPTER 9

THE SONGS

While there existed in early Tudor England thriving centers of urban culture, only the royal court in London nurtured an "international" French style, whose roots lay in medieval chivalry and courtly pastimes, and which remained the mark of elegant breeding and gentility until it was superseded in the 1540s by the growing influence of Italian artists and ideas. That style is found in Tudor papers, letters, books, collections, accounts, histories, romances and poems that have come down to us in countless numbers. It is documented too in some 200 vernacular songs of the early Tudor court. These are found mainly in three sources: Lbl 5465 and 31922 (the Fayrfax and Henry VIII Manuscripts), compiled at the court in the first fifteen years of the sixteenth century[1], and in Lbl 5665 (the Ritson Manuscript), a provincial manuscript much of whose repertory came from composers at the court.[2]

John Stevens has distinguished three main groups of poems which were set as songs.[3] One, found in the carols of Lbl 5465 and 5665, deals with religious and moral subjects. The Ritson carols, straightforward, often didactic, are set in strongly accented triple meter, with harmonies of thirds and sixths supporting florid, syncopated treble voices. In contrast, the intense and dramatic Fayrfax Book carols are set to music of greater rhythmic variety and contrapuntal complexity in a prevailing duple meter, and their texts treated with considerable sensitivity.

A second group of lyrics, political and topical, seems to have been written for specific occasions or as poetic trivia. These poems are found in all three songbooks, and their settings conform to the general musical idioms found there.

The largest group of poems, few of them in carol form, are love lyrics displaying the devices and attitudes of a courtly tradition, on chivalric subjects such as absence, parting and service to the lover. Those in Lbl 5465 tend to cultivate a high Latinate style, often in the rhyme royal stanza (ababbcc) derived from the *ballade* and associated with that style. They do not scan in any consistent manner according to the system of feet and syllables perfected by Chaucer, but instead follow an older tradition of prosody, "based on a line of interminate length in which the pattern was established by a fixed number of strongly accented syllables linked by alliteration and divided by a strong caesura in the middle of the line."[4] The poet's conception of style as adornment and decoration is reflected and matched by the composer. One conventional but distinctive musical pattern predominates: a line of text begins on a simple "point" introduced by the voices in imitation and developed in rhythmic intensity until it breaks out, at the last syllable, into a contrapuntal melisma leading to a cadence. This procedure begins again at the next line of text. Stevens, calling these melismas "roulades," notes that they are "the counterpart in music to the ornate 'figures,' the 'rethoryke' and 'termes eloquent' of courtly verse, and perhaps also to visual decorations."[5] The analogy is apt: a "high" musical style, serious, abstract and sophisticated, and abounding in conventions, characterizes much of the music of Lbl 5465. Typically, these songs have a bisectional form in which a break occurs after the fourth line of text, irrespective of what that break does to the sense of the poem. The love lyrics of Henry VIII's Book are rather different. Their courtly language is less elevated and alliterative, and more playful and direct. In some cases it is derived from popular poetry; rhyme royal verses are rare. The verses are generally short and easily scanned according to the foot and syllable system. These lyrics shape their musical settings, which feature equal voices, balanced phrases, and strong duple meter. Their charming tunes are set concisely and cast generally in block chords, with little trace of elaborate counterpoint or artful line-ending melisma.

The variety of text and form in Taverner's four extant songs, and the care which he took in setting them, indicate a lively interest on his part in the different types of literary expression in courtly circles during the early years of Henry VIII's reign. *In women is rest peas and pacience / No season*, found in a two-part setting in the late sixteenth-century manuscript inscribed by John Baldwin of Windsor, lets forth a tirade against women, in the complex guise of a punctuation poem. The perspective of women--more precisely, of a certain group of women--is found in *The bella, the bella*, a cheerful carol set for four voices. *Love wyll I and leve*, for three voices, is again the man's complaint, but the rhetoric of the Baldwin Manuscript song has given way to an ironic, detached tone, in a Chaucerian rhyme royal stanza. *Mi hart my mynde*, also for three voices, declares the lover's devotion to his mistress in conventional chivalric terms, in a strophic poem bound together by a refrain.

Unfortunately, the latter three songs have come down to us in an incomplete state. Their common source is the book of *XX songes*, a set of four small partbooks in the library of Westminster Abbey, and one copy of the complete bass part-book (Lbl K. 1. e. 1.).[6]

In women is rest peas and pacience / No season

Three punctuation poems were written down early in the sixteenth century in a manuscript collection of French legal essays.[7] One of them was set to music by Taverner. This type of poem is syntactically ambiguous: it can be read either straight through to yield one meaning or in part to yield a quite different and sometimes opposite meaning. The form of the poem is borrowed from the high Latinate medieval tradition, with its long nonscanning lines divided by a pause or "virga." Through that pause and the strong internal rhyme scheme accompanying it, the poem achieves its ambivalent meaning:

> In women is rest and peas and pacience
> No season / for-soth outht of charite
> Bothe by night and day / thei have confidence
> All wey of treasone / Owt of blame thei be
> No tyme as men say / Mutabilite
> They have without nay / but stedfastnes
> In theym may ye never fynde Y gesse / Cruelte
> Suche condicions they have more and lesse.[8]

The rhyme scheme of the poem, which when read in its entirety is a tribute to women, is ababbcbc. But one can also arrange the poem as a seven-line rhyme royal (ababbcc) by reading from one caesura to the next; read thus, it is transformed into a diatribe against women.

This poem is a rhetorical *tour de force*, sophisticated and steeped in courtly convention. It and others like it were written by professional poets for an aristocratic audience, not for the pleasure of merchants and country squires. Taverner could have found such material only at the court or through someone in touch with it.

One other punctuation poem, *Nowe the lawe is led be clere conciens*, was set to music for two voices, of which only one is extant:

> Nowe the lawe is led be clere conciens
> Full sylde / covetise hath dominacion
> In every place / ryght hath residens
> Nethir in towne ne fylde / simulacion
> Ther is trewly in every case / consolacion
> The pore pepull no tyme hath / but ryght
> Men may fynd day ne nyght / adulacion
> Now raynyth trewly in every mannys syght.

The lyric itself is remarkably similar to the Taverner set in its language and figures ("by night and day," "no tyme," and "ye never fynde" have their equivalents in "day ne nyght," "no tyme," and "Men may fynd") and identical in poetic structure, length, and rhyme scheme. It hides a denunciation of the law in a rhyme royal within a larger poetic unit praising the law. The eight-line stanza coheres through a double-rhyme scheme and alliteration rather than through meter.

The setting of *Nowe the lawe is led* was composed by Richard Davy.[9] His setting is found in the Fayrfax Book, the court manuscript in which the most cultivated lyrics and artificial musical settings are found. Since his and Taverner's are the only known surviving settings of punctuation poems, one might have expected Taverner's setting to have found its way, like Davy's, into a songbook associated with the court. If it did, that book has been lost. Taverner's song does not appear in any contemporary manuscripts, let alone a court manuscript. We know of it only through Baldwin's musical commonplace book.[10] The song is found midway in the book among a group of two- and three-part compositions which Baldwin, with his interest in problems of rhythmic proportions, took pains to copy out. The representation of composers--from the fifteenth-century John Bedyngham through Taverner, Nathaniel Giles and Baldwin himself--attests to an abiding interest by English composers over a number of generations in these monstrously difficult pieces (the Giles work has proportions such as 8:3, 21:4, 32:5, 16:7 and 21:8).[11] Baldwin had problems in merely copying the Taverner song. At one point late in the work he miscopied part of a sequential passage, while earlier he inadvertently skipped a section of music in the tenor part and had to insert it at the bottom of the page. He indicated both the inserted passage and the place in the song where it belongs by a hand with a pointing second finger, used frequently throughout the manuscript (Plate 22).

Baldwin's version of the song[12] has a text slightly different from that of the original poem, but the additions (in italics)--"both by night and *by* day" (countertenor part only), "for sooth out of charitie *they be*," "such conditions they have *both* more and lesse"--and one deletion--"*peas and pacience*" (both parts)--have no effect upon either the rhyme scheme or the meaning of the poem. Furthermore, since (in this poem as in many of the love lyrics of Lbl 5465) the number or regularity of feet is of no account, these alterations make no difference. But one ambiguity on Baldwin's part tells all. Baldwin has set down the title (and part of the first line) under the beginning of the first staff of each voice part. The countertenor part begins "In women is rest:-." and is sung to those words. The tenor part begins "In women ^no season^ is rest & pacience:-."; here, though, it makes no sense to sing the words. "In women is rest & pacience," set in darker and larger script, is clearly a title: it was common practice for Elizabethan scribes to enter first the title of the work to be copied, then the music, and finally the words.[13] The words "no season" do not belong in the title, but begin the second

line. The musical context makes it clear that they alone are to be sung
to the first notes of the tenor part, and demonstrates that Taverner knew
very well both what kind of poem he was dealing with and how to set it.
The result is a musical clarification of the double-meaning which the
poet has so cleverly imbedded in his verse: "In women is rest
(countertenor) no season" [tenor]. These sung words point the text with
an immediacy which the spoken words cannot achieve, because their
setting exploits the possibilities of simultaneity and succession which
inhere in music alone. Thus the opening point, a lovely musical prelude
sung by the countertenor alone, is mocked and broken by the tenor
counterpoint "no season," in a delightful example of musical humor.
Taverner then continues to bring out the double meaning of the poem by
adhering scrupulously to the caesuras in the middle of each line, in this
manner giving the internal rhyme scheme the same weight as the end-
line rhyme scheme.

The similarity of Taverner's song to the settings of the love lyrics
in Lbl 5465 is remarkable--so close, in fact, that one can entertain little
doubt that it was written during the same brief period and at the same
place as they were. Each half-line of text is introduced by a clearly
articulated point, one note to each syllable, which is then taken up by the
second voice. There follows an increasing rhythmic activity as the point
develops, until at the last syllable of each half-line the notes break away
from the text into speedy roulades and arrive at a cadence.[14] Through
much of the point, or all of it if no roulade intervenes, there is close
matching of verbal and musical accent patterns; in this song, the
prominence of anapests certainly influences the rhythmic structure of the
points. The song is set in duple meter, until it breaks into $\frac{6}{8}$ at the coda.

A spirit of play pervades the entire song. Where he can,
Taverner invents points to reflect the mood of the words. "In women is
rest" is set with the lower voice at rest; "they have confidence" is set to
two pairs of repeated notes separated by an upward leap of the fourth
(countertenor) and to a simply repeated c' (tenor), all in a "confident"
rhythmic formula; the word "more" elicits the longest melisma of the
song, followed by a solitary note at the word "less."

The two voices seem to play with one another at the beginning
of each point, now the tenor leading, now the countertenor. The manner
in which they succeed each other varies with each new point. "Always
of treason" is a virtually exact melodic imitation at the unison, "such
conditions" is imitative melodically (at the fifth) and rhythmically, "for
soothe out of charitie" is only loosely imitative, "both by night and day"
is sequential but not at all imitative, while "they have without nay" is
sung by the two voices almost exactly together.

The song is set firmly in the Ionian mode; its two voices moving
in a succession of almost continual thirds and sixths with barely a trace

of harmonic motion, regenerated at each new point and impelled by their exuberant counterpoint. Dissonance plays no role at all, and whatever tension exists here is created and released through the ebb and flow of rhythmic motion. The interest of *In women is rest peas and pacience / No season* lies centrally in the wit of its text and in the musical illumination of that wit. The two-part scoring of the song, while unusual in a repertory the vast majority of whose contents were in three parts, is not rare. Once again, there seems to be a close relationship with the Fayrfax Book: that manuscript contains thirteen such songs (including Davy's *Nowe the lawe is led*), the Ritson Manuscript has five, while Henry VIII's Manuscript has none.

dence al- way

al- way of trea-

of trea- son owt of blame they be

- son out of blame they be

no tyme as men say

no tyme as men say

mu-ta-bi- li- tie they have without nay

mu-ta-bi- li-tie they have without nay but

but sted- fast-nes

sted- fast-nes in

In women is rest: Corrigenda and addenda
   Measure 52: ꜱ
  M. 56: Original of top line reads: a′ e′ f′ e′ f′ d′ e′ d′ e′ b′ c′ b′

Love wyll I and leve

Like the Baldwin Book song, *Love wyll I and leve* treats of the disillusionment of a lover. But this poem, a single rhyme royal stanza, vaunts a high, detached moral tone. There is no sarcasm here, nor bitterness. It lies squarely in the medieval courtly tradition, cultivated, artificial and conventional,[15] yet not at all cold.

> Love wyll I and leve, so yt may befall,
> I hold yt great wysdom in that governaunce;
> a hard thing it is, prove it who so shal,
> A mannys thought to know by hys countenaunce.
> Sum tyme I was in lovys daunce
> and cowde not beward tyll I dyd aspy
> how that I rode on mocke full preuely.[16]

With only the bass part of the original three parts extant,[17] we cannot know how, if at all, the high courtly tone of the poem influenced Taverner's setting of it. Nevertheless, several observations are in order. The song is through-set in two sections with the break after the fourth line of text, a procedure found commonly in the rhyme royal settings of Lbl 5465. As in *In women is rest / No season*, the musical rhythm matches the iambic meter and accent patterns of the poetry. The handling of line seems rather restrained perhaps to reflect the seriousness of the text, at least until the final musical phrase, where the rhythm breaks into triplets. The use of triplets to intensify the drive to the final cadence, while not conventional in Tudor song, is nevertheless common enough.[18] Still, here the uncommon instance upon the specific figure

♩₃♪ cannot be written off, with its "galloping" rhythm for the words "I rode on mocke full preuely."

It has been noted above that musical settings to poetry of this kind inevitably break off after the fourth line of text, no matter what effect his procedure had on the meaning of the poem. On the very slim evidence of the bass part, Taverner seems to have conformed to this tradition; but here the result certainly reinforces the meaning and thrust of the poem.

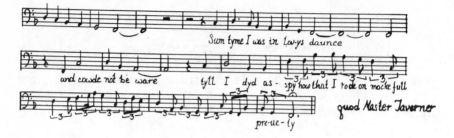

Mi hart my mynde

Mi hart my mynde is a love lyric whose chivalric subject--the lover's service to his mistress--places it firmly within the same courtly tradition as *Love wyll I*. Its words are not the polysyllables of the aureate tradition, and lack artifice or allegorical significance. Their meaning is explicit, and the lines they make up are easily scanned iambic tetrameters. Yet while its language is more direct and accessible to the modern reader than *Love wyll I*, it is the less attractive poem. The four rhyme royal stanzas with their seventh-line refrain--here the relationship to the ballade is unmistakable--are stiff and distant in their conventional declarations and dogged rhythms. They betray an impoverished imagination.

A version of the text alone, Lbl 18752, is generally similar to the text in *XX songes* except for minor variants in orthography. Other differences are noted in the bracketed lines.[19]

> Mi hart my mynde and my hole poure
> my servyce trew wyth all my myght
> on lond or see in strome and shour
> I geve to you be day and nyght
> and eke my body or to fyght
> > [and yoke my body for you to fyghte]
> My goods also be at your plesur
> > Take me and myne as your owne tresure.
>
> When your wyll is by nygt or day
> > [When your wyll is both nyght or daye]
> to ryde or go I wyll be prest
> and not to refuse that I do may
> to perysh the hart wythin my brest
> adversant trobles at your request
> shall me not dere but to be pleasure
> > Take me and myn as your owne tresure.

Yf ye fare well great myrth I make
yf you mysfare the contrary
      [...the contrary do I]
my grefe doth grow my myrth doth slake
      [my payne doth grow...]
and redy I am strayt for to dye
as ye do fare evyn so fare I
your wo my payn your Joy my plesur
      Take me and myne as youre own treasure.

Yow for to please it ys my mynd
and you to serve my well yt ys
what shuld I more thus wast my wynd
I have no thyng that you can myse
nor ought can do wyth my servyce
      [that I can do by my trew servyce]
and shall be at your pleasure
      [but is and shall be at your plesure]
    Take me and myne as youre owne treasure.[20]

The fact that we lack the two upper voices of *Mi hart my mynde* precludes any analysis of its setting and structure, but the bass part does offer us a glimpse of Taverner's aims and methods.[21] The song is in transposed Dorian mode, and indeed a modal quality seems to stand out more prominently here than in his other song settings. The handling of the text is prevailingly syllabic, although short melismas trail off from the last words of some lines and longer melismas punctuate each statement of the refrain.[22] Taverner ignored the structural significance of the four statements of the refrain, and instead composed straight through the first and third statements, allowing a full break only after the second statement in his intention to write a bisectional song. He articulated the scheme through an almost exact correspondence of musical line in the second and final statements of the refrain. This division of a song into two sections, each ending with a musically "rhyming" melisma, is found commonly in the songs of Lbl 5465.[23]

On the other hand, Taverner was aware of the textual significance of the refrains (his melismas demonstrate that), and of that of the lines which precede them and connect them by rhyme to the rest of each stanza. Thus the music for the third statement of the refrain borrows a passage from the above musical excerpts:

take me   and myne as youre, own trea- sure

the penultimate lines of the first and second stanzas share the same musical phrase:

(a) my goods al-so   be at your ple- sur

(b) shal me not dere but to be plea-sure

and an unmistakable similarity informs the opening of the first statement of the refrain and the phrase preceding its third statement:

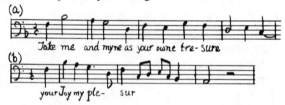

(a) Take me and myne as your owne tre- sure

(b) your Joy my ple-   sur

The pattern of a rising third or fourth followed by a stepwise motion downwards is of course a commonplace; here it recurs so often, however, that it seems to bind the disparate phrases into a unified whole and colors one's memory of the bass part. We are dealing here not with the musician's apprehension and articulation of the poem, but with his use of purely musical devices and correspondences. Note, for instance, the settings of the following passages:

(a) be day and nyght and eke my body for to fyght

(b) that I do may

(c) wyth-in   my brest

(d) yow for to please it ys my mynd

Repetition through ostinato and sequence, and variation of melodic and rhythmic figures appear commonly in this song, sometimes within the phrase

and at other moments quite clearly for the purpose of bringing out the meaning of the text:

The bass part lacks the melodic mobility and expressive freedom that must have characterized the two missing upper voices it supported; it boasts some passages elegant in their sense of pacing and line, impressed upon the listener through correspondence and variation, and with its repetitions of shorter melodic formulas it gives the sense of being all of a piece, the product of sustained and consistent intention. We can only regret that so little remains of *Mi hart my mynde.*

finis Taverner

The bella, the bella

The medieval carol was a song containing several uniform stanzas and a burden, the latter a repeated element standing apart from the stanza pattern as an autonomous formal unit. The burden, sung before the first stanza and usually after each following one, is usually a couplet, sometimes longer, only rarely shorter. Often a refrain appears at the end of (and therefore as an integral part of) each stanza; in certain carols, usually those with tail-rhyme stanzas, it is linked to the burden by rhyme.[24] In *The bella, the bella* Taverner found a carol whose "low" subject and colloquial language must have delighted him, for he gave it a wonderful setting, buoyant, light and tuneful. It is a song sung by prostitutes, vigorous and forthright but ending with a sobering warning. Carols, R.L. Greene has noted, are courtly in origin and popular in destination.[25] Perhaps this poem was intended to cut the other way: ostensibly about women who sell their bodies, it would certainly embarrass or discomfort women of courtly status or manner. Although its author is unknown, the sexually frank language is reminiscent of similar verses (*My darling dear*, for example, or *Mannerly Margery*) by the greatest of early Tudor poets, John Skelton (ca. 1460-1529), a court poet and tutor to the young Henry VIII.

A collation of the existing sources of the song--*XX songes* and a few fragments bound as flyleaves into a set of early seventeenth-century partbooks now in the Drexel collection of the New York Public Library--enables us to reconstruct the poem almost completely for the first time. *XX songes* contains the bass part. A flyleaf placed upside-down at the beginning of NYpl 4143 (Quintus) contains fragments of a treble voice. A second flyleaf preceding the main body of Nypl 4184 supplies still more material: the recto (NYpl 4184/1) and the lower half of the verso (NYpl 4184/2b) have words and music for the mean voice, while the upper half of the verso (NYpl 4184/2a) has words and music for a treble voice (Plates 1-3).[26]

	XX songes	NYpl 4183	NYpl 4184/1	NYpl 4184/2a	NYpl 4184/2b
The bell-a the bell-a we maydyns bere the bell-a	*		*		
the bell-a the bell-a we maydyns bere the bell-a	*		*		
we maydyns bere the bell-a the bell-a	*		*		

	XX songes	NYpl 4183	NYpl 4184/1	NYpl 4184/2a	NYpl 4184/2b
We be maydins fayr and free			*		
come nere young men behold and see			*		
how praty and proper now that we be	*				
so comely under / kell-a	* /*				
the bell-a / the bell-a we maydyns bere the bell-a	*	*/	*		
we maydyns bere the bell-a	*		*		
We be maydyns fayr and gent	*		*		
wyth yes grey and browys bent	*		*		
we be cum for thys intent	*	*	*		
our selfys / now for to sell-a	*	*	*/		
the bell-a the bell-a we maydyns bere the bell-a	*		*		
the bell-a the bell-a we maydyns bere the bell-a	*		*		
we maydyns bere the bell-a	*		*		
. . . .					
. . . .[27]					
assay you then non of ther spyce	*	*			
for it wyl make your bely to swell-a	*	*			
the bell-a the bell-a we maydyns bere the bell-a	*		*		
we maydyns bere the bell-a	*		*		
Syster loke that ye be not forlorn				*	*
for then every man wyl lagh you to skorn	*				*
and say: "kytt hath got a clap under a thorne"	*			*	
alack wher shal we then dwell-a	*			*	
the bell-a the bell-a we maydyns bere the bell-a	*		*	*/	
the bell-a the bell-a we maydyns bere the bell-a	*		*		
we maydyns bere the bell-a[28]	*		*		

The use of nonsense syllables as suffixes in light poetry was common in England at that time (it appears in the refrain lines of a fifteenth-century carol printed by Greene: "I shuld not tell-ey...And rofe my bell-ey...I was begyled-ay...To beyre a childe-ey...A long while-ey."[29]), and the tradition has continued among folk-singers in England into this century.[30] The name Kytt identifies the girls in the poem as country maids or serving girls; it occurs as well in the charmingly erotic text of a carol found in Lbl 58, *Kytt hath lost hur key*.[31]

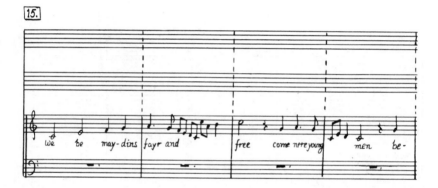

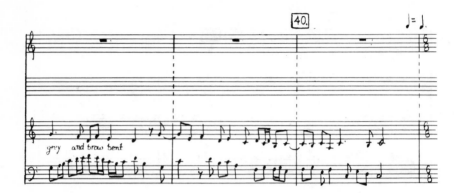

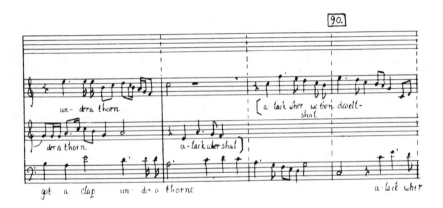

The bella the bella: Corrigenda and Notes

measure 8:   *XX songes* gives final note as f.

mm. 9-10:   NYpl 4184/1 gives final c′ of phrase as breve.

mm. 21-25:   NYpl 4184/1 gives length of rest as ▆▆▆ instead of ▆▆▆

m. 25:   NYpl 4184/1 gives second g′ value of minim instead of semibreve.

m. 41:   NYpl 4183 and 4184/1 and *XX songes* indicate change of time signature to ⊃.

m. 46:   *XX songes* gives final note value of minim instead of semiminim.

m. 47:   NYpl 4183 and *XX songes* omit return to original time signature.

mm. 68-69:   NYpl 4183 gives melisma on "spyce" as series of black minims preceded by black semibreve, instead of as series of black semiminims preceded by black minim.

mm. 90-96:   NYpl 4184/2a places entire passage too high by interval of a third.

m. 91:   NYpl 4184/2a gives third note, written as b′ in ms. but properly g′, value of black minim instead of white minim.

The primary value of the Drexel fragments lies in their contribution towards a reconstruction of the musical setting. They do far more than add bits and pieces to the complete bass part found in the book of *XX songes*; they help reveal some of the melodic and contrapuntal fertility of the song, a skeleton of its structure, and, most important, a sense of the original shape of the burden and of all but one of the verses. They also make us aware of some errors in the printed bass part in *XX songes*, which after all was the first (and, for a generation, sole) attempt at printing mensural polyphony in England.

On the other hand, these fragments raise several problems which render hazardous even a partial reconstruction of *The bella, the bella*. They were inscribed by a rough early sixteenth-century hand as two folios of an earlier set of partbooks, then were cut or torn out of that set, and finally were cut further for use as flyleaves when the present Drexel set was originally bound. As a result, we lack the extreme left side of the staves of the flyleaf verso in NYpl 4184 (with their time and key signatures and perhaps other information), and the extreme right side of the flyleaf verso in NYpl 4184 and the flyleaf in Drexel 4183, the upper staves of the flyleaf in NYpl 4183, and the lower staves of the flyleaf verso in NYpl 4184. Furthermore, the scribe has been discouragingly careless in his notation of single notes, whole passages, proportions and the length of rests.

In the preceding transcription and reconstruction, I have corrected all obvious errors in the manuscript and printed parts, noting these in a list following the music; placed in brackets reconstructions of passages based on similar passages in other verses and statements of the burden; and set down the music on four staves, in order to render clear exactly what proportion of the music has come down to us.

I have chosen to set down the music on four staves, not three, because of the very remote chance that the two treble fragments give us the music for two treble parts, not one. If this were so, we would have at least some representation for each of the four parts which this song is noted to have in the table of contents of *XX songes*. This identification of two treble parts rests on slim evidence: the length of the rest following the second verse in the treble part in NYpl 4183 indicates that it enters the burden only in the seventh measure, while the notation of notes and rests following the final verse in the treble part in NYpl 4184/2a indicates that it enters the burden in the fourth measure. If we assume that the statements of the burden were set to the same music, we seem thus to have two different treble parts, and four parts altogether.

Nevertheless, it is extremely probable that the two treble fragments represent only one voice. They present music for different verses: NYpl 4183 gives the end of the first verse and all of the second and third verses, while NYpl 4184/2a gives the fourth verse. That fact alone seems compelling evidence that we have here the source for one almost complete voice rather than for two dovetailing voices. It is only in material for the burden that the fragments seem not to fit together. The fact that they give this conflicting material for different statements of the burden might lead us to wonder whether Taverner wrote each statement independently. To do so, however, would have been highly unorthodox: the very structure of the carol, and the way it was set in the middle ages, argue against this possibility. And the habit of the scribe and the printer of not bothering to note down the music for all statements of the burden after the first one, a habit both traditional and sensible, certifies that the music of the burden in *The bella, the bella* was repeated without variation.

In all probability, then, we are dealing here with a scribal error: the treble voice should rest for the first three, not five, measures of the burden.[32] To understand the problem, let us examine the burden as set out in a four-voice scheme, as if there were no error. It opens with a perfectly rounded phrase of three measures, in which the mean voice carries a simple melody supported by a triplet-dominated bass part. There follow three measures of rest for these voices, during which the second treble voice sings a figure, apparently alone, for which only a fragment remains. Then the mean reiterates its melody, slightly telescoped and accompanied by a simpler bass line and a new melodic figure in the top voice, in another three-measure phrase. This in turn leads directly into an elaborate coda of five measures, dominated by triplets and cross-rhythms.

Now in this scheme, measures four to six make little sense. For Taverner to have had only one voice singing here would have gone against the firm tradition of setting the burden, that part of a carol associated originally with choral performance, contrasted against the solo setting of verses. It would have also gone against the architecture of this particular burden, destroying its momentum and its sense of direction. A duet of the two upper voices would suit this passage far better, a duet which tied the first and third phrases together by repeating the opening melody and setting it against a modified accompaniment. The three notes extant in the fourth measure give the beginning not of a solo melody but of an accompaniment, a variant of the opening bass figure which would support a reiteration of the melody. If this be the case, as I posit in the following reconstruction, then the missing part is indeed a treble part; in fact, it is the top vocal part in the song.

A phrase somewhat along these lines would flow naturally into the third phrase and coda, probably scored for four voices, as well as give the entire burden a logical, symmetrical and dramatic shape: three statements of a melody which is repeated, yet enlivened through a changing accompaniment and through its being set first *alternatim* and then in full scoring.

My transcription of the song on four staves, then, does not attempt to convey the probable scoring of the song, and should not be thought of as an incomplete working score. Its purpose is to present accurately the remains of the song, as they have come down to us in a printed part and three manuscript fragments.

Taverner composed the last eight measures of the burden as an autonomous unit capable of supporting the function of a burden alone: he used the entire burden to open the song and to punctuate the second and fourth verses, and the last eight-measure section, to punctuate the first and third verses. He so fashioned it that in both treatments it completes the musical sense of the stanzas dovetailed into it, just as the textual burden rounds off and completes the rhyme scheme of each stanza. For the simple text he wrote a delectable tune, in a popular idiom, utterly appropriate to the characters that text depicts. The broad structure which he built upon the tune, and the way he molded this structure for use as two alternate statements, impress upon one his care and imagination in setting this song.

The stanzas are articulated as the quatrains they are, but in a manner not anticipated by the text. Taverner ignores the rhyme scheme (aaab) and instead divides each verse into two pairs of lines, and sets all but one of these couplets to individual musical ideas quite irregular in length (six and four, eight and the equivalent of two, seven and four, and five and nine measures in the four respective stanzas). He sets off each couplet from its partner by a change in the underlying rhythm (from duplets to triplets) and a contrast of melodic material. Only in the final quatrain does he forego movement by triplets in the second couplet, with good reason and to good effect. The lines themselves will not bear the light, rollicking tone which triplets suggest, so instead he sets them in one sustained and serious contrapuntal phrase, the longest phrase in the song.

Despite the fact that Taverner's setting ignores the strophic possibilities suggested by the carol, *The bella, the bella* nevertheless coheres through certain structural bonds and unvarying characteristics, and functions clearly as a carol through the behavior of the burden. The reiteration by the mean at the beginning of the first verse of a melodic figure from the burden (m. 15) and the reflection of the opening bass figure in the bass passage at "how praty and proper" illustrate the correspondence between the burden and first stanza. A far closer relationship exists between the first and third stanzas, whose ending couplets are set to almost identical music. All four stanzas end in spirited melismas which dovetail into the burden, completing their thought and providing them with another link.

A felicitous handing of imitation binds the voices and animates their movement: imitation at the beginning of a phrase (as at "so comely under kella," mm. 22-23), imitation and sequence within the phrase in varying degrees of strictness (mm. 34-36, 39-40), and imitation which pervades a phrase from beginning to end, as in the second couplet of the final quatrain. Finally, the entire setting is anchored in the Ionian mode, bound by strings of consonant thirds and sixths, and articulated by simple triadic melodies. Our lack of the upper voice deprives us of most of these melodies, but what little we do have gives us a taste of the delights that Taverner composed for this, the most elaborate of his song settings.

Let us return now to the provenance of these four songs, the place and period of their composition. Certainly Taverner could have written such works for his own diversion or for informal gatherings at any time in his life, whether in London, in the little community of musicians at Tattershall (remember *The Cry of Calais* copied there), in the academic surroundings of Oxford, or for colleagues in the city of Boston. But for these particular songs, the evidence points overwhelmingly to London during the second decade (or even late in the first decade) of the sixteenth century.

The documentary evidence alone points to London as their city of origin, and to ca. 1505-1510 as their date. *The bella, the bella* is found in the Drexel fragments, which we can reasonably assign to London in ca. 1505-1510. That song is found again, with *Love wyll I* and *Mi hart my mynde*, in the 1530 London print, *XX songes*, whose repertory is decidedly old-fashioned, antedating considerably the print itself.

Sixteen of the twenty works found in *XX songes* are attributed to eight composers. Five of these men--William Cornysh junior (with four works), Robert Cowper (with three), Fayrfax (with two), Robert Jones (with one) and Richard Pygot (with one)--were associated with the royal court; a sixth, Thomas Ashewell (with one; d. ca. 1518?) may also have been in the royal service, while the two others Taverner (with three) and John Gwynneth (with one; d. ca. 1562) spent some time in and around London. By the time of the publication of *XX songes* in 1530, Ashewell, Cornysh and Fayrfax had died, and Taverner had long ago left London. Jones (whose life has not been traced beyond 1520) and Cowper were also probably dead by 1530. The print appeared long after the high tide of song production at the court had passed: to our knowledge, no major manuscript of secular English music was produced for presentation and use at the court after 1520.

The repertory confirms the conservative nature of the print suggested by its selection of composers. Four songs are settings of rhyme royal stanzas, a fashion that marked Lbl 5465 but had become dated by Lbl 31922: Taverner's *Mi hart my mynde* and *Love will I*, Cowper's *So gret unkyndnes*, and Cornysh's *Concordans musycall*. Ten songs (including all four unattributed works in the print) are carols. One of these, Jones' *Who shall have my fayr lady*, is a moralization in carol-form of the text of the same-named song in Lbl 5465. A second carol,

Gwynneth's devotional *And I mankynd have not in mynd*, is related in similar fashion to the Cornysh song *My love sche morneth* found in Lbl 31922. The text of a third carol, the anonymous *And wyll ye serve me so*, bears a striking resemblance to the poem *And wylt thou leve me thus* by Sir Thomas Wyatt (1503-1542), one of the poets at the royal court.[33] Two devotional carols, Cowper's macaronic *In youth in age* and Ashewell's *She may be callyd a soverant lady*, are, with Gwynneth's, probably also of early date (ca. 1500-1510): the genre, richly represented in Lbl 5665 and 5465, is found only once in Lbl 31922.[34] Two other songs, Cornysh's *Pleasure yt ys* and Fayrfax's *My hartes lust*, are given *termini ad quem* by the death dates of their composers, 1523 and 1521, respectively; the devotional text of the former and aureate language of the latter, moreover, once again relate them to Lbl 5465, the earlier of the two court manuscripts. Finally, there are a *Pater noster* by Cornysh and three instrumental works by Cornysh, Fayrfax and Cowper. An extended version of the first of these, Cornysh's *Fa la soll*, is found in Lbl 31922.[35]

This review of the composers and repertory represented in *XX songes* indicates that it was a compilation of music composed and circulated at the court and in London during the period ca. 1505-1520 (indeed, more closely related to the ca. 1505 of Lbl 5465 than to the ca. 1515 of Lbl 31922), music for which a demand later developed among a wider circle of musical amateurs of the city.[36]

The presence of Taverner's *The bella, the bella, Love wyll I* and *Mi hart my mynde* in *XX songes* would seem to place them, then, in the period ca. 1505-1520. The aureate language of *Love wyll I*, the bipartite construction of *My hart my mynde*, the rhyme royal stanzas of both of these settings, the manuscript evidence of *The bella, the bella*, and the striking relationship between *In women is rest / No season* and Davy's *Nowe the lawe is led*, all point so strongly to the repertory in Lbl 5465 that we may securely narrow that date to ca. 1505-1515 and place their origin in London.

The following review of fundamental elements of poetic and musical form and style in Taverner's songs reinforces this thesis.

1.   *Punctuation poem, consisting of eight-line stanza masking a rhyme royal (In women is rest / No season)*. Only one other is found set to music, its structure, length and rhyme scheme are identical: Lbl 5465 (*ETSC*, no. 30).

2.   *Rhyme royal poem (Love wyll I, Mi hart my mynde)*. Two each are found in Lbl 5665 (*ETSC*, nos. 4, 13) and 31922 (*MCH*, nos. 106, 108); twenty one found in Lbl 5465 (*ETSC*, nos. 2, 23-25, 27-28, 31-43, 48).

2a. *Rhyme royal through-set in two sections with "rhyming" melisma (Mi hart my mynde).* None is found in Lbl 5665 or 31922;[37] fifteen are found in Lbl 5465 (*ETSC*, nos. 21, 23-25, 27-28, 31-34, 37-40, 48).

3. *Carol, set strictly (with strophic verses) or in modified form (with new music to each verse) (The bella, the bella).* These are found in all three songbooks; but *The bella, the bella* is the one Taverner song whose manuscript evidence tends to relate it to Lbl 5465.

4. *Song set for two voices (In women is rest / No season).* Five are found in Lbl 5665 (*ETSC*, nos. 5, 6, 10, 13, 17), none in Lbl 31922, and thirteen in Lbl 5465 (*ETSC*, nos. 21-31, 35, 36).

5. *Song set for four voices (The bella, the bella).* None is found in Lbl 5665, fourteen are found in Lbl 31922 (*MCH* nos. 2, 8-10, 12, 22, 42, 45, 56, 67, 68, 82, 92, 105), and four in Lbl 5465 (*ETSC*, nos. 51-54). But refine the definition:

5a. *Carol set for four voices (The bella, the bella).* None is found in Lbl 5665, one in Lbl 31922 (*MCH*, no. 105), and four are found in Lbl 5465 (*ETSC*, nos. 51-54).

Still, can we be certain that these songs of Taverner's were written in early Tudor London? Were not such songs possible in the provincial estates of the nobility who imitated the culture of the King's circle? After all, Richard Davy, the composer of *Nowe the lawe is led*, is known to have been in Oxford and probably Exeter, but not in London. And the Ritson Book apparently was produced far from London, in the west of England. Surely, one could continue, Taverner would have heard and composed such music in Tattershall, whose surviving accounts from the turn of the century mention the copying of songs, or at Oxford, which had a flourishing musical community. True, the evidence points towards London. Taverner's songs share some characteristics with the provincial Ritson Book as well as with Henry VIII's Manuscript; but they are closest by far to the repertory of the Fayrfax Book, produced at or near the royal court around 1505. One of them, furthermore, is found in manuscript fragments closely related to the Fayrfax Book, and dating probably from about the same time as does Lbl 5465. Three are found in a retrospective London print from 1530, and the fourth (*In women is rest / No season*) was copied some fifty years after Taverner's death by a musician living at the royal chapel in Windsor who was familiar with London music.

But none of this is hard evidence. An argument based on formal or stylistic properties or on the city of a scribe or printer is no substitute for one absolutely secure piece of documentary evidence. And we lack that piece of evidence. Taverner's songs are found nowhere among the major collections of English court songs. No existing document, account or list gives evidence that Taverner was ever at court. It is just conceivable that the Drexel fragments were copied at a second remove, elsewhere than in London; and that the printer of *XX songes* somehow found his Taverner songs in a provincial manuscript and included them for his London market, even though a name unknown in London would not help sales there; and that Baldwin, the Windsor scribe, found a copy of *In Women is rest / No season* in a similar source. It is possible, too, that Taverner was not in London during the 1510s, that court songs found their way to Tattershall or Oxford and there were imitated by him; though we may wonder where he might have found (and how he would have grasped so marvelously) a poem so intricate and "hidden" as *In women is rest / No season*, and why he would have set these texts not in the popular and novel style of the Lbl 31922 but rather in the dated style of Lbl 5465. It is even possible that Baldwin misattributed *In women is rest / No season*, as he did a few other works.

But we see what is involved in the argument for locating these songs anywhere else but in early Tudor London. One must dismantle a great deal of interlocking evidence, explaining away its elements as if they were not related to one another--and here we are not considering the chain of evidence discussed earlier, linking Taverner to London through the register of the Fraternity of St. Nicholas, *Sospitati dedit aegros*, the *Western wind* Mass, and presence of his sacred music in two manuscripts probably copied in London around 1520. Then one must construct a series of hypotheses grounded in no positive evidence, not even circumstantial evidence of the most indirect nature, all the while brushing aside the issues of poetic and musical form and style.

That way lies fantasy, not history. The documentary evidence that we have supported by our analysis of their form and style, leaves us no choice but to conclude that Taverner's songs belong firmly to the repertory of the early Tudor court, and that they were written at or close to the court circle during the period ca. 1505-1515.

AFTERWORD

I am aware that I have not provided this study with a conclusion. That is because I cannot find it in myself to provide one. We are not ready for conclusions, we have not yet earned them. Biographical lacunae remain, but they are not the issue. Our problem is centered around the music of Taverner and his contemporaries. We have unearthed, examined and transcribed it. We have described its form, structure, mechanics and surface style. But we have not penetrated its substance, we have not mastered--by the evidence of our published work--its fundamental compositional principles and procedures. Symptomatic of our ignorance is the continuing disagreement within the scholarly community over such vital matters as attribution, chronology, and a host of performance practice problems.

Such disagreement is a sign of robust health. The controversies on subjects such as pitch, musica ficta, tempo and meter in the pages of English musicological journals, spurred in good part by the Early English Church Music series (of which the new Taverner edition will be a part), give reason for hope that the evolution of our knowledge and attitudes will issue in comprehensive studies on these and other matters of style and performance practice. Associated with them, indeed prerequisite to them, is a sustained analysis of the musical manuscripts. Related to them as well is the continued exhumation, analysis and publication of the archival documents of Tudor institutions bearing on composers, music, musical education and performance practice. In addition, we sorely need a comprehensive study on the relationship of the liturgy and ritual of the Sarum church to the polyphony that adorned it. Harrison's exploration of these subjects in *Music in Medieval Britain* was an inspiration, after all, because it opened the field with its sustained and detailed methodology, not because it closed it. But if the promise of the present scholarly activity is fulfilled, we may look forward to the day when the study of a man such as Taverner will not rest so heavily on the words "perhaps," "possibly" and "probably."

Today, however, we remain very much in the middle of our work, and our attitudes seem unsettled and open. Much is still to be discovered. Some of the material in this study is presented for the first time: the transcriptions of the songs in the Drexel fragments, *XX songes*, and the Baldwin book; some of the Tattershall accounts; the Ipswich episode; the Cardinal College lists; the suit between Taverner's heirs; and other documents and letters illuminating his life. Known material is newly interpreted. Concerning the early years in Tattershall and London, and the late years in Boston, our collective attitudes are still very much in flux. But these are precisely the areas previously cut off from question by the Foxe-Fellowes tradition; we have had to explore them anew, opening Taverner's life to the possibility of rational biography and accounting for the growth and achievement of his music. He was not a composer for only five years of his life, from the later Tattershall years to Oxford. Fellowes created an historical figure of great dramatic power, and it may be seen as a shame that in unmasking his distortions we have dismantled the drama. But Taverner was not the dramatic material of which myths or operas are made. He was a decent and practical man living in times of turmoil and adjusting to them with reasonable success, a man set apart from his contemporaries only by the genius of his music. If the man has been diminished, the composer has been set free.

APPENDIX A

SAMPLE SCHEDULES OF FINES AT TATTERSHALL COLLEGIATE CHURCH

The table below is compiled from the precentor's accounts at Tattershall for the years 1495-96, 1496-97 and 1498-99. All sums are listed in pence. A fine of ½d was imposed for each absence, with the exception of absences from matins, and from dirge in 1496-97, when the fine for chaplains only was 1d. Maltby, Preston and Pykering had not paid their fines for 1495-96 when the accounts for that year were drawn up. The fines for Charles were not specified in 1498-99. Charles was not yet a clerk in 1495-96, while Howard resigned in 1498-99.

	1495-96					1496-97						1498-99					
	Matins	Mass	Vespers	Requiem Mass	TOTAL	Matins	Mass	Vespers	Dirge	Requiem	TOTAL	Matins	Mass	Vespers	Dirge	Obsequies	TOTAL
Henry Porter	0	0	0	0	0	0	½	½	0	0	1	0	0	0	0	0	0
Thomas Bundy	0	2	1	0	3	0	3	1	1	0	5	0	1	1	1	0	3
Thomas Gibon	3	2½	3½	0	9	10	6½	9	0	0	25½	0	0	½	1½	0	2
William Maltby	2	2½	7½	½	12½	0	4	5	0	0	9	4	2½	5½	0	0	12
David Preston	2	1½	4½	1	9	3	2½	4	0	0	9½	1	1	2	0	0	4
Andrew Tott	2	½	3½	½	6½	0	1	8½	1	0	10½	0	1	1	0	0	2
John Charles	—	—	—	—	—	6	11	10½	½	½	29½	?	?	?	?	?	48
Thomas Howard	½	2	5	0	7½	½	½	1½	0	0	2½	—	—	—	—	—	—
John Litster	½	1	2½	0	4	0	½	3	0	0	3½	½	1½	2	0	0	4
Robert Lounde	3	0	1½	1	5½	2	1	1	½	0	4½	1	0	½	0	0	1½
Robert Lynne	5½	7	5	0	17½	4	5½	6	0	0	15½	0	½	1½	0	0	2
Edward Oky	0	0	0	0	0	0	0	1½	0	0	1½	½	0	0	0	0	½
John Pykering	3	4	5	0	12	1	2	4½	0	0	7½	½	1½	4	0	1	7
Total in Pence	21½	23	39	3	86½	26½	38	56	3	½	124	7½	9½	19	1	1	86
Absences of Chaplains	9	18	40	4	71	13	35	46	2	0	96	5	12	22	2	0	41
Absences of Clerks	25	28	38	2	93	27	41	56	2	1	127	5	7	16	0	2	126

In shillings and pence, the yearly totals of fines were 7s.2½d for 1495-96, 10s.4d for 1496-97, and 7s.2d for 1498-99. Fine totals listed in two other accounts were 7s.4d for 1500-1501, and 3s.4d for 1503-1504.

APPENDIX B

CHAPLAINS, CLERKS AND CHORISTERS AT
CARDINAL COLLEGE, OXFORD, DURING "THE FIFTH YEAR"

The names of chaplains and clerks at Cardinal College in "the fifth year" (October 1529 to September 1530) are found in a list of payments to these men in Lpro E/36/104, f. 8. The names of fourteen chaplains are given, although the highest number employed during any one week of that year was thirteen. One of these men probably replaced another who left during the year. The order of names is that found in the manuscript.

The names of some of the choristers are found in the same manuscript, on f. 21.[1]

Chaplains	Clerks	Choristers
Goffe	Evans	Leonard
Stafforde	Garlonde	Jo. Smythe
Tapitow	Londer	Sharpe
Whitbrok	Nobull	Godale
Lawney	Wolnall	Tailor
Lyster	Raynolde	Rambrige
Marshall	Alexander	
Harsty	Radley	
Mason	Lentall	
Hewell		
Clement		
Browne		
Spyer		
Kyttley		

APPENDIX C

INQUISITION POST MORTEM: JOHN TAVERNER (1546)[2]

Lincoln.

Inquisition . . . taken at Donington in the parts of Holland in the country aforesaid on 5 October 38 Henry VIII [1546] . . . after the death of John Taverner . . . Who say on their oath that he the aforesaid John Taverner . . . long before his death was seised in his demesne as of fee of and in seventeen acres of land, eleven acres of pasture with appurtenances in Skirbek in the country aforesaid. And being so seised the same John Taverner by the name of John Taverner of Boston in the county of Lincoln, gentleman, by his indented charter bearing the date 8 August 37 Henry VIII . . . gave . . . to certain Richard Goge and Richard Gilman . . . the aforesaid seventeen acres of land and eleven acres of pasture with appurtenances among other things, by the name of all those his messuages, lands, tenements, meadows, feedings, pastures, rents, reversions, services and hereditaments whatsoever with their appurtenances situated, lying and being in the fields and territories of Skirbek. To have and hold the aforesaid seventeen acres of land and eleven acres of pasture with appurtenances in Skirbek aforesaid to the aforesaid Richard Goge and Richard Gilman, their heirs and assigns to the proper use and behoof of the aforesaid Richard and Richard and their heirs and assigns for ever. Under condition that the aforesaid Richard and Richard of the one of them who should happen to survive or the heir of him who should happen to survive, before the 20 August then next following after the date of the aforesaid charter, at the request or desire of the aforesaid John Taverner or Rose, then his wife, should make or cause to be made . . . to the aforesaid John Taverner and the aforesaid Rose a good and lawful estate in law of and in the aforesaid seventeen acres of land and eleven acres of pasture with appurtenances, to have and hold to the aforesaid John and Rose and the heirs of the body of John lawfully begotten, and for default of such issue to remain to the aforesaid Rose, her heirs and assigns, to the proper use and behoof of Rose, her heirs and assigns for ever . . . By virture of which enfeoffment the same Richard Goge and Richard Gilman · entered into the aforesaid seventeen acres of land and eleven acres of pasture with appurtenances and were seised thereof in their demesne as of fee tail. And they being so seised . . . the same Richard Goge and Richard Gilman by the names of Richard Goge and Richard Gilman, by their indented charter bearing the date the 10th day of August year 37 Henry VIII abovesaid . . . at the request and desire of the aforesaid John Taverner, handed over, demised and by the same charter delivered to the aforesaid John and Rose the aforesaid seventeen acres of land and eleven acres of pasture with their appurtenances in Skirbek aforesaid, to have and hold all and singular the premises with their appurtenances to the aforesaid John Taverner and Rose and the heirs of the body of the aforesaid John Taverner lawfully begotten. And for default of such issue the remainder thereof to the aforesaid Rose, her heirs and assigns to the proper use and behoof of the aforesaid Rose, her heirs and assigns for ever. By virtue of which gift and feoffment the aforesaid John and Rose entered into the aforesaid seventeen acres of land and eleven acres of pasture with their appurtenances in Skirbek aforesaid, and were seised thereof in their demesne as of fee tail, and the same John and Rose being so seised of the premises, the aforesaid John Taverner died seised thereof of such estate, and the aforesaid Rose survived him and held herself within by right of survivorship, and is still in full life, namely at Boston in the county aforesaid. And further . . . that six acres of land, parcel of the aforesaid seventeen acres of land and eleven acres of pasture in Skirbek aforesaid are held, and at the time of the death of the aforesaid John Taverner were held of the heirs of Charles, Duke of Suffolk, as of his manor of Leke in the county aforesaid, parcel of his honor of Richmond, by fealty and rent of 8d, but by what other services the jury aforesaid do not know. And are worth by the year in all issues after reprises 15s. And that the aforesaid seventeen acres of land and eleven acres of pasture, the residue of the aforesaid seventeen acres of land and eleven acres of pasture in Skirbek aforesaid, are held and at the time of the death of the aforesaid John Taverner were held of the Warden and College of St. Peter, Westminster, as of their manor of Rucheforth Towre [Rocheforth Tower, E. 150/580/18.] by fealty and rent of 14d, but by what other services the jury aforesaid do not know. And are worth by the year . . . £3.13.4. And further . . . that the said John Taverner . . . died 18 October last past, and that William Taverner is kinsman and next heir of the aforesaid John Taverner, namely brother of the same John Taverner. And they say that the aforesaid William Taverner at the time of death of the aforesaid John Taverner was aged forty years and more. And further . . . that the aforesaid John Taverner . . . on the day of his death had nor held nor any other or others had nor held to his use, of the said lord King nor of any other or others any other or more lands, tenements and hereditaments in the county aforesaid. . . .

APPENDIX D

THE WILL OF WILLIAM TAVERNER
OF TATTERSHALL (1556)[3]

In the name of God Amen, the iij day of March in the year of our Lord 1556. I, William Taverner of Tattershall . . . my body to be buried in the church yard of Tattershall aforesaid. Item I bequeath unto the church work of Lincoln iiij^d. Item I bequeath unto the church of Tattershall xij^d. Item I bequeath unto William Taverner, my son, half my crop now growing in west croft and in Skylgate, restoring unto his mother half the seed that I sow on the same grounds. Item I bequeath unto my said son William ij loads wood, my wain and mine old cart. Item I bequeath to John Taverner, my son, ij oxen, the one black broken [broked] and the other red marked, ij mares, the one gray and the other bay, and my new cart. Item I will that my draught be not broken, but shall remain whole for the space of iij years unto the use or uses of Katherine, my wife, and John, my son. Item I will that William, my son, have the occupying of my said draught for the said space of iij years and he to receive half the profits increasing of the same, paying half the charges and Katherine, my wife, and John, my son, to have the other half of the said profits and pay the other half of the charges during the said time. Item I bequeath unto Wenefride Taverner, my daughter, iij loads wood and five hundred kids. And all the residue of my goods not bequeathed I give to Katherine, my wife, to pay my debts and honestly to bury my body. Also I do make and constitute George Martyne my full executor of this my last will, unto whom I bequeath for his pains to be herein taken, over and above the allowance of his reasonable charges iij^s.iij^d. These being witnesses, John Wilkinson, clerk, and William Metcalf with others.

APPENDIX E

SUIT: ROGER HODGE VS. EME SALMON[4]

To the Right Honorable Sir Nicholas Bacon, knight, Lord Keeper of the Great Seal of England.

Humbly complaining showeth unto your good Lordship your orator Roger Hodge of the City of London that whereas one Rose Taverner of Boston [in the county of] Lincoln, widow, deceased, was in her lifetime lawfully possessed of certain goods and chattels and likewise held for a number of years a certain fulling mill [ ] and so being possessed by her last will and testament bearing date the first day of May in the year of our Lord God 155[3] bequeathed all her said goods and chattels unto the use and behoove of her daughters' children, and willed by the same will that the same goods and chattels so bequeathed [ ] equally and indifferently divided amongst her said daughters' children by her executors, of which said will and testament she made, named and appointed your said orator [Roger Hodge and . . . Stephen] Salmon her executors and died of the said goods and chattels possessed, after whose death your said orator and the said Stephen Salmon [ ] last [ ] of the said Rose took upon them the executorship of the same according to the true intent and meaning of the said Rose and according to the trust reposed in them, your said orator and the said Stephen Salmon, her said executors, equally divided between the daughters' children of the said Rose [ ] goods and chattels amongst the which divisions, partition and allotment the said executors made a division and allotment of the fulling mill standing [ ] Spilsby aforesaid, that is to say that Stephen or his farmer and occupier should pay a yearly rent out of the said fulling mill during the continuance of [ ] unto the daughters' children of the said Rose of the clear yearly value of £4.10.0 of lawful money of England over and besides [ ] reserved upon the said lease rent, the lessor and his heirs, videlicet that one of the daughters' children of the said Rose should have yearly 45s of the said yearly rent of £4.10.0 and the other of her daughters' children the other 45s, the other half and [ ] said mill's rent. After which division and allotment so had and made the said Stephen Salmon made and declared his last will and testament and thereof named and [ ] one Eme Salmon, one of the said Rose's daugh[ters], his wife, his executrix and died having in his custody and possession the said ground lease, after whose death the said [Eme] Salmon proved the will of her said husband and took upon her the execution of the same.. But so it is . . . that your orator [ ] the said Rose's daughters and by her hath diverse children of young and tender years, unto whom what in the lifetime of the said Stephen Salmon and sin[ce] his [   ] there is behind and unpaid to be answered unto the said children eleven years' rent of the said fulling mill, the which arrearages, although your said orator hath a [   ] sundry times required the said Eme to content, satisfy and pay unto your said orator as guardian [   ] unto his said children and also to deliver the said [   ] for that he was executor with her husband unto the said Rose and now surviveth after his death and standeth charged to pay and satisfy as well [   ] as also unto the said Stephen Salmon's children all the said legacies and bequests when they shall attain and come unto their full and lawful age, and also [   ] is to see to the safety of the ground lease of the said fulling mill which is casually come to the hands of the said Eme, which she utterly refuseth [   ] reason of [   ] to compound with him in whom the reversions of the said fulling mill remaineth, and so to surrender the same [   ] to the utter undoing of the said poor infants contrary to all right, equity and conscience. In consideration whereof and for that your said orator can have no remedy by the order and course of the common laws of this realm for the recovery of the same and for that the said Stephen Salmon in his lifetime and the said Eme since his death hath ever received the rent of the said mill and hath put one into the occupation of the said mill utterly and altogether unknown [   ] orator what he is or whence he came. And for that the said Eme hath goods and chattels sufficient of her said husbands to pay and discharge [   ] arrearages his debts and legacies . . . .

(Square brackets refer to illegible passages in the original document.)

APPENDIX F

A SURVEY OF CONTINENTAL MUSIC IN MANUSCRIPTS IN ENGLAND DURING THE REIGN OF HENRY VIII

The earliest evidence of Continental music during the reign of Henry VIII is found in Lbl 31922, a court songbook produced in ca. 1515 whose contents are overwhelmingly English, including instrumental works, puzzle canons, and rounds. Among its 112 compositions are two dozen attributed to men of Fayrfax's generation: fourteen by Cornysh, two by Fayrfax himself, seven by Farthyng, and three by John Lloyd (d. 1523). A younger generation is represented as well: thirty-five works by the young king, three by Robert Cowper (d. ca. 1530), and one by Richard Pygot (d. 1552).[5] All these men (aside from Henry himself, of course) were gentlemen of the Chapel Royal. The Continental compositions in the songbook include two each by Hayne van Ghizeghem (d. after 1472) and Heinrich Isaac (d. 1517), and isolated works by Jacques Barbireau (d. 1491), Antoine Busnois (d. 1492), Alexander Agricola (d. 1506), Jean Prioris (d. after 1512), Antoine de Févin (d. 1512), and Loyset Compère (d. 1518).[6] Added to these are perhaps a half-dozen anonymous works of clearly Continental origin, and at least four works attributed to Henry VIII which are simply reworkings of Franco-Flemish originals.

Contemporaneous with Lbl 31922 is a Continental manuscript produced for Henry's court at the atelier of Alamire in 1516, Lbl 11 E.xi.[7] It contains seven works: two motets in praise of Henry, one of them by Richard Sampson; three Marian antiphons, two by Sampson and Benedictus de Opitiis; and two anonymous psalm settings of Franco-Flemish origin.[8]

In a second Alamire manuscript copied in ca. 1520-22, Lbl 8 G.vii,[9] there are thirty-six four-part motets and votive antiphons, and two secular works, including prayers for Catherine of Aragon and Emperor Charles V. All but five of these have been attributed to known Continental composers, among them Févin, Isaac, Pierre de la Rue (d. 1518), Josquin des Prez (d. 1521), Jean Mouton (d. 1522), Jean Ghiselin (called Verbonnet, d. ca. 1535), and Pierkin Therache.

Josquin, Mouton and Therache are represented as well in an earlier Franco-Flemish manuscript, Cm 1760.[10] Copied and presented to Henry and Catherine in ca. 1516,[11] it contains thirty motets, votive antiphons, responds, sequences and settings of the Lamentations, and twenty-seven chansons. Twenty-two of its works are by Févin, others by Jacob Obrecht (d. 1505), Jean Prioris, Antoine Brumel (d. 1520), Hilaire Penet (d. after 1522), Jean Richafort (d. 1548), Bontemps, Matthieu Gascongne, Ninon le Petit, and Jean Brunet.

A fourth Continental source is the set of five partbooks--four of them at the Newberry Library in Chicago, MS VM 1578.M91, and the recently discovered alto book in Sutton Coldfield in England--produced in Florence and presented to Henry in ca. 1528.[12] Of its thirty-one motets, votive antiphons, responds and psalm settings and thirty madrigals, thirty-four have been ascribed to Philippe Verdelot (d. 1527 or later), and another ten may be his. Other composers represented are Andreas de Silva (d. after 1522), Jean Conseil (1498-1535), Maistre Jhan (d. after 1543), Jean Lhéritier (d. after 1552), Claudin de Sermisy (d. 1562), and Adrian Willaert (d. 1562).

Lcm 1070, copied in London and very probably in Anne Boleyn's court circle in ca. 1533-36,[13] contains an almost entirely Franco-Flemish repertory of thirty-nine motets, antiphons, hymns, responds, sequences and psalm settings,, and three chansons. Ten works are by Josquin, nine by Mouton, and others by Obrecht, Févin, Compère, Brumel, Claudin and Therache. Of particular interest is the evidence this manuscript provides that, contrary to the view generally held, Marian antiphons were considered perfectly acceptable in the reformist group led by Archbishop Cranmer and patronized by Anne Boleyn during her brief reign as Queen of England. More than a third of the pieces in the collection are settings of Marian texts.

Five other manuscripts of unknown provenance, but probably all copied during the reign of Henry VIII, are major sources of Continental music in England during this period. The chansonnier Lbl 35087 contains some sixty-five songs in French, Italian, Dutch and Latin, and fourteen motets, antiphons, responds and psalms.[14] Their three part scoring is unusual: most of the music in these manuscripts is in four parts. The composers represented--among them, Agricola, Benedictus Appenzeller, Prioris, Josquin, Févin, Compère, Mouton, Ghiselin, Gascongne and Ninon--and the repertory (including Mouton's *Salve mater salvatoris*, with its prayer for Charles V) indicate a date for the manuscript of ca. 1530.

The surviving partbook Lbl 19583 of an otherwise lost set contains twenty motets, antiphons, responds, sequences, hymns, and psalm settings, and four chansons by Mouton, La Rue, Josquin, Andreas (de Silva?), Antonius Divitis (d. after 1526), Elzéar Genet (Carpentras) and other composers active in the first two decades of the century, as well as by a later generation of composers including Richafort, Costanzo Festa (d. 1545) and Willaert.[15] It may date, therefore, from the 1530s or 1540s.

Three chansonniers containing mostly three-part chansons date apparently from the early years of the sixteenth century: Ob 831, one of whose four songs is Spanish;[16] Lbl 20 A.xvi, with twenty-nine chansons by Hayne van Ghizeghem, Agricola, La Rue, Josquin and others;[17] and by Hayne van Ghizeghem, Agricola, La Rue, Josquin and others;[17] and Lbl 5242, with thirty-one chansons by Agricola, Brumel (d. 1520), Févin, Gascongne, and others.[18]

These surviving manuscripts represent the known extent of Continental music in London during the period ca. 1510-40.[19] This repertory, overwhelmingly Franco-Flemish, consists of some 400 compositions, of which about 180 are sacred, 220 secular, by some thirty composers. Braithwaite examined some 140 sacred works, limiting his study to five manuscripts he considered of Continental provenance: Lbl 8 G.vii, 19583, and 35087; Lcm 1070 (in fact an English manuscript); and Cm 1760. (He excluded Lbl 11 E.xi, misattributing it to an English scribe.) Among these works, he identified forty-five antiphons, twenty-one hymns and sequences, nine psalm settings, nineteen general prayers, ten settings of Biblical texts, and eight settings or representations from Vergil. Some fifty works apparently have no concordances in the manuscripts of Continental libraries; this English group of Continental works, then, constitutes a unique source of a large repertory of Continental polyphony. But many other compositions found here have concordances in Petrucci and Attaingnant prints, and in manuscripts in Continental libraries. Furthermore, the concordances within the English group of manuscripts are widespread. Josquin, Mouton and Févin are particularly well represented. Josquin's *Virgo salutiferi genitrix intacta*, Mouton's *Adiutorium nostrum in nomine Domini*, Févin's *Sancta Trinitas unus Deus*, and Therache's *Verbum bonum et suave* are all found in Lbl 8 G.vii, Cm 1760, and Lcm 1070, while Févin's chanson *Je le laire* is found in Lbl 5242 and 35087, and in Cm 1760.

Interestingly, in all these manuscripts we find not one setting of the mass ordinary.[20] It is possible, of course, that prints containing Continental Masses circulated in Henrician England; but we do not know which of them may have circulated where or when.[21]

The impact of Continental music and musicians was felt increasingly strongly during the early years of Henry VIII's reign, until by ca. 1530-40 its presence in English manuscripts was substantial. Its influence was limited for the most part to London and court circles. With a few notable exceptions, that influence has been described only in general terms. But musical influence does not work that way. It works through the course of particular composers, compositions, manuscripts and prints from one court or city to another. To ascribe a general Franco-Flemish influence to a particular English composer or composition on stylistic grounds backed by no specific documentary evidence may perhaps be necessary; but it is at best an uncertain undertaking, for it begs the question of what in a given composer's development is the result of internal change, and what the result of his absorption of a foreign idiom or technique. We have here a body of work whose substance and impact upon Tudor music has yet to be studied in comprehensive fashion; the further analysis of these manuscripts and prints, their repertory and filiation, is needed to trace the transmission and absorption of specific Continental tests, compositions and practices into the mainstream of Henrician polyphony.

NOTES

CHAPTER 1

[1]Two of Taverner's Masses were adapted to English texts for a short-lived Protestant liturgy early in the reign of Edward VI (1547-53). The bulk of the extant music has come down to us from the isolated efforts of later Tudor and Stuart scribes--of varying degrees of competence--who compiled partbooks for use during the Catholic interregnum of Mary Tudor (1553-58), for private Catholic devotional observances during the reigns of Elizabeth and James I (1558-1625), or occasionally for performance as vocal and instrumental chamber music.

The only music of Taverner's which circulated widely, in a variety of guises, was the "in nomine" section of his Mass *Gloria tibi Trinitas.* An instrumental transcription of this passage, along with several other composers' settings based on the same cantus firmus, appeared in the Mulliner Book not long after Taverner's death (a modern edition by Denis Stevens was published as the first volume of MB [2nd rev. ed., London: Stainer and Bell, 1966]. The printer John Day published it in 1560 (and again in 1565) in his collection of Anglican music as the anthem *In trouble and adversity.* Gustave Reese, "The Origin of the English 'In Nomine,'" *Journal of the American Musicological Society* 2 (1949): 7-22; and Robert Donington and Thurston Dart, "The Origin of the 'In Nomine,'" *Music and Letters* 30 (1949): 101-106.

[2]9th ed. (3 vols.; London: Company of Stationers, 1684), 2:251.

[3]Meres, *Palladis Tamia* (1598; reprint ed., New York: Scholars' Facsimiles and Reprints, 1938), p. 288: Morley, *A Plain and Easy Introduction to Practical Music* (1597), ed. R.A. Harman, 2nd ed., London: J.M. Dent, 1963), pp. 123, 255.

[4]*The Church-History of Britain* (6 books in 1 vol.; London: John Williams, 1655-56), Book 5, p. 170.

[5]New edition in 5 vols., ed. Philip Bliss (London: F.C. & J. Rivington, 1813-20), 5, column 45.

[6]Wood, *Athenae Oxoniensis* 5, cols. 297-300.

[7]New ed., 2 vols. (London: Novello, 1853; reprint ed., New York: Dover, 1963), 1:354-55. Hawkins copied the entire composition in his manuscript of Tudor church music (Lbl 5059, ff. 48-62v); his source must have been the Sadler partbooks Ob 1-5, the only sixteenth-century source containing the complete text.

[8]1935 edition by Frank Mercer, 2 vols. (reprint ed., New York: Dover, 1957), 1:786-90. Burney copied three canons and a four-part passage on "Qui tollis" from the Mass, as well as *Dum transisset Sabbatum,* in his manuscript (Lbl 11586); his source was Och 984-88.

[9]*History of English Music* (London: J. Curwen, 1895), p. 108.

[10]"John Taverner," *The Catholic Encyclopedia,* 15 vols. (New York: The Encyclopedia Press, 1913), 14:466.

[11]"John Taverner," *DNB* 19: 392-93.

[12]"New Light on Early Tudor Composers. XII--John Taverner," *The Musical Times* 61 (1920): 597-98.

[13]*TCM* 1: *John Taverner c. 1495-1545* 1.

[14]*TCM* 3: *John Taverner c. 1495-1545* 2.

[15]Dom Anselm Hughes, "Sixteenth Century Service Music," *Music and Letters* 5 (1924): 145-54, 335-46; Sylvia Townsend Warner, "Doubting Castle," *Music and Letters* 5 (1924): 155-68; H.B. Collins, "John Taverner's Masses," *Music and Letters* 5 (1924): 322-34, and "John Taverner--Part II," *Music and Letters* 6 (1925): 314-29.

[16]In *Tudor Church Composers* (London: Oxford University Press, 1925).

[17]*TCM: Appendix with Supplementary Notes* (London: Oxford University Press, 1948).

[18]"John Taverner," *Grove* 8:323-24.

[19]*Tudor Church Music*, 2nd ed. (London: Faber and Faber, 1966).

[20]"John Taverner," *MGG* 13: cols. 152-56; "John Taverner, *Essays in Musicology in Honor of Dragan Plamenac*, ed. Gustave Reese and Robert J. Snow (Pittsburgh: University of Pittsburgh Press, 1969) pp. 331-39.

[21]*The Religious Orders in England 3: The Tudor Age* (Cambridge: University Press, 1961), p. 20.

[22]London: Boosey and Hawkes, 1972.

[23]Paul Doe, "Latin Polyphony under Henry VIII," *Proceedings of the Royal Musical Association* 95 (1968-69): 87.

CHAPTER 2

[1]The name Taverner was a fairly common one in medieval and Tudor England. References to it can be found in Charles Bardsley, *A Dictionary of English and Welsh Surnames* (1901; reprint ed., Baltimore: Genealogical Publishing, 1967); C. L'Estrange Ewen, *A History of Surnames of the Brtitish Isles* (London: K. Paul, Trench, Trubner, 1931); James Fairbairn, *Fairbairn's Crests*, rev. Lawrence Butters, ed. Joseph Maclaren (1911; reprint ed., Baltimore: Genealogical Publishing, 1963); Gustav Fransson, *Middle English Surnames of Occupation 1100-1350* (London: Williams and Norgate, 1935); the publications of the British Record Society and the Harleian Society, and the various registers of Oxford and Cambridge Universities, among other sources.

For Lincolnshire, see C.W. Foster's editions of *Calendars of Lincoln Wills* 1, 1320-1600 (Publications of the British Record Society 28 (London: British Record Society 1902), and *The Parish Registers of Boston in the County of Lincoln* 1, 1557-1599, Publications of the LRS, Parish Register Section 1 (Horncastle: LRS, 1914). For the renowned Taverner family of Norfolk, of whom Richard Taverner, early translator of the Bible and a colleague of the composer at Oxford during the late 1520s, was a member, see Augustus George Legge, ed., *The Ancient Register of North Elmham, Norfolk, from A.D. 1538 to A.D. 1631* (Norwich: Agas H. Goose, 1888).

The principal archives that I examined in a vain attempt to trace the ancestry of the composer are the Lincoln Archives Office in Lincoln, the Library of the Society of Genealogists in London, and the Borthwick Institute of Historical Research at St. Anthony's Hall in York.

[2]See Chapter 4.

[3]See Chapter 6.

[4]See pp. 103-105.

[5]See the *Inquisition post mortem*, pp. 106-108, and Appendix C.

[6]His will, dated 3 March 1556 and probated in the following year, is found in LIao Consistory Court Wills 1557, 3, f. 28, where he is described as a farmer, probably of yeoman class. He left a son, John. *Calendars of Lincoln Wills* 1:304; *TCM* 1:li. See Appendix D.

Two Taverner families in Lincoln contemporary with the composer may be related to him. The head of one was Thomas Taverner, who died at Lincoln in 1528 and left a wife Joan and four children: William, Annas, Alice, and Ame (*LP* 4, no. 4083). A second Thomas Taverner, an innkeeper, died in 1557 at Billingborough, a town some fifteen miles west of Boston. He left a brother Bartholomew and two sons, John and Hugh (LIao Consistory Court Wills 1557, 3, f. 150; *Calendars of Lincoln Wills* 1:304; *TCM* 1:li). Among his bequests was one to William's son John, indicating that he was a close relative of William and therefore of the composer as well.

[7]Connections between Tattershall and Boston were close in any case. The latter, the only town of any size between Lincoln and Norwich, was at the time still a major North Sea port. Tattershall, some eleven miles up the Witham River from Boston and situated on a tongue of land formed by the confluence of the Witham and its tributary, the Bain, was a seat of nobility around which developed a little market town that depended for its livelihood on Boston. Its decline followed closely the decline of that town. Indicative of the close link is the fact that the owners of Tattershall Manor were frequently enrolled in the fraternity of the Guild of Corpus Christi in Boston, which Taverner too was to join. The manor itself was part of the parish of St. Botolph's, whose seat was the parish church in Boston.

[8]The only exception was the son of one of the college clerks.

[9]The most complete account of Tattershall Manor is found in H. Avray Tipping, *Tattershall Castle, Lincolnshire* (London: Jonathan Cape, 1929). Brief historical surveys are found in John George Hall, *Notices of Lincolnshire* (Hull: Eastern Morning News, 1890), pp. 131-41; and Alexander Hamilton Thompson, *Tattershall: The Manor, the Castle, the Church* (Lincoln: J. W. Huddock, 1928).

[10]William Douglas Simpson, ed., *The Building Accounts of Tattershall College, 1434-1472*, Publications of the LRS 55 (Hereford: LRS, 1960), xi.

[11]A chapel existed here as early as 1298. The will (1416) of Maud Cromwell, grandmother of the third Lord Cromwell, provided for seven priests to say masses for ten years in the Chapel of the Holy Cross, and for executors to provide for twelve poor men and women in the almshouse. Tipping, *Tattershall Castle* pp. 32, 71-72. Both this chapel and the later one of Cromwell's foundation are mentioned in the

Valor Ecclesiasticus of 1534, ed. John Caley and Joseph Hunter; 6 vols. (London: Record Commission, 1810-34), 4:42.

[12]For these accounts in the original Latin and in English translation, see Simpson, *Building Accounts*, pp. 1-37, 41-77.

[13]Simpson, *Building Accounts*, pp. xxviii-xxix. John Harvey has suggested that Tattershall Castle was the prototype of later Tudor brick architecture (Gothic England [London: B.T. Batsford, 1947], p. 102). It is mentioned in a list of fortifications and fortified cities in an elegy to Edward IV written by John Skelton soon after the King's death in 1483. The speaker is the dead king:

> I had enough, I held me not content,
> Without remembrance that I should die;
> And more ever to increase was mine intent,
> I knew not how longe I should it occupy:
> I made the Tower stronge, I wist not why;
> I knew not to whom I purchased Tattershall;
> I amended Dover on the mountain high,
> And London I provoked to fortify the wall;
> I made Nottingham a place full royall,
> Windsor, Eltham, and many other mo:
> Yet, at the last, I went from them all,
> *Et, ecce, nunc in pulvere dormio.*

(Philip Henderson, ed., *The Complete Poems of John Skelton* [3rd ed.; London: J.M. Dent, 1959], p. 2.) Tattershall Castle had fallen forfeit to Edward on the death in battle of Humphrey Bourchier, the fourth Lord Cromwell, in 1471.

[14]William Dugdale, *Monasticon Anglicanum*, trans. and ed. John Stevens (London: D. Browne and J. Smith, 1718), p. 368.

[15]Tipping, *Tattershall Castle*, p. 83; *Calendar of the Patent Rolls . . . Henry VI* (6 vols.; London: His Majesty's Stationery Office, 1901-1910) (1436-41): 292.

[16]HMC *Report on the Manuscripts of Lord De L'Isle and Dudley Preserved at Penshurst Place* 1, HMC Reports on Collections of Manuscripts 77 Part 1 (London: His Majesty's Stationery Office, 1925) pp. 172-73.

[17]More was a former fellow of Peterhouse and a Doctor of Theology from Cambridge. The years of his tenure as warden of Tattershall, 1444-56, coincide with those he spent as canon of York Cathedral, the latter post providing him with a handsome additional income. Buried at Tattershall, he donated his library to Peterhouse. A.B. Emden, *A Biographical Register of the University of Oxford to A.D. 1500* (3 vols.; Oxford: Clarendon Press, 1957-59), 2:410; John and J.A. Venn, *Alumni Cantabrigienses* 1: From the Earliest Times to 1751 (4 vols.; Cambridge: University Press, 1922-27), 3:208.

[18]A memorandum for Cromwell's executor from ca. 1456 includes the following item: "For the conclusion with the heirs that the College might have the new place that Thomas Wolwune dwelled in . . ." See HMC *Report*, p. 185.

[19]HMC *Report*, p. 179, taken from the De L'Isle and Dudley Manuscript MAk U1475 Q 21/2.

[20]Since these final statutes confirm William More as master, they can be dated from some time after Cromwell's death in January 1456 to before More's by October 1456. HMC *Report*, p. 179, erroneously gives ca. 1460 as the date of these statutes (pp. 179-84); they exist only in a final version for a draft which is lost. See Roger Bowers, Choral Institutions within the English Church: Their Constitution and Development, 1340-1500 (Ph.D. University of East Anglia, 1975), p. 5063n.

[21]For a detailed rendering of the origins and execution of this clause in the statutes, see Bowers, Choral Institutions, pp. 5064-65.

[22]HMC *Report*, pp. 181-82.

[23]From a clerk's salary, £3.0.8 was deducted for commons and 10s for livery. Bowers, Choral Institutions, p. 5067 note 2.

[24]In his will of 1451, Lord Cromwell had left money for 3000 masses to be said for his soul, 1000 to the Holy Trinity, 1000 to the Virgin, and 1000 requiem masses. See Alfred Gibbons, *Early Lincoln Wills* (Lincoln: James Williamson, 1888), p. 182.

[25]"Item Capellano seu clerico ludenti ad orgona [sic] in diebus dominicis festis maioribus et principalibus ac ad missam beate marie virginis." Bowers, Choral Institutions, p. 5099.

[26]Harvey, *Gothic England*, p. 102.

[27]The late start in construction is attested by the following stipulation in Lord Cromwell's will of 30 September 1454: "The Collegiate Church of Tateshale and the College are to be built out of his moveable goods. . . . The College is to be completely newly built" (Harvey, *Gothic England*, p. 210). A memorandum from ca. 1456 from Cromwell's executors mentions specifications of dorsers at high doors in the college hall, so that by that year the hall was nearing completion (HMC *Report*, p. 186).

[28]HMC *Report*, p. 198, shows payments to his widow.

[29]HMC *Report*, pp. 198-99.

[30]Tipping, *Tattershall Castle*, pp. 109-110. The fact that Waynflete entrusted this task to Gigur suggests, in the absence of documentary evidence, that Gigur was responsible for the erection of the college and grammar school.

[31]HMC *Report*, pp. 175-76, for the indenture of 14 January 1486 between Gigur and the Tattershall carpenter Henry Halsebroke, providing for the wood of the almshouse.

[32]Lbl 1210. For a list of the music, see Augustus Hughes-Hughes, *Catalogue of Manuscript Music in the British Museum*. 3 vols. (London: British Museum, 1906-1909; reprint ed., 1964-66), 1:255-56; and Friedrich Ludwig, "Die mehrstimmige Messe des 14. Jahrhunderts," *Archiv für Musikwissenschaft* 7 (1925):429.

[33]*DNB* 20:996-1000.

[34]Nikolaus Pevsner and John Harris, *The Buildings of England: Lincolnshire* (London: Penguin, 1964), p. 387.

[35]Harvey, *Gothic England*, pp. 119-20.

[36]HMC *Report*, pp. 198-99. Simpson suggests that the tower and roodscreen were not build until the end of the century (p. xiii). Note, however, that materials for the tower were being assembled in 1482.

[37]Pevsner and Harris, *Buildings: Lincolnshire*, pp. 387-88. The authors add: "One walks through it and stays in it and never quite forgets the Treasurer's badge, which is a purse."

[38]Thompson, *Tattershall*, p. 29.

[39]HMC *Report*, p. 175.

[40]Thompson, *Tattershall*, p. 25; quoted in Simpson, *Building Accounts*, p. xiv, with corrections.

[41]A.B. Emden, *A Biographical Register of the University of Cambridge to 1500* (Cambridge: University Press, 1963), p. 285; Venn and Venn, *Alumni* 2:300.

[42]*DNB* 6:1260-61; Venn and Venn, *Alumni* 2:407; C.H. and T. Cooper, *Athenae Cantabrigienses* (Cambridge: Macmillan, 1858), 1:19.

[43]These MSS are the property of the Viscount De L'Isle, V.C., K.E. The receiver's accounts are De L'Isle and Dudley MSS U 1475 Q 16/1-3; the precentor's accounts are DLD MSS U1475 Q 19/2-8.

[44]HMC *Report*, pp. 194-97. The numbering system found there is, for receiver's accounts: 203 (1492-93), 204 (1495-96), and 205 (1507-1508); for precentor's accounts: 200 (1495-96), 201 (1496-97), 202 (1498-99), 199 (1500-1501), and 208 (1507-1508).

[45]William Lounde, son of Robert Lounde, one of the hired clerks (Tattershall account 203).

[46]HMC *Report*, pp. 176-77.

[47]HMC *Report*, pp. 184-85.

[48]Dates of death are found in a list of gravestones in the church, in Gervase Holles, *Lincolnshire Church Notes*, ed. R.E.G. Cole, LRS 1 (Lincoln: LRS, 1911), p. 143. I have been able to identify only one of these men. Gibon was a fellow of Magdalen College, Oxford, Waynflete's foundation. He received the M.A. by 1484, and later was rector of Wyberton, a village near Boston (Emden, *Oxford* 2:839 (Thomas Gybbons).

[49]Dr. Bowers' recent research has yielded new evidence which, when published, will require revision of some of this material. One discovery already in print establishes that Thomas Ashewell, a well-known Tudor composer, was a singing clerk at Tattershall in 1502-1503 (*Early Tudor Masses* 2, EECM 16, ed. John D. Bergsagel, p.x). Ashewell was a boy chorister at St. George's Chapel, Windsor, in the early 1490s, master of the children at Lincoln Cathedral in 1508, and master of the Lady chapel choir at Durham Cathedral in 1513. His only complete surviving works are two Masses found in Ob 376-81 (modern edition of the two Masses in *Early Tudor Masses* 1 and 2, EECM 1 and 16). Since Ob 376-81 were compiled for and probably under the supervision of Taverner in Oxford during the late 1520s, and since their selection of Masses cannot have been haphazard, we may ascribe the presence of Ashewell's Masses in those partbooks to an earlier association between Ashewell and Taverner, an

association that may have been formed at Tattershall when Ashewell was a clerk there and Taverner, a boy chorister.

[50]All but two of these entries are found in the precentor's accounts of 1496-97 and 1498-99; the other two are in the less detailed precentor's account of 1495-96.

[51]*Gaudent in caelis* is the antiphon to the fifth psalm (*Lauda Jerusalem Dominum*: Psalm 147) at vespers on the Feast of Relics (*Breviarium ad usum...Sarum*, ed. Francis Procter and Christopher Wordsworth 3 vols.; Cambridge: University Press, 1879-86, 3:451), and the antiphon as well to *Magnificat* at vespers on the Feast of Martyrs (*Breviarium* 2:396).

[52]Identified by Bowers as probably *Hierusalem respice*, a trope to the ritual antiphon *En rex venit*. Choral Institutions, pp. 6024 note 3.

[53]A setting for two voices of the verse *Dicant nunc Judei* of *Christus resurgens* is found in Cm 1236 (*The Music of the Pepys MS 1236*, ed. Sydney Robinson Charles, Corpus Mensurabilis Musicae 40 [Rome: American Institute of Musicology, 1967], pp. 80-81), and another for three voices in Lbl 3307 (*British Museum Manuscript Egerton 3307*, ed. Gwynn McPeek [London: Oxford University Press, 1963], pp. 86-88).

[54]Three settings in two parts by John Tudor are found in Cm 1236 (*Music of the Pepys MS 1236*, pp. 145-46, 152-54, and 154-55). Two anonymous settings in two and three parts are found in Lbl 3307 (*The British Museum Manuscript Egerton 3307*, pp. 9-92 and 90-91, respectively).

[55]*The Eton Choirbook*, 3 vols., ed. Frank Ll. Harrison, *MMB* 10-12 (London: Stainer and Bell, 1956-61), 2:62-72, 181; Bowers, Choral Institutions, p. 6021.

[56]Of the eighteen "Gaude" texts, eleven are *Gaude flore virginali*, four are *Gaude virgo mater Christi*, two are *Gaude virgo saluta*, and one is *Gaude rosa sine spina*.

[57]The Eton choirbook contains two incomplete settings of the *Magnificat* in four parts by Baldwin.

[58]*The Worcester Fragments*, ed. Luther Dittmer, Musicological Studies and Documents 2 (Dallas: American Institute of Musicology, 1957), No. 27, is a polyphonic setting of an *Alleluia* whose top voice has a Marian trope beginning with the words "Parens Alma." The Tattershall text may be a Marian antiphon.

[59]For its dating, see Charles Hamm, *A Chronology of the Works of Guillaume Dufay* (Princeton: Princeton University Press, 1964), pp. 152, 169.

[60]The "Burton" mentioned in the Tattershall accounts is almost certainly the same Burton who was paid £1 by Henry VII for making a Mass in 1494 and joined the Chapel Royal in 1509. See Lester Brothers, "Avery Burton and his Hexachord Mass," *Musica Disciplina* 28 (1974): 154.

[61]The provost, chosen annually from among the clerks, seems to have acted as an assistant to the precentor, one of his duties being collection of fines for absences from services. For schedules of fines at Tattershall, see Appendix A.

[62]*Chapter Acts of the Cathedral Church of St. Mary of Lincoln A.D. 1536-47*, ed. R.E.G. Cole, LRS 13 (Horncastle: LRS, 1917), p. 31; translated in Harrison, *MMB*, p. 177. For Horwood's successors and their duties, see Harrison, *MMB*, pp. 178-79.

[63]The complete deed of appointment is given in the original Latin (Harrison, *MMB*, pp. 429-30). A free translation of part of it is found in David Knowles, *The Religious Orders in England 3: The Tudor Age* (Cambridge: University Press, 1961), pp. 17-18. The deed is virtually identical to the one drawn up at Durham for Thomas Foderly (1496) and John Tildesley (1502), while these three differ from the deed of John Stele (1447) only in that they include the teaching of organ and square-note, and add *Salve regina* to the musical portion of the service in which the cantor took part. Harrison, *MMB*, p. 187.

[64]M.A. Oxford by 1476-77, fellow and later bursar of Magdalen College; fellow of Eton 1482-89; D.Th. Oxford 1493; dean of the Chapel Royal 1508; succeeded Wolsey as Bishop of Lincoln 1514, died 1521. Margaret Bowker, ed., *An Episcopal Court Book For the Diocese of Lincoln 1514-1520*, LRS 61 (Lincoln: LRS, 1967), pp. xvii-xviii.

[65]*Visitations in the Diocese of Lincoln 1517-1531* 3, ed. A.H. Thompson, LRS 37 (Hereford: LRS, 1947), p. 111. The second complaint was that the clerks (*clerici socii*) dressed like laymen rather than in clerical habit. An appropriate injunction followed.

CHAPTER 3

[1]"A London Gild of Musicians, 1460-1530," *Proceedings of the Royal Musical Association* 83 (1956-57): 15-28.

[2]Notably by Denis Stevens in his Taverner entry in *MGG 13*, cols. 152-56, and an expanded version of that essay in *Essays in Musicology in Honor of Dragan Plamenac*, ed. Gustave Reese and Robert J. Snow (Pittsburgh: University of Pittsburgh Press, 1969), p. 331. It is on the basis of the 1514 register entry that Stevens first proposed the revision of Taverner's birthdate from ca. 1495 back to ca. 1490.

[3]Nan Cooke Carpenter (*Music in the Medieval and Renaissance Universities* [Norman: University of Oklahoma Press, 1958]), notes a payment in the Magdalen College, Oxford, accounts of 1512-13 "Iohanni Tabourner pro lusione in interludio Octavis Epiphaniae" (to John Tabourner for playing the interlude of the octave of the Epiphany) and suggests that this man "is probably the same John Taverner who became organist of Cardinal College in 1525" (p. 174). Her suggestion is incorrect. The preceding entry in the accounts is "Petro Pyper pro piping in interludio nocte Sancti Iohannis," indicating that these payments were made to a piper and a tabor player (a common pairing: see *Grove 6*: 775-76) for participation in a Christmastide entertainment. Such payments are found frequently in medieval English records. Thus, among the early sixteenth-century accounts of the parish of St. Laurence, Reading, we find payments "to a taberer on Philips day," "to the taberer at Whitsuntide," and to "Thomas Taberer for the King play at Whitsuntide" (John Charles Cox, *Churchwardens' Accounts* [London: Methuen, 1913], pp. 282-83).

Furthermore, genealogical evidence militates against the association of the name Taverner and its variants on the one hand, and Tabourner or Taberner and its variants on the other. The one remaining possibility of positive association of the two names might have lain in a paleographic error--"b" for "v"--at the printed source. Ms. Carpenter cites as her source Frederick Boas's *University Drama in the Tudor Age* (Oxford: Clarendon Press, 1914), and Boas cites as his, William Macray's *Register of the Members of St. Mary Magdalen College, Oxford* 1 (London: Henry Frowde, 1894). Macray's trancription has been confirmed by Mr. Neil Ker, reader in paleography at

Magdalen College, who has written that "'Iohanni Tabourner pro lusione . . .' can mean no more than that John the tabor player was paid six pence. There is no doubt that the third letter is *b* and not *v.* The people writing our accounts at this time seem to write regularly in this form; Christian name and name of profession, John the piper, Gerald the smith, so and so the glover, or the barber. There is no trace of John Taverner here, I fear" (Letter to author, 28 February 1968).

[4]"A description of England in an early Italian 'Relation,' ca. 1500," reprinted in *English Historical Documents* 5: 1485-1558, ed. C. H. Williams (London: Eyre and Spottiswoode, 1967), p. 200.

[5]The "Relation" (report) by the Venetian Ambassador Ludovico Falier in 1531, in *Calendar of State Papers, Venetian*, ed. Rawdon Brown, Cavendish Bentinck and Horatio. Brown. 38 vols. (London: Her (His) Majesty's Stationery Office, 1864-1947), 4:296.

[6]There were approximately 10,500 inhabitants in Bristol and 8,000 in Norwich and York. *English Historical Documents* 5:8.

[7]Several musicians of the king's household chapel lived at Greenwich, among them Gilbert Banester, William Colman, William Newark and Richard Pygot. See Hugh Baillie, "A London Gild," p. 16.

[8]St. George's Chapel at Windsor (incorporated by royal charter in 1352 and reconstituted by 1482-83 into the symmetrical complement of thirteen canons, vicars, clerks and choristers each) and the chapel at nearby Eton College, lying almost twenty-five miles west of London, constituted a community in their own right; musicians there remained, by and large, quite apart from the musical life of the city.

[9]See, for instance, John Charles Cox, *Churchwardens' Accounts from the Fourteenth Century to the Close of the Seventeenth Century* (London: Methuen, 1913). Baillie notes that St. Anthony's and St. Bartholomew's hospitals and the colleges of Whittington and St.-Martin-le-Grand "had substantial choirs and made a useful contribution to London music" ("A London Gild," p. 17n).

[10]Harrison, *MMB*, pp. 197-98, 200.

[11]For records of music at St. Mary's, see Henry Littlehales, ed., *The Medieval Records of a London City Church (St. Mary at Hill) A.D. 1420-1559*, Early English Text Society, Original Series 128 (London: Kegan Paul, Trench, Trubner, 1905), and Baillie, "A London Church in Early Tudor Times," *Music and Letters* 36 (1955): 55-64.

[12]Edward Pine, "Westminster Abbey: Some Early Masters of the Choristers," *The Musical Times* 94 (1953): 258-59; Harrison, *MMB*, pp. 43, 288. Mundy would later serve at St. Mary-at-Hill.

[13]Harrison, *MMB*, pp. 12-14.

[14]One such occasion was a mass celebrated by Wolsey in the presence of the king and the French ambassador in November 1527, "which was sung with the king's chapel & the choir of Paul's" (George Cavendish, *The Life and Death of Cardinal Wolsey* in *Two Early Tudor Lives*, ed. Richard S. Sylvester and Davis P. Harding [New Haven: Yale University Press, 1962], pp. 66-67). Another occurred that same year when Wolsey led "Te Deum, the which was solemnly sung with the king's trumpets &

shawms as well Englishmen as Venetians" (William Dugdale, *History of St. Paul's Cathedral* [London: Thomas Warren, 1658], p. 32; Harrison, *MMB*, p. 217). During another service, celebrated in honor of the birth of Edward VI, "Paul's choir sang an anthem of the Trinity, with *Te Deum*, and the ninth respond of the Trinity [*Summae Trinitati simplici Deo*], with the collect of the same. Then the king's waits and the waits of London played with the shawms" (Charles Wriothesley, *Chronicle of England during the Reigns of the Tudors*, in *English Historical Documents* 5:726).

[15]Walter Woodfill, *Musicians in English Society* (Princeton: Princeton University Press, 1953), pp. 33-51. The aldermen raised their salary to £3.6.8 in 1524, the year in which it was decreed that all church dedications be celebrated on the same day, 3 October, and to £6 in 1536, when the number of holidays was reduced further. Woodfill connects the loss of opportunity to make music which resulted from these conditions to the increase in waits' salaries. The figures themselves point to the probability that extra activities added many times over to the waits' basic salary.

[16]Woodfill, *Musicians in English Society*, pp. 1-31.

[17]Cavendish, *Life and Death of Cardinal Wolsey*, pp. 20-21; quoted in *English Historical Documents* 5:409.

[18]The incident is documented in *LP* 2, nos. 4023-25, 4053, 4044. Although no. 4044 precedes no. 4053 in *LP*, it was written at least a day after the latter entry. Nos. 4024 and 4044 are found complete in *Original Papers, Illustrative of English History*, ed. Henry Ellis, 3rd series; 4 vols. (London: Bentley, 1846), 1:49-54. As Henry snatched a treble from Wolsey, so Wolsey took a bass from William Warham, Archbishop of Canterbury: *Original Papers*, 3rd series 1:54-55.

[19]*Calendar of State Papers, Venetian* 4: 300.

[20]Woodfill, *Musicians in English Society*, pp. 177-93.

[21]For these and other payments, see Harrison, *MMB*, p. 172.

[22]Among the lists of liveried musicians at his father's funeral are such foreign names as Hakenett de Lewys, Stephen de Lalaunde, and Jayn Marquesyn. See *The King's Musick*, ed. Henry Cart de Lafontaine (London: Novello, 1909; reprint ed., New York: Da Capo, 1973), pp. 2-3.

[23]Wilibald Nagel, *Annalen der englischen Hofmusik 1509-1649 von der Zeit Heinrichs VIII. bis zum Tode Karls I.* (Leipzig: Breitkopf und Härtel, 1894), p. 4.

[24]The list of instruments is published in the Lady Mary Trefusis, *Songs, Ballads and Instrumental Pieces Composed by King Henry the Eighth* (Oxford: privately printed by the University Press, 1912), pp. xiii-xxx. For foreign musicians at the court, see for instance, Sebastian Giustiniani, *Four Years at the Court of Henry VIII*, trans. and ed. Rawdon Brown (London: Smith, Edler, 1854), 1:80-81; and John Izon, "Italian Musicians at the Tudor Court," *The Musical Quarterly* 44 (1958): 329-31.

[25]Martin Picker, *The Chanson Albums of Marguerite of Austria* (Berkeley and Los Angeles: University of California Press, 1965), p. 34; and James Braithwaite, The Introduction of Franco-Netherlandish Manuscripts to Early Tudor England: The Motet Repertory, 5 vols. (Ph.D. Boston University, 1967), 1:31-37.

[26]J. J. Scarisbrick, *Henry VIII* (Berkeley and Los Angeles: University of California Press, 1968), p. 73.

[27]*Calendars of State Papers, Venetian* 2:247.

[28]*MGG* 8, cols. 228-29.

[29]Picker, *Chanson Albums*, p. 28.

[30]Baillie, "A London Gild," pp. 17-18.

[31]Brothers, "Avery Burton," pp. 156-57.

[32]Among the English singers were Burton, Cornysh, Crane, Thomas Farthyng, Robert Jones, and John Lloyd.

[33]Joycelyne Russell, *The Field of Cloth of Gold* (London: Routledge and Kegan Paul, 1969), pp. 171-75, 214; Edwin B. Warren, *Life and Works of Robert Fayrfax 1464-1521*, Musicological Studies and Documents 20 ([Rome]: American Institute of Musicology, 1969), p. 28.

[34]Quoted in Harrison, *MMB*, p. 172 (where, however, no mention is made of the boys), and in *Original Papers*, 3rd Series 2:48-49.

[35]Harrison, *MMB*, pp. 20, 268.

[36]General accounts of the fraternity are found in James Christie, *Some Accounts of Parish Clerks* (London: privately printed by J. Vincent, 1893), and Ernest Arthur Ebblewhite, *The Parish Clerks' Company and its Charters* (London: privately printed, 1932). Briefer, and musically oriented, is Hugh Baillie, "A London Gild," pp. 15-28. A broad study of the parish clergy of the period is found in Peter Heath, *The English Parish Clergy on the Eve of the Reformation* (London: Routledge and Kegan Paul, 1969).

[37]Christie, *Some Accounts*, p. 25.

[38]The Charter of 1442 has the following passage: "fearing and deeply considering that the said fraternity which hitherto never had a beginning of due and lawful foundation although it has been piously and devoutedly continued as is aforesaid should in no wise for this cause be able to endure." Ebblewhite, *The Parish Clerks' Company*, p. 12.

[39]Ebblewhite, *The Parish Clerks' Company*, pp. 12-13.

[40]Christie, *Some Accounts*, p. 27.

[41]For later charters, namely, those of 1553 (which was applied for and received after the Act for the Suppression of Chantries brought into doubt the legality of guilds whose functions were non-commercial), 1612, 1636 and 1639, see Ebblewhite, *The Parish Clerks' Company*, pp. 16-19.

[42]These ordinances were approved in 1529 and were entered into the records of the Corporation of the City of London on 8 February 1530.

[43]Christie, *Some Accounts*, pp. 71-72.

[44]For the induction feasts, see Philip Norman, *The Ancient Halls of the City Guilds* (London: George Bell and Sons, 1909), p. 109. For the other duties see Christie, *Some Accounts*, pp. 69-71, 126-29, and Baillie, "A London Gild," pp. 22-24.

[45]Christie, *Some Accounts*, p. 71.

[46]Christie, *Some Accounts*, pp. 58-64.

[47]In 1449, the year in which the company received its amended charter, three lists were made containing the names of the masters for that year and all living members, the names of former members now dead, and the names of deceased clerks. In 1458 the classification of priests, clerks, laymen and laywomen was adopted, and thirteen years later it was applied to deceased members. Succeeding scribes would handle the task of listing these names in a variety of modes which frustrates the scholar today, sometimes with minute sub-classification, sometimes with none at all. In general, however the guidelines established in 1458-71 were kept. The register ends abruptly in 1521, with the list for the deceased members of that year missing. The folio containing that list, and another for the year 1523, had been sold on the private market by the time Christie wrote his book.

[48]To name a few: Bishop John Alcock, Chancellor of England (joined 1467, died 1501) and friend of Henry VII; William Caxton (joined 1480, died 1492), Richard Pynson (joined 1497), Barnard Flower, glazier to Henry VII (joined 1503), and William Blount, Lord Mountjoy, friend of Thomas More (joined 1515). Christie, *Some Accounts*, pp. 40-42, and Baillie, ".A London Gild," p. 21.

[49]These are the names listed in Baillie, "A London Gild," pp. 20-22. The classifications are found in the register itself. Horwood and a later master of the fraternity, John Cooke, both contributed to a manuscript of polyphonic Masses now at the Borthwick Institute in York. The fact that these two men are the only composers named in the endleaves containing Masses has led Baillie to connect them directly with the fraternity.

[50]"Some Biographical Notes on English Church Musicians, Chiefly Working in London (1485-1569)," *Royal Musical Association Research Chronicle* 2 (1962): 18-57.

[51]*MMB*, pp. 454-65.

[52]For instance, there are several entries for John Browne: two for Thomas Knyght (unclassified, joined 1496; layman, joined 1520); and two for John Wendon (clerk, joined 1507; layman, joined 1520). A clerk named Thomas Taverner joined in 1521.

[53]For instance, John Morgan (layman, joined 1508, died 1517); John Ambros (layman, died 1514); John Kemp (layman, joined 1515); John Sheppard (layman, joined 1519).

[54]Nothing is known of this woman. Between 1514, when she and her husband joined the Fraternity of St. Nicholas, and in 1521, when the fraternity register ends, there is no mention of either of them. Since deaths, but not registrations, were noted in the register (Christie, *Some Accounts*, pp. 41-42), they were both alive in 1520, and were either residing in London and still members, residing there but no longer members, no longer residing there but still members, or no longer in London and no longer members. If this John Taverner was the composer, Annes must have died some time between 1520 and 1526, by which year he was looking forward to the prospect of another marriage.

[55] *LP* 2, no. 2550.

[56] *LP* 3:1545.

[57] *LP* 4, no. 136.

[58] *LP* 4, nos. 5774, 5791. He is noted as a "citizen of London."

[59] *LP* 19, Part 2, no. 340, grants 36, 59.

[60] Joined 1469; organist of St. Dunstan-in-the-East, 1495-99.

[61] Joined 1500; parish clerk of St. Dunstan-in-the-West, 1516-36.

[62] Entered in the register twice, 1514 and 1518; conduct of St. Margaret Pattens, 1524-25.

[63] Joined 1515; conduct of St. Mary-at-Hill, 1529-30.

[64] Joined 1515; sexton of St. Mary Magdalene, Milk Street, 1518-28, and clerk of St. Dunstan-in-the-West, 1534-42.

[65] Joined 1515; "singing man," at Christ Church, Canterbury, 1535; clerk of St. George's, Windsor, 1547.

[66] Joined 1517, re-entered as a clerk, 1521; conduct of Whittington College, 1547.

[67] The most complete list of surviving records of London institutions employing musicians is found in Baillie, "Some Biographical Notes," pp. 19-23.

[68] A modern edition of Lbl 5465 (and of the songs of the Ritson Manuscript, Lbl 5665) is found in *ETSC*. See also John Stevens's *Music and Poetry in the Early Tudor Court* (London: Methuen, 1961).

[69] Modern edition in *MCH*. See also John Stevens's "Rounds and Canons from an Early Tudor Songbook," *Music and Letters* 32 (1951): 29-37, and his *Music and Poetry*, *passim*.

[70] For contents and description, see Stevens, *Music and Poetry*, pp. 426-28. For *The bella, the bella,* see Chapter 9.

[71] Stevens, *Music and Poetry*, p. 426, nos. 1, 5, 9, 12, 4, respectively.

[72] Stevens, *Music and Poetry*, p. 426, nos. 3, 4, 13.

[73] Stevens, *Music and Poetry*, p. 426, nos. 2, 5.

[74] Stevens, *Music and Poetry*, p. 426, no. 8.

[75] For description and contents, see Montague Rhodes James, *A Descriptive Catalogue of the Manuscripts in the Library of St. John's College Cambridge* (Cambridge: University Press, 1913), pp. 273-74; and *A Catalogue of the Manuscripts Preserved in the Library of the University of Cambridge*, 5 vols. (Cambridge: University Press, 1856-67), 5:588.

[76] The manuscript is dated ca. 1525-30 by Edwin Warren in the Critical Notes (p. I) to his edition of *Robert Fayrfax: Collected Works* 1: The Masses, Corpus Mensurabilis Musicae 17 ([Rome:] American Institute of Musicology, 1959).

[77] *Grove* 5:409.

[78] *Grove* 1:245; Harrison, *MMB, p. 29.*

[79] Baillie, "Some Biographical Notes," pp. 48-49.

[80] It is found next in Cp 471-74 (ca. 1540-47).

[81] Misled by the presence of this earlier music, Warren dates the MS from "before 1509" (*Life and Works of Robert Fayrfax*, p. 54).

[82] For Gwynneth, see Baillie, "A London Gild," p. 18; David Harris, "Musical Education in Tudor Times," *Proceedings of the Royal Music Association* 65 (1938-39): 125; and *MGG* 5: cols. 1138-39.

[83] Harrison, *MMB*, pp. 432-33.

[84] *Pontifices almi* is the seventh antiphon at matins, *O per omnia* is the fifth antiphon at lauds, *Summe Dei* is the seventh respond at matins and *Qui tres pueros* is its verse, and *Congaudentes exsultemus* is the sequence of the mass.

[85] Harrison, *MMB*, p. 458.

[86] Hughes-Hughes, *Catalogue* 1:139, 204, 212; 2:123-24; 3:57, 103, 181, 235, 313, 375; Henry Davey, *History of English Music* (London: J. Curwen, 1895), p. 133; Kenton Parton, "On Two Early Tudor Manuscripts of Keyboard Music," *Journal of the American Musicological Society* 17 (1964): 81-83; John Ward, "The Lute Music of Ms. Royal Appendix 58," *Journal of the American Musicological Society* 13 (1960: 117-25).

[87] Lbl 58, f. 5. Rossell Hope Robbins notes that this "single quatrain . . ., often erroneously cited as a choice specimen of popular verse, is quite a sophisticated piece." *Secular Lyrics of the XIVth and XVth Centuries*, 2nd ed. (Oxford: Clarendon Press, 1956), p. xxxviii.

[88] Stevens, *Music and Poetry*, p. 130.

[89] See the useful comparative table of musical examples in Nigel Davison, "The *Western Wind* Masses," *The Musical Quarterly* 57 (1971): 432-33.

[90] Davison postulates that the king came upon the *Western wind* tune in about 1510 and set it as a three-part song, placing the tune in the tenor part. Taverner then took the king's treble part and used it as the cantus firmus of his own Mass. It is a fascinating hypothesis. But Davison does not go on from there to place Taverner's Mass in the second decade of the century. Instead, he invokes the rarity of secular cantus firmus settings in England, and wonders if Taverner did not adopt the continental practice "when Henry's reforms, and the 1549 Act of Uniformity in particular, effectively stifled further progress." Then he backs off and places Taverner's setting "some time shortly before 1530, when he gave up music for a less honorable career" (pp. 433-35). The leap from the 1510s to the 1540s is incorrect, as we shall see. But even were it not, Davison's subsequent retreat from that period back to the 1520s would be weakly based, for there were no "reforms" before 1530. His argument bears sad witness to the fact that the arguments of John Foxe and E. H. Fellowes continue to paralyze the work of scholars of Tudor music.

[91]Ff. 17v-18. The identification was made by John Caldwell in a letter in *Music and Letters* 44 (1963): 208-209. For the contents of Lbl 56, see Hughes-Hughes, *Catalogue* 1:205, 460; 3:79, 315.

CHAPTER 4

[1]For Longland, who succeeded Bishop Atwater in 1521, see Derek Wilson, *A Tudor Tapestry* (Pittsburgh: University of Pittsburgh Press, 1972), pp. 37-54.

[2]*Visitations in the Diocese of Lincoln 1517-1531* 3: 11-13.

[3]Cambridge, D. Can. L. 1496. Cunstable succeeded Henry Horneby as warden in 1518. He may have been educated at St. John's College, where he endowed a scholarship. Emden, *Cambridge*, p. 155; Venn and Venn, *Alumni* 1:380.

[4]Educated at Cambridge, he later became a chaplain at Cardinal College. Venn and Venn, *Alumni* 3:52.

[5]Cambridge, B. Civ. L. 1517-18 (?). Venn and Venn, *Alumni* 3: 147.

[6]Oxford, B.A. 1514, D. Theol. 1522. Joseph Foster, *Alumni Oxonienses: the Members of the University of Oxford, 1500-1714.* 4 vols. (Oxford: Clarendon Press, 1891-92), 2:1231.

[7]Cambridge, B.A. 1506, B. Theol. 1518. Penbroke College, fellow 1506. Venn and Venn, *Alumni* 4:123.

[8]Oxford, Magdalen College, B.A. 1510; All Souls, fellow 1511; D. Theol. 1515; Eton, fellow 1518. Foster, *Alumni* 2:1601.

[9]*Visitations in the Diocese of Lincoln 1517-1531* 1:xcvi.

[10]*Visitations* 3:12.

[11]John Tonnard, probably his father, had been a conduct at Tattershall in 1495-96.

[12]H. Salter, ed., *A Subsidy Collected in the Diocese of Lincoln in 1526,* Oxford Historical Society 53 (Oxford: B.H. Blackwell, 1909), p. 52. The listing of payments here suggests by its order that the master of the choristers and the organist were chosen from among the chaplains. Such was almost certainly not the case. These men must have been clerks, as there were in the earlier Tattershall accounts.

[13]*Valor ecclesiasticus* 4:42-44. See also Edward Cutts, *Parish Priests and their People in the Middle Ages in England* (London: Society for Promoting Christian Knowledge, 1898), pp. 392-407.

[14]Cambridge, B. Can. L. 1510; incorporated at Oxford 1522. Dean of Lincoln 1528-44. Venn and Venn, *Alumni* 2:354.

[15]Oxford, B.A. 1525: Foster, *Alumni* 2:1267.

[16]Oxford, B.A. 1520 (?); Foster, *Alumni* 1:834.

[17]At the end of its report on Tattershall, the *Valor* lists the obits of the collegiate church. The context makes it clear that all the men whose obituary anniversaries were celebrated were members of the foundation: among those mentioned here John Gigur, Thomas Gibons, Henry Horneby, Thomas Howard, Edward Oky, Henry Porter and Andrew Tott were all found in earlier lists of chaplains and clerks at the college. We may infer, then, that the following men, found only in the *Valor* obit list, were at one time members of the foundation: Thomas Bradbrige, Robert Collyn, Richard Englyshe, John Madenwell, Robert Mawr, William Newbride, Richard Parker (perhaps the same man who was *informator* at Magdalen College, 1500-1503), John Pyllyt, Thomas Ryby, Robert Sudbury, William Symson, Richard Westby, Robert Whallay and John Wynman.

[18]Bishop Longland took refuge in the castle during the uprising, but it too fell to the rebels for a few days. Hennage, who two years earlier had led the fellows of the college in signing the oath of supremacy (*LP* 7, nos. 891, 1121), was suspected by Henry of wavering loyalties until Suffolk cleared his name (*LP* 11, nos. 552, 567, 1043, 1084). For an analysis of the uprising and the role played in it by the Lincolnshire gentry, see M. E. James, "Obedience and Dissent in Henrician England: The Lincolnshire Rebellion 1536," *Past and Present*, No. 48 (August 1970): 3-78.

CHAPTER 5

[1]Emden, *Oxford* 1:xxxiii-xxxiv.

[2]A. R. Myers, *England in the Late Middle Ages (1307-1536)*, 2nd rev. ed. (London: Penguin, 1963), p. 161; Knowles, *Religious Orders* 3:157.

[3]A complete list of the powers of his papal instrument is given in A.G. Dickens, *The English Reformation* (New York: Schocken, 1964), p. 39.

[4]*LP* 4, no. 650.

[5]For the surrender of St. Frideswide's, see *LP* 4, no. 1137. Instances of gifts are found in the same source, nos. 3838, 4452, 4483, 5144, 5593.

[6]Knowles, *Religious Orders*. pp. 161-62, 470. A particularly ugly attempt at blackmail by Longland on Wolsey's behalf is recorded in *LP* 4, no. 2378.

[7]Henry's concern in the matter is documented in *LP* 4, nos. 4509, 4513; in the *State Papers, King Henry VIII* (II vols,; London: His (Her) Majesty's Stationery Office, 1830-52), 1:317; and in *Original Papers, Illustrative of English History*, ed. Henry Ellis, 2nd series (4 vols.; London: Harding & Lepard, 1827), 2:17-21.

[8]*LP* 4, nos. 376, 432.

[9]*Original Papers*, 1st series (3 vols.; London: Harding, Triphook & Lepard, 1824), 1:180-84; abstracted in *LP* 4, no. 995.

[10]A mutilated document in the Public Record Office in London (abstracted in *LP* 4, no. 1087) through which Wolsey leased the lands of a dissolved priory incorporated by his college to one George Throckmorton on 14 February 1525 indicates the Cardinal's concern in staffing his college chapel and his efforts to enlist aid in doing so: "Ten marks will be allowed to him [Throckmorton] for the finding of . . . yearly to sing in

the priory." "The priory" can only refer to the chapel of the former priory of St. Frideswide's.

[11]*LP* 4, no. 1499.

[12]*LP* 4, no. 1499, items 18, 1 and 26, respectively. Various drafts of the statutes are found in Lpro E 36/102-103. The original statutes, various emendations and an amended set dating from 1527 are printed in *Statutes of the Colleges of Oxford* (3 vols.; Oxford: J.H. Parker, 1853), 2, no. 11 (pp. 1-121). One contemporaneous copy includes changes that were, according to the unnamed editor, "apparently intended as adaptations of the Statutes of a College at Cambridge" that Wolsey wished to found (p. 3).

[13]John Harvey, "The Building of Cardinal College, Oxford," *Oxoniensia* 8-9 (1943-44): 138-39.

[14]Walter George Hiscock, *A Christ Church Miscellany* (Oxford: University Press, 1946), pp. 2, 198.

[15]Harvey, "The Building of Cardinal College," pp. 145-52.

[16]*LP* 4, no. 2734 (29 December 1526).

[17]*LP* 4, no. 1845 (30 December 1525).

[18]Harvey, "The Building Works and Architects of Cardinal Wolsey," *Journal of the British Archaeological Association*, 3rd series, 8 (1943): 54.

[19]Foxe, *Acts and Monuments* 2:250.

[20]W. Gordon Zeeveld, *Foundations of Tudor Policy* (London: Methuen, 1969), pp. 18-19.

[21]The boys were promoted to petty canons when their voices changed. *Statutes of the Colleges of Oxford* 2:49.

[22]Regarding the officers of the chapel, see *Statutes of Oxford* 2:49-51.

[23]Leonard Hutten, who entered the college in 1574 (it was then Christ Church College), became a canon there in 1599, and was later one of the contributors to the King James Bible. Hutten's list is printed in *Elizabethan Oxford*, ed. Charles Plummer, Oxford Historical Society 8 (Oxford: Clarendon Press, 1887), pp. 58-59.

[24]For more complete information and dates concerning these men and others mentioned in this chapter, consult the following biographical registers: Charles William Boase, *Register of the University of Oxford* 1, Oxford Historical Society 1 (Oxford: Clarendon Press, 1885); Cooper, *Athenae Cantabrigienses*; Emden, *Cambridge* and *Oxford*; Joseph Foster, *Alumni Oxonienses: the Members of the University of Oxford, 1500-1714* (4 vols.; Oxford: Clarendon Press 1891-92); Venn and Venn, *Alumni Cantabrigienses* 1.

[25]Surely he is Baggard.

[26]Shorton received the degree of D. Theol. from Cambridge in 1512 and became master of Pembroke Hall in 1516, which position he held until coming to Oxford. He was a canon of Lincoln Cathedral and St. George's Chapel, Windsor.

[27]On 17 February 1527, Shorton was reimbursed £11.2.0, the expenses he incurred in bringing "sundry scholars from Cambridge to Oxford." *LP* 4, no. 3534.

[28]Zeeveld, *Foundations of Tudor Policy*, pp. 29-30.

[29]This list has been compiled from the biographical registers mentioned above (see note 24) as well as from the following sources: Anthony à Wood, *Fasti Oxonienses*, Part 1: 1500-1640, ed. Philip Bliss (London: F. C. and J. Rivington, 1815); John Strype, *The Life and Acts of Matthew Parker* (3 vols.; Oxford: Clarendon Press, 1821); and Strype, *Memorials of John Cranmer*, new ed. (2 vols.; Oxford: Clarendon Press, 1812). Information concerning the precise identification of Bayley, Goodman, Harman and Wotton is either incomplete or contradictory in these sources. Among the names in the list in Strype's *Parker* (p. 10) is "Flor. Dominick," who Zeeveld suggests may be Florentius Volusene, a tutor of Wolsey's natural son Thomas Winter (p. 28). Zeeveld's list (pp. 28-29) relies heavily on Wood and Strype--misidentifying the man Bayley as Richard Baily, and accepting Wood's mention of John Taverner as a canon without comment--and should not be accepted without question.

[30]The career and theological writings of this extraordinary man are discussed in William A. Clebsch, *England's Earliest Protestants, 1520-1535* (New Haven: Yale University Press, 1964), pp. 78-153.

[31]*LP* 13, no. 817.

[32]*LP* 13, no. 817.

[33]*DNB* 7:741.

[34]Strype, *Parker*, p. 11.

[35]Strype, *Cranmer*, p. 3.

[36]The others were Laurence Barber (philosophy), Thomas Brynknell (theology), Matthew Calphurne (Greek), John Clement, a friend of Erasmus and son-in-law of More, and then Thomas Lupset (humanity), Nicholas Kratzer, friend of Durer and Holbein (mathematics), and Thomas Musgrave (medicine). Andrew Clark, *The Colleges of Oxford* (London: Methuen, 1891), p. 306; for Lupset, see Zeeveld, *Foundations of Tudor Policy*, p. 25.

[37]Lpro S. P. 1/39, f. 118; abstracted in *LP* 4, no. 2457.

[38]Harrison discusses Newark College and clarifies the long-muddled biography of Aston in *MMB*, pp. 27-30.

[39]Lpro S. F. 1/39, f. 139; abstracted in *LP* 4, no 2564. "Dene" may refer to Higden, who is referred to in order sources as "Mr. Dene" or "Mr. Dean." Hiscock, p. 215, notes that "a pair of organs" (i.e., an organ) in the chapel is mentioned in records of the Priory of St. Frideswide and the city of Oxford in 1545 and 1546. Whether the latter reference is to the former priory's organ or to a new instrument obtained by Wolsey on Longland's suggestion is unknown.

[40]Something is amiss here: Longland's letter was written, remember, on 17 October, only *two* days before the Feast of St. Frideswide. Might Wolsey have been referring to the next festival in her honor, the Feast of the Translation of St. Frideswide four months later on 11 February? Very probably not, for Longland's letter speaks with a palpable

sense of urgency; with four months on hand, he would have had more than enough time to find a suitable candidate for the post, not merely an interim man from within the chapel.

[41]Note, however, that contrary to the original statutes of the college, the organist would also be director of the choir, rather than chosen from among the clerks.

[42]The editors of *TCM* state that Taverner arrived at Oxford by November 1526, citing Lpro M/36/102 as the source of their information (1:xlviii). I have been unable to find the corroboration of that statement there.

[43]Lpro E/36/102, ff. 2-4. John Lubyns was being paid a salary of £10, plus 12d for each day he spent at the site, in 1528. Wolsey apparently considered the post of *informator* equivalent in stature to that of chief architect of the college. For Lubyns, see Harvey, "The Building Works," p. 57.

[44]*LP* 4, no. 3576 (13 November 1527), in which the Bishop of Exeter encloses in a letter to Wolsey a note from a young scholar praising the college. See also no. 3804 (14 January 1528).

[45]*Calendar of State Papers, Venetian* 4:515.

[46]*VCH Oxford* 3, ed. H. E. Salter and Mary Lobel (London: Oxford University Press, 1954), pp. 228-29.

[47]*LP* 4, nos. 1836 (23 December 1525) and 2258 (18 June 1526).

[48]*LP* 4, no. 4603. The Earl's letter is printed in full, and his chapel choir described in detail, in Sir John Hawkins, *A General History of the Science and Practice of Music* 1:384-86.

[49]*Statutes of Oxford* 2:56-58.

[50]*Statutes of Oxford* 2:165. This antiphon is listed only in the revised statutes of July 1527.

[51]*Statutes of Oxford* 2:59-68, 135-36.

[52]*Grove* 8:323.

[53]See John Bergsagel, "The Date and Provenance of the Forrest-Heyther Collection of Tudor Masses," *Music and Letters* 44 (1963):240-48.

[54]Oxford, B.A. 1518; Cambridge, M.A. 1523; B. Theol. and D. Theol.

[55]For a brief discussion of the rise of the Lollards and their connections with English Lutherans, see Dickens, *The English Reformation,* Chapter 2 ("The Abortive Reformation").

[56]*LP* 4, nos. 3962, 3968, 3999, 4004, 4017, 4073-75, 4125, 4135, 4150; *Original Papers,* 2nd series, 2:17ff.; 3rd series (4 vols.; London: Bentley, 1846), 1:239ff., 2:77ff., 138ff. A sensitive account of the episode is found in H. C. Maxwell Lyte's *History of the University of Oxford from the Earliest Times to the Year 1530* (New York: Macmillan, 1886), pp. 459-68. The quotations of Dalaber's story are from Foxe, *Acts and*

Monuments 2:438-41. Related material is found briefly in Foxe's treatment of John Frith in 2:250-51.

[57]Dalaber's account erroneously gives the year as 1526.

[58]Lyte, *History of the University of Oxford* p. 465 (from Ob M3 282 [Register FF]).

[59]The letters (*LP* 4, nos. 3962, 3968) were written on 24 and 26 February. The later letter, dated Ash Wednesday, was assigned the incorrect date of 25 February by the editors of *LP*, who apparently did not take into account the fact that 1528 was a leap year.

[60]And from there to London in Wolsey's custody, according to Lyte, *History of the University of Oxford*, p. 466.

[61]*DNB* 8:276.

[62]*LP* 4, no. 4175 (19 March 1528).

[63]On 3 March, Longland sent a note to Wolsey urging the arrest of Farman and Gough (*LP* 4, no. 4004). As both officials were then in London, the note was probably delivered within an hour of its dictation, and the arrests must have followed immediately. A connection between the interrogation of these Lutherans and the arrest of Fryer in London on the following day (*LP* 5, no. 4017) is therefore probable.

[64]*LP* 4, no 4511.

[65]Foxe, *Acts and Monuments* 2:251. In the original edition of 1563, Foxe referred to Taverner as "a man very singular in music;" this phrase was replaced in later editions by "the good musician."

[66]Denis Stevens, "New Light on Taverner," paper delivered before the Greater New York Chapter of the American Musicological Society in New York City on 13 March 1965.

[67]Lpro. S. P. 1/47, f. 111; abstracted in *LP* 4, no. 4704.

[68]*LP* 4, no. 4125.

[69]*LP* 4, no. 4075.

[70]The men named in Foxe (2:251) as having marched in this procession are Betts, Clerk, Dyott, Edon, Radley, Sumner, Taverner, and Udal, two Benedictines, two Cistercians, and two Augustinians.

[71]*Original Papers*, 3rd series, 2:139; abstracted in *LP* 4 no. 4135. This report contrasts remarkably with one given by Higden at the height of the trouble. Having prepared the reformed statutes of the college, Higden asked on 24 February that Wolsey add another statute concerning

> the good ordering of the ministers of the chapel; for diverse of them are very negligent, and often absent, especially from matins and the mass of requiem "daily both in holidays, and also from matins in principal feasts." [He] wishes a statute for the choir, and a fine of 2d. for absence from matins, from prime ld., from high

mass 2d., from evensong 1d., from compline and the hours 1/2d., holy water on Sundays 3/4d., from procession 2d.....*LP* 4, no. 3961.

[72]*LP* 4, no 6100.

[73]John Charles Fox, *The Parish Registers of England* (London: Methuen, 1910), p. 142.

[74]Foxe maintained that their deaths were caused by a six-month long diet of salt fish and incarceration in "a deep cave . . . through the filthy stench thereof they were all infected." This explanation loses its credibility in the fact of the contradictory account contemporary with the events in a letter of 1 September 1528 from Thomas Byrd, a chaplain at Magdalen, to Cromwell, abstracted in *LP* 4, no. 4690.

[75]Fryer's letter of 16 September is abstracted in *LP* 4, no. 4741. A recent speculation upon the connection between Edward Fox (see p. 58), Fryer, and Edward Higgons, the probable scribe of the Lambeth and Caius choirbooks, appears in Geoffrey Chew's "The Provenance and Date of the Caius and Lambeth Choir-books," *Music and Letters* 51 (1970):107-17. For biography of Fryer, see *DNB* 20:301. Chew's tentative dating of the two choirbooks as "not before the late 1520's" (p. 117), based in good part on the confusing of two unrelated men named John Fryer, rests on sand.

[76]Foxe, *Acts and Monuments* 2:251.

[77]The list of these monasteries, whose members numbered five or fewer and whose total income (including that of St. Peter and St. Paul) was perhaps £400, is in Knowles, *Religious Orders* 3:470. For dates and other information concerning their suppressions between 13 April and 31 May, see *LP* 4, nos. 4229, 4259, 4297, 4307, 4424, 5076.

[78]Emden, *Oxford* 3:2080; *VHC Suffolk*, ed. William Page (2 vols.; London: Archibald Constable, 1907, 1911), 2:142-43.

[79]*Original Papers*, 1st series, 1:185-90. Capon's letter ends with information concerning the gifts of food sent for the dinners held at the college and in the town on the feast-day, a payment of 6s.8d to the curates of the town "for the pains and labors taken in our procession," the receipt of 175 tons of Caen stone, and the expectation of 1100 tons more before the coming Easter, for the buildings of the college.

One Nycolas Lentall joined the Fraternity of Parish Clerks in London in 1516 as a layman; a clerk named William Lentall joined the guild in 1517 (Lgl 4889). One of these men may have been the Ipswich Lentall.

[80]An entry in *LP* 4, no. 6788, noting payment by Cardinal College, Oxford, of 5s.1d. for a "dinner of Mr. Lentall and others" on 23 September 1530; probably refers to Philip Lentall, a clerk to the auditor of the college (*LP* 4, no. 6748) and later an auditor of the attainted lands of the monastery of Jervaulx (*LP* Addenda, nos. 1268, 1385, 1475, 1591). It probably does not refer to the musician Lentall, who would have received his commons annually as a member of the chapel. See Appendix B.

[81]*LP* 4, no. 5052.

[82]Letter of 10 January from William Goldwin, the schoolmaster, to Wolsey, in which he enclosed examples of the script of certain boys who would soon be able to speak Italian; abstracted in *LP* 4, no. 5159.

[83]*LP* 4, no. 5792.

[84]*LP* 4, nos. 1944, 4661, 4778, 4793, 6447; Addenda, no. 238. Alvard, appropriately, was appointed keeper of York Place in 1530 (*LP* 4, nos. 6301, 6709). Like Cromwell, he remained loyal to Wolsey during the brief period between the cardinal's fall and his death in November 1530 (no. 6225).

[85]Lpro S. P. Hen. VIII 235, f. 290; abstracted in *LP* Addenda, no. 599.

[86]Letter from John Harvey to the author, 16 March 1968. Mr. Harvey suggested there: "What happened to the second master, John Lebons or Lovyns, after that date, we do not know (in my *English Mediaeval Architects*, p. 158, there is an error in the last paragraph; the whole entry ascribed to 1537 should be referred to 1515). So there may have been urgent need for Wolsey to get into touch with the new man who was putting on Redman's shoes."

[87]The story of the divorce case, the canonic and diplomatic issues involved, and Wolsey's role in the proceedings, is told in J. J. Scarisbrick, *Henry VIII* (Berkeley and Los Angeles: University of California Press, 1968), Chapters 6-8. Wolsey's last months are recounted in A. F. Pollard, *Wolsey* (rev. ed.; New York: Harper, 1966), Chapter 7.

[88]See, for example, *LP* 4, no. 5749, and Pollard, *Wolsey*, p. 236.

[89]*Calendar of State Papers, Spanish, 1485-1558*, ed. Gustav A. Bergenroth *et al.* (15 vols.; London: Her (His) Majesty's Stationery Office, 1862-1954), 4, no. 211.

[90]*LP* 4, no. 6076.

[91]*LP* 4, nos. 6574-78.

[92]*LP* 4, no. 6579.

[93]Lpro E/36/104, f. 8. See Appendix B.

[94]*LP* 4, no. 6788, item viii, notes a payment to Mr. Burgis, the chanter, of £6 "pro libris in torto cantu factis" and £6.5.0 "pro libris infracti cantus."

[95]Lpro E/36/104, ff. 3-6v.

[96]F. 7v. Two chaplains, Mason and Tapitow, replaced him for the third term, and were paid the sum of 18s.7d. His successor, John Benbow, arrived for the fourth term, and received two pounds for that term. (The MS gives this last sum as ten pounds; but this is a mistake, for the total sum that follows is £7.18.7.)

[97]F. 11v: "Pro diversis que apparent in billa sua." See also *LP* 4, no. 6788, item 7.

[98]F. 12; *LP* 4, no 6788, item 7.

[99]F. 13: "Pro expensis Domini Whitbroke equitantis pro Benbow ad mandatum Domini decani. 20 Junij. vi^{s}viij^d." See also *LP* 4, no. 6788, item 7.

[100]Baillie, "Some Biographical Notes," p. 56.

[101]*LP* 5, no. 47.

[102]*LP* 5, no. 185.

[103]*LP* 5, no. 1647.

[104]*Statutes of Oxford* 2:149-94.

[105]*Elizabethan Oxford*, p. 59.

[106]Nor was there provision for a choirmaster, whose duties were transferred to a vicar who was to be precentor. But music was well provided for; one statute requires that all members of the college be able to play an instrument and be competent in plainsong. *Statutes of Oxford* 2:192-94; Nan Cooke Carpenter, *Music in the Medieval and Renaissance Universities* (Norman: University of Oklahoma Press, 1958), pp. 169-70.

CHAPTER 6

[1]Eilert Ekwall, *The Concise Oxford Dictionary of English Place-names.* 4th ed. (Oxford: Clarendon Press, 1960), p. 54.

[2]For this evidence, see the following: J.W.F. Hill, *Medieval Lincoln* (Cambridge: University Press, 1947), pp. 314 ff; Pevsner and Harris, *Lincolnshire*, pp. 462-77; Thompson's comprehensive *History and Antiquities of Boston*; and *VHC Lincoln*, 2 vols. (1: London and Lincoln: John Saunders, 1834; 2: ed. William Page: London: James Street, 1906), *passim*. For the port of Boston, see Winifred I. Haward, "The Trade of Boston in the Fifteenth Century," *Lincolnshire Architectural and Archaeological Society* 41 (1932-33): 169-78; and E.M. Carus-Wilson and Olive Coleman, *England's Export Trade, 1275-1547* (Oxford: Clarendon Press, 1963).

[3]I.e., the Witham.

[4]A reference, in all probability, to the Guild of the Blessed Virgin.

[5]Lucy Toulmin Smith, ed. *The Itinerary of John Leland in or about the Years 1535-1543*, 4 parts in 5 vols. (London: Centaur Press, 1964), 5:33-34.

[6]Smith, *Leland*, 4:114.

[7]Lbl 4795, Register of the Guild of Corpus Christi in Boston: "Johannes Tavernar de Boston" was admitted in 1537, f. 63v; "Johannes Taverner" named treasurer from 1541 to 1543, f. 64r-v. Taverner's tenure of one of the two treasurers' posts for three successive years was unusual practice for the guild, and may indicate that the guild experienced difficulty in finding someone else willing to assume the responsibility. George Cutteler, the other treasurer appointed in 1542, also remained in that post in 1543. A decline of the guild, and probably also of the town, may be seen in the shrinking list of admissions to the fraternity: three in 1536, inexplicably, for the guild in Boston was spared dissolution during the reign of Edward VI.

[8]Records for the Guild of the Blessed Virgin are scant. No register of membership exists. When Thompson wrote his massive history in the mid-nineteenth-century, he had recourse to the annual account books of the guild for the years 1514-46 (which

included the names of aldermen and treasurers only), and an inventory of goods made in 1534. Fifty years later, the editor of *VCH Lincoln* 2 could find only an account for the year 1525-26 and rent rolls for 1540 and 1545-46.

[9]C.W. Foster and A.H. Thompson, "The Chantry Certificates for Lincoln and Lincolnshire, Returned in 1548 (continued)," *Associated Architectural Societies' Reports and Papers* 37 Part 2 (1925): pp. 258-60. The complete report on Boston is found on pp. 255-72.

[10]Thompson, *Boston*, pp. 141-46.

[11]Thompson, *Boston*, pp. 136-37 and 183n.

[12]Thompson, *Boston*, p. 138.

[13]LIao Bailiffs' *Compoti*, Guild of the Blessed Virgin, Boston, 1518-19; summary in LIao Miscellaneous Donations 169; published abstract in *Archivists' Report*, no. 13 (Lincoln: Lincoln Archives Committee, 1961-62), pp. 11-12.

[14]*VCH Lincoln* 2:452.

[15]These payments were supported by endowed funds. Thus, for instance, John Robinson, merchant of the Staple of Calais who died in March 1525, "fundavit duos Capellanos in Gilda beatae Mariae Virginis in Ecclesia Parochialis Sancti Botulphi de Boston imperpetuum celebraturos pro animabus etc." Gervase Holles, *Lincolnshire Church Notes*, ed. R.E.G. Cole, LRS 1 (Lincoln: LRS, 1911), p. 155.

[16]Foster and Thompson, "Chantry Certificates," pp. 258-60; also A.F. Leach, *English Schools at the Reformation 1546-8* (New York: Russell and Russell, 1968), Part 2, p. 136.

[17]As "master of the plays," Harrison was probably charged with the production of the festivities for the Feast of Corpus Christi as well as other entertainments given in the town. Evidence of where these entertainments were held is found in an order of 1578 that "there shall be no more plays nor interludes in the church, nor in the chancel, nor in the hall, nor in the school house" (Thompson, *Boston*, pp. 210-11).

[18]"Dominus Andree Hedley" and "Willelmo Harison" are listed among the 12 chaplains at St. Botolph's in the account of Bishop Atwater's visitation there on 5 July 1519. Bowker, *An Episcopal Court Book*, p. 118.

[19]Leach, *English Schools* 2:15. The grammar master was not numbered among the chaplains. One of the clerks functioned as organist.

[20]Leach, *English Schools* 2:87. Neither song master nor grammar master is listed among the chaplains or clerks.

[21]Leach, *English Schools* 2:135. The master of the grammar school, John Goodall, was paid the large sum of £20. The master of the choristers, Ralph Waderson, whom I have included among the clerks, received £10.

[22]For "maintenance" (*exhibitio*).

[23]He may be identified with one or both of the entries for a John Wendon in the Fraternity of St. Nicholas in London: clerk, joined 1507; layman, joined 1520. See p. 224 note 52.

[24]*LP* 8, no. 29. The same gift was sent to Cromwell by Robert Pulvertoft (*LP* 5, no. 1204), a member of one of the leading families in Boston; it seems to have been a common token either in anticipation of or in thanks for a favor of some size.

[25]*LP* 18 Part 1, no. 346; 21 Part 1, no. 643.

[26]Boston, Town Hall, Council Minutes 1, ff. 1r-v; also *LP* 20, Part 1, no. 846.

[27]Thompson, *Boston*, pp. 156-57, 454.

[28]LIao Consistory Court Wills 1554-56, f. 182. His will of 18 November 1554 was probated on 3 February 1555. *Calendars of Lincoln Wills* 1:330.

[29]*LP* 14 Part 2, Appendix, no. 23.

[30]*LP* 14 Part 2, Appendix, no. 24.

[31]Gillmyn was also serving the Guild of the Blessed Virgin and Corpus Christi in Stamford, Lincolnshire, in that year. The incumbents, according to the 1548 Chantries Commission report (Foster and Thompson, "The Chantry Certificates . . . ," *Associated Architectural Societies' Reports and Papers* 37 Part 1 [1923-24]: 101; also, G.A.J. Hodgett, ed., *The State of the Ex-Religious and Former Chantry Priests in the Diocese of Lincoln, 1547-1574*, LRS 53 [Hereford: LRS, 1959], p. 24) were William Norwood, of the age of 60 years, by no means fit to serve the cure, and Richard Gilmen, of the age of 42 years, by no means fit to serve the cure." Norwood's salary was £5.6.8, Gillmyn's was £5. "Richard Gilman, singingman" of Boston, died there soon after and was buried in St. Botolph's churchyard. His will, dated 12 December 1548, was probated on 2 March 1549 (LIao Consistory Court Wills 1547-49, f. 187). He should not be confused with the Richard Gilmyn of London, a yeoman of the guard, who is referred to in several entries in *LP* (5:313; 6, no. 562; 10, no. 597, grant 17; 12 Part 2, no. 1311, grant 9; 14 Part 2, nos. 70, 625), or with the Richard Gylman who was a clerk at the parish church of St. Matthew, Friday Street, in 1553-54 (Baillie, "Some Biographical Notes," p. 38).

[32]*LP* 13 Part 2, no. 1211.

[33]A published summary of the contents of the register is found in Thompson, *Boston*, pp. 115-22.

[34]William Boothby, Robert Freeman, Robert Smith, Humphrey Spencely, William Stevenson and John Stowell. One chaplain is not named. Thompson, *Boston*, p. 133.

[35]Edward L. Cutts, *Parish Priests and their People in the Middle Ages in England* (London: Society for Promoting Christian Knowledge, 1898), p. 475.

[36]Thompson, *Boston*, pp. 115-34, 749-53. The Feast of Corpus Christi was traditionally associated with mystery plays, processions and banquets. Several notices of payments to musicians and players for performing on this day and others are found in J. Charles Cox, *Churchwardens' Accounts* (London: Methuen, 1913), *passim*.

[37] The definitive account of the suppression of the friars is found in Knowles, *Religious Orders*, Chapter 28 (pp. 360-66).

[38] For a history of the Boston friars, see *VCH Lincoln* 2:213-17.

[39] The will of William Cawod of Boston (d. 1478), a merchant of the staple of Calais, serves as an example of the integral position of the guilds and friaries in the town. Cawod left 20s each to the Corpus Christi and St. Peter's guilds; 13s.4d to the Guild of the Blessed Virgin; 6s.8d each to the Guilds of St. George and St. Catherine; and "to every other guild in the same church of Boston, 3s.4d to pray for my soul." To the Austin friars, in whose cemetery his wife Anneys was buried, he gave 40s; to the Frey and White friars, 13s4d each; and to the "Friars Preachers," 20s. The cathedral church at Lincoln received 33s.4d. C.W. Foster, "Lincolnshire Wills Proved in the Prerogative Court of Canterbury, 1471-1490," *Associated Architectural Societies' Reports and Papers* 41 (1932-33): 180.

[40] Derek Wilson, *Tudor Tapestry*, p. 151.

[41] Lpro Letters and Papers, Henry VIII, 136, ff. 133-34; printed in *TCM* 1:liv-lv; abstracted in *LP* 13 Part 2, no. 328.

[42] I am indebted to Dr. G.R. Elton (Clare College, Cambridge) for the interpretation of this passage. Dr. Elton notes that the confusion of genders was "quite common in early Tudor language, especially when a (personified) image is in question." Letter to the author, 17 February 1972.

The seventh injunction of the set drawn up by Cromwell in the early autumn, and published in October, ordered "that such feigned images as ye know of in any of your cures to be so abused with pilgrimages or offerings of anything made thereunto, ye shall, for avoiding of that most detestable sin of idolatry, forthwith take down . . ." *English Historical Documents* 5:812.

[43] Lpro Letters and Papers, Henry VIII, 142, ff. 101-102; printed in *TCM* 1:lv; abstracted in *LP* 14 Part 1, no. 101.

[44] Thomas Wright, *Three Chapters of Letters Relating to the Suppression of the Monasteries*, Camden Society 26 (London: Camden Society, 1843), pp. 191-92; abstracted in *LP* 14 Part 1, no. 348, where the date is given incorrectly as 23 February. Knowles' statement (p. 364) that Ingworth "moved north from London at the end of February" on his way to Boston must be modified in light of the dates of Ingworth's and Paynell's letters.

[45] *Original Papers*, 3rd series 3:170-72; abstracted in *LP* 14, Part 1, no. 342.

[46] Perhaps the reference to "tile" was used to mislead Cromwell, to cover up the real (and far more valuable) material of the roofing.

[47] Dickens, *The English Reformation*, pp. 154-60.

[48] There is no record, either, of Taverner's having been involved in the dissolutions of the Lincolnshire monasteries in 1536 and 1539, or of his having taken part in the land speculation that followed these suppressions. See Gerald A.J. Hodgett, The Dissolution of the Monasteries in Lincolnshire (M.A. University of London, 1947).

[49] *VCH Lincoln* 2: 213-17.

[50] Lpro Letters and Papers, Henry VIII, 159, ff. 253-54; printed in *TCM* 1:lv-lvi; abstracted in *LP* 15, no. 628.

[51] *LP* 12 Part 1, no. 1207, item 13. "Chr. Yerburgh" is listed among the members of the Lincolnshire grand jury panel that indicted Lord Darcy, but the name is crossed out.

[52] Charles Bardsley, *A Dictionary of English and Welsh Surnames* (1901, reprint ed., Baltimore: Genealogical Publishing, 1967), pp. 832, 834; Henry Harrison, *Surnames of the United Kingdom: A Concise Etymological Dictionary*, 2 vols. (London: Morland Press, 1912-18), 2:316.

[53] *LP* 3, no. 3282; *LP* 4, no. 547.

[54] *LP* 17, no. 882.

[55] Llao Consistory Court Wills 1543-45, ff. 170v-175v. The will, dated 15 March 1544, was probated on 27 September 1544. It does not mention Taverner's name. *Calendars of Lincoln Wills* 1:347-48.

[56] Boston, Town Hall, Council Minutes, 1, f. lv; *LP* 20, no. 846, grant 38. The number of other positions held by these men gives added evidence of the prestige associated with the executive council. Bollys, Margarie and Spynke were aldermen of the Guild of the Blessed Virgin; Felde, Hoode and Tupholme were constables of the staple; Tupholme, Wendon and Kyd, respectively, followed Nicholas Robertson as mayor of the borough. Most if not all of these men held extensive property in and around Boston. Robertson was a member of the wealthiest family in early sixteenth-century Boston.

[57] Lpro *Inquisitions post mortem*, MS C. 1442/74/130, and MS E. 150/580/18. These two copies are identical except for minor orthographic variants. See Appendix C. The language of these documents is explained in Sir Frederick Pollock, *The Land Laws*, 3rd ed. (London: Macmillan, 1896), pp. 74-76.

[58] See her will of 1553, pp. 108-109.

[59] Thompson, *Boston* pp. 121, 139; *LP* 3, no. 2411. No single document establishes the relationship between Rose and Thomas Parrowe as one of daughter to father, but the cumulative evidence is unmistakable. Between 1490 and 1550, only two men of that name, Thomas and John, are found in Boston, and they are a generation apart. Both held land and official positions in the town. They must have been father and son. In her will, Rose mentioned John as her brother. Thomas must therefore have been her father.

[60] Boston, Town Hall, List of Records of the Borough of Boston, no. 4/A/1/2, p. 26.

[61] Evidence of his land holdings is documented for the years 1545 (*LP* 20 Part 1, no. 846, grant 87) and 1563 (Boston, Town Hall, Council Minutes, 1 [1 June 1545-1 May 1607], f. 51; *Calendar of the Patent Rolls . . . Philip and Mary*, ed. M.S. Giuseppi. 4 vols. (London: His Majesty's Stationery Office, 1936-39), 2:153.

[62] Boston, Town Hall, Council Minutes 1, f. 44.

[63]C.W. Foster, ed., *The Parish Registers of Boston in the County of Lincoln* 1, 1557-99, LRS, Parish Record Section 1 (Horncastle: LRS, 1914), p. 110.

[64]The date is given in the *Inquisition post mortem.* See Appendix C.

[65]See Rose Taverner's will, pp. 108-109.

[66]Smith, *Leland* 4:182.

[67]See p. 9.

[68]See Appendix D.

[69]LIao Consistory Court Wills 1551-53, f. 271; and 1552-56, f. 177; collated and printed in *TCM* 1:lvi-lvii; *Calendars of Lincoln Wills* 1:304.

[70]Geoffrey Parrowe of Boston (d. 1592) and his wife Rebecca (d. 1595) had two sons, William (b. 1577) and Richard (1581): Foster, *The Parish Registers of Boston* 1:53, 59, 135, 138.

[71]*Calendar of Patent Rolls . . ., Philip and Mary* 2:153.

[72]LIao Consistory Court Wills 1569, 1, f. 48, where he is described has a yeoman of Bamburgh (Baumber). Emma Salmon died 1599, f. 150. *Calendars of Lincoln Wills* 1: 274.

[73]Lpro C. 3/95/53, m. 1-3. It is addressed to "Sir Nicholas Bacon, knight, Lord Keeper of the Great Seal of England." Therefore it dates from no later than 20 February 1579, the date of Bacon's retirement from that post. The first and longest of the three parchment sheets (m. 1: Hodge's suit) is badly crumpled and damaged on the right-hand side, so that a good part of the text is impossible to read. Still, enough of the text remains legible to allow us to understand the suit. See Appendix E. The second and third sheets (m. 2-3: Emma's and Hodge's replies) are much shorter. The ink is very faint on all three sheets.

[74]For patterns of landholdings in England in the 1530s and 1540s, see R.B. Smith, *Land and Politics in the England of Henry VIII* (Oxford: Clarendon Press, 1970), Tables VIII, IX, XIV, and *passim*. Investment in land represented some protection against the inflation that set in during the mid-1530s; see *ibid.*, Table IV, as well as B. H. Phelps Brown and S. V. Hopkins, "Seven Centuries of the Price of Consumables Compared with Builders' Wage-Rates," *Economica*, new series 23 (1956): 296-314.

[75]But remember that such terms as "conservative" and "liberal" are necessarily vague. Bishop Longland and Dr. London, too, were religious conservatives. They cooperated with Cromwell not out of religious conviction but out of loyalty to the king, following the terms of the evolving Henrician settlement wherever those took them. When the settlement approached Protestantism for Dr. London, he went to prison rather than compromise further.

CHAPTER 7

[1]Note, for instance, the diminished octave in the treble towards the beginning of the Mass *Corona spinea* (1:157, fourth measure from the end) that results from their accepting a late sixteenth-century source (Lcm 2035) reading rather than the original

one in Ob 376-81. Such decisions, unfortunately common throughout the edition, deface the musical text.

[2]"John Taverner's Masses," *Music and Letters* 5 (1924): 322-34, and "John Taverner--Part II," *Music and Letters* 6 (1925): 314-29.

[3]These figures refer to volume:page in *TCM*.

[4]Harrison, *MMB*, p. 334.

[5]See p. 243 note 34.

[6]*A Plain and Easy Introduction to Practical Music*, ed. R. A. Harman, 2nd ed. (London: J. M. Dent, 1963), pp. 258-59.

[7]Benham, *LCM*, p. 156.

[8]This fragment was identified and transcribed by Professor Margaret Bent, who graciously permitted its inclusion here.

[9]See p. 226 note 83.

[10]This list excludes the Sarum processional flyleaf noted above, as well as all sources that contain alone among Taverner's compositions the "in nomine" section taken from the *Benedictus* of his Mass *Gloria tibi Trinitas*, in various vocal and instrumental adaptations dating from ca. 1560 until well into the seventeenth century. Nine of these sources are listed in Denis Stevens's edition of *In Nomine. Altenglische Kammermusik für vier und fünf Stimmen*, Hortus Musicus 134 (Kassel: Bärenreiter, 1956), p. 4. To that list should be added the partbook Tsm 389 (late sixteenth century) and the printed books in Lbl, Royal Music Library K. 7. e. 7 and 8: John Day (printer), *Certaine notes set forthe in foure and three parts* (London, 1560), reprinted as *Mornyng and Evenyng Prayer and Communion* (London, 1565).

[11]The information below has been gathered from the manuscripts as well as from the following catalogues: *A Catalogue of the Harleian Manuscripts in the British Museum*, 4 vols. (London: 1808); G.E.P. Arkwright, *Catalogue of Music in the Library of Christ Church Oxford*, 2 vols. (London: Oxford University Press, 1915, 1923); E. H. Fellowes, *The Catalogue of Manuscripts in the Library of St. Michael's College Tenbury* (Paris: Louise Dyer, 1934); Dom Anselm Hughes, *Catalogue of the Musical Manuscripts at Peterhouse Cambridge* (Cambridge: University Press, 1953) and *Medieval Polyphony in the Bodleian Library* (Oxford: Bodleian Library, 1951); Augustus Hughes-Hughes, *Catalogue of Manuscript Music in the British Museum*; 3 vols., M. R. James, *A Descriptive Catalogue of the Manuscripts in the Library of St. John's College Cambridge*; and *A Catalogue of the Manuscripts Preserved in the Library of the University of Cambridge*, 5 vols.

Valuable information concerning Tudor manuscripts is found in the general histories of Benham, Henry Davey, Harrison, Le Huray and Denis Stevens, as well as in numerous articles, critical editions and associated reviews. Indexes of individual collections will be noted at the appropriate places.

[12]Transcribed and edited by Hugh Benham (London: Stainer and Bell, 1971).

[13]Transcribed and edited by Philip Brett (London: Stainer and Bell, 1962).

[14]Edited and arranged by Dom Anselm Hughes, in *Short Mass for three voices* (London: Stainer and Bell, 1961).

[15]The first and second settings, as set out in *TCM* 3, are found as Kyrie eleison and Christe eleison, respectively, in *Short Mass for three voices*.

[16]Edited with an English text by R. R. Terry (London: Oxford University Press, 1921).

[17]Found as Benedictus in *Short Mass for three voices*.

[18]Edited by E. H. Fellowes (London: Oxford University Press, 1936).

[19]Edited with an alternative English text by Philip Brett (London: Stainer and Bell, 1964).

[20]Transcribed and edited by Hugh Benham (London: Stainer and Bell, 1969); and by Edmund Harding in *The Treasury of English Church Music* 1: 1100-1545, ed. Denis Stevens (London: Blandford, 1965), 197-210.

[21]Edited by Hugh Benham (London: Stainer and Bell, 1969).

[22]Edited by Philip Brett (London: Oxford University Press, 1975).

[23]Transcribed and edited in David Josephson, "John Taverner: Smaller Liturgical Works," *American Choral Review* 9 No. 4 (Summer 1967): 34-37.

[24]Transcribed and edited by Hugh Benham (London; Stainer and Bell, 1969).

[25]See W. H. Frere, "Edwardine Vernacular Services," *A Collection of his Papers on Liturgical and Historical Subjects*, Alcuin Club Collections 35 (London: Oxford University Press, 1940), pp. 5-21.

[26]See John Bergsagel, "The Date and Provenance of the Forrest-Heyther Collection of Tudor Masses," *Music and Letters* 44 (1963): 240-48; and the introductions to his editions of *Early Tudor Masses* 1 and 2, EECM 1 and 16 (London: Stainer and Bell, 1962, 1976).

[27]See Paul Doe, "Latin Polyphony under Henry VIII," *Proceedings of the Royal Musical Association* 95 (1968-69): 82-83; and Nicholas Sandon, "The Henrician Partbooks at Peterhouse, Cambridge," *Proceedings of the Royal Musical Association* 103 (1976-77): 106-140.

[28]See Frere, "Edwardine Vernacular Services," pp. 5ff.; E. H. Fellowes, *English Cathedral Music*, 5th ed., rev. by J. A. Westrup (London: Methuen, 1969), pp. 34-40; and Dom Anselm Hughes, "Sixteenth Century Service Music," *Music and Letters* 5 (1924): 335–46.

[29]See Roger Bray, "British Museum Add. Mss. 17802-5 (The Gyffard Part-Books): An Index and Commentary," *Royal Musical Association Research Chronicle* 7 (1969): 31-50. Bray suggests that the MSS may have been compiled over a period of forty years, from the 1540s to the 1580s; he offers good reasons for the latter date, not for the former. Harrison believes that they were compiled during the reign of Mary Tudor, 1553-58 (*MMB*, pp. 288-89).

[30]See the introduction to *Christopher Tye, The Instrumental Music*, ed. Robert Weidner (New Haven: A-R Editions, 1967). See also Ernst Hermann Meyer, *Die mehrstimmige Spielmusik des 17. Jahrhunderts in Nord- und Mitteleuropa* (Kassel: Bärenreiter, 1934); Jeremy Noble, "Le Repertoire Instrumental Anglais: 1550-1585," *La Musique Instrumentale de la Renaissance*, ed. Jean Jaquot (Paris: Editions du Centre National de la Recherche Scientifique, 1955), pp. 91-114; and Warwick A. Edwards, "The

Performance of Ensemble Music in Elizabethan England," *Proceedings of the Royal Musical Association* 97 (1970-71): 113-23.

[31]On f. 46 of Ob 983; Baldwin writes: "Mr. John Tavernor, of Cardinal Wolsey's chapel, who died at Boston and there lieth." On f. 112v of Ob 981, he calls him "homo memorabilis." See Roger Bray, "The Part-Books Oxford, Christ Church, MSS 979-83: An Index and Commentary," *Musica Disciplina* 25 (1971): 179-97.

[32]Edwards, "Performance of Ensemble Music," p. 120.

[33]See Roger Bray, "British Museum MS Royal 24 d. 2 (John Baldwin's Commonplace Book): An Index and Commentary," *Royal Musical Association Research Chronicle* 12 (n.d.): 137-51.

[34]This setting of *Ave regina caelorum* is also found in Lcm 2089, where it is attributed to "Mr. Birde," and in Tsm 369-73. See Joseph Kerman's letter in the *Journal of the American Musicological Society* 16 (1963): 110.

[35]Excluding the little one-voice Kyrie fragment found on the flyleaf of the printed Sarum processional discussed earlier.

[36]Philip Brett, "Edward Paston (1550-1630): A Norfolk Gentleman and his Musical Collection," *Transactions of the Cambridge Bibliographical Society* 4 Part 1 (1964): 51–69.

CHAPTER 8

[1]*Ave Maria* and *Sancte Deus, sancte fortis,* both of which have come down to us with two parts lacking, were almost certainly fully scored throughout; *Sub tuum praesidium,* also missing two parts, may have been fully scored throughout as well.

[2]A detailed discussion is found in his "Formal Design and Construction of Taverner's Works," *Musica Disciplina* 26 (1972): 189-209.

[3]*LCM,* pp. 45, 46.

[4]Excluding final chords with fermatas followed by the double bar. Benham explains: "Where the signature is $\emptyset$ a 'bar' consists of three semibreves; where it is $\mathcal{C}$ of four. $\frac{\phi}{3}$ has two dotted breves to a bar." *LCM,* pp. 226-27.

[5]The relationships in the six-part *Magnificat* are worked out in Benham, "The Formal Design and Construction of Taverner's Works," p. 199.

[6]See p. 66.

[7]"The Problem of Pitch in Sixteenth-Century English Vocal Polyphony," *Proceedings of the Royal Musical Association* 93 (1966-67): 97-112.

[8]A selective list of recommended readings includes, besides Wulstan's article, the introductory and editorial notes in John Bergsagel's editions of *Early Tudor Masses* 1 and 2 (EECM 1, 16); Philip Brett's edition of William Byrd's *Mass for five voices* (London: Stainer and Bell, 1973), with its suggestions for the pronunciation of the Latin mass text; David Chadd's edition of *John Sheppard* 1--*Responsorial Music*

(EECM 17); Paul Doe's edition of *Early Tudor Magnificats* 1 (EECM 4); Frank Harrison's edition of *The Eton Choirbook* 1 (MB 10); and Nicholas Sandon's edition of *John Sheppard* 2--*Masses* (EECM 18). See also David Fallows's review of EECM 16-18 in *The Musical Times* 118 (1977): 949-52; Nigel Davison's review of EECM 16 in *Music and Letters* 57 (1976): 446-48; Sandon's review of EECM 16 in *Early Music* 4 (1976): 325-29; Wulstan's review of EECM 18 in *Music and Letters* 58 (1977): 369-71; Roger Bray's review of EECM 18 in *Early Music* 5 (1977): 233-35, with Sandon's and Bray's correspondence following on pp. 595-99; Doe's review of Davison's edition of the *Western wind* Mass by Christopher Tye, in *The Musical Times* 113 (1972): 487, and subsequent related letters from Davison, Doe and Brett on pp. 768-69 and 972. Recent articles and discussions in books include Bray, "The Interpretation of Musica Ficta in English Music *c.* 1490-*c.* 1580," *Proceedings of the Royal Musical Association* 97 (1970-71): 29-45; Doe, "Another View of Musica Ficta in Tudor Music," *Proceedings of the Royal Musical Association* 98 (1971-72): 113-22; Benham, *LCM*, pp. 28-37; Peter Le Huray, *Music and the Reformation in England 1549-1660* (New York: Oxford University Press, 1967), pp. 90-134; and Peter Phillips, "Performance Practice in 16th-Century English Choral Music," *Early Music* 6 (1978): 195-98.

[9]Fallows notes, for instance, in his review of Sandon's and Chadd's editions of Sheppard for EECM, that as a result of their divergent editorial decisions in the matter of accidentals, "the Sheppard of Sandon's volume sounds entirely different from the Sheppard of Chadd's." *The Musical Times* 118 (1977): 952.

[10]*A Plain and Easy Introduction to Practical Music*, ed. R. Alec Harman (London: J. M. Dent and Sons, 1952), pp. 243-45.

[11]*The Eton Choirbook* 1:xxi.

[12]Clement A. Miller, "Erasmus on Music," *The Musical Quarterly* 52 (1966): 339.

[13]Le Huray, *Music and the Reformation in England 1549-1660*, p. 7.

[14]For evidence of Marian music in Anne Boleyn's circle, see Appendix F. Marian observances continued unabated in the Chapels Royal into the 1540s. When Dr. London purged the royal household at Windsor in March 1543, two of the men accused of heresy were musicians in St. George's Chapel, John Marbeck and Robert Testwood. Marbeck was accused of making an English concordance of a Latin book; he alone among the heretics escaped the stake through the king's intervention. Testwood, a superb singer who had enjoyed Cromwell's patronage, was undone by what seems to have been a sharp sense of humor and love of pranks. On one occasion he ripped the nose off an image of the Blessed Virgin. On another,

> he was set to sing against a famous singer of the King's Chapel, who happened to be in Windsor. The anthem chosen contained a long and elaborate counter verse, addressed to the Virgin, beginning "O Redemptrix et Salvatrix," and in this the singers were to try their skill. As the two voices rose in the air, repeating and combining the words in bouts and turns of intricate sweetness, it was heard that Testwood changed the *O* into *Non*, and the *et* into *nec.* As often as the one singer cried *Oh*, the other answered *No*: each exerted his powers to the utmost in the struggle for the

mastery: and the piece came to an end in a furious combat of sound and doctrine, to the scandal of the congregation.

(Richard Watson Dixon, *History of the Church of England from the Abolition of the Roman Jurisdiction.* 6 vols. [London: G. Routledge, 1881-1902], 2:330.)

[15]Le Huray, *Music and the Reformation in England 1549-1660*, p. 4.

[16]Harrison, *MMB*, p. 251.   See also Lewis Lockwood, "A Continental Mass and Motet in a Tudor Manuscript," *Music and Letters* 42 (1961): 336-47.

[17]The seven settings by Ludford, and probably also William   Mundy's and William Whytbroke's Masses *Upon the square.* See Benham, *LCM*, pp. 10-11.

[18]For surviving examples, see Harrison, *MMB*, pp. 274-80.

[19]See Dom Anselm Hughes, "Sixteenth Century Service Music," *Music and Letters* 5 (1924): 151-52; Ruth Hannas, "Concerning Deletions in the Polyphonic Mass Credo," *Journal of the American Musicological Society* 5 (1952): 155-86; Jeremy Noble's letter, Hannas's reply, and the editor's comment in the *Journal of the American Musicological Society* 6 (1953): 91-93; and Denis Stevens, *Tudor Church Music*, pp. 26-27.

[20]Benham, *LCM*, p. 13.

[21]Other Tudor Masses with this omission include Fayrfax's *Regali* and *O quam glorifica*, and Sheppard's *Be not afraid, Cantate* and *Frences* Masses.

[22]Also in Fayrfax's *O quam glorifica* and *Albanus* Masses, Ashewell's *Jesu Christe*, and Sheppard's *Western wind.*

[23]As do those in Aston's *Videte manus meas* and *Te Deum* Masses, Marbeck's *Per arma justitiae*, Norman's *Resurrexit Dominus* and Sheppard's *Cantate* and *Frences* Masses.

[24]See also Alwood's *Praise Him praiseworthy* Mass, Sheppard's *Be not afraid*, Tallis's *Salve intemerata* and four-part Masses, and the Masses of Christopher Tye. Benham points out that these Masses were all composed after ca. 1525. *LCM*, p. 13.

[25]These numbers refer to volume:page in the *Tudor Church Music* edition.

[26]*Antiphonale Sarisburiense*, pl. 567; Harrison, *MMB*, p. 271; Stevens, *Tudor Church Music*, p. 32.   It was also sung at Procession before Mass when the Feast of St. Michael in Monte Tumba fell on Sunday (Benham, *LM*, p. 49).   During Taverner's adulthood (ca. 1510-45) that occurred in 1513, 1519, 1524, 1530 and 1541.

[27]For example, the openings of the first three movements, and the quartet on "Laudamus te" in the Gloria (1:194-95).

[28]At "pleni sunt caeli" and "dona nobis pacem."

[29]*LCM*, p. 149.

[30]*TCM* 1:lxiii, and Collins, "John Taverner's Masses," p. 331.

[31]For these, see the footnote corrections in the *TCM* editions of *Corona spinea* and Hugh Aston's *Videte manus meas*, and the critical commentaries in John Bergsagel's editions of Richard Alwood's *Praise Him praiseworthy* and Thomas Ashewell's *Ave Maria* (EECM 1), Nicholas Sandon's edition of Sheppard's *Cantate* (EECM 18), and John Satterfield's edition of Tye's *Euge bone* (Christopher Tye, *The Latin Church Music* 1: The Masses [Madison, Wisconsin: A-R Editions, 1972]).

[32]The *TCM* editors, while correcting several of them, knowingly left others intact (*TCM* 1:lxiii) and apparently missed the rest. It is no more necessary to accept their authority here than in the cases of the *Plainsong* Mass, the four-part *Magnificat*, and the *Kyrie Le Roy*--all found in Lbl 17802-805--whose faulty passages have been corrected by Collins and others.

[33]Benham finds rather less to admire in this passage, declaring it "mechanical in a way which Taverner would normally have avoided." *LCM* p. 149.

[34]Charles Burney declared this canon "the finest of all the compositions which I have seen of this author." *A General History of Music* (1776-82; reprint of ed. by Frank Mercer, 2 vols., New York: Dover, 1957), 1:790.

[35]It is placed on the fourth staff from the top in *TCM*, between a countertenor whose range is c-g″ and a tenor whose range is G-b. Its compass of c-d′, while falling within both countertenor and tenor ranges, is closer to the higher voice than to the lower.

[36]The second "Qui tollis" and "tu solis Dominus" of the Gloria, the opening "Sanctus and "caeli et terra" of the Sanctus, and "qui tollis" of the first Agnus Dei.

[37]For instance, at "Et incarnatus est" in the Credo, "qui venit" in the Sanctus, and the second Agnus Dei.

[38]*Tudor Church Music*, p. 32.

[39]At "mundi" (treble, 1:161), "miserere nobis" (treble, 1:161; note its use as a sequential point), "deprecationem" (tenor, 1:162), "nostram" (treble, 1:162), "tu solus" (tenor, 1:164), and retrograde at "Amen" (tenor and bass, 1:166).

[40]*Antiphonale Sarisburiense*, ed. W. H. Frere (London: Plainsong & Mediaeval Music Society, 1901-1926), plate 286.

[41]Benham notes precedents for this unusual voice placement in the ritual music of William Pasche and John Browne, *LCM*, p. 148.

[42]At "tu solus altissimus Jesu Christe" (1:134), "miserere nobis" of the (1:153-54), and "Pleni sunt caeli et terra" (1:146-47).

[43]The first countertenor should enter on e′, not f′ (measure 9).

[44]I have proposed elsewhere that William Byrd knew this famous passage and quoted it in his five-part Mass. Josephson, letter to *The Musical Times* 117 (1976): 739.

[45]The trio of *Western wind* Masses by Taverner, Tye and Sheppard is given a close comparative analysis in Davison, "The *Western Wind* Masses," pp. 427-43.

[46]Doe, "Latin Polyphony," pp. 88-90. The argument is refuted on stylistic grounds in Benham, *LCM*, pp. 150-51.

[47]See pp. 41-44.

[48]See Appendix F.

[49]York, Borthwick Institute of Historical Research, MS Mus. 1.

[50]Baillie has recorded the payment of 4d in 1513 to Raymond Blake, a clerk at St. Thomas' Chapel on London Bridge, "for a masse of iiij parts in pryksonge." "Some Biographical Notes," p. 26.

[51]The reader is warned, however, that this is a minority opinion. The *Western wind* Mass was esteemed highly enough in its own day to elicit new settings by Sheppard and Tye. It remains popular and highly regarded today, the only Mass of Taverner's sung with some frequency, and recorded by a major recording company.

[52]Harrison, letter in *Music and Letters* 46 (1965): 382.

[53]Harrison has found in the *York Processional* and a Sarum Book of Hours an antiphon beginning "O Willelme pastor bone" and continuing with words virtually identical to those of *Christe Jesu pastor bone. MMB*, p. 341. Benham adds that the same antiphon found its way into "several Sarum Primers, including those of 1511 and 1528." *LCM*, p. 229.

[54]See p. 60.

[55]Stevens, *Tudor Church Music*, p. 16.

[56]The editors of *TCM* have provided a generally sensitive substitute tenor.

[57]Benham suggests that "the tercentenary of St. William's canonisation, on 21 March 1526-27, three or four months after Taverner's arrival at Oxford, is a possible occasion for the first performance of the Mass." *LCM*, p. 152.

[58]Here the figuration of the editorial tenor part in *TCM* seems unnecessarily busy.

[59]For a detailed discussion of the parody technique in this Mass, see Benham, "The Formal Design and Construction of Taverner's Works," pp. 202-208.

[60]It is found at "gratias agimus" (treble, 1:99), "[prop]ter magnam gloriam" (countertenor, bass, treble, 1:99-100), "Domine fili" (mean, 1:100), the second "Qui tollis" of the Gloria (bass, countertenor, and probably tenor, 1:102), "Qui sedes" (treble, countertenor, 1:103), "in gloria Dei patris" (treble, 1:105), "et ex patre natum (the full contrapuntal quotation, 1:107), "et propter nostram (probably all voices, 1:108), "secundum scripturas" (treble, 1:110), the final imitative point shared by all four (probably five) voices at "[sa]baoth" (1:115), "Osanna" and "[in ex]celsis" (1:117), "in

nomine Do[mini.] Osan[na in] excelsis" (1:119-20), "qui tollis peccata" (1:123-24), and "dona nobis pacem" (1:124-25).

[61]In this Mass the editors of *TCM* have declined to provide a substitute part because of the ambiguity of "the tonality and the structure of the music" (1:lxi).

[62]It is found in Lbl 17802-805, its lone source, among a group of nine Masses (nos. 24-32 in the partbooks). The first three are the *Western wind* Masses by Taverner, Tye and Sheppard, respectively. While these Masses posed no problems of nomenclature for the scribe, the rest apparently did. They are, in order: Sheppard's *Frences Mass* and *Be not afraid*, whose titles remain puzzling (*John Sheppard 2: Masses*, ed. Nicholas Sandon, EECM 18, pp. x-xi), an untitled four-part Mass by Tallis, Taverner's *Plainsong Mass*, Sheppard's *Plainsong Mass for a mean*. Such titles are found in no other sources or Masses of the period, a fact which may suggest that these Masses were, like Tallis's, originally *Missae sine nomine* to which the scribe of LBl 17802-805 added his own descriptive titles.

[63]The "plainsong" in Sheppard's *Plainsong Mass for a mean* refers as well to its notation, which is in plainsong symbols. In Taverner's Mass, the symbols are the conventional ones of white mensural notation.

[64]Cp 471-74 and Ob 420-22.

[65]CHe 1 and Tsm 1464.

[66]At the unison and the upper and lower third, fourth, fifth and octave as well as the more unusual lower tritone ("miserere nobis" [1:52]) and lower seventh ("suscipe" [1:53]). Note the following sequence of entries on the rising point at "in nomine" (1:64-65): d-a-c'-a'-d-c'-g-f-c'.

[67]There is an alternate version of the second Agnus Dei (1:69), but it is the only duet in the Mass, and it seems far less appropriate stylistically than the second Agnus Dei printed in the body of the Mass in *TCM* (1:67).

[68]In Ob 420-22.

[69]Nigel Davison, "Structure and Unity in Four Free-composed Tudor Masses," *Music Review* 34 (1973): 328-38.

[70]Several of these squares are found in LBl 462, ff. 151v-152. See Baillie, "Squares," *Acta Musicologica* 32 (1960): 178-93, and Harrison, *MMB*, pp. 290-92.

[71]*Graduale Sarisburiense*, ed. W. H. Frere (London: Bernard Quaritch, 1894), pl. 227.

[72]Harrison illustrates the placement of the polyphony in the ritual form in *NOHM* 3:341.

[73]*MMB*, p. 292. Harrison notes, however, that the cantus firmus "resembles both *Salve virgo* and *Virga Jesse floruit* [for the Saturday Lady Mass] but is not identical with either." See also his article, "Music for the Sarum Rite; MS 1236 in the Pepys Library, Magdalene College, Cambridge," *Annales Musicologiques* 6 (1958): 110. Both plainchants are found in the printed Sarum Graduals of 1507 ("Commune Apostolorum," ff. 43 and 44v, respectively), and 1532 ("Commune Sanctorum," ff. 50

and 51v, respectively), in virtually identical versions. The two Alleluias are quite distinct. Certain passages of Taverner's cantus firmus are identical to one chant and others to the other chant. Taverner's cantus firmus is probably a direct and faithful borrowing of a chant whose identity we have not been able to establish, or of another version of one of these chants.

[74]*Processionale Sarum*, ed. W. G. Henderson (Leeds: M'Corquodale, 1882), pp. 24-25; *The Use of Sarum* 2:157.

[75]Harrison, *MMB*, p. 392.

[76]*Missale Sarum*, ed. F. H. Dickinson (Burntisland: J. Parker, 1861-63), col. 850.

[77]*Missale Sarum*, col. 752*.

[78]*Missale Sarum*, col. 848.

[79]Harrison suspects the attribution to Taverner "on account of Baldwin's errors in similar cases (*MMB*, p. 381), but both the melodic contour--especially the descending octave passages--and rhythmic thrust of the two lower lines are consistent with that attribution.

[80]There are settings by Fayrfax, Tallis and Marbeck, as well as by an anonymous composer in the Lambeth choirbook.

[81]The third line of the seventh stanza is almost identical to the opening words of the Introit for the Lady Mass from Purification to Advent: "Salve sancta parens enixa puerpera. . . ."

[82]"Te Deum laudamus, te Dominum confitemur;" "Te eternum Patrem omnis terra veneratur;" "[Sanctus, sanctus,] sanctus, Dominus Deus sabaoth;" "Tu rex gloriae, Christe;" "In te Domine speravi, non confundar in aeternum."

[83]Harrison, *MMB*, p. 331; Benham, *LCM*, p. 152.

[84]Harrison notes the same pun in Josquin's *Virgo prudentissima*; that work is not found in any of the manuscripts of Continental music known to have been in England during the period. *MMB*, p. 331.

[85]As Harrison warns, however, these repetitions may be the work of scribes; all three sources for *O splendor gloriae* date from the last twenty years of the sixteenth century.

[86]The abbreviations are for treble (Tr), mean (M), countertenor (C), tenor (T), bass (B), and full (F).

[87]Perhaps because of its advanced idiom, the late sixteenth-century scribe John Baldwin attributed *O splendor gloriae* to Taverner and Christopher Tye in his partbooks Och 979-83. In Lbl 24 d.2, he attributed the trio on "Et cum pro nobis duram tolerasses vitam" specifically to Tye. H. B. Collins found the dual attribution convincing ("John Taverner--Part II," p. 315), but I find it suspect. While Baldwin's attributions have proved not entirely trustworthy, John Sadler, an unusually reliable scribe, attributed the antiphon in his partbooks Ob 1-5 to Taverner alone.

[88]E. H. Fellowes, in his later edition of the antiphon (London: Oxford University Press, 1936), replaced the substitute tenor provided in *TCM* with a more appropriate one.

[89]See p. 142.

[90]See p. 60.

[91]They are found in Cp 472-74.

[92]The numbers refer to the voices in order as counted from the highest part in the *TCM* edition. (F) stands for full scoring.

[93]By Tallis (only a single part survives), Sheppard, and an anonymous composer.

[94]Benham takes issue with its "unnecessarily frequent departures from equal-note presentation." *LCM*, p. 229.

[95]A final E must be added to (the set) verses eight, nine, ten, thirteen and fourteen.

[96]*MMB*, p. 389.

[97]But the several editorial F sharps on interior cadences that cause cross relations such as those on "quoque" (3:29) should be ignored.

[98]Benham finds the harmonic language of this composition so atypical of Taverner that, citing Baldwin's other misattributions, he "is tempted to wonder if [it] is in fact by [Tallis or Sheppard]." *LCM*, p. 156.

[99]*Antiphonale Sarisburiense*, p. 567 (music); *The Use of Sarum*, ed. W. H. Frere, 2 vols. (Cambridge: University Press, 1898, 1901) 1:120-21 (text and rubrics).

[100]Harrison, *MMB*, p. 107; Benham, *LCM*, p. 18.

[101]Found in Lbl 17802-805, with other settings by Tallis and Sheppard.

[102]The relationship between plainsong and polyphony is worked out in the musical example in Harrison, *New Oxford History of Music* 3:342-43.

[103]The first mean part is stated in Lbl 17804 to be an optional part ("pars ad placitum") by [William] Whytbroke, a claim made plausible by the fact that Whytbroke was a chaplain at Cardinal College, but nonetheless certainly incorrect.

[104]*Antiphonale Sarisburiense*, pl. 50; *The Use of Sarum* 2:57; Harrison, *MMB*, pp. 62, 98; Benham, *LCM*, p. 18. No setting by Taverner has survived for the second Lenten compline respond, *In manus tuas*, although it was set frequently by Tudor composers.

[105]Lbl 17802-805, where it is found with other settings by Tallis, Sheppard, Blytheman and Tye.

[106]Benham, noting that the rubrics call for the chant to be sung by a clerk on feasts and by a boy on other days, concludes from the placement of the cantus firmus that

Taverner wrote his setting for final days at Lenten compline. "The music of Taverner; A Liturgical Study," *Music Review* 33 (1972): 272.

[107]The entire liturgical setting, including the choral plainchant sections, is printed in the Benham edition of this respond.

[108]*Antiphonale Sarisburiense*, pl. 47; *The Use of Sarum* 2:30; Harrison, *MMB*, p. 107; Benham, *LCM*, p. 18.

[109]Found in Lbl 17802-805, with other settings by Cowper, Sheppard and Tallis.

[110]The cantus firmus notes on "[De]o" should be 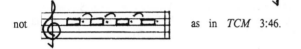 not as in *TCM* 3:46.

[111]*Antiphonale Sarisburiense*, pl. 236; *The Use of Sarum* 2:71; Benham, "The Music of Taverner," p. 272; Harrison, *MMB*, p. 98.

[112]We do not know why he chose this particular text, but many settings of it followed his, and his may have provided the model. The concluding treble motive at "Alleluia" in both of Taverner's five-part settings is used at the same place by John Stanbridge (Och 979-83) and Tallis (*Cantiones Sacrae*, 1575).

[113]*MMB*, p. 369.

[114]Found here with settings by Robert Barber and Robert Johnson.

[115]Thus, for instance, the countertenor point at "Maria Magdalene" in the five-part version is transferred to the treble in the four-part setting.

[116]The same passage in the four-part version seems cramped in comparison.

[117]For the relationship between these two surviving sources, see Roger Bray, "The Part-Books Oxford, Christ Church, MSS 979-983: An Index and Commentary," p. 195. Benham wonders whether this setting "originated as an instrumental piece" (*LCM*, p. 155); but we have no firm evidence to suggest that Taverner wrote any instrumental music.

[118]*Antiphonale Sarisburiense*, pl. 360; *Breviarium ad usum...Sarum*, ed. Francis Proctor and Christopher Wordsworth, 3 vols. (Cambridge: University Press, 1879-86), 3:36; Harrison, *MMB*, p. 69.

[119]This discussion is indebted to Harrison, *MMB*, pp. 395-97 and *NOHM* 3:343.

[120]The edition in *TCM* (3:110-16) is supplied with an editorial bass part. The original is found in the *TCM Appendix*, pp. 34-35.

[121]Collins first proposed this identification more than fifty years ago. "John Taverner-- Part II," p. 316.

[122]Its darkness, though not its severity, would be removed if following Wulstan's prescription it were transposed up a fourth.

[123]*MMB*, p. 345.

[124]See, for example, Benham, *LCM*, p. 155.

CHAPTER 9

[1]See p. 37.

[2]These three manuscripts have been transcribed and edited by John Stevens. *Medieval Carols*, MB 4, contains the Ritson carols; *ETSC*, MB 36, the rest of the Ritson songs and the entire Fayrfax Book; and *MCH*, MB 18, King Henry VIII's Manuscript.

[3]*Music and Poetry*, pp. 9-21.

[4]Maurice Evans, *English Poetry in the Sixteenth Century*, 2nd ed. (New York: Norton, 1967), p. 39.

[5]Stevens, *Music and Poetry*, p. 17.

[6]The book's history is given in H.M. Nixon, "The Book of XX Songs," *British Museum Quarterly* 16 (1951-52): 33-35; its contents, in Howard Mayer Brown, *Instrumental Music Printed Before 1600, A Bibliography* (Cambridge, Mass.: Harvard University Press, 1965), pp. 34-35; its song texts, in Rudolph Imelmann, "Zur Kenntnis der vor-shakespearischen Lyrik: I. Wynkyn de Wordes 'Song Booke,' 1530, II. John Dayes Sammlung der Lieder Thomas Whythornes, 1571, *Jahrbuch der deutschen Shakespeare- Gesellschaft* 39 (1903): 121-140.

[7]Cu Hh. 2. 6. See Rossell Hope Robbins, ed., *Secular Lyrics of the XIVth and XVth Centuries*, 2nd ed. (Oxford: Clarendon Press, 1956), p. 263.

[8]The text is reprinted in Stevens, *Music and Poetry*, pp. 162, 442; in Robbins, *Secular Lyrics*, p. 102; and in Carleton Brown and R.H. Robbins, eds., *The Index of Middle English Verse* (New York: Columbia University Press, 1943), no. 1593.

[9]*ETSC*, no. 30.

[10]Lbl 24 d. 2. Baldwin, a composer and singer, left his post as a lay-clerk at Windsor in 1594 to join the Chapel Royal, where he remained until his death in 1615. His fame rests, however, on the valuable collections of music which he copied out in his superb script. Studies by the late Ernest Brennecke ("A Singing Man of Windsor," *Music and Letters*, 33 [1952]: 33-40, and "The Entertainment at Elvetham, 1591," *Music in English Renaissance Drama*, ed. John Long [Lexington: University of Kentucky Press, 1968], pp. 32-56) have documented Baldwin's contribution to an entertainment for Queen Elizabeth. Other articles on Baldwin are found in *Grove* 1:369-70 and *MGG* 1: columns 1101-1102. For his manuscript, see Roger Bray, "British Museum MS Royal 24 d. 2. (John Baldwin's Commonplace Book): An Index and Commentary," *Royal Musical Association Research Chronicle* 12 (1974): 137-51.

[11]Thus the statement by Stevens in *MCH* that no musical texts "of the early Tudor court-songs occur in later manuscripts" (p. xxii) must be modified. His conclusion, though, still stands: by Elizabeth's reign there was "an almost total collapse of the traditional court-culture. If these songs were symptoms of a 'renaissance' in English song, one might expect to find them used and built upon by later composers." One cannot find them thus used and built upon. Baldwin, in his commonplace book, demonstrates conservative taste and specialized interests as a compiler and anachronistic leanings as a composer, and his labor of love is more a splendid aberration than a reflection of the interests of musicians of his era.

[12]Lbl 24 d. 2, ff. 99v-100. The final section of the song, beginning at the words "such conditions," is in major prolation without augmentation ($\mathbb{C}$). It is in black notation, the void notes (λ) lasting half the length of the full notes ($\blacklozenge$). Baldwin's error occurs in measure 56 in the countertenor part, where his first five notes read a-e-f-e-f.

[13]See, for instance, the account by Philip Brett and Thurston Dart of "Songs by William Byrd in Manuscripts at Harvard," *Harvard Library Bulletin* 14 (1960): 346.

[14]Both the origins and performance practice of this peculiar stylistic trait are open to speculation. Bruce Pattison suggests: "It is probable, though not certain, that these runs were performed by instruments, which doubled the voice parts while the words were being sung" (*Music and Poetry of the English Renaissance*, 2nd ed. [London: Methuen, 1970], p. 85). In Taverner's song, the placement of the last word or the last note of the song shows that the melisma must have been sung. But in the songs of Lbl 5465, Pattison's suggestion seems reasonable, for there the texts end on a cadential resolution just as the fast melismatic passages begin.

[15]Two similar poems are *Love woll I with-oute eny variaunce* (*Secular Lyrics*, No. 151, p. 148) and *Luf will [i] with variance* (*Secular Lyrics*, No. 152, p. 149). Fifteenth-century settings of both are found in *Early Bodleian Music* 2, ed. John Stainer (London: Novello, 1901).

[16]*Leve*: grant, believe. *Governaunce*: conduct, control, *Preuely*: bravely, gallantly. The poem is found without music in Ob 88, f. 93v. It is published in Ewald Fluegel, "Liedersammlungen des XVI. Jahrhunderts, besonders aus der Zeit Heinrich's VIII., II," *Anglia* 12 (1889): 595; and in Rudolf Imelmann, "Zur Kenntnis der vor-shakespearischen Lyrik: I. Wynkyn de Wordes 'Song Booke.' 1530, II. John Dayes Sammlung der Lieder Thomas Whythornes, 1571," *Jahrbuch der deutschen Shakespeare-Gesellschaft* 39 (1903): 132-33.

[17]*XX songes*, no. 13, ff. G. 4v to H. lv.

[18]For instance, two songs by Henry VIII in Lbl 31922 (*MCH*, nos. 23, 64) and two in Lbl 5665 (*ETSC*, nos. 10, 13) use the device. But once again the chief reference is to the songs of Lbl 5465: there nine songs by Browne, Davy, Fayrfax, Newark and Turges (*ETSC*, nos. 22, 23, 30, 33, 34, 39, 40, 48, 59) with triplet-rhythm codas. One of these, it might be noted, is Davy's *Nowe the lawe is led.*

[19]Lbl 18752, f. 72. This manuscript, dating from the first half of the sixteenth century, contains poems, treatises and five essays on music from the compendium *Secretum philosophorum*, first copied down in the fourteenth century.

[20]Published in Fluegel, "Liedersammlungen," p. 594, and Imelmann, "Zur Kenntnis," p. 132. The penultimate line of the poem is clearly lacking a foot. Fluegel reconstructs

it as "and [so I] shall be at your pleasure," Imelmann as "and [ever] shall be at your pleasure." The apparently original complete line in Lbl 18752, is found above in brackets.

[21] *XX songes*, no. 12, ff. G. lv to G. 4v.

[22] One unclear moment occurs in the untexted passage before "My goods also be at your plesur." Surely the notes here were sung to some syllable. Since nowhere else in the song does a melisma on a syllable continue after a rest, we may assume that these notes were sung not to "fyght" but to "my · goods." The present transcription, nevertheless, follows the passage in *XX songes*, and that source seems quite firm in its prosodic intentions during this passage.

[23] See, for instance, *ETSC*. nos. 21, 23, 24, 25, 31, 33, 34, 37, 38, 39, 40, 46, 48, 49.

[24] Richard Leighton Greene, ed., *The Early English Carols* (Oxford: Clarendon Press, 1935), pp. xxiii, xciii, cxxxiii-cxxxviii.

[25] Greene, *Early English Carols*, p. xciii.

[26] *XX songes*, no. 6, ff. C. 3v to D. 2; and from NYpl 4180-85, the front flyleaves from NYpl 4183 (Quintus), and NYpl 4184 (Sextus). Text alone, incomplete, published in Fluegel, "Liedersammlungen," p. 591, and in Imelmann, "Zur Kenntnis," pp. 128-29. For the complete list of the fragments of fifteen early Tudor songs and instrumental works in NYpl 4180-85, see Stevens, *Music and Poetry*, pp. 426-28.

[27] These two lines are lacking in all the manuscripts.

[28] *Bella*: bell, with the nonsense syllable "a" added. *Bere the bell*: be the best. *Kell*: woman's head-dress or garment. *Clap*: perhaps a *double entendre* is meant here, *clap* meaning both blow (or stroke) and gonorrhea. *XX songes* has as variants of *bere* (bear), "berth" and "beryth."

[29] Greene, *Early English Carols*, p. 309, no. 456.

[30] During the course of his research into English folksong some sixty years ago, the Australian composer Percy Grainger noted that the "custom of adding meaningless syllables to words in order to avoid singing one syllable to more than one note, is very generally prevalent amongst North Lincolnshire singers." See his article, "Collecting with the Phonograph," *Journal of the Folk-Song Society* 3 (1908-1909): 162.

[31] Published in Greene, *Early English Carols*, p. 310, no. 458.

[32] Carelessness with rests is not uncommon among Tudor musical scribes.

[33] Stevens, *Music and Poetry*, pp. 437, 459, 433.

[34] Pygot's macaronic carol, *Quid petis, o fily?*

[35] One other interesting coincidence may be noted. At the end of the printed part, the bass parts to two songs have been added in manuscript. The second of these, *By a bancke as I lay*, is found in Lbl 58, and was said to have been sung by Henry VIII. Sir Thomas Phillipps, ed. "The life of Sir Peter Carew," *Archaeologia* 28 (1840):13.

[36] Harrison *MMB*, p. 420

[37]Four songs in Lbl 5665 (*ETSC*, nos. 5-8) and one in Lbl 5465 (*ETSC*. no. 46) are through-set in two sections with "rhyming" melismas, but they are not settings of rhyme royal stanzas. Two songs in Lbl 31922 (*MCH*, nos. 106, 108) and one in 5465 (*ETSC*, no. 41) are rhyme royal stanzas through-set in two sections, but their melismas do not "rhyme."

APPENDIX NOTES

[1]Selected entries from the MS are published in *LP* 4, no. 6788.

[2]Lpro *Inquisitions post mortem*, C.142/74/130 and E.150/580/18. Originals in Latin.

[3]Llao Consistory Court Wills 1557, 3, f. 28.

[4]Lpro C.3/95/53, m. 1-3.

[5]Other English composers represented are William Daggere, John Kemp, and Rysbye, of whom nothing is known, and John Dunstable (d. 1453).

[6]Five of these songs are found in Petrucci's *Odhecaton A* (1501), as is the melody of a sixth, Henry's *Taunder naken*.

[7]An authoritative treatment of the manuscript and its provenance is found in Albert Dunning, *Die Staatsmotette 1480-1555* (Utrecht: A. Oosthoek, 1970), pp. 121-30. The MS contents are listed in Hughes-Hughes, *Catalogue* 1:259 and 2:1, 193. They are discussed briefly in Harrison, *MMB*, pp. 338-40.

[8]Psalm settings by English composers do not appear before ca. 1540.

[9]The contents are listed in Hughes-Hughes, *Catalogue* 1:140, 259, and 2:1, 193; and with attributions in James Braithwaite, The Introduction of Franco-Netherlandish Manuscripts to Early Tudor England: The Motet Repertory (Ph.D. Boston University, 1967), 2:9-11. For its provenance see Dunning, *Staatsmotette*, p. 125. The works are described in Braithwaite, Introduction of Franco-Netherlandish Manuscripts, 1:30-40, and in Edward E. Lowinsky, "A Music Book for Anne Boleyn," *Florilegium Historiale: Essays Presented to Wallace K. Ferguson*, ed. J. G. Rowe, and W. H. Stockdale (Toronto: University of Toronto Press, 1971), p. 162. The manuscript probably was brought by Charles V as a gift to Henry and Catherine on one of his two visits to England in 1520 and 1522, or at their meeting at Gravelines in 1520, after Henry had left the Field of Cloth of Gold.

[10]The manuscript is described, and its contents listed, in A. Tillman Merritt, "A Chanson Sequence by Fevin," *Essays on Music in Honor of Archibald Thompson Davison* (Cambridge, Mass.: Harvard University, 1957), pp. 91-99. Partial listings are found in Braithwaite, Introduction of Franco-Netherlandish Manuscripts, 2:19-21 and in Montague R. James, *Bibliotheca Pepysiana: A Descriptive Catalogue of the Library of Samuel Pepys* 3: *Mediaeval Manuscripts* (London: Sidgwick and Jackson, 1923), pp. 36-68. A description is found also in Braithwaite, Introduction of Franco-Netherlandish Manuscripts, 1:52-54.

[11]Lowinsky, "A Music Book," pp. 162-64, 222n. His revision of the usual date given for the MS (before 1509) seems indisputably correct.

[12]The Newberry partbooks are authoritatively examined and transcribed in Colin Slim, *A Gift of Madrigals and Motets*, 2 vols. (Chicago: University of Chicago Press, 1972). For the altus book, see Slim, "A Royal Treasure at Sutton Coldfield," *Early Music* 6 (1978): 57-71.

[13]Lowinsky, "A Song Book," pp. 160-235.

[14]Hughes-Hughes, *Catalogue* 1:262 and 2:128; Braithwaite, Introduction of Franco-Netherlandish Manuscripts, 1:55-57 and 2:22-23.

[15]Hughes-Hughes, *Catalogue* 1:244, 261-62, and 2:128; Braithwaite, Introduction of Franco-Netherlandish Manuscripts, 1:50-52.

[16]Dom Anselm Hughes, *Medieval Polyphony in the Bodleian Library*, pp. 6-7.

[17]Hughes-Hughes, *Catalogue*, 2:127-28.

[18]Hughes-Hughes, *Catalogue*, 2:122-23.

[19]A Scottish source of early sixteenth-century Continental music--twenty compositions, two identified as works of Josquin and Jaquet of Mantua--is the set of five Dunkeld partbooks Edinburgh, University Library MS Db. I.7. Harrison, *MMB*, p. 194.

[20]The evidence of Continental Masses in England during Henry's reign is scant, and it is found entirely in British manuscripts (which presumably were copied from Continental sources in England now lost). In Lbl 31922 there is an instrumental arrangement of part of the Credo from Isaac's Mass *O praeclara*; but the textless form of the transcription strips it of its identity. In the partbooks Cp 471-74 (ca. 1540-47) there is a Mass by Lupus Italus (Lewis Lockwood, "A Continental Mass and Motet in a Tudor Manuscript," *Music and Letters* 42 (1961): 336-47). Dufay's Mass *L'homme armé* is found in the early sixteenth-century Carver choirbook, Edinburgh, National Library of Scotland, Advocates' Library MS 5.1.15 (Harrison, *MMB*, pp. 193-94); but this is a Scottish source, copied probably at the royal court in Edinburgh, not an English one.

[21]Our ignorance in this matter, and the absence of Continental Masses in the manuscripts, throws doubt on, say, Benham's discovery of a model in the opening of Josquin's *Missa de Beata Virgine*, and "an obvious precedent in a section such as the 'Dona nobis pacem'" of his Mass *Pange lingua*, for Taverner's *Mean* Mass (*LCM*, pp. 140-142, respectively). He may be correct; but our scholarship, in its present state, has not earned the right to make such positive attributions.

BIBLIOGRAPHY

A. Books and Periodicals

Analecta Hymnica Medii Aevi 32, ed. Guido Maria Dreves. 1899; reprint ed., New York: Johnson, 1961.

Arkwright, G.E.P. *Catalogue of Music in the Library of Christ Church Oxford.* 2 vols. London: Oxford University Press, 1915, 1923.

Baillie, Hugh. "A London Church in Early Tudor Times," *Music and Letters* 36 (1955): 55-64.

_____. "A London Gild of Musicians, 1460-1530," *Proceedings of the Royal Musical Association* 83 (1956-57): 15-28.

_____. "Some Biographical Notes on English Church Musicians, Chiefly Working in London (1485-1560)," *Royal Musical Association Research Chronicle* 2 (1962): 18-57.

_____. "Squares", *Acta Musicologica* 32 (1960): 178-93.

Bardsley, Charles. *A Dictionary of English and Welsh Surnames.* 1901; reprint ed., Baltimore: Genealogical Publishing, 1967.

Benham, Hugh. *Latin Church Music in England 1460-1575.* London: Barrie and Jenkins, 1977.

_____. "The Formal Design and Construction of Taverner's Works," *Musica Discipline* 26 (1972): 189-209.

_____. The Music of John Taverner--A Study and Assessment. Ph.D. University of Southampton, 1969.

_____. "The Music of Taverner: A Liturgical Study," *Music Review* 33 (1972): 251-74.

Bergsagel, John. "The Date and Provenance of the Forrest-Heyther Collection of Tudor Masses," *Music and Letters* 44 (1963): 240-48.

Boas, Fredrick. *University Drama in the Tudor Age.* Oxford: Clarendon Press, 1914.

Boase, Charles William, ed. *Register of the University of Oxford* 1. Publications of the Oxford Historical Society 1. Oxford: Clarendon Press, 1885.

Bowker, Margaret, ed. *An Episcopal Court Book for the Diocese of Lincoln, 1514-1520.* Publications of the Lincoln Record Society 61. Lincoln: Lincoln Record Society, 1967.

Bowers, Roger. Choral Institutions within the English Church: Their Constitution and Development, 1340-1500. Ph.D. University of East Anglia, 1975.

Braithwaite, James R.   The Introduction of Franco-Netherlandish Manuscripts to Early Tudor England: The Motet Repertory. Ph.D. Boston University, 1967.

Bray, Roger.   "British Museum Add.   Mss.   17802-5 (The Gyffard Part-Books):   An Index and Commentary," *Royal Musical Association Research Chronicle* 7 (1969): 31-50.

_____.   "British Museum MS Royal 24 d 2 (John Baldwin's Commonplace Book): An Index and Commentary," *Royal Musical Association Research Chronicle* 12 (1974): 137-51.

_____.   "The Interpretation of Musica Ficta in English Music c.1490-c.1580," *Proceedings of the Royal Musical Association* 97 (1970-71): 26-45.

_____.   "The Part-Books Oxford, Christ Church, MSS 979-83: An Index and Commentary," *Musica Disciplina* 25 (1971): 179-97.

Brennecke, Ernest.   "A Singing Man of Windsor," *Music and Letters* 33 (1952): 33-40.

_____.   "The Entertainment at Elvetham, 1591," *Music in English Renaissance Drama.* Ed. John Long. Lexington: University of Kentucky Press, 1968. Pp. 32-56.

Brett, Philip.   "Edward Paston (1550-1630): A Norfolk Gentleman and his Musical Collection," *Transactions of the Cambridge Bibliographical Society* 4 Part 1 (1964): 51-69.

_____   and Thurston Dart.   "Songs by William Byrd in Manuscripts at Harvard," *Harvard Library Bulletin* 14 (1960): 343-65.

Breviarium ad usum...Sarum.   Eds. Francis Proctor and Christopher Wordsworth. 3 vols. Cambridge: University Press, 1879-86.

Brothers, Lester D.   "Avery Burton and his Hexachord Mass," *Musica Disciplina* 28 (1974): 153-76.

Brown, Carleton and R.H. Robbins, eds. *The Index of Middle English Verse.* New York: Columbia University Press, 1943.

Brown, Howard Mayer.   *Instrumental Music Printed Before 1600, A Bibliography.* Cambridge, Mass: Harvard University Press, 1965.

Brown, Phelps E.A. and S.V. Hopkins.   "Seven Centuries of the Price of Consumables Compared with Builders' Wage-Rates," *Economica*, new series 23 (1956): 296-314.

Burney, Charles.   *A General History of Music* (1776-89).   Ed. Frank Mercer (1935). 2 vols. Reprint ed., New York: Dover, 1957.

Calendar of the Patent Rolls...Henry VI.   6 vols. London: His Majesty's Stationery Office, 1901-10.

Calendar of the Patent Rolls...Philip and Mary.   Ed. M. S. Giuseppi. 4 vols.   London: His Majesty's Stationery Office, 1936-39.

Calendar of State Papers, Spanish, 1485-1558. Ed. Gustav A. Bergenroth *et al.* 15 vols. London: Her (His) Majesty's Stationery Office, 1862-1954.

Calendar of State Papers, Venetian. Eds. Rawdon Brown, Cavendish Bentinck and Horatio Brown. 38 vols. London: Her (His) Majesty's Stationery Office, 1864-1947.

Calendars of Lincoln Wills 1, 1320-1600. Ed. C. W. Foster. Publications of the British Record Society 28. London: British Record Society, 1902.

Carpenter, Nan Cooke. *Music in the Medieval and Renaissance Universities.* Norman: University of Oklahoma Press, 1958.

Carus-Wilson, E. M. and Olive Coleman. *England's Export Trade, 1275-1547.* Oxford: Clarendon Press, 1963.

A Catalogue of the Harleian Manuscripts in the British Museum. 4 vols. London, 1808.

A Catalogue of the Manuscripts Preserved in the Library of the University of Cambridge. 5 vols. Cambridge: University Press, 1856-67.

Cavendish, George. *The Life and Death of Cardinal Wolsey,* in *Two Early Tudor Lives.* Eds. Richard S. Sylvester and Davis P. Harding. New Haven: Yale University Press, 1962.

Chapter Acts of the Cathedral Church of St. Mary of Lincoln A.D. 1536-47. Ed. R.E.G. Cole. Publications of the Lincoln Record Society 13. Horncastle: Lincoln Record Society, 1917.

Chew, Geoffrey. "The Provenance and Date of the Caius and Lambeth Choir-books," *Music and Letters* 51 (1970): 107-17.

Christie, James. *Some Accounts of Parish Clerks.* London: privately printed by J. Vincent, 1893.

Clark, Andrew. *The Colleges of Oxford.* London: Methuen, 1891.

Clebsch, William A. *England's Earliest Protestants, 1520-1535.* New Haven: Yale University Press, 1964.

Collins, H.B. "John Taverner--Part II," *Music and Letters* 6 (1925): 314-29.

_____. "John Taverner's Masses," *Music and Letters* 5 (1924): 322-34.

Cooper, C.H. and T. *Athenae Cantabrigienses.* 2 vols. Cambridge: University Press, 1858-61.

Cox, John Charles. *Churchwardens' Accounts from the Fourteenth Century to the Close of the Seventeenth Century.* London: Methuen, 1913.

Cutts, Edward L. *Parish Priests and their People in the Middle Ages in England.* London: Society for Promoting Christian Knowledge, 1898.

Davison, Nigel. "Structure and Unity in Four Free-composed Tudor Masses," *Music Review* 34 (1973): 328-38.

_____."The *Western Wind* Masses," *The Musical Quarterly* 57 (1971): 427-43.

Davey, Henry. *History of English Music.* London: J. Curwen, 1895.

_____. "John Taverner," *Dictionary of National Biography.* Eds. Leslie Stephen and Sidney Lee. 21 vols. London: Oxford University Press, 1917. 19: 392-93.

Dickens, A. G. *The English Reformation.* New York: Schocken, 1964.

Dixon, Richard Watson. *History of the Church of England from the Abolition of the Roman Jurisdiction.* 6 vols. London: G. Routledge, 1881-1902.

Doe, Paul. "Another View of Musica Ficta in Tudor Music." *Proceedings of the Royal Musical Association* 98 (1971-72): 113-22.

_____. "Latin Polyphony under Henry VIII," *Proceedings of the Royal Musical Association* 95 (1968-69): 81-96.

Donington, Robert and Thurston Dart. "The Origin of the 'In Nomine,'" *Music and Letters* 30 (1949): 101-106.

Dugdale, William. *History of St. Paul's Cathedral.* London: Thomas Warren, 1658.

_____. *Monasticon Anglicanum.* Trans. and ed. John Stevens. London: D. Browne and J. Smith, 1718.

Dunning, Albert. *Die Staatsmotette 1480-1555.* Utrecht: A. Oosthoek, 1970.

Ebblewhite, Ernest Arthur. *The Parish Clerks' Company and its Charters.* London: privately printed, 1932.

Edwards, Warwick A. "The Performance of Ensemble Music in Elizabethan England," *Proceedings of the Royal Musical Association* 97 (1970-71): 113-23.

Ekwall, Eilert. *The Concise Oxford Dictionary of English Place-Names.* 4th ed. Oxford: Clarendon Press, 1960.

Emden, A.B. *A Biographical Register of the University of Cambridge to 1500.* Cambridge: University Press, 1963.

_____. *A Biographical Register of the University of Oxford to A.D. 1500.* 3 vols. Oxford: Clarendon Press, 1957-59.

English Historical Documents 5: 1485-1558. Ed. C. H. Williams. London: Eyre and Spottiswoode, 1967.

Evans, Maurice. *English Poetry in the Sixteenth Century.* 2nd ed. New York: Norton, 1967.

Ewen, C. L'Estrange. *A History of Surnames of the British Isles.* London: K. Paul, Trench, Trubner, 1931.

Fairbairn, James. *Fairbairn's Crests.* Rev. Lawrence Butters, ed. Joseph Maclaren (1911). Reprint ed., Baltimore: Genealogical Publishing, 1963.

Fellowes, E. H.   *The Catalogue of Manuscripts in the Library of St. Michael's College Tenbury.* Paris: Louise Dyer, 1934.

_____.   *English Cathedral Music.*   5th ed.   Rev. by J. A. Westrup.   London: Methuen, 1969.

_____.   "John Taverner," *Grove's Dictionary of Music and Musicians.* 5th ed. Ed. Eric Blom. 9 vols. London: Macmillan, 1954. 8: 323-24.

Flood, W. H. Grattan.   "John Taverner," *The Catholic Encyclopedia.* 15 vols. New York: The Encyclopedia Press, 1913. 14: 466.

_____.   "New Light on Early Tudor Composers. XII--John Taverner," *The Musical Times* 61 (1920): 597-98.

_____.   *Tudor Church Composers.* London: Oxford University Press, 1925.

Fluegel, Ewald.   "Liedersammlungen des XVI. Jahrhunderts, besonders aus der Zeit Heinrich's VIII., II," *Anglia* 12 (1889): 585-97.

Foster, C. W.   "Lincolnshire Wills Proved in the Prerogative Court of Canterbury, 1471-1490." *Associated Architectural Societies' Reports and Papers* 41 (1932-33): 179-218.

_____, ed. *The Parish Registers of Boston in the County of Lincoln* 1, 1557-1599. Publications of the Lincoln Record Society, Parish Register Section 1.   Horncastle: Lincoln Record Society, 1914.

_____   and A. H. Thompson.   "The Chantry Certificates for Lincoln and Lincolnshire, Returned in 1548," *Associated Architectural Societies' Reports and Papers* 37 (1923-25): 18-106, 247-275.

Foster, Joseph.   *Alumni Oxonienses: the Members of the University of Oxford, 1500-1714.* 4 vols. Oxford: Clarendon Press, 1891-92.

Fox, John Charles. *The Parish Registers of England.* London: Methuen, 1910.

Foxe, John.   *Acts and Monuments (1563).* 9th ed. 3 vols. London: Company of Stationers, 1684.

Fransson, Gustav. *Middle English Surnames of Occupation 1100-1350.* London: Williams and Norgate, 1935.

Frere, W. H.   "Edwardine Vernacular Services," *A Collection of his Papers on Liturgical and Historical Subjects* (Alcuin Club Collections 35). London: Oxford University Press, 1940. Pp. 5-21.

Fuller, Thomas. *The Church-History of Britain.* 6 books in 1 vol. London: John Williams, 1655-56.

Gibbons, Alfred. *Early Lincoln Wills.* Lincoln: James Williamson, 1888.

Giustiniani, Sebastian. *Four Years at the Court of Henry VIII.* Trans. and ed. Rawdon Brown. London: Smith, Edler, 1854.

Grainger, Percy. "Collecting with the Phonograph," *Journal of the Folk-Song Society* 3 (1908-1909): 147-242.

Greene, Richard Leighton, ed. *The Early English Carols.* Oxford: Clarendon Press, 1935.

Hall, John George. *Notices of Lincolnshire.* Hull: Eastern Morning News, 1890.

Hamm, Charles E. *A Chronology of the Works of Guillaume Dufay.* Princeton: Princeton University Press, 1964.

Hannas, Ruth. "Concerning Deletions in the Polyphonic Mass Credo," *Journal of the American Musicological Society* 5 (1952): 155-86; related correspondence, 6 (1953): 91-93.

Harris, David. "Musical Education in Tudor Times," *Proceedings of the Royal Music Association* 65 (1938-39): 109-39.

Harrison, Frank Ll. "English Polyphony (c. 1470-1540)," *The New Oxford History of Music* 3: Ars Nova and the Renaissance 1300-1540. Ed. Dom Anselm Hughes and Gerald Abraham. London: Oxford University Press, 1960. Pp. 303-348.

————. "Music for the Sarum Rite, MS 1236 in the Pepys Library, Magdalene College, Cambridge, " *Annales Musicologiques* 6 (1958-63): 99-144.

————. *Music in Medieval Britain.* 2nd ed. London: Routledge and Kegan Paul, 1963.

————. "The Eton Choirbook," *Annales Musicologiques* 1 (1953): 151-75.

Harrison, Henry. *Surnames of the United Kingdom: A Concise Etymological Dictionary.* 2 vols. London: Morland Press, 1912-18.

Harvey, John. *Gothic England.* London: B. T. Batsford, 1947.

————. "The Building of Cardinal College, Oxford," *Oxoniensia* 8-9 (1943-44): 137-53.

————. "The Building Works and Architects of Cardinal Wolsey," *Journal of the British Archaelogical Association*, 3rd series 8 (1943): 50-59.

Haward, Winifred I. "The Trade of Boston in the Fifteenth Century," *Lincolnshire Architectural and Archaeological Society* 41 (1932-33): 169-78.

Hawkins, John. *A General History of the Science and Practice of Music* (1776). New edition in 2 vols. London: Novello, 1853. Reprint ed., New York: Dover, 1963.

Heath, Peter. *The English Parish Clergy on the Eve of the Reformation.* London: Routledge and Kegan Paul, 1969.

Henderson, Philip, ed. *The Complete Poems of John Skelton.* 3rd ed. London: J. M. Dent, 1959.

Henry, Charles and Thompson Cooper. *Athenae Cantabrigienses.* Cambridge: Macmillan, 1858.

Hill, J. W. F. *Medieval Lincoln.* Cambridge: University Press, 1948.

Hiscock, Walter George. *A Christ Church Miscellany.* Oxford: University Press, 1946.

Historical Manuscripts Commission. *Report on the Manuscripts of Lord De L'Isle and Dudley Preserved at Penshurst Place* 1. H. M. C. Reports on Collections of Manuscripts 77 Part 1. London: His Majesty's Stationery Office, 1925.

Hodgett, Gerald A. J. The Dissolution of the Monasteries in Lincolnshire. M.A. University of London, 1947.

_____, ed. *The State of the Ex-Religious and Former Chantry Priests in the Diocese of Lincoln, 1547-1574.* Publications of the Lincoln Record Society 53. Hereford: Lincoln Record Society, 1959.

Holles, Gervase. *Lincolnshire Church Notes.* Ed. R. E. G. Cole. Publications of the Lincoln Record Society 1. Lincoln: Lincoln Record Society, 1911.

Hughes, Dom Amselm. *Catalogue of the Musical Manuscripts at Peterhouse Cambridge.* Cambridge: University Press, 1953.

_____. *Medieval Polyphony in the Bodleian Library.* Oxford: Bodleian Library, 1951.

_____. "Sixteenth Century Service Music," *Music and Letters* 5 (1924): 145-54, 335-46.

Hughes-Hughes, Augustus. *Catalogue of Manuscript Music in the British Museum.* 3 vols. London: British Museum, 1906-1909. Reprint ed., 1964-66.

Imelmann, Rudolf. "Zur Kenntnis der vor-shakespearischen Lyrik: I. Wynkyn de Wordes 'Song Booke,' 1530, II. John Dayes Sammlung der Lieder Thomas Whythornes, 1571," *Jahrbuch der deutschen Shakespeare-Gesellschaft* 39 (1903): 121-78.

Izon, John. "Italian Musicians at the Tudor Court," *The Musical Quarterly* 44 (1958): 329-337.

James, Montague Rhodes. *A Descriptive Catalogue of the Manuscripts in the Library of St. John's College, Cambridge.* Cambridge: University Press, 1913.

_____. *Bibliotheca Pepysiana: A Descriptive Catalogue of the Library of Samuel Pepys* 3: *Mediaeval Manuscripts.* London: Sidgwick and Jackson, 1923.

James, M. E. "Obedience and Dissent in Henrician England: The Lincolnshire Rebellion 1536, " *Past and Present*, No. 48 (August 1970): pp. 3-78.

Josephson, David. "In Search of the Historical Taverner," *Tempo*, No. 101 (1972): 40-52.

_____. "John Taverner: An English Renaisssance Master," *American Choral Review* 9 No. 2 (Winter 1967): pp. 6-15.

_____. "John Taverner: Smaller Liturgical Works," *American Choral Review* 9 No. 4 (Summer 1967): pp. 26-41.

_____. "The Festal Masses of John Taverner," *American Choral Review* 9 No. 3 (Spring 1967): pp. 10-21.

Knowles, David. *The Religious Orders in England* 3: *The Tudor Age.* Cambridge: University Press, 1961.

Lafontaine, Henry Cart de, ed. *The King's Musick.* London: Novello, 1909. Reprint ed., New York: Da Capo, 1973.

Leach, A. F. *English Schools at the Reformation 1546-8.* New York: Russell and Russell, 1968.

Legge, Augustus George, ed. *The Ancient Register of North Elmham, Norfolk, from A.D. 1538 to A.D. 1631.* Norwich: Agas H. Goose, 1888.

Le Huray, Peter. *Music and the Reformation in England 1549-1660.* London: Herbert Jenkins, 1967.

Letters and Papers, Foreign and Domestic, of the Reign of Henry VIII. Eds. J. S. Brewer, James Gairdner and R. H. Brodie. 21 vols. and Addenda. London: Her (His) Majesty's Stationery Office, 1862-1932.

(Lincoln) *Archivists' Report.* No. 13. Lincoln: Lincoln Archives Committee, 1961-62.

Littlehales, Henry, ed. *The Medieval Records of a London City Church (St. Mary at Hill) A.D. 1420-1559.* Early English Text Society, Original Series 128. London: Kegan Paul, Trench, Trubner, 1905.

Lockwood, Lewis. "A Continental Mass and Motet in a Tudor Manuscript," *Music and Letters* 42 (1961): 336-47.

Lowinsky, Edward E. "A Music Book for Anne Boleyn," *Florilegium Historiale; Essays Presented to Wallace K. Ferguson,* ed. J. G. Rowe and W. H. Stockdale (Toronto: University of Toronto Press, 1971), pp. 160-235.

Ludwig, Friedrich. "Die mehrstimmige Messe des 14. Jahrhunderts," *Archiv für Musikwissenschaft* 7 (1925): 419-35.

Lyte, Maxwell. *History of the University of Oxford from the Earliest Times to the Year 1530.* New York: Macmillan, 1886.

Macray, William, ed. *Register of the Members of St. Mary Magdalen College, Oxford.* New Series 1. London: Henry Frowde, 1894.

Meres, Francis. *Palladis Tamia* (1598). Reprint ed., New York: Scholars' Facsimiles and Reprints, 1938.

Merritt, A. Tillman. "A Chanson Sequence by Févin," *Essays on Music in Honor of Archibald Thompson Davison.* Cambridge, Mass.: Harvard University, 1957.

Messenger, Thomas. "Texture and Form in Taverner's 'Western wind' Mass," *Journal of the American Musicological Society* 22 (1969): 504-507.

_____. "Texture and Form in the Masses of Fayrfax," *Journal of the American Musicological Society* 24 (1971): 282-85.

Meyer, Ernst Hermann. *Die mehrstimmige Spielmusik des 17. Jahrhunderts in Nord- und Mitteleuropa.* Kassel: Bärenreiter, 1934.

Miller, Clement A. "Erasmus on Music," *The Musical Quarterly* 52 (1966): 332-49.

Missale Sarum. Ed. F. H. Dickinson. Burntisland: J. Parker, 1861-63.

Morley, Thomas. *A Plain and Easy Introduction to Practical Music* (1597). Ed. R. A. Harman, 2nd ed. London: J. M. Dent, 1963.

Myers, A. R. *England in the Late Middle Ages (1307-1536).* 2nd rev. ed. London: Penguin, 1963.

Nagel, Wilibald. *Annalen der englischen Hofmusik 1509-1649 von der Zeit Heinrichs VIII. bis zum Tode Karls I.* Leipzig: Breitkopf und Härtel, 1894.

Nixon, H. M. "The Book of XX Songs," *British Museum Quarterly* 16 (1951-52): 33-35.

Noble, Jeremy. "Le Répertoire Instrumental Anglais: 1550-1585," *La Musique Instrumentale de la Renaissance.* Ed. Jean Jacquot. Paris: Editions du Centre National de la Recherche Scientifique, 1955. Pp. 91-114.

Norman, Philip. *The Ancient Halls of the City Guilds.* London: George Bell and Sons, 1903.

Original Papers, Illustrative of English History. 3 series in 11 vols. Ed. Henry Ellis. London: Harding, Triphook and Lepard, 1824; Harding and Lepard, 1827; Bentley, 1846.

The Oxford History of Music 2: The Polyphonic Period, Part 2. Ed. H. E. Wooldridge. Oxford: Clarendon Press, 1905.

Parton, Kenton. "On Two Early Tudor Manuscripts of Keyboard Music," *Journal of the American Musicological Society* 17 (1964): 81-83.

Pattison, Bruce. *Music and Poetry of the English Renaissance.* 2nd ed.   London: Methuen, 1970.

Pevsner, Nikolaus and John Harris. *The Buildings of England: Lincolnshire.* London: Penguin, 1964.

Phillips, Sir Thomas, ed. "The Life of Sir Peter Carew," *Archaeologia* 28 (1840): 96-151.

Picker, Martin. *The Chanson Albums of Marguerite of Austria.* Berkeley and Los Angeles: University of California Press, 1965.

Pine, Edward. "Westminster Abbey: Some Early Masters of the Choristers," *The Musical Times* 94 (1953): 258-60.

Plummer, Charles, ed. *Elizabethan Oxford.* Publications of the Oxford Historical Society 8. Oxford: Clarendon Press, 1887.

Pollard, A. F. *Wolsey.* Rev. ed. New York: Harper, 1966.

Pollock, Sir Frederick. *The Land Laws.* 3rd ed. London: Macmillan, 1896.

Processionale Sarum. Ed. W. G. Henderson. Leeds: M'Corquodale, 1882.

Reese, Gustave. *Music in the Renaissance.* Rev. ed. New York: W. W. Norton, 1959.

_____. "The Origin of the English 'In Nomine,'" *Journal of the American Musicological Society* 2 (1949): 7-22.

Robbins, Rossell Hope, ed. *Secular Lyrics of the XIVth and XVth Centuries.* 2nd ed. Oxford: Clarendon Press, 1956.

Russell, Joycelyne. *The Field of Cloth of Gold.* London: Routledge and Kegan Paul, 1969.

Salter, H., ed. *A Subsidy Collected in the Diocese of Lincoln in 1526.* Oxford: B. H. Blackwell, 1909.

Sandon, Nicholas. "The Henrician Partbooks at Peterhouse, Cambridge," *Proceedings of the Royal Musical Association* 103 (1976-77): 106-140.

Scarisbrick, J. J. *Henry VIII.* Berkeley and Los Angeles: University of California Press, 1968.

Simpson, William Douglas, ed. *The Building Accounts of Tattershall College, 1434-1472.* Publications of the Lincoln Record Society 55. Hereford: Lincoln Record Society, 1960.

Slim, H. Colin. *A Gift of Madrigals and Motets.* 2 vols. Chicago: University of Chicago Press, 1972.

_____. "A Royal Treasure at Sutton Coldfield," *Early Music* 6 (1978): 57-71.

Smith, Lucy Toulmin, ed. *The Itinerary of John Leland in or about the Years 1535-1543*, 4 parts in 5 vols. London: Centaur Press, 1964.

Smith, R. B. *Land and Politics in the England of Henry VIII.* Oxford: Clarendon Press, 1970.

State Papers, King Henry VIII. 11 vols. London: His (Her) Majesty's Stationery Office, 1830-52.

Statutes of the Colleges of Oxford. 3 vols. Oxford: J. H. Parker, 1853.

Stevens, Denis. "John Taverner," *Die Musik in Geschichte und Gegenwart.* Ed. Friedrich Blume. 14 vols. Kassel: Bärenreiter, 1949-68. 13, cols. 152-56.

_____. *The Mulliner Book, A Commentary.* London: Stainer and Bell, 1952.

_____. "John Taverner," *Essays in Musicology in Honor of Dragan Plamenac.* Ed. Gustave Reese and Robert J. Snow. Pittsburgh: University of Pittsburgh Press, 1969. Pp. 331-39.

_____. *Tudor Church Music.* 2nd ed. London: Faber and Faber, 1966.

Stevens, John. *Music and Poetry in the Early Tudor Court.* London: Methuen, 1961.

_____. "Rounds and Canons from an Early Tudor Songbook," *Music and Letters* 32 (1951): 29-37.

Strype, John. *The Life and Acts of Matthew Parker.* 3 vols. Oxford: Clarendon Press, 1821.

_____. *Memorials of John Cranmer.* New ed. 2 vols. Oxford: Clarendon Press, 1812.

Thompson, Alexander Hamilton. *Tattershall: The Manor, the Castle, the Church.* Lincoln: J. W. Huddock, 1928.

Thompson, Pishey. *The History and Antiquities of Boston.* Boston, Lincs.: John Noble, 1856.

Tipping, H. Avray. *Tattershall Castle, Lincolnshire.* London: Jonathan Cape, 1929.

Two Early Tudor Lives. Eds. Richard S. Sylvester and Davis P. Harding. New Haven: Yale University Press, 1962.

The Use of Sarum. Ed. W. H. Frere. Cambridge: University Press, 1898, 1901.

Valor Ecclesiasticus (1534). Eds. John Caley and Joseph Hunter. 6 vols. London: Record Commission, 1810-34.

Venn, John and J. A. *Alumni Cantabrigienses* 1: From the Earliest Times to 1751. 4 vols. Cambridge: University Press, 1922-27.

Victoria History of the County of Oxford 3.   Eds. H. E. Salter and Mary Lobel. London: Oxford University Press, 1954..

Victoria History of the County of Lincoln. 2 vols.   Vol. 1:   London and Lincoln: John Saunders, 1834; Vol. 2, ed. William Page: London: James Street, 1906.

Victoria History of the County of Suffolk.   Ed. William Page.   2 vols.   London: Archibald Constable, 1907-1911.

Visitations in the Diocese of Lincoln 1517-1531.   3 vols. Ed. A. H. Thompson. Publications of the Lincoln Record Society 33, 35, 37.   Hereford: Lincoln Record Society, 1940-47.

Ward, John.   "The Lute Music of Ms. Royal Appendix 58."   *Journal of the American Musicological Society* 13 (1960): 117-25.

Warner, Sylvia Townsend.   "Doubting Castle," *Music and Letters* 5 (1924): 155-68.

Warren, Edwin B.   *Life and Works of Robert Fayrfax 1464-1521*, Musicological Studies and Documents 20.   Rome: American Institute of Musicology, 1969.

Williams, C. H. ed.   *English Historical Documents* 5:   1485-1558. London: Eyre and Spottiswoode, 1967.

Wilson, Derek.   *A Tudor Tapestry.* Pittsburgh: University of Pittsburgh Press, 1972.

Wood, Anthony à.   *Athenae Oxoniensis.*   New ed. in 5 vols.   Ed. Philip Bliss.   London: F. C. and J. Rivington, 1813-20.

_____.   *Fasti Oxoniensis,* Part 1: 1500-1640.   Ed. Philip Bliss.   London: F. C. and J. Rivington, 1815.

Woodfill, Walter.   *Musicians in English Society.*   Princeton: Princeton University Press, 1953.

Wright, Thomas.   *Three Chapters of Letters Relating to the Suppression of the Monasteries.* Camden Society 26. London: Camden Society, 1843.

Wulstan, David.   "The Problem of Pitch in Sixteenth-Century English Vocal Polyphony," *Proceedings of the Royal Musical Association* 93 (1966-67): 97-112.

Zeeveld, W. Gordon.   *Foundations of Tudor Policy.* London: Methuen, 1969.

B. Published Music

Antiphonale Sarisburiense. Ed. W. H. Frere. London: Plainsong & Mediaeval Music Society, 1901-1926.

The British Museum Manuscript Egerton 3307. Ed. Gwynn McPeek. London: Oxford University Press, 1963.

Dufay, Guillaume. *Opera Omnia.* Ed. Heinrich Besseler. *Corpus Mensurabilis Musicae* 1. Rome: American Institute of Musicology, 1966-

Early English Church Music. Vols. 1-. London: Stainer and Bell, 1962-.

Early Tudor Magnificats 1. Ed. Paul Doe. Early English Church Music 4. London: Stainer and Bell, 1962.

Early Tudor Masses. Ed. John Bergsagel. 2 vols. Early English Church Music 1, 16. London: Stainer and Bell, 1962, 1976.

Early Tudor Songs and Carols. Ed. John Stevens. Musica Britannica 36. London: Stainer and Bell, 1975.

The Eton Choirbook. Ed. Frank Ll. Harrision. Musica Britannica 10-12. London: Stainer and Bell, 1956-61.

Fayrfax, Robert. *Collected Works.* Ed. Edwin B. Warren. 1: The Masses; 2: Magnificats and Motets; Missa Sponsus Amat Sponsam. *Corpus Mensurabilis Musicae* 17. Rome: American Institute of Musicology, 1959, 1964.

Graduale Sarisburiense. Ed. W. H. Frere. London: Bernard Quaritch, 1894.

In Nomine. Altenglische Kammermusik für vier and fünf Stimmen. Ed. Denis Stevens. Hortus Musicus 134. Kassel: Bärenreiter, 1956.

Medieval Carols. Ed. John Stevens. Musica Britannica 4. London: Stainer and Bell, 1952.

The Mulliner Book. 2nd rev. ed. Ed. Denis Stevens. Musica Britannica 1. London: Stainer and Bell, 1966.

Musica Britannica. Vols. 1-. London: Stainer and Bell, 1952-.

Music at the Court of Henry VIII. Ed. John Stevens. Musica Britannica 18. London: Stainer and Bell, 1962.

The Music of the Pepys MS 1236. Ed. Sydney Robinson Charles. *Corpus Mensurabilis Musicae* 40. Rome: American Institute of Musicology, 1967.

Sheppard, John. *John Sheppard.* 2 vols. 1: Responsorial Music. Ed. David Chadd. 2: Masses. Ed. Nicholas Sandon. Early English Church Music 17, 18. London: Stainer and Bell, 1977, 1976.

The Treasury of English Church Music 1: 1500-1545. Ed. Denis Stevens. London: Blandford, 1965.

Trefusis, Lady Mary. *Songs, Ballads and Instrumental Pieces Composed by King Henry the Eighth.* Oxford: privately printed by the University Press, 1912.

Tudor Church Music. Eds. P. C. Buck, E. H. Fellowes, A. Ramsbotham. R. R. Terry and S. T. Warner. 10 vols. London: Oxford University Press, 1923-29. Vols. 1 and 3: *John Taverner c. 1495-1545,* Parts 1 and 2. *Appendix with Supplementary Notes.* Ed. E. H. Fellowes. Oxford: University Press, 1948.

Tye, Christopher. *The Instrumental Music.* Ed. Robert Weidner. New Haven: A-R Editions, 1967.

          Ed. John Satterfield. *The Latin Church Music.* 1: The Masses; 2: The Shorter Latin Works. Madison: A-R Editions, 1972.

The Worcester Fragments. Ed. Luther Dittmer. Musicological Studies and Documents 2. Dallas: American Institute of Musicology, 1957.

GENERAL INDEX

INDEX OF TITLES